Framing Devices and Global Legal Traditions

This collection explores prefaces, prologues, paratexts, and other types of framing devices. Across world history, these devices have introduced the law, articulated its context and audience, identified the basis of legal and moral authority, critiqued existing conditions, or even tried to "restore" something that never was. Scribes, lawmakers, and legal theorists also used frames to position the law in time and space, purporting to define populations and their identities. Despite the ubiquity and complexity of these phenomena, few studies have drawn out methods for studying their role in constructing, fortifying, or reimagining legal frameworks within legal cultures or traditions. This volume offers new ways to consider the significance of framing apparatuses regarding how and why they are created, remembered, forgotten, utilized, and recovered within legal traditions. The studies range from the ancient world to the modern nation-state system, aiming to explore the intersections and collisions between juridical and political interpretation practices.

The book will be of interest to academics and researchers in the areas of legal history, comparative law, legal cultures and traditions, legal theory, jurisprudence, constitutional law and legislative drafting.

Laura Culbertson (Ph.D., University of Michigan, Ann Arbor, Near Eastern Studies) is Professor of Middle East Studies at American Public University.

Susan Longfield Karr (Ph.D., University of Chicago, History) is Associate Professor of History at the University of Cincinnati.

Routledge Studies in Comparative Legal History

This series covers the general area of comparative legal history, including contributions focusing on both 'internal' legal history, i.e., doctrinal and disciplinary developments in the law, and 'external' legal history, i.e., legal ideas and institutions in wider contexts. Considering the various legal traditions worldwide, the series also welcomes works dealing with other laws and customs from around the globe. Temporal or geographical in approach, the series will consider both legal and similar law-like normative traditions. Works encompassing views from different schools of thought and contributions from comparative and transnational historiography, including interdisciplinary approaches, are encouraged. With a focus on higher level research in the form of monographs and edited collections, proposals for supplementary reading and textbooks are also welcomed.

Series editors:

Aniceto Masferrer is Professor of Legal History and teaches legal history and comparative law at the Faculty of Law, University of Valencia, Spain. He has published extensively on criminal law from an historical and comparative perspective, as well as on the codification movement and fundamental rights in the Western legal tradition.

Heikki Tapio Pihlajamäki is Professor of Comparative Legal History, Faculty of Law, University of Helsinki, Finland. He has published widely, in a number of languages, on various aspects of comparative legal history.

Titles in this series

Tracing British West Indian Slavery Laws
A Comparative Analysis of Legal Transplants
Justine K. Collins

State Liability and the Law
A Historical and Comparative Analysis
Bartłomiej Wróblewski

Nazi Antisemitism and Jewish Legal Self-Defence
The Turn to Law in Liberal Democracies, 1932–39
David Fraser

English Law, the Legal Profession, and Colonialism
Histories, Parallels, and Influences
Edited by Cerian Griffiths and Łukasz Jan Korporowicz

Borders of the Early Modern Ius Commune
England, Venice and Scandinavia
Edited by Dolores Freda, Mario Piccinini, Heikki Pihlajamäki, and Chiara Maria Valsecchi

Framing Devices and Global Legal Traditions
From the Ancient World to the Modern Nation State
Edited by Laura Culbertson and Susan Longfield Karr

For more information about this series, please visit: www.routledge.com/Routledge-Studies-in-Comparative-Legal-History/book-series/COMPLEGHIST

Framing Devices and Global Legal Traditions

From the Ancient World to the Modern Nation State

Edited by Laura Culbertson and Susan Longfield Karr

Routledge
Taylor & Francis Group
LONDON AND NEW YORK

First published 2026
by Routledge
4 Park Square, Milton Park, Abingdon, Oxon OX14 4RN

and by Routledge
605 Third Avenue, New York, NY 10158

Routledge is an imprint of the Taylor & Francis Group, an informa business

British Library Cataloguing-in-Publication Data
A catalogue record for this book is available from the British Library

ISBN: 978-1-032-84944-7 (hbk)
ISBN: 978-1-032-87859-1 (pbk)
ISBN: 978-1-003-53481-5 (ebk)

DOI: 10.4324/9781003534815

Typeset in Galliard
by Apex CoVantage, LLC

Contents

About the authors

Adam M. Bishop obtained his Ph.D. in medieval studies from the University of Toronto in 2011. From 2011–2012 he was a postdoctoral researcher for the project "The Legal Status of Religious Minorities in the Euro-Mediterranean World (5th–15th Centuries)" at the Université de Nantes, France. He is currently an independent scholar whose research focuses on the Assizes of Jerusalem, the collection of legal texts used by the High Court and Burgess Courts of the crusader Kingdoms of Jerusalem and Cyprus. He is also the author of *Robert of Nantes, Patriarch of Jerusalem (1240–1254)* in Routledge's "Rulers of the Latin East" series (2024).

Christoffer Bovbjerg is Associate Director of the Interdisciplinary Humanities Center at the University of California, Santa Barbara. He earned his Ph.D. in History from the University of California, Berkeley. He studies medieval Japan, specializing in the law, administration, and governance of the Kamakura shogunate.

Frédéric Constant is a professor of legal history at Université Nice Côte d'Azur (France). His primary research interests are in Chinese law and comparative legal history, with emphasis on the interactions between Chinese law and legal institutions and those of other Asian countries. His most recent works currently focus on Chinese jurisprudence and the history of law codification in China. He also leads a research project on the history of crime in China. He is the author of *Le droit chinois* (2013), *Le droit mongol dans l'État sino-mandchou* (2019), and *Le Traitré juridique du Livre des Jin* (2025).

Jorge L. Contreras is a Distinguished University Professor, the James T. Jensen Endowed Professor for Transactional Law and Director of the Program on Intellectual Property and Technology Law at the University of Utah S.J. Quinney College of Law. His academic research focuses, among other things, on intellectual property, antitrust law, technical standards, and science policy. He is the author or editor of fourteen books and has published more than 150 scholarly articles and book chapters. He is the recipient of numerous awards and honors, including the University of Utah's Distinguished Research Award, and is an elected member of the American Law Institute. He has previously testified before committees of the U.S. Senate and House of Representatives, the Federal Trade Commission, the European Commission, and courts in North and South America, Europe, and Asia and is regularly quoted by news outlets such as The New York Times, The Wall Street Journal, The Economist, Bloomberg, Law360, and CNN. He is an honors graduate of Harvard Law School (J.D.) and Rice University (B.S.E.E., B.A.), and he clerked for Chief Justice Thomas R. Phillips of the Texas Supreme Court.

Nicholas D. Cross is Assistant Professor of Ancient Mediterranean History at the United States Naval Academy. His research interests include ancient diplomacy and warfare, religions, numismatics, and epigraphy. He is the author of several publications on interstate relations in the ancient world. His current monograph project, *The Roots of Cooperation: Constructing Interstate Alliances in the Ancient Greek World*, is the first full-length inquiry into the diplomatic, social, religious, and military traditions involved in ancient Greek alliances. He is also the co-editor of the forthcoming volume *Playing the Classics: The Ancient World and Rock Music of the 1960s and 1970s.*

Matthew Crow is Professor of History and Director of the Law and Society program at Hobart and William Smith Colleges in Geneva, New York. He is the author of *Thomas Jefferson, Legal History, and the Art of Recollection* (Cambridge, 2017), and in addition to continuing research on natural law, maritime literature, political theology, and the history of the book, he is finishing a book project on Herman Melville, legal imagination, and oceanic history.

Laura Culbertson (Ph.D. Michigan, Near Eastern Studies) is a professor of Middle East Studies at American Public University. Her background is in ancient Near Eastern history and archaeology, and her recent research interests include slavery and ancient law. On the topic of slavery, she edited *Slaves and Households in the Near East* and co-edited *Society and the Individual in Mesopotamia*, which includes a contribution on Mesopotamian slavery. Her other recent publications discuss legal pluralism and the social contexts of Mesopotamian law.

Elizabeth Lhost is a historian of modern South Asia whose research focuses on the intersections of law, history, and archives. Her first book, *Everyday Islamic Law and the Making of Modern South Asia* (University of North Carolina Press 2022), won the 2023 Karwaan Book Prize. It provides a bottom-up history of Islamic law and legal practice in 19th and 20th century South Asia. Her new research focuses on the production, translation, and circulation of law books in British India. She currently works as Program Manager for the Modern Endangered Archives Program at the University of California Los Angeles Library where she supports efforts to document and digitize at-risk cultural heritage collections around the world. Lhost holds a Ph.D. in History and South Asian Languages and Civilizations from the University of Chicago.

Susan Longfield Karr's (Ph.D. University of Chicago, History) teaching and research focuses on state- and empire-state formation and the emergence of the so-called modern rule of law within communities (constitutions) and between them (international law) from the late medieval through the early modern period. Her work gives particular attention to the meaning and significance of legal vocabularies within cultural, political, and juridical frameworks that accompany the history and development of rights (customary, civic, and natural) in the context of state and empire formation in Italy, Germany, France, and England. Most recently, she published *On Justice and Right: Jus gentium in Humanist Jurisprudence*, wherein she explored the transformation of fundamental categories of Roman law such as ius and ius gentium by the fathers of legal humanism, Guillaume Budé, Ulrich Zasius, and Andrea Alciati (Brill, 2022). Dr. Longfield Karr is Associate Professor of History at the University of Cincinnati.

Andrew Rabin is a professor of English at the University of Louisville. His research examines the law and literature of early medieval Britain. His books include *Crime and Punishment in Anglo-Saxon England* (Cambridge University Press, 2020), *Wulfstan: Old English Legal Writings* (Harvard University Press, 2020), *The Disputatio Puerorum: A Ninth-Century Monastic Instructional Text* (Pontifical Institute of Medieval Studies, 2017), and *The Political Writings of Archbishop Wulfstan of York* (Manchester University Press, 2015). In addition, he has edited multiple essay collections on early medieval law and published articles in such journals as *Early Medieval Europe, English Historical Review*, and *Speculum.* He is a fellow of the Royal Historical Society and the London Society of Antiquaries.

Daimeon Shanks-Dumont is a Ph.D. candidate at the University of California, Berkeley, School of Law's Jurisprudence and Social Policy Program and holds a J.D. from the University of Colorado Law School. An historian by training, Shanks-Dumont focused his dissertation research on the contested histories of sovereign equality and international hierarchy in international law and the relationship among historical energy regimes, world economic systems, and inter-sovereign relations. He has published on a range of theoretical areas, including the self-funding structures of U.S. administrative agencies, the aesthetic dimensions of law and legal order, the early histories of international humanitarian law, international environmental law, and the criminalization of ecocide.

1 More than marginal

The complex work of framing devices

Laura Culbertson and Susan Longfield Karr

1 Introduction

This volume presents essays exploring texts that are often underemphasized within the broader contours of legal history and theory: prefaces, prologues, epilogues, and other types of framing devices. Such texts range from a few words in the margins to lengthy expositions. They occupy the beginning, end, and sometimes the middle of documents, letters, and stories within multiple legal traditions. Working on media from ancient stelae to modern prints, their authors crafted them to help contemporary and subsequent audiences understand how to approach the laws and ideas laid out in their accompanying works. Some such texts, like the opening paragraphs of the 1776 American Declaration of Independence and the Preamble of the 1789 Constitution of the United States, have acquired an exalted status in the global imagination that far exceeds the political contexts in which they were written or the legal documents to which they were attached.[1] However, most framing devices—despite their foundational and enduring effects on legal traditions across the globe—are not as well known even though they have shaped numerous legal traditions for thousands of years.

Although framing texts are well known by legal scholars and practitioners, the fact that framing texts of distinct legal traditions are not well known (or even known at all) across legal traditions disguises how ubiquitous framing devices are within legal contexts. The relative absence of cross-cultural knowledge among scholars about these texts also tends to rob the few that are well known of their historicity. For example, extracted from their time, place, and context, the Code of Hammurabi (ca. 1750 BCE), the Cyrus Cylinder (539 BCE), and the Magna Carta (1215) have become improbable stepping stones in a linear and progressive history of freedom, punctuated by the 1948 Universal Declaration of Human Rights, within the Western legal tradition and are, by

1 See David Armitage, *The Declaration of Independence: A Global History* (Cambridge, MA: Harvard University Press, 2008); Akhil Reed Amar, *America's Constitution: A Biography* (New York: Random House, 2005), and Amar, America's *Unwritten Constitution: The Precedents and Principles We Live By* (New York: Basic Books, 2012).

DOI: 10.4324/9781003534815-1

extension, a global legal tradition of rights.[2] As attractive as such narratives may be, they are not only fictive but also distorting. They can no sooner provide us with a historical perspective about the global cultures and traditions that shape our world today than they can educate and inform us about why specific texts were crafted as they were, why and how they were displayed, what problems they were meant to address, what aspirations they were meant to announce, or even whether these texts were meant to be read as legal documents at all.

The ease by which these ideas and documents are folded into grand narratives should raise questions for modern students and scholars of legal history, practice, and culture. However, repositioning the texts—and the theories anchored within them—is challenging given our general lack of exposure to all of the inaugural framing devices in legal traditions that span the globe outside of them. We wondered what a historical study of different framing devices might look like if, instead of squinting in attempt to trace the reception and influence of one tradition on another, we turned our gaze to explore what these devices did not only for those who produced them but also for those who used, misused, remembered, misremembered, interpreted, and misinterpreted them after they were created. Questions emerged from these points: What might we learn if we invited scholars from various disciplines and specialties to explore the role of framing devices within legal documents, theories, and cultures without expecting the resulting chapters to neatly interlock? What might we gain by asking why lawgivers, lawyers, and jurists were so attentive to how their ideas, theories, laws, and practices were framed and reframed in the first place? By extension, what do we lose if/when we flip past the frames or when we encounter these devices and read the texts that they frame for other purposes? How can we understand how and why subsequent generations reimagined or purposefully misremembered ideas that underpinned such texts to defend or critique existing conditions? Finally, what might this undertaking lend to broader discussions of comparative legal history and the ever-increasing interest in global legal history, particularly given the diversity of images and understandings of the law involved?[3]

2 See Paul Gordon Lauren, *The Evolution of International Human Rights: Visions Seen*, 3rd ed. (PA: University of Pennsylvania Press, 2011), specifically, Chapter 7; Micheline Ishay, *The History of Human Rights: From Ancient Times to the Globalization Era* (CA: University of California Press, 2008), 47f; and "Replica of 'Edict of Cyrus' Gifts," United Nations. For an understanding of the Cyrus Cylinder and its context, see Amelie Kuhrt, "Cyrus the Great of Persia: Images and Realities," in *Representations of Political Power: Case Histories from Times of Change and Dissolving Order in the Ancient Near East*, eds. Marlies Heinz and Marian H. Feldman (PA: Penn State University Press, 2007), 169–192.

3 For these methods, theories, and concepts, see Thomas Duve, "What Is Global History?," *Comparative Global History* 8 no. 2 (2020): 73–115; Olivier Moréteau, Aniceto Masferrer, and Kjell A. Modéer (eds.), *Comparative Legal History* (Edward Elgar, 2019), John G. H. Hudson and William Eves, "Introduction: Situating, Researching, and Writing Comparative Legal History," in *Introduction to Common Law, Civil Law, and Colonial Law: Essays in Comparative Legal History from the Twelfth to the Twentieth Centuries*, eds. William Eves, John Hudson, Ingrid Ivarsen, and Sarah B. White (Cambridge: Cambridge University Press, 2021), 1–24.

These were among the questions that we asked ourselves and our contributors as this project transformed from a series of engaging workshops to a collection of essays, each illuminating the importance of framing devices from multiple vantage points, at various times, and from within different traditions. As the project developed, several compelling themes emerged. These common themes went beyond using these devices to establish authorship, intention, and the purpose of the materials attached to explore questions of audience, placement, history, memory, and culture. Before turning to these and other themes, we provide a brief discussion of our approach and the relevant terminology, drawing on the scholarship that informed this undertaking.

2 On fractured texts

In recent decades, historians, codicologists, and philologists have drawn all kinds of framing texts from the margins into the foreground.[4] The resulting scholarship offers an opportunity for legal historians to harvest insights while revisiting their own source material with the previous questions in mind.[5] As noted already, it is easy to overlook how foundational legal texts are framed, no matter how skillfully a scribe or lawgiver constructs their introductions, no matter how well these devices infuse the whole text with meaning and authority, or no matter how much subsequent jurists and scholars draw on them in their own legal and political thought and texts. We can note several reasons for this—aside from the general tendency of today's readers to skip material such as front matter—ranging from function, to format, to genre. First, when it comes to legal sources, framing devices may seem extraneous to the "binding" parts of the composition: the articles, laws, resolutions, or statutes—the parts that help to put law into operation.[6] In some cases, the

4 Andreas Görke and Konrad Hirschler, in *Manuscript Notes as Documentary Studies* (Beirut: Ergon, 2011), 13–14, made the case for taking "manuscript notes" in Arabic manuscripts seriously as a genre. See also the contributions in Antonella Brita, Giovanni Ciotti, Florinda De Simini, and Amneris Roselli (eds.), *Copying Manuscripts: Textual and Material Craftsmanship* (Naples: UniorPress, 2020) and Liv Ingeborg Lied and Hugo Lundhaug (eds.), *Snapshots of Evolving Traditions: Jewish and Christian Manuscript Culture, Textual Fluidity, and New Philology* (Berlin: De Gruyter, 2017). On colophons, see Christopher D. Bahl and Stefan Hanß, *Scribal Practice and the Global Culture of Colophons, 1400–1800* (Palgrave Macmillan, 2022). See George Anton Kiraz and Sabine Schmidtke, *Literary Snippets: Colophons Across Time and Space* (Gorgias Press, 2023). Other important contributions are cited throughout, though not exhaustively.

5 Recent studies on prefaces to legal texts include Anya Adair, "Narratives of Authority: The Earliest Old English Law-Code Prefaces," *Law and Humanities* 15 no. 1 (2021): 4–24; Thom Gobbitt, "Liutprand's Prologues in the Edictus Langobardorum," in *Law, Book, Culture in the Middle Ages*, ed. Thom Gobbitt (Leiden: Brill, 2021), 71–97.

6 Gerhard Reis, *Prolog und Epilog in Gesetzen des Altertums* (München: C.H. Beck, 1983), 1–2, described the prologues of ancient, biblical, and classical law codes as the "*nichtdispositiven*" or "*nichtjuristischen*" components of the law, which could be misinterpreted as excusing prologues from relevance.

tone and character of prefatory or paratextual material differs from the "content" to the extent that they read with dissonance, like generically different compositions fastened together.[7] The material location of paratextual content in particular—positioned in margins or as colophons—can encourage modern readers to regard this content as distinctive from the other parts, even if the original authors did not view the components as fractured.

These kinds of perspectives lead to a false conclusion that the backbone of a foundational legal text resides in the parts in-between the frames, even though the framing content itself articulates the essence of the whole composition. Such a dichotomous view of the sources—*the frames are ceremonial, while the content is immutable*—also reflects an anachronistic interpretation of the legal topography of these texts. The laws of a code, for example, may emerge from an intentional legislative process, but in many traditions, the collected laws hold an unclear relevance to practice and legislation, standing instead as theoretical constructs, evidence for claims of moral and political authority, markers of prestige, or non-binding examples meant to advise judges or magistrates.[8] That we ascribe greater legislative agency to such cases reflects a problematic point of departure: a modern and Western assumption that the

7 For example, the Edict of Horemheb (ancient Egypt, 18th Dynasty), has been described as consisting of "an introduction, a legal part, and an administrative part" with "no unity of construction or style," (Kurt Pflüger, "The Edict of King Haremhab," *Journal of Near Eastern Studies* 5 no. 4 (1946): 260). Yet, the introduction is critical for establishing the authority and legitimacy of Horemheb, a pharaoh of non-royal descent, after the tumult of the previous period (Amarna). Another example is found in William F. Edgerton, "The Nauri Decree of Seti I: A Translation and Analysis of the Legal Portion," *Journal of Near Eastern Studies* 6 no. 4 (1947): 219–230, in which the prologue and epilogue were omitted on the grounds of being "long" and "rhetorical" (as opposed to legal). Such dissonance has also been observed regarding the Laws of Hammurabi, whose prologue and epilogue exhibit a literary character, whereas the "laws" themselves are formulaic casuistic statutes, giving an impression of two different genres. Pamela Barmash, *The Laws of Hammurabi: At the Confluence of Royal and Scribal Traditions* (Oxford University Press, 2020), reconciled these components.

8 A number of studies have noted gaps between the provisions of ancient and medieval codes and the ways in which criminal or civil legal matters were handled. For an exploration of the complexities, see Brian E. McKnight, "T'ang Law and Later Law: The Roots of Continuity," *Journal of the American Oriental Society* 115 no. 3 (1995), who described Tang and Song codes as "icebergs" (p. 420), and Norman Ho, "Understanding Traditional Chinese Law in Practice: The Implementation of Criminal Law in the Tang Dynasty (618–907)," *UCLA Pacific Basin Law Journal* 32 no. 2 (2015): 145–180 for comments on the "inconsistencies and discrepancies." For an English translation of the introductory chapter of the Tang code, see Wallace Johnson, *The T'ang Code, Volume I, General Principles* (Princeton University Press, 1979), 49ff. Raymond Westbrook provided a similar consideration on whether codes had much to do with normative legislation in the ancient Near East in "Codification and canonization," in *Ex Oriente Lex: Near Eastern Influences on Ancient Greek and Roman Law* (Johns Hopkins University Press, 2015), 184ff. Regarding Roman codes, J. Harries explored similar questions in "Roman Law Codes and the Roman Legal Tradition," in *Beyond Dogmatics: Law and Society in the Roman World*, eds. Cairns and du Plessis (Edinburgh University Press, 2007), 86. See also Bishop, Culbertson, Longfield Karr, and Rabin in this volume.

framed content is dispositive, justiciable, stable, and firmly connected to society and legal practice in a given context. By tracing the threads of legal traditions, the studies in this volume remind us that the legal content itself is often unstable, contestable, aspirational rather than normative, and subject to cycles of revision, reproduction, and reinterpretation, including misinterpretation.[9] Concerns about inconsistency, diversity, and instability no doubt inspired the need for framing material across many disparate traditions in the first place. To this point, framing components are often attempts to take new or tenuous collections of laws, procedures, or ideas and pin them into constructs of time, society, and place, sometimes with great finesse and innovation and other times lacking the authority to prevent later reframing. They serve as sites of constructed and collective memory as much as artifacts of history and culture.

Of course, this is not everything that scribes and authors set out to do with their framing texts. The particular functions vary across traditions, as we will see throughout the volume, utilizing a variety of strategies and calling upon different sources of authority. Thus, despite the allure of a comparative study on the strikingly ubiquitous phenomenon of framing devices, we find that variables of culture, social norms, written traditions, and political dynamics limit the exportability of many insights—not to mention the different ideas about where these compositions stand in terms of law. In fact, it is precisely because these compositions are embedded in carefully crafted frames (written or unwritten) that they cannot be classified into groups of equivalents. The purpose in this introduction is therefore not to synthesize studies into one master archetype of what framing devices do but to uncover themes that may help sharpen insights on specific traditions—to suggest approaches and themes for discovering the particulars and finding common ground to discuss and compare very disparate traditions.

First, an additional point about legal traditions is needed. It is well understood that intertextual readings are an "insistent task" of legal historians.[10] The sources under discussion are not treated as individual compositions in the ensuing chapters but as products of strategic, lengthy, and sometimes contentious editorial processes that involved systematizing lineages of texts, discourses, and ideas into new innovations.[11] Each act of textual appropriation or translation witnesses the injection of new cultural assumptions and ideas about

9 Some preambles in fact spell out the necessity and indeed the expectation of altering the content ongoingly. For example, the preamble of the first code of Nepal (1854) states that portions may be corrected, erased, or rejected, and the code was thus understood as a living text, "as a process, rather than as a fixed code;" Rajan Khatiwoda, Simon Cubelicand, and Axel Michaels, *The Mulukī Ain of 1854: Nepal's First Legal Code* (Heidelberg University Publishing, 2021), 4.

10 Steven Wilf, "Law/Text/Past," *Irvine Law Review* 1 (2011): 550.

11 Legal texts, if we are to pinpoint one aspect of their character, are "often intentionally derivative, moving forward across time through constantly gesturing toward commonly accepted terms of art," as Steven Wilf put it, in "Law/Text/Past," *Irvine Law Review* 1 (2011): 550.

law.[12] In many traditions, interaction with the preceding legal sources was critical for establishing legitimacy, in contrast to modern common law, in which older laws are discarded.[13] Framing texts themselves have complex histories, as mixtures of "echoes, borrowings, reworkings, and innovations."[14] To make things more complicated, these streams of succession are neither unbroken nor continuous but often ruptured and incomplete. All chapters touch on the ways that the sources originate in contexts like the textualization of unwritten traditions, codification processes, constitution drafting, or attempts at legal unification in moments of conquest, upheaval, and empire.[15] Therefore, we have multiple dimensions of prefacing to consider, both in the framing of a source, and in the engagement with all the received ideas that preface and frame the drafting itself. This requires some attention to terminology.

3 Key concepts in modern scholarship

Narrowing down terminology for phenomena that span many cultural and textual traditions—particularly through the mediation of modern concepts—is impossible. Everyone has a notion of what a prologue, preamble, or epilogue entails, but the particulars of how such texts were executed vary according to tradition and genre. Transposing definitions or expectations of a distinct textual category carries a risk of naturalizing intentions or expectations that may not belong to the original sources. This is especially important to keep in mind when different legal genres may seem to overlap or interrelate in ways that differ from modern categories. For example, scholars debate about whether Qin-era (221–206 BCE) decrees, ordinances, and statutes—sources that appear to overlap and intersect—represent distinct genres of legal texts or "different evolutionary stages in an ongoing process of codification."[16] We cannot

12 For example, as noted by Ada Maria Kuskowski, "Translating Justinian: Transmitting and Transforming Roman Law in the Middle Ages," in *Law and Language in the Middle Ages*, eds. Matthew W. McHaffie, Jenny Benham, and Helle Vogt (Leiden: Brill, 2018), 32.

13 For modern common law systems, "what is past is not prologue, but extraneous material, irrelevant to practice" according to Philippa Byrne, "Medieval Violence, the Making of Law and the Historical Present," *Journal of the British Academy* 8 no. 3 (2020): 136, who also pointed out that "We [modern readers] are not accustomed to imagining law on the basis of a series of historical relationships: a provision either is current or it is not" (ibid.).

14 This phrase is taken from Anya Adair, "Narratives of Authority," 32.

15 Here, we use "codification" as a general term to encapsulate a variety of curation processes, some of which are better termed as "collections" or "consolidations" (lacking in authority of enforcement). "Codification," for example, was not conceived as such until recent centuries; we do not mean to suggest that there were Napoleonic-style processes across time from the ancient world until now.

16 See Thies Staack, "From Copies of Individual Decrees to Compilations of Written Law: On Paratextual Framing in Early Chinese Legal Manuscripts," in *Copying Manuscripts: Textual and Material Craftsmanship*, eds. Antonella Brita, Giovanni Ciotti, Florinda De Simini, and Amneris Roselli (Naples: UniorPress, 2020), 187, for sources relevant to this debate. Staack argues for the latter interpretation.

answer this debate by superimposing assumptions about what these types of texts entail. For that matter, what a decree, ordinance, or statute is in the Qin setting differs from what we might call a decree, order, or statute in the Roman legal tradition, or within an Ancient Near Eastern setting, and so on. The transposition of a modern Western term to diverse sources suggests similarity across time and space that might not exist, and we face the same problem when talking about "prefaces," "prologues," "preambles," and so forth. Here, we can therefore only offer some engagement with relevant concepts as they are utilized in modern scholarship and throughout the volume, taking these terms as mediators for variations rather than a fixed glossary.

To start, "prefaces" and "prologues" in general have long received attention as components of historical and literary works, whether ancient, medieval, or modern.[17] Prefaces are difficult to define and typologize not only because of variations of goals, content, and rhetorical strategies but also because not all traditions formalized prefaces into standard formulae.[18] Studies on prefaces have explored what these elements must entail to be considered prefaces as opposed to other types of introductory material and whether they comprise a specific "class" on their own or even a genre, meaning "groups of mutually connected texts."[19] A prologue, similarly, is a distinct piece of material that precedes the narrative portion of a composition, but this concept also lends to variation by text and genre and can precede non-narrative texts, such as a law collection. Across traditions, content described as prefaces or prologues may also consist of non-prose components, for example, titles, tables of contents, calendars, dedications, or images, though some scholars may describe these as paratexts.

Preambles are generally understood as statements introducing that which they precede, but "in the realm of [modern] law, a slightly more specific definition intrinsically links preambles with statements of the motivations and

17 For examples of how scholars describe the particulars of prefaces and prologues in specific traditions, see Reis, *Prolog und Epilog*; Justin Lake, *Prologues to Ancient and Medieval History: A Reader* (University of Toronto Press, 2013), especially "Introduction," xi–xviii; Lane J. Sobehrad provided a discussion of prologues in relation to history in *The Past in Prologues: The Origins, Form, and Function of Introductory Material in Medieval English Historical Works* (Texas Tech University dissertation, 2017).

18 For general questions about what prefaces do and how they exist, see Jacques Derrida, *La dissémination* (London: The Athlone Press, 1971). (See the 1981 edition translated by Barbara Johnson, pages 7–8). Discussing the difficulty of pinning down what a preface is or does, he wrote, "Prefaces, along with forewords, introductions, preludes, preliminaries, preambles, prologues, and prolegomena, have always been written, it seems, in view of their own self-effacement. Upon reaching the end of the *pre*-. . . the route which has been covered must cancel itself out" (p. 9).

19 Tore Janson, *Latin Prose Prefaces: Studies in Literary Convention* (Stockholm: Almquist and Wiksell, 1964), 14. See also 13–16.

objectives that inform the legal document they introduce."[20] Though preambles attach to a specific range of legal texts (treaties, constitutions, laws, and so on), the degree of their justiciability or "legal effect" is less concrete.[21] They are often dismissed as symbolic or descriptive "window dressing," with disregard to their "performative, laudatory, and exhortatory" aspects and overarching political charge.[22] A preamble is sometimes identified in terms of functionality, such as that of defining the aspirations and identity of a people in a constitution (*We, The People Of*).[23] Preambles have a socio-political character,[24] and in many traditions, preambles have a historical aspect, providing a narrative to frame a scenario.[25] At least, these kinds of features encourage historians to employ the term "preamble" for texts showcasing these characteristics. To reiterate, there is nothing innate in these terms so far that we must expect from each source; herein, they are springboards for discussing and mediating between sources of different traditions, but they do not inherently hold specific sets of expectations themselves apart from what individual authors identify according to the particulars of the traditions that they are engaged with.

Regardless, these terms do not suit all examples. We next turn to literary critic Gérard Genette's elaboration on the concept of "paratexts," which means all of the material surrounding a text—the title, the author's name, a preface, and other adornments such as illustrations—all of the things that "ensure the text's presence in the world."[26] A paratext is what enables a text to become what it is and to become this to the public. Genette described them as "thresholds," neither part of the text nor separate from it. Thresholds shape the audience's understanding of a work, serving as spaces through which the audience must pass in order to understand the content they are about to

20 Max H. Hulme, "Preambles in Treaty Interpretation," *University of Pennsylvania Law Review* 164 no. 5 (2016): 1288. See also Nomi Claire Lazar, "Time Framing in the Rhetoric of Constitutional Preambles," *Law and Literature* 33 no. 1 (2021): 3.

21 Max H. Hulme, "Preambles in Treaty Interpretation," 1288.

22 See Nomi Claire Lazar, "Time Framing in the Rhetoric of Constitutional Preambles," 3, who also points out that even symbolic purposes "may be intensely political, even violent" (5).

23 Of course, such claims of consensus about identity may reflect conflict and division. The implicit claim of consensus about the vision of the state may also be subject to contestation; see Hanna Lerner, *Making Constitutions in Deeply Divided Societies* (Cambridge University Press, 2011).

24 Neha Ummareddy and Aniket Alam, "What Do Preambles Do? A Study in Constitutional Intent and Reality," *Studies in Indian Politics* 9 no. 2 (2021): 221.

25 For example, in Hittite vassal treaties of the ancient Near East, "preambles" preceded or included a sometimes lengthy historical "prologue" to the treaty; see Gary Beckman, *Hittite Vassal Treaties* (Atlanta: Scholars Press, 1996) for the treaties and Amnon Altman, "The Role of the 'Historical Prologue' in the Hittite Vassal Treaties: An Early Experiment in Securing Treaty Compliance," *Journal of the History of International Law* 6 (2004): 43–64, for a discussion of how the historical prologues established the obligations and political subordination of the second party of the treaty (and are thus not extraneous to the "legal effect" of the text).

26 Gérard Genette, *Paratexts: Thresholds of Interpretation*, Translated by Jane E. Lewin. Literature, Culture, Theory 20 (Cambridge University Press, 1997), 1.

encounter.[27] The concept of paratext has been exported from literary studies to a variety of fields, and it is particularly valuable for material approaches to texts, manuscript studies, and codicological approaches;[28] plus it can describe textual elements that do not fit into Western categories starting with *pre-*. To that point, the concept of paratext also lends to the study of theory, insofar as such devices enable their authors to fix conceptual or normative frames by which the attached text should be understood, utilized, or interpreted. Still, the term "paratext" itself requires parsing and theorization for new applications, and one should be careful not to presume that historical authors considered *para*textual content to be *marginal*.[29]

In fact, a question following this brief survey is whether the authors of our sources considered prefaces, prologues, preambles, or paratexts separate from the "body" of a work to the extent that these can be stripped off without compromising meaning or legal effect. The premise of the volume is that meaning, context, and purpose is indeed lost without these elements, whether or not they were considered distinctive portions of a composition. Besides, textual framing elements are only one manifestation of longer processes of how authors prefaced and framed the driving ideas—via editing, revising, collecting, synthesizing, or textualizing unwritten laws. The sources do not achieve a "final" form given the vagaries of appropriation, reproduction, and editing by subsequent actors with their own innovative agendas or competing understandings of what should be preserved.[30] This brings us to the concept

27 This spatial conceptualization or analogy was explored by Jean Nicole Mellon Saint Laurent, who examined the connection of these concepts to space in the concept of a "literary narthex;" see "Prologues as Narthexes in Syriac Hagiography," in *Syriac Hagiography: Texts and Beyond*, eds. Sergey Minov and Flavia Ruani (Leiden: Brill, 2021), 17–55.

28 To note but a few important works of interest: Giovanni Ciotti and Hang Lin (eds.), *Tracing Manuscripts in Time and Space through Paratexts* (Berlin: Walter de Gruyter, 2016) included a variety of studies on manuscript cultures, colophons, and framing texts in Africa, South Asia, and East Asia. Antonella Brita, Giovanni Ciotti, Florinda De Simini, and Amneris Roselli's volume *Copying Manuscripts: Textual and Material Craftsmanship* (Naples: UniorPress, 2020). Laura Janson (ed.), *The Roman Paratext: Frame, Text, Readers* (Cambridge University Press, 2014), particularly the chapter on law books by Matthijs Wibier.

29 Following the caveats and italics of Charlotte Cooper, "What Is a Medieval Paratext?," *Marginalia* 19 (2015): 37–50. See also Patrick Andrist, "Toward a Definition of Paratexts and Paratextuality: The Case of Ancient Greek Manuscripts," in *Bible as Notepad: Tracing Annotations and Annotation Practices in Late Antique and Medieval Biblical Manuscripts*, eds. Liv Ingeborg Lied and Marilena Maniaci (Berline: De Gruyter, 2018), 132 for a discussion of how Gennette's ideas connect to manuscript studies (with additional scholarly sources of interest) and a discussion of theory.

30 Here, we recall Cooper's phrasing on how paratexts are constantly "recast and recreated with each new edition" in processes that "endlessly add to the layers of paratext" ("What is a Medieval Paratext?" 46). For a discussion of paratexts and copying in general, see the contributions in Antonella Brita, Giovanni Ciotti, Florinda De Simini, and Amneris Roselli (eds.), *Copying Manuscripts: Textual and Material Craftsmanship* (Naples: UniorPress, 2020) and various contributions in Liv Ingeborg Lied and Hugo Lundhaug (eds.), *Snapshots of Evolving Traditions: Jewish and Christian Manuscript Culture, Textual Fluidity, and New Philology* (Berlin: De Gruyter, 2017).

of "framing device" itself, which may better mediate among all of the documented phenomena here.

The concepts of "frames" and "framing" are modern and often anchored in Western studies, especially as adapted from the highly influential 1974 study of sociologist Erving Goffman, *Frame Analysis: An Essay on the Organization of Experience*. Scholars of numerous fields have adopted/adapted Goffman's core concepts for different applications, such that most of the literature on frames and framing ventures far from the subjects of this volume. Recent studies have recruited important elements of Goffman's ideas for studies of ancient texts.[31] Goffman explained that our experiences with reality are mediated through "frames." Frames are understood as "cognitive structures that serve to classify and categorize all kinds of experiences, perceptions, and acts of communication."[32] These are dynamic structures that change as actors interact through communications.

> To apply frame theories means to disentangle such communication processes in order to understand the relationship between smaller pieces of information—and especially to think about how such information is embedded into the pre-existing frame network, i.e., how communication is framed by the background knowledge of the author and (target) audience, and their respective knowledge, experiences, and expectations.[33]

Legal historians cannot adopt such frame theories wholesale for studies of wide-ranging traditions, particularly not when we lack access to author knowledge or intentions, not to mention the kind of mass media environments Goffman and his scholarly successors have at their disposal. The matter of audience adds a complexity that also limits how we might apply the theory. However, we can extrapolate a few points of insight.

Application of frame theories involves looking for culturally specific elements within communicative processes, which means that studying frames is appropriate for application to different cultures and potentially liberates us from the restrictions of some of the above terminology. The idea of a framing device, here taken as a component of a long communicative process, also helps us maneuver

31 Günther, Elisabeth and Sven Günther (eds.), *Frames and Framing in Antiquity I: Selected Papers from the First Frames and Framing in Antiquity Conference 16–18 October 2020*. Supplements to the *Journal of Ancient Civilizations* 9 (Changchun, 2022), 3. These authors expanded on other influences in frame theory in relevance to sources from beyond the modern world, including Charles J. Fillmore (linguistics) and Marvin Minsky (cognitive science). Scholarship on frames and framing in general is numerous and rich—far too numerous to cite there.

32 Günther and Günther, *Frames and Framing in Antiquity*, 3. See also R. M. Entman, "Framing: Towards a Clarification of a Fractured Paradigm," *Journal of Communication* 43 no. 4 (1993): 51–58.

33 Günther and Günther, *Frames and Framing in Antiquity*, 4.

beyond just the textual/paratextual dichotomy and consider the trajectory of communication with legal traditions as part of the prefacing of texts. The reception, transmission, translation, appropriation, editing, telling, retelling, etc.—all of this comprises part of the prefacing process, with many parts unwritten. Prefaces, prologues, preambles, epilogues, and all kinds of paratexts can all be understood as strategies of "framing," all artifacts of processes of appropriation and reproduction of law. They express the background knowledge and ideas of the author and formulate this knowledge to convey arguments, context, purpose, authority, legitimacy, and history to a target audience. Moreover, the idea of framing devices lets us expand our range of sources, drawing in sources that we would exclude if we adhered to an idea of the "final draft" or narrowed the study to only prologues or preambles or the like. Here, we can include compositions such as Hōjō Yasutoki's letters on codification in medieval Japan, Jefferson's introductions, and appeals by Renaissance jurists to more abstract ideas, for example, theories of justice, early modern and modern.[34] All of these frame new arguments for reform by appealing to existing laws, inventing new ones, or offering ideas for alternative legal frameworks.

To sum up, we are adapting the idea of a "framing device" to encapsulate various prefacing material, whether attached to a specific legal composition or part of the trajectory of its production, whether introductory or complementary, whether written or unwritten, whether legal or historical. Above all, the Western forms that we surveyed earlier can be studied as framing devices, but this concept can also include forms from non-Western traditions.

4 Themes of the volume

Regarding these elements as forms of communication, what we find in the context of law is that framing and re-framing devices are laden with all kinds of claims. Indeed, their objective is to convey these claims, imparting the composition with authority, longevity, and resonance. This brings us to a synopsis of insights gathered from the essays of this volume and other sources on legal traditions. As noted in the opening, neglect of context (social, political, and historical) comes with a risk of subscribing to grand narratives that are themselves constructs (of frame authors and of modern scholarly discourses). All of the following thematic areas intersect and interrelate but do not form an "archetype" of a legal framing device.

Claiming Cohesion, Stability, and a Common Understanding of Law: First, any kind of anthology or collection requires a framing device of some type to introduce and explain the contents, and a legal product is

34 See Bovbjerg (Japan), Crow (Jefferson), and Longfield Karr (Renaissance jurists).

no exception.[35] Framing texts can serve to pin an unstable assortment of things and ideas into place, advancing a claim that they belong together. Most of the ensuing chapters note how framing components are replete with such claims of cohesion, continuity, and stability, even if what they frame are curations, collections, or fictions. The arguments about cohesion have two dimensions. First, the claims argue for a smooth integration of texts and traditions,[36] or even having achieved a new level of textual stability, having ironed out a mess of received ideas and sources and composed, as Matthew Crow puts it, "a narrative of legal continuity." Second, the claims may pertain to a fractured geography of law on the ground, a setting of plurality and competing normative systems. Framing texts may depict this plurality as problematic or even dangerous (representing a colonizer's view) and then advance claims of having overcome or managed this plurality, achieving a common understanding of the law[37] or even establishing a common identity.[38] For some framers, these goals comprised a moral imperative to rescue populations from the uncertainty and vulnerabilities that come from legal disparities.[39] After all, what is law if not a means to stave off conflict and violence? Whether reality supports these depictions of law—or the notion of pluralism as the cause of violence—is another matter. Such claims help framers establish legal authority, including supremacy over *other* competing texts. A composition such as a law code, after all, has no purpose unless it positions itself as the *only* code.[40] Additionally, reconciling scattered and fragmented customs and laws along with new ones created more systematic (and thus less malleable) legal frameworks and legal norms, while simultaneously (and likely unintentionally) laying the groundwork for some to fundamentally misinterpret them by (opportunistically) misreading and reworking them to suit their own time and purposes. Moreover, in doing so, this disregards the markers that the authors of the devices so carefully crafted for their intended audiences (contemporary and future) to understand them.

Construction of Contexts and Legal Landscapes: Harmonization strategies vary widely: sometimes, they swallow up sources from prior traditions and other times, skillfully ignore or erase them; sometimes, they present predecessor

35 This is not solely an expectation of written legal traditions; see the possibly-thirteenth-century "Hunter's Oath" from Mali (not to be conflated with the Charter of Kurukan Fuga), which has a preamble; Gregory Mann, "The World Won't Listen: The Mande "Hunters' Oath" and Human Rights in Translation," *Humanity* 13 no. 2 (2022): 136.

36 See Frédéric Constant's discussion of *Comments to the Tang Code* and the imperative to "harmonize and strike the balance" (this volume).

37 For other examples, see Bishop, Bovbjerg, Culbertson, Lhost, Longfield Karr, and Rabin, this volume.

38 See Cross, Crow, and Longfield Karr, this volume.

39 These kinds of arguments are showcased in the chapters by Bobvjerg and Lhost.

40 Raymond Westbrook 2000/2015. "Codification and Canonization."

sources as venerated pillars of authority and other times, denounce them as flawed, incomplete, or outdated. All of this pertains to how the framers wish to depict the context into which they will stake the supremacy of their new composition. A framing device helps to construct and communicate this context, building the cosmos[41] in which the law will live just as much as innovating the law itself (or claiming to). Framing texts even define an antiquity against which to set their depictions of the present by painting the past as a golden age[42] or a time of corruption to correct.[43] It is tempting to conceive of context as something fixed and anchored in a tangible reality, when in fact, "context" is not an essential object, and we should not adopt a positivist view that assumes that context refers to a permanent space. On the contrary, context creation is a politically charged process, involving claims of either continuity or chaos, like those mentioned in the previous paragraph, and it shifts the instant a successive audience receives the composition and repositions it within their own objectives. As noted earlier, a stream of succession does not drive itself; for some of the framing narratives, context creation involves a written presentation of the curated genealogy of texts, defining linkages between the "ancient" and "current" legal sources. The presentation is steeped in fictitious or even propagandistic depictions of state, history, or society. Meanwhile, framing devices identify aspirations and serve as blueprints for an idealized relationship between law and society, the structure of state and society, or the order of the cosmos itself.

Defining the Bases of Authority: With so many claims bursting from these sources—claims about law, state, society, and history—framing texts often must establish who holds the prerogative to consolidate law in the first place and, just as important, posit its source of authority (moral or historical). The sources call upon the authority of the gods, emperors, kings, nature, or legislators to announce how the laws, procedures, and ideas fit into a tradition or break from it. In some traditions, authors define their personal status in the framing content vis-a-vis their patrons, commissioners, social standing, scribal or judicial authority, or their grasp of the very concepts that frame and guide the law.[44] Appealing to time as a

41 See Bishop, Culbertson, Longfield Karr, this volume.

42 For example, see various Chinese legal traditions holding that "ancient times were a golden age from which there has been a steady decline" (Johnson, *The T'ang Code*, 9); see also the "imperial preface" to the Great Ming Code (finalized after a lengthy revision process in 1397), promulgated by Emperor Zhu Yuanzhang with the opening statement: "I have the realm and govern it by imitating antiquity," translation of Yonglin Jiang *The Great Ming Code/Da Ming lü* (University of Washington Press, 2004), p. lii and p. 3.

43 For example, ancient Near Eastern law codes preface their laws as correcting all kinds of social evils, such as debts and other crises.

44 Like the concept of *dōri*, discussed in Bovbjerg's chapter on medieval Japanese warrior law, the idea of reason could mean a combination of morality, justice, and the lived experience of the law. Hōjō Yasutoki could draw upon the concept in making his case for a strategic update to the law.

chronological marker and conceptual space, several framing devices use history to appeal to authorities that went beyond naming one's patron or protector. Authority can derive from a fixed community or institution, which reinforces and is reinforced by political structures. The basis of authority can also change.[45] While some framing texts offer insights into the scope of legal knowledge that the documents were establishing or calling on, others referred to the kinds of figures mentioned previously, referencing an already long-established tradition or noting how they were fundamentally breaking with it to create something new.

Temporal Framing and Mytho-Historical Narratives: Throughout the examples cited here and throughout the volume, we see that authority is often borrowed from the past, both historical and imagined. This may involve an appeal to venerated traditions, for example, the ways that European traditions engaged with emperor Justinian's code or how the Song Dynasty and other successor traditions engaged with the Tang Code of 737.[46] A source may even purport to derive from the past itself as a means to frame its own authority.[47] Many framing devices rely on historical narratives or archaizing language because they serve as the vehicle by which past or foreign elements are picked up and relocated into the present. In addition, an appeal to history—lived, remembered, recorded, and imagined—could infuse existing legal frameworks and cultures with gravitas, especially when changes in form, structure, or content were either being introduced or disseminated in new ways. They could also be used to critique corruption and tyranny. Just as important, appeals to history were used to distract and absorb the shock of announcing the creation of something entirely new, whether made necessary by the advent of new regimes, powers, and constitutions or to merely replace procedures, practices, and institutions that no longer served their intended purpose or had fallen out of use entirely. Some of these histories were secular; some were religious. Some were grounded in fact; others were wholly fictive. Some imparted historical authority to authors, legislatures, and ancestors; others supplied moral authority to arguments aimed at resisting or implementing sweeping changes in legal codes and cultures. A few of the texts explored

45 See Bishop, Longfield Karr, and Rabin in this volume.

46 The comparison is limited to the ways in which these codes were received by subsequent audiences, see Brian E. McKnight, "T'ang Law and Later Law: The Roots of Continuity," *Journal of the American Oriental Society* 115 no. 3 (1995): 410.

47 One example is the "Pact of 'Umar" (*shurūṭ Umar*), a letter claiming legal authority and a pact between the Caliph 'Umar and the Patriarch of Jerusalem, which purports to derive from the 7th century but contains features of a 9th-century composition not associated with the reign of 'Umar. Yet, it is the 7th-century textures that impart authority and legal effect to the text, even without a preamble. See Milka Levy-Rubin, *Non-Muslims in the Early Islamic Empire: From Surrender to Coexistence* (Cambridge University Press, 2011), 60f on the dating of this text and a discussion of it in a legal context; see pages 171–176 for translations.

in this volume also appealed to the power of the past to offer harrowing postscripts and preludes of what it would cost communities to ignore and disregard them. Most combined appeals to the past, present conditions, and visions of the future to foreshadow and emphasize the necessity of harmonizing existing laws and procedures in order to alleviate discord and confusion and to promote social cohesion and stability in society. Whether restricting the terms and time of peace treatises[48] or establishing limits on conduct in war,[49] attempting to solidify cultural norms and aspirations[50] or demarcating the penalties and procedures for punishment,[51] each text offers illuminating insights into the political and social contexts that the prefaces and epilogues emerged from and attempted to preserve and secure.

Audience and Identity Construction: Next, we come to the matter of who these compositions were for. Framing devices presume a specific audience and sometimes explicitly invoke them. On the one hand, audiences could be narrow and carefully circumscribed, consisting only of scribal communities, an aristocracy who either had a stake in judicial decision making or feared the repercussions of reforms, or divine benefactors who entrusted the lawgivers with their roles. On the other hand, the audience could be universal. In any case, one important role of framing devices is to satisfy expectations about the new composition and to ensure its acceptance and adoption. After all, law cannot be enforced only from the top-down. Its enforcement requires vast networks of legal practitioners, public officials, magistrates, judges, archivists, and scribes—all of these people must accept the claims of authority and that is why framing devices address these audiences. Part of convincing them of their stake in the law is defining a common identity or postulating a unity of diverse identities within the legal space.[52]

Political Power, State-Making, and Empire: By now, it is clear that all sources under discussion have ideological charges as much as legal character. Codes, for example, are manifestations of power, instruments to justify conquest and colonization, efforts to circumscribe power in new ways—or even outright challenges to political paradigms.[53] Their frames contain appeals to memories of powers that reinforce the claims of political authority—often in the service of new kings, regimes, or states. The

48 See especially Cross, this volume.

49 Shanks-Dumont, this volume.

50 Contreras, Crow, Longfield Karr, this volume.

51 Lhost, this volume.

52 See Bishop, Bovbjerg, Constant, Culbertson, Longfield Karr, and Rabin in this volume.

53 For example, see Łukasz Niesiołowski-Spanò, "Some Considerations on the Socio-Political Aspects of the Law-Codification in the Province of Yehud in the Persian Period. A View through a Roman Lens," *Palamedes. A Journal of Ancient History* 13 (2022): 307–313, for a discussion of whether codification can be a political and social act (p. 310).

political and ideological aspects of our texts may be so bombastic as to convince modern scholars that some of these sources were truly more propagandistic than practical,[54] and historians may question the historicity of events recounted in texts such as conquest narrative prologues.[55] Whether anchored in real events or hyperbole, the effect of framing narratives could be consequential and effective for defining the structure of power—and its limits. It bears emphasizing that many of these legal texts emerged at points of state formation, colonization, conquest, and consolidation or following periods of major political upheavals and crises. Some texts even serve to challenge a hegemon.[56] The texts play a role in creating the identity of the state, its leaders, and its subjects and charting the structure of authority, even if only to point out the centrality of a royal figure or imperial core. To that point, they articulate royal or imperial ideologies and ideals, exemplifying rhetorical strategies and tropes associated with claims of power.[57] But they also articulate the limits by involving justice, right, nature, history, or god.

5 Volume organization and chapter overview

This volume is split into two parts, each consisting of essays that complement rather than supplement one another. Taken together, these essays and the primary sources in the appendix aim to encourage readers to consider the enduring effects of framing devices in legal cultures within and beyond those featured here.

The essays in **Part One: Pulling Together** explore prefaces as sites of harmonization, solidification, and dissemination of legal precedents, norms, and knowledge. From Ancient Greek interstate treaties (7th–6th centuries BCE) to the creation of a modern Indian Penal Code (1837), the materials explored in Part One are examples of successful codifications and systemizations of legal customs, practices, and frameworks. The framing devices affixed

54 For example, see Norman Yoffee's analysis of the Code of Hammurabi in *Myths of the Archaic State* (Cambridge University Press, 2005), 109, in which he argued that the code was "designed, or better adapted as a piece of political propaganda to win the hearts and minds of citizens of formerly autonomous city-states" after a unification process.

55 Amnon Altman discussed historical narratives and conquest claims that appear in the prologue of a treaty between the Hittite King Tudhaliya IV and Šaušgamuwa, the King of Amurru. He noted how "historical prologues" in Hittite vassal treaties establish relationships of subordination to the Hittite rulers, serving "not to present a literary-historiographic treatise, but rather to marshal legal arguments and facts in order to justify the terms of subordination set forth in the stipulatory section." See "Rethinking the Hittite System of Subordinate Countries," *Journal of the American Oriental Society* 123 no. 4 (2003): 744.

56 See Lhost, this volume.

57 For example, see Thom Gobbitt's discussion of "Liutprand's Prologues in the *Edictus Langobardorum*," 71. This chapter also provides another example of a complex reception history and re-invention of the laws.

to documents—whether set in stone, written on parchment, or presented in typeset—not only rationalized legal processes and relationships for their contemporaries and subsequent jurists within their legal cultures but also sometimes served as guides to others. The chapters in Part One, as studies of stable texts, also explore how and why some prefaces and epilogues not only serve to proscribe legal principles but also serve as vessels of political and cultural history. These essays shed light on how and why prefaces and epilogues stand as monuments to power, explanations for amending or changing legal traditions, and signposts to the future. They achieved what they were meant to achieve.

The essays in **Part Two: Breaking Apart** discuss prefaces that, even though they influenced subsequent legal traditions—including their own—were not always received or applied with their intended purpose in mind. These devices—documentary and theoretical—had these results for various reasons, including a misalignment between the work that the prefaces and prologues were intended to accomplish and the uses to which their immediate audiences put them. Imprecise terms, heavy-handed prose, and unrealistic expectations invited criticism from their contemporaries or subsequent readers. These issues also inadvertently encouraged those who rediscovered or recovered them to misinterpret their legal and cultural significance and, in some cases, assimilate them into traditions that they were otherwise alien to or ignore the history and theory (ancient or modern, real or imaginary) that they carried with them. Part Two includes essays exploring debated understandings of ancient legal-literary works, such as the Code of Hammurabi (1755–1750 BCE) or the purposeful forgetting of the social justice preamble in the Utah State Constitution (1992). These chapters illuminate the complicated reception histories of framing texts as much as the instability of their original contexts.

Part One begins with a detailed analysis of the use of preambles to create and announce new relationships by setting forth their expectations among Archaic Greek city-states. Nicholas Cross, in his "The preambles to archaic Greek interstate treaties at Olympia: a study in the diffusion of diplomatic language," shows how these framing devices and their placement in prominent public spaces enabled the proliferation of language and an understanding of identity between the seventh to fifth centuries BCE, ultimately leading to the creation of formulaic language in interstate agreements among Greek states across the Mediterranean. While the main body of Greek treaties contained clauses familiar to modern readers—such as provisions for mutual defense, future amendments, and the specification of leadership roles—Cross explores specific terms and language to show how the preambles illuminate embedded religious and social features of the societies that made them. Drawing on the international relations theory of constructivism and its view of states, Cross contends that common features within the preambles ultimately reflect an emerging Greek identity.

In Chapter Three, "Prefaces of legal documents in Late Imperial China," Frédéric Constant likewise argues for the significance of prefaces to cultural understanding. In this case, however, the prefaces of legal texts did not create shared practices so much as they exhibited them. Most Chinese works, regardless of genre, contained prefaces or afterwords in which the authors stated their reasons for writing the text, such as paying homage to tradition, establishing or confirming the cultural capital of the author or printer, and, in some cases, announcing that the text to which the preface or afterword was attached was ordered by the emperor. The prefaces to legal codes or regulatory texts also contained the imperial edicts that solicited them. Those attached to collections of cases, commentaries, and legal treaties often included the authorial intentions behind writing and publishing the text, especially those that aimed at celebrating the judicial skills of magistrates. Some framing devices offered their readers a historical understanding of the law that stretched back to high antiquity, infusing the law with legitimacy while asserting both its relevance and social prestige. Others, intended to be used by subsequent jurists, offered guidelines and explanations on how the general principle of law could be applied to address specific issues. Attention to the prefaces attached to such collections reveals, like the preambles in the first chapter, a common understanding of the law, and, thus, Constant argues, they constitute an essential resource for understanding Chinese legal theory.

In "The conservative case for warrior law: legal change in medieval Japan," Christoffer Bovbjerg explores the importance of framing to establish new legal frameworks. Chapter Four focuses on what Bovbjerg calls Japan's 1232 "Magna Carta moment," when the first shogunate adopted the *goseibai shikimoku*, a code outlining legal philosophy and principles with relevance to the samurai or warrior class. Bovbjerg points to an astonishing aspect of its articles: they restricted and circumscribed the power of this elite community, establishing accountability. Widely distributed in writing, this foundation enabled a common understanding of law and held a lasting influence in legal education for centuries. But how did it accomplish this status, let alone compel an elite imperial administration to embrace restrictions to their authority? Bovbjerg argues that acceptance of the code stemmed from the rhetorical finesse of its compiler, the shogunal regent Hōjō Yasutoki, who played up its traditional nature. Yasutoki employed the concept of *dōri* ("reason") to explain deviations from prior traditions, downplaying breaks from tradition and crafting continuity. Analyzing two letters of Yasutoki as framing devices, Bovbjerg shows how Yasutoki cleverly assured imperial elites that reforms would secure stability and order.

In "Bodies of law in early medieval England and Scotland," Andrew Rabin also addresses the dynamics between legal expertise and political power while exploring a different kind of feudal legal framework: the transmission and dissemination of injury schedules across time and cultures within the Western legal tradition. Given their long lives, injury schedules were as much legal repositories as reflections of power grappling; they were sites of "proxy battles" for political authority. A central discussion of Chapter Five is how Rabin accounts for a surprising discovery: a copy of the twelfth-century Scottish legal tract *Leges inter Brettos et Scottos* bound within a fifteenth-century recension that was, itself, promulgated some six to nine hundred years earlier. Rabin lends insight to this unexpected medieval injury schedule by situating it within its genre and history, showing more broadly how injury schedules were living texts received across time and cultures in decentralized settings. Rabin explores their "tangled history of reception," showing how these texts were aspirational and ideological (i.e., not practical for applied law). Their function was to stake a monopoly on legal authority and expertise for the sovereign by demonstrating his "knowledge and control over the legal history of his kingdom." To that point, scribes preserved the form and structure of the laws—the appearance of legal authority. This explains how the text survived despite the enormous changes of history and politics across its lifespan.

Part One concludes with a chapter that investigates a legal framework centered on punishments far more systematic than those found within the *Leges inter Brettos et Scottos*. In "Promises and Perils of Macaulay's Preface to the Indian Penal Code," Elizabeth Lhost explores the first Indian Penal Code drafted by Thomas Macaulay in 1837 before several revisions. Lhost points to the exceptional success of the code and its far-reaching acceptance and reproduction across and beyond South Asia. Despite the original commissioners' emphasis on uniformity, the code's success resulted in its proliferation—a sprouting up of "spin-off" princely state codes inspired by the first drafts—which eventually raised questions about the code's authority, originality, uniformity, and even British hegemony. To understand these phenomena, Lhost explores editions and receptions of the code after examining Macauley's framing arguments. The exploration solidifies the questions of Part One: how ideas about law traveled across legal, cultural, and political boundaries; the role that texts and frames play in their transmission; and the question of whether transmission and reproduction indicate success or instability. Lhost shows how the mobility of this code shaped understandings of codification, codes, and colonial rule as she charts the balance between the code's stability and adaptation.

Part Two: Breaking Apart examines how framing devices affixed to seminal legal texts or that underpin legal and political thought tend to be overlooked or misunderstood and thus misinterpreted by those who read them without regard to their original context and by those who fold them into narratives that elide their revolutionary character.

In Chapter Seven, "(Re-)framing Hammurabi's laws: worldbuilding with prologues and epilogues in the Ancient Near East," Laura Culbertson investigates why early law collections from the Ancient Near East, such as the so-called Code of Hammurabi, can be framed and reframed in many ways, both today and in antiquity. Such codes are simultaneously precursors to future framing strategies and culminations of ancient traditions. But how did their original framers make the case for their position in time and space? Cautiously drawing on the concepts of frames and framing as used in modern media and communication studies, this chapter explores how the authors of the law collections themselves argued for their positioning in history by revisiting the often-skipped prologues and epilogues. Culbertson notes that these framing texts had complex and multidimensional purposes, serving as conveyances of legal ideas and ideological frameworks to state elites and scribes. To frame claims of authority, the prologues and epilogues contained complete revisions of history, geography, and legal authority.

In Chapter Eight, "Prefaces in the legal texts of the crusader Kingdoms of Jerusalem and Cyprus," Adam M. Bishop also examines how framing language in legal documents was used to map geographies of authority within juridical spaces and demarcate the boundaries of states in the Near East. Such medieval Catholic feudal states, founded in conquest and political intrigue, were unstable and short-lived. The chapter focuses on the kingdoms based in Acre and Cyprus, whose thirteenth-century Crusaders constructed ideas of a "legendary past" to frame their codes, claiming that the codes came from 1099 unchanged. To inject the codes with legitimacy and longevity, they anchored them in long-standing Byzantine and Latin Christian traditions and mythologized glorified Crusader authorities. Bishop pushes back at the claims of historical continuity, showing how they were imagined histories crafted to serve present political purposes. Bishop recounts the scattered, competing, and incoherent networks of legal sources that informed the codes and describes how framing devices set out to explain them through specific rhetorical strategies. By situating the Crusader codes in these complex traditions, Bishop illuminates how the rhetorical strategies drew on language and history to position the codes in the service of the states.

Imagined histories are also central to Susan Longfield Karr's "No mere metaphor: the state of nature as a framing device." Rather than use legends to justify the existence of new states, Renaissance jurists used them to anchor their calls for fundamental legal and political reforms. In this way, they conjured ideas of the state of nature—rooted in the history and memory of *ius gentium* (the law of nations)—to offer their audiences visions of the past with which they could measure corruptions in their present. In the first half of Chapter Nine, Longfield Karr suggests why the idea of the state of nature and the collective memory that it carries with it serves as a significant framing device within the "Western legal tradition" itself. As such, Longfield Karr attempts to illuminate how the metaphor and idea construct and shore up legal frameworks, past and present. The second half of the chapter offers a series of brief case studies in which Renaissance jurists utilized the state of nature as a framing device to transliterate legal theory into legal history. Longfield Karr argues that they appealed to an imagined past to elucidate why the future depended on legal and political reforms in their present, even though the past that they invoked to accomplish this relied on collective—and constructed—memory rather than empirical evidence.

With "Jefferson's preambles, prefaces, and persistence," Matthew Crow shifts our attention from imagined history to troubled ones, focusing on Thomas Jefferson. One of the most prolific writers in early American history, Jefferson is overlooked for his contributions to the intellectual history of law and constitutions. Crow demonstrates that Jefferson was in fact a serious constitutional theorizer. He reconstructs Jefferson's eccentric understanding of constitutions as instantiations of "collective political life" and carefully situates Jefferson's thinking within the intellectual culture of colonial Virginia. In this atmosphere of fractured thinking about constitutions, Jefferson collected, queried, and tinkered with inherited sources to explore constitutional culture and grapple with questions about constitutional authority and identity—about who held the authority to read the law and whether it should be everyone. Crow introduces Jefferson's lengthy and seemingly overwritten constitutional drafts to show the evolution of thinking about ideas of constitutions, the notion of citizenship and how it relates to constitutions, and indeed, the evolution of the drafts themselves. The sources reveal Jefferson's anxieties over who controls historical narratives and the role of the past in politics and how these questions informed the alternative paths that Jefferson framed and constructed—paths ultimately not taken.

Tensions between memory and myth also weave into Daimeon Shanks-Dumont's argument in Chapter Eleven, "Martens Clause and ambiguity at the birth of modern humanitarian law." Shanks-Dumont recounts a traditional narrative: a clause formulated for the preamble of the 1899 Hague Convention—named the Martens Clause after Russian lawyer and diplomat Feodor Martens—was the foundation and catalyst for the development of modern international humanitarian law. Across the ensuing century, scholars and courts alike have recruited and restated this clause, pointing to its foundational importance for humanitarian concerns, even while competing interpretations and ambiguities persist to this day. Shanks-Dumont counters the narrative and reframes it as a myth. He shows how the clause has been stretched into something it never was—arguing that its original meaning had little to do with humanitarian concerns—and shows how its import has "expanded and contracted" as determined by interpretations in later legal and political contexts. By repositioning the clause within its original legal context, political history, and the events surrounding its formation and by reconciling contradictory depictions of Martens' motivations and role, Shanks-Dumont explores how the clause is a "shaky foundation as a source of normative legal doctrine."

Finally, in Chapter Twelve, "Searching for meaning in the Utah Constitution's Free Market Preamble," Jorge L. Contreras focuses on the Constitution of Utah (1895) to show what happens when the intended meaning behind a framing clause is purposefully forgotten and then, once remembered, artfully co-opted to serve competing political interests. US state constitutions receive less scholarly attention than the US Constitution, and a striking component among them is Utah's one-of-a-kind Free Market Clause (drafted 1992), which uniquely establishes links between economic efficiency and the general public's welfare. The clause reflects the ideas of Professor John J. Flynn, a progressive antitrust theorist, who constructed the provision with the intentions to promote antitrust regulation for the sake of social justice and equality and to preserve democratic institutions, based on his interaction with Rawlsian ideas. Contreras points to a fascinating institutional "memory lapse" since the clause's adoption, whereby it has not only been forgotten but misremembered and then essentially gutted of its justiciability, as best illustrated by the case *Tesla Motors v. Utah Tax Commission*. By reconstructing the background and journey of the clause all the way back to the formation of the state Constitution, the chapter concludes by considering not only what, if anything, can be done when such significant constitutional text is purposefully stripped of its potential but also the "interpretive coin toss" in the future of this clause.

6 Summary, limitations, and future questions

Ideally, a study on framing texts across legal traditions would include many traditions, including those less represented in the grand narratives of law that we discussed at the opening. The absence of other traditions from this volume was not by design but rather by the chances of timing, contributor availability, and the impact of a pandemic. But the discussion so far only underscores the promise of expanding the scope. New queries concern the question of whether the current assemblage of essays demonstrates the possibility of a comparative methodology in the future, particularly on the sticking question of how compilations or "codes" are used in different settings and how their consolidation occurred.

Altogether, the aim of this book is neither to attempt to be comprehensive nor historically exhaustive but rather to start a conversation. We hope that this collection suggests directions for scholars working with framing texts. We also hope that this volume inspires others to explore the role of these framing devices beyond the purposes—and for more expansive audiences—than the authors in this book have hitherto discussed, alluded to, or observed. Finally, we hope that such studies help scholars and students better understand the many purposes that framing devices have served within legal traditions, from ancient times to the present, across the globe.

References

Adair, Anya. "Narratives of Authority: The Earliest Old English Law-Code Prefaces." *Law and Humanities* 15, no. 1 (2021): 4–24. https://doi.org/10.1080/17521483.2020.1847455.

Altman, Amnon. "Rethinking the Hittite System of Subordinate Countries." *Journal of the American Oriental Society* 123, no. 4 (2003): 741–756. https://doi.org/10.2307/3589966.

Altman, Amnon. "The Role of the 'Historical Prologue' in the Hittite Vassal Treaties: An Early Experiment in Securing Treaty Compliance." *Journal of the History of International Law* 6 (2004): 43–64. https://doi.org/10.1163/157180504773805838.

Amar, Akhil Reed. *America's Constitution: A Biography*. New York: Random House, 2005.

Amar, Akhil Reed. *America's Unwritten Constitution: The Precedents and Principles We Live by*. New York: Basic Books, 2012. https://doi.org/10.5860/choice.50-5275.

Andrist, Patrick. "Toward a Definition of Paratexts and Paratextuality: The Case of Ancient Greek Manuscripts." In *Bible as Notepad: Tracing Annotations and Annotation Practices in Late Antique and Medieval Biblical Manuscripts*, edited by Liv Ingeborg Lied and Marilena Maniaci, 130–150. Manuscripta Biblica 3. Berlin: De Gruyter, 2018. https://doi.org/10.1515/9783110603477-001.

Armitage, David. *The Declaration of Independence: A Global History.* Cambridge, MA: Harvard University Press, 2008. https://doi.org/10.2307/j.ctv1ks0hkk.

Bahl, Christopher D. and Stefan Hanß. *Scribal Practice and the Global Culture of Colophons, 1400–1800.* London: Palgrave Macmillan, 2022. https://doi.org/10.1007/978-3-030-90154-7.

Barmash, Pamela. *The Laws of Hammurabi: At the Confluence of Royal and Scribal Traditions.* Oxford: Oxford University Press, 2020. https://doi.org/10.1093/oso/9780197525401.001.0001.

Beckman, Gary. *Hittite Diplomatic Texts.* Society of Biblical Literature: Writings from the Ancient World Series. Atlanta: Scholars Press, 1996. https://doi.org/10.2307/606683.

Byrne, Philippa. "Medieval Violence, the Making of Law and the Historical Present." *Journal of the British Academy* 8, no. 3 (2020): 133–154. https://doi.org/10.5871/jba/008s3.133.

Cooper, Charlotte E. "What Is a Medieval Paratext?" *Marginalia* 19 (2015): 37–50.

Derrida, Jacques. *La dissémination.* 1981 edition. Translated by Barbara Johnson. London: The Athlone Press, 1973.

Duve, Thomas. "What Is Global History?" *Comparative Global History* 8, no. 2 (2020): 73–115.

Edgerton, William F. "The Nauri Decree of Seti I: A Translation and Analysis of the Legal Portion." *Journal of Near Eastern Studies* 6, no. 4 (1947): 219–230. https://doi.org/10.1086/370843.

Entman, R. M. "Framing: Towards a Clarification of a Fractured Paradigm." *Journal of Communication* 43, no. 4 (1993): 51–58. https://doi.org/10.1111/j.1460-2466.1993.tb01304.x.

Genette, Gérard. *Paratexts: Thresholds of Interpretation*, Translated by Jane E. Lewin. Literature, Culture, Theory 20. Cambridge: Cambridge University Press, 1997.

Gobbitt, Thom. 2021. "Liutprand's Prologues in the Edictus Langobardorum." In *Law, Book, Culture in the Middle Ages*, edited by Thom Gobbitt, 71–97. Leiden: Brill, 2021. https://doi.org/10.1163/9789004448650_002.

Goffman, Erving. *Frame Analysis: An Essay on the Organization of Experience.* Cambridge, MA: Harvard University Press, 1974.

Görke, Andreas and Konrad Hirschler (eds.). *Manuscript Notes as Documentary Studies.* Beirut: Ergon, 2011.

Günther, Elisabeth and Sven Günther (eds.). *Frames and Framing in Antiquity I: Selected Papers from the First Frames and Framing in Antiquity Conference 16–18 October 2020.* Supplements to the *Journal of Ancient Civilizations* 9. Changchun: Institute for the History of Ancient Civilizations, 2022.

Harries, J. "Roman Law Codes and the Roman Legal Tradition." In *Beyond Dogmatics: Law and Society in the Roman World*, edited by John W. Cairns and Paul J. du Plessis, 85–104. Edinburgh: Edinburgh University Press, 2007. https://doi.org/10.1017/upo9780748631773.007.

Ho, Norman. "Understanding Traditional Chinese Law in Practice: The Implementation of Criminal Law in the Tang Dynasty (618–907)." *UCLA Pacific Basin Law Journal* 32, no. 2 (2015): 145–180. https://doi.org/10.5070/p8322029214.

Hudson, John G. H. and William Eves. "Introduction: Situating, Researching, and Writing Comparative Legal History." In *Introduction to Common Law, Civil Law, and Colonial Law: Essays in Comparative Legal History from the Twelfth to the Twentieth Centuries*, edited by William Eves, John Hudson, Ingrid Ivarsen, and Sarah B. White. Cambridge: Cambridge University Press, 2021.

Hulme, Max H. "Preambles in Treaty Interpretation." *University of Pennsylvania Law Review* 164, no. 5 (2016): 1281–1343.
Ishay, Micheline. *The History of Human Rights: From Ancient Times to the Globalization Era.* CA: University of California Press, 2008.
Janson, Laura (ed.). *The Roman Paratext: Frame, Text, Readers.* Cambridge: Cambridge University Press, 2014.
Jiang, Yonglin. *The Great Ming Code/Da Ming lü.* WA: University of Washington Press, 2004.
Johnson, Wallace. *The T'ang Code, Volume I, General Principles.* NJ: Princeton University Press, 1979.
Kuhrt, Amelie. "Cyrus the Great of Persia: Images and Realities." In *Representations of Political Power: Case Histories from Times of Change and Dissolving Order in the Ancient Near East*, edited by Marlies Heinz and Marian H. Feldman, 169–192. PA: Penn State University Press, 2007.
Kuskowski, Ada Maria. "Translating Justinian: Transmitting and Transforming Roman Law in the Middle Ages." In *Law and Language in the Middle Ages*, edited by Matthew W. McHaffie, Jenny Benham, and Helle Vogt, 30–51. Medieval Law and Its Practice 25. Leiden: Brill, 2018.
Lake, Justin. *Prologues to Ancient and Medieval History: A Reader.* University of Toronto Press, 2013.
Lauren, Paul Gordon. *The Evolution of International Human Rights: Visions Seen*, 3rd ed. PA: University of Pennsylvania Press, 2011.
Lazar, Nomi Claire. "Time Framing in the Rhetoric of Constitutional Preambles." *Law and Literature* 33, no. 1 (2021): 1–21.
Lerner, Hanna. *Making Constitutions in Deeply Divided Societies.* Cambridge: Cambridge University Press, 2011.
Levy-Rubin, Milka. *Non-Muslims in the Early Islamic Empire: From Surrender to Coexistence.* Cambridge: Cambridge University Press, 2011.
Lied, Liv Ingeborg and Hugo Lundhaug (eds.). *Snapshots of Evolving Traditions: Jewish and Christian Manuscript Culture, Textual Fluidity, and New Philology.* Berlin: De Gruyter, 2017.
Łukasz Niesiołowski–Spanò. "Some Considerations on the Socio-Political Aspects of the Law-Codification in the Province of Yehud in the Persian Period. A View through a Roman Lens." *Palamedes. A Journal of Ancient History* 13 (2022): 307–313.
Mann, Gregory. "The World Won't Listen: The Mande 'Hunters' Oath' and Human Rights in Translation." *Humanity* 3, no. 2 (2022): 129–145.
McKnight, Brian E. "T'ang Law and Later Law: The Roots of Continuity." *Journal of the American Oriental Society* 115, no. 3 (1995): 410–420.
Moréteau, Olivier, Aniceto Masferrer, and Kjell A. Modéer (eds.). *Comparative Legal History.* Edward Elgar, 2019.
Pflüger, Kurt. "The Edict of King Haremhab." *Journal of Near Eastern Studies* 5, no. 4 (1946): 260–276.
Reis, Gerhard. *Prolog und Epilog in Gesetzen des Altertums.* München: C.H. Beck, 1983.
"Replica of 'Edict of Cyrus' Gifts." *United Nations.* www.un.org/ungifts/replica-edict-cyrus#:~:text=On%2014%20October%201971%2C%20the,of%20the%20country%20of%20Iran.
Sohebrad, Lane J. "The Past in Prologues: The Origins, Form, and Function of Introductory Material in Medieval English Historical Works." Texas Tech University dissertation, 2017.
Staack, Thies. "From Copies of Individual Decrees to Compilations of Written Law: On Paratextual Framing in Early Chinese Legal Manuscripts." In *Copying Manuscripts: Textual and Material Craftsmanship*, edited by Antonella Brita, Giovanni Ciotti, Florinda De Simini, and Amneris Roselli, 183–240. Naples: UniorPress, 2020.

Ummareddy, Neha and Aniket Alam. "What Do Preambles Do? A Study in Constitutional Intent and Reality." *Studies in Indian Politics* 9, no. 2 (2021): 221–238.
Westbrook, Raymond. "Codification and Canonization." In *Ex Oriente Lex: Near Eastern Influences on Ancient Greek and Roman Law*, edited by Raymond Westbrook, Deborah Lyons, and Kurt Raaflaub, 181–193. MD: Johns Hopkins University Press, 2015.
Wibier, Matthijs. "The Topography of the Law Book: Common Structures and Modes of Reading." In *The Roman Paratext: Frame, Texts, Readers*, edited by Laura Jansen, 56–72. Cambridge: Cambridge University Press, 2014.
Wilf, Steven. "Law/Text/Past." *Irvine Law Review* 1 (2011): 543–564.
Yoffee, Norman. *Myths of the Archaic State.* Cambridge: Cambridge University Press, 2005.

Part I

Pulling together

2 The preambles to archaic Greek interstate treaties at Olympia

A study in the diffusion of diplomatic language

Nicholas D. Cross

1 Introduction

Over the course of the archaic Greek period (700 BCE–480 BCE), the various communities spread out across the Mediterranean embraced common diplomatic practices and vocabulary. They recorded their interstate agreements on stone or metal and exhibited them in their civic centers. Often, they displayed copies of those inscriptions at Panhellenic centers, where visitors could see them and then adopt the same language for their own community's agreements. This essay considers this process of diffusion through the case studies of the three oldest extant interstate treaties in Greece. In the sixth and early fifth centuries, the communities of Elis and the Ewaoioi, Sybaris and the Serdaioi, and the Anaitoi and Metapioi made respective alliances and displayed these agreements at Olympia. Most of these cities were not large, geopolitically significant cities. Two (Elis and Sybaris) were regional powers, and four were small communities about which little is known today. Nevertheless, the language of these early treaties spread and eventually became the basis for diplomatic documents throughout the Mediterranean.

The preambles to these treaties therefore served two introductory functions. First, they literally introduce the treaties and prepare the reader for how to regard the texts. The main body of each text contains clauses that are similar to modern ones, such as provisions for mutual defense or penalties for noncompliance, but it is the preambles that frame how contemporaries would conceive these treaties. With their announcements of the titular designations and durations of the treaties, the preambles reflect the social character of the agreements, and it is in these terms that the Greeks understood them just as much as in political or military terms. Second, these preambles introduce the Greek world to how to articulate and display interstate documents. They function, metaphorically, as the preambles to the development of a common Greek diplomatic vocabulary. By examining the language and the influence of these preambles, this essay sheds light on how the Greeks themselves would have understood them and later interstate agreements, a perspective that the conclusion connects to a constructivist reading of international relations. From

DOI: 10.4324/9781003534815-3

this two-pronged investigation—of the preambles themselves and of the ripple effects on later treaties—this essay emphasizes that these shared prefatory elements give a unique insight into the spread of a standard vocabulary of diplomacy and the creation of a common understanding of legal norms during the archaic period and beyond.

2 Preambles

The preambles to ancient Greek treaties naturally appear at the top of inscriptions. Although there are no spaces between words, one can still distinguish the preambles from the rest of the documents. Stone stelae are usually tapered at the top so that the preambles are visually separated from the main texts. Due to the narrower space at the top, the opening material contains more letters per line, and these lines are closer together. But in the case of bronze plaques, the material on which the three treaties at Olympia—between Elis and the Ewaoioi, Sybaris and the Serdaioi, and the Anaitoi and Metapioi—were inscribed, there are linguistic dividers. By the end of the archaic period, preambles became so formulaic that even if inscriptions survive in fragmentary condition, it is possible to reconstruct them on the basis of the dimensions of the inscriptions and by comparison with other preambles.

Since there is a comparative wealth of extant documentation from the classical Greek period (480 BCE–323 BCE), it is possible to enumerate the common prefatory components of the interstate treaties of that later time. These include (1) an invocation of the gods; (2) a heading announcing the subject matter; (3) a prescript containing the names of the presiding officials involved, the date, and the name of the proposer; and (4) a motivation clause and an enactment formula.[1] But these standard elements were the product of many years and many intercommunal interactions. Earlier archaic treaties, though more rudimentary with only the first and second components, set precedents for the preambles and texts to come. The main contents of the three treaties at Olympia have been the subject of much discussion in modern scholarship, but few have looked closely at their preambles—or their physical features and their display locations, for that matter.[2] These often-overlooked aspects are

1 Margherita Guarducci, *Epigrafi di carattere pubblico* (Roma: Istituto poligrafico dello Stato, 1969), 11–19; Peter J. Rhodes, *The Athenian Boule* (Oxford: Clarendon Press, 1972), 64–68; Alan S. Henry, *The Prescripts of Athenian Decrees* (Leiden: Brill, 1977), 1–18; Peter J. Rhodes and David M. Lewis, *The Decrees of the Greek States* (Oxford: Clarendon Press, 1997), 4–5.

2 On interstate treaties at Olympia in general, see Francesca Mello, "Ἀ ϝράτρα τοῖς ϝαλείοις. Rhetra e le wratrai olimpiche," *Zeitschrift für Papyrologie und Epigraphik* 167 (2008): 50–66; V. Alonso Troncoso, "Olimpie et la publication des traités internationaux," *Rivista di diritto ellenico* 2 (2012): 3–26; Paulina Komar, "Epigraphic Culture in Olympia," in *Epigraphic Culture in the Eastern Mediterranean in Antiquity*, ed. Krzysztof Nawotka (New York: Routledge, 2021), 68–80; Nicholas Cross, *The Roots of Cooperation: Constructing Interstate Alliances in Ancient Greece* (forthcoming).

important because they shed light on how the original audience viewed the inscriptions and interpreted the nature of those agreements.

2.a Eleans and Ewaoioi

The oldest extant alliance treaty in Greece was between Elis and the Ewaoioi in the late sixth century. It was once thought to be between Elis and the Heraeans, a community in Arcadia, until James Roy and Damian Schofield, using three-dimensional computer technology, showed that the inscription reads the Ewaoioi, an otherwise unknown community in the Elean region.[3] Elis was the dominant city in the northwestern region of the Peloponnesus, with several dependent communities in the area, including the Ewaoioi. Indeed, by the sixth century, Elis had control over Olympia, its sanctuary and its games, placing the city in a position of geopolitical prominence.[4] Many of Elis' own laws were posted at Olympia.[5] It was only natural, therefore, for Elis to display its treaty with the Ewaoioi at the same place.

The treaty was inscribed on a bronze plaque measuring 10 cm high x 20 cm wide x 0.65 cm deep. It reads as follows:

> ἀ ϝράτρα τοῖρ Ϝαλείοις : καὶ τοῖς Ἐυϝαοίοις : συνμαχία κ' ἔα ἐκατὸν ϝέτεα: ἄρχοι δέ κα τοΐ : αἰ δέ τι δέοι : αἴτε ϝέπος αἴτε ϝάργον : συνέαν κ' ἀλ(λ)άλοις : τά τ' ἄλ(λ)<α> καὶ παρ πολέμō : αἰ δὲ μὰ συνέαν : τάλαντόν κ'ἀργύρō : ἀποτίνοιαν : τοῖ Δὶ Ὀλυνπίοι : τοὶ κα(δ)δαλε̄́μενοι: λατρειο̄́μενον : αἰ δέ τιρ τὰ γράφεα : ταῒ κα(δ)δαλέοιτο : αἴτε ϝέτας αἴτε τελεστὰ : αἴτε δᾶμος: ἐν τἐ̄πιάροι κ' ἐνέχοιτο τοἰνταυτ' ἐγραμ(μ)ένοι.
>
> The agreement of the Eleans and the Ewaoioi. There will be an alliance for one hundred years. It will begin from this year. If there is any need, either in word or in deed, they shall stand together in all things, especially in war. If they do not stand together, the wrong-doers shall pay a talent of silver to Olympian Zeus for dedication. If anyone does harm to this writing, whether the community or an official or private citizen, he shall be liable to the sacred penalty which here is written down.[6]

3 James Roy and Damian Schofield, "*IvO* 9. A New Approach," *Horos* 13 (1999): 155–165; cf. Sophie Minon, *Les inscriptions éléennes dialectales (VIe-IIe siècle avant J.-C.)*, vol. 1 (Geneva: Droz, 2007), 73–84.

4 James Roy, "Elis," in *An Inventory of Archaic and Classical Poleis*, eds. Mogens Herman Hansen and Thomas Heine Nielsen (Oxford: Oxford University Press, 2004), 494–498; Matt Kõiv, "Early History of Elis and Pisa: Invented or Evolving Traditions?," *Klio* 95 (2013): 329–332.

5 cf. Minon, *Les inscriptions éléennes dialectales.*

6 *IvO* 9. For commentary on the text, see Robert A. Bauslaugh, *The Concept of Neutrality in Classical Greece* (Berkeley: University of California Press, 1991), 58–59; Ernst Baltrusch, *Symmachie und Spondai: Untersuchungen zum griechischen Völkerrecht der archaischen und klassischen Zeit* (Berlin: de Gruyter, 1994), 9–11; Roy and Schofield, "*IvO* 9"; Minon, *Les inscriptions éléennes dialectales*, 73–83.

The preamble contains the designation and duration of the agreement. The document is described as a *fratra* (ϝράτρα), the Elean dialectal form of *rhetra* (ῥήτρα), which literally means "compact, treaty." Francesca Mello, on the basis of comparative evidence, thinks that *fratra/rhetra* refers to a treaty dictated by one superior party to another.[7] In this case, the superior party would be Elis, which at the time was also the hegemon of the Elean League.[8] This treaty may have been signed when the Ewaoioi became a member of this multistate alliance. That there was a hegemonic power, however, does not necessarily mean that the alliance was exploitative. The preamble describes the condition of the association between the two parties as a *synmachia* (συνμαχία), which literally means "a fighting together." This is the first appearance of this noun in the Greek language but it would become the standard descriptor for alliances later in the fourth century. Previously, in archaic literature, alliances were called *philia* (φιλία, friendship), *xenia* (ξενία, guest-friendship), or other socially charged metaphors.[9] Jonathan Hall suspects that *synmachia* "arose initially within the orbit of the connections that early archaic élites forged with one another, indicating an *ad hoc* arrangement between individuals or groups of individuals designed to address a specific military need."[10] Ernst Baltrusch considers the emergence of *synmachia* to be an indication that interstate relations had moved from personal contacts to legal contracts concluded by communal political entities.[11] That may be the case, but the break with the past terminology would never be complete. Although the word *synmachia* is associated with military affairs, it still raised connotations of the earlier words. Although the people of Ewa were probably a small community within the region controlled by Elis and a member of the Elean League, the language in the preamble indicates that their relationship was not wholly political or one-sided and that it was characterized by social features.

"There will be a *symmachia*," the treaty announces, "for one hundred years. It will begin from this year." It is comparatively rare for later Greek treaties of this sort to carry a specific time limit. Most are designated to last forever. Nevertheless, a century is a lengthy period of time. The signatories did not consider their alliance to be merely a temporary expedient. Instead, they intended it to endure beyond their own lifetimes. Furthermore, the alliance would address more than just military or political aims. The particle *de* (δέ) marks a division between the heading and the main text of the treaty. Following the preamble, there is the first appearance in Greek treaties of a generalized

7 Mello, "Ἀ ϝράτρα τοῖς ϝαλείοις."

8 James Roy, "The *Perioikoi of Elis*," in *The Polis as an Urban Centre and as a Political Community*, ed. Mogens H. Hansen (Stuttgart: Franz Steiner Verlag, 1997), 292–295.

9 Cross, *The Roots of Cooperation*.

10 Jonathan M. Hall, "International Relations," in *The Cambridge History of Greek and Roman Warfare*, vol. 1, eds. Philip Sabin, Hans van Wees, and Michael Whitby (Cambridge: Cambridge University Press, 2007), 101.

11 Baltrusch, *Symmachie und Spondai*, 14.

mutual defense clause ("if there is any need, either in word or in deed, they shall stand together in all things, especially in war"), which will become a principal element of classical alliance treaties. The clause highlights collaboration in war but leaves open the possibility for other unspecified cooperative activities. The wide range indicates that the signatories saw their *synmachia* embracing collaboration in any activity: military, political, social, economic, religious, or otherwise. This choice of *symmachia* in the preamble is notable; it evidently contained a multivalent meaning for the parties. Beyond the preamble and the mutual defense clause, the agreement contains a monetary fine for violation of the treaty terms and a religious punishment for defacing the inscription, both common clauses in later treaties.

2.b Sybarites and Serdaioi

A contemporary treaty is the one between Sybaris and the Serdaioi.[12] Sybaris was an Achaean colony founded on the southern coast of Italy in the late eighth century. Because of its fertile territory and busy port, the city became known for luxury and excess, as reflected in the modern English word "sybarite." By the end of the sixth century, it had positioned itself as the hegemon of the Greeks in the region, including the Serdaioi.[13] Outside of this treaty, the only other evidence for the Serdaioi is a rare issue of silver coinage from this period.[14] Apparently, the Serdaioi's dependency on the Sybarites did not preclude the minting of coins.

The brief treaty was inscribed, in Achaean script and Doric dialect, on a bronze plaque measuring 8.9 cm high x 15.7 cm wide x 0.5 cm deep. It reads as follows:

> ἁρμόχθεν οἱ Συβαρῖται κ' οἱ σύνμαχοι κ' οἱ Σερδαῖοι ἐπὶ φιλότατι πιστᾶι κ' ἀδόλοι ἀείδιον· πρόξενοι ὁ Ζεὺς κ' Ὀπόλον κ' ὀλλοι θεοὶ καὶ πόλις Ποσειδανία.
>
> The Sybarites and their allies and the Serdaioi agreed to friendship, faithful and without deceit, forever. The protectors are Zeus, Apollo, the other gods, and the city of Poseidonia.[15]

12 On the date of this treaty, see Mario Lombardo, "Il trattato tra i Sibariti e i Serdaioi: problemi di cronologia e inquadramento storico," *Studi di Antichità* 12 (2008): 49–60.

13 Strabo 6.1.13; cf. Tobias Fischer-Hansen, Thomas Heine Nielsen and Carmine Ampolo, "Italia and Kampania," in Hansen and Nielsen, *An Inventory of Archaic and Classical Greek Poleis*, 253–254. Ove Hansen, "The Coins with the Legend MEP and the Origin of the Etruscans," *Parola del Passato* 45 (1990): 447–448 argues that the Serdaioi were Etruscan, not Greek.

14 N. Keith Rutter, *Historia Numorum: Italy* (London: British Museum Press, 2001), 142–143; Emanuele Greco, "Serdaioi," *Annali di archeologia e storia antica* 12 (1990): 39–57.

15 *SdA* 120. For commentary on the text, see Maurizio Giangiulio, "La φιλότης tra Sibariti e Serdaioi (Meiggs-Lewis, 10)," *Zeitschrift für Papyrologie und Epigraphik* 93 (1992): 31–44; Giangiacomo Panessa, *Philiai: l'amicizia nelle relazioni interstatali dei greci* (Pisa: Scuola Normale Superiore, 1999), 92–101; Lombardo, "Il trattato tra I Sibariti e i Serdaioi"; Sarah Bolmarcich, "Communal Values in Ancient Diplomacy and Culture," in *Valuing Others in Classical Antiquity*, eds. Ralph M. Rosen and Ineke Sluiter (Leiden: Brill, 2010), 117–119.

As in the previous treaty, the preamble contains the designation and duration of the alliance. It opens with the verb *armochthen* (ἁρμόχθεν) that means "put together, fit well, betroth," which has prompted some scholars to think that the two parties were entering into an arrangement that was entirely new for them.[16] The preamble continues by stating that the Sybarites and their existing allies (*synmachoi*) agreed to join with the Serdaioi in a *philotēs* (φιλότης), an archaic word for friendship. The treaty fails to mention the expected duties of the new allies in this *philotēs*, so it is impossible to determine how things might be different for them than for the unspecified *synmachoi*, but some distinction is presupposed. Maurizio Giangiulio claims that this treaty refers to a hegemonic symmachy ("una simmachia egemoniale"), suggesting that the alliance was both exploitative and hierarchical.[17] Emanuele Greco thinks that this treaty is evidence not only for hegemony but also for a "Sybarite empire" (*impero sibarita*) in Italy.[18]

A close look at the language of the preamble, however, raises doubts that this *philotēs* reflected such a situation any more than the Elean-Ewaoioi *symmachia* did. In addition to *philia* and *xenia*, the Greeks had characterized some of their earliest alliances as *philotēs*.[19] Peter Karavites considers its use to be analogous to that of "brotherhood" in Near Eastern treaties from the Bronze Age, though with a broader application.[20] Kurt Raaflaub suggests that *philotēs* is the communal equivalent to *xenia*, an intimate relationship between individuals.[21] Its meaning is close to that of *symmachia* in that it refers to a union of peoples for any sort of collective action.

There is an expressed commitment on the part of the two parties to the friendship "*pistai k'adoloi*" (faithfully and without deceit), an early form of what Everett Wheeler calls an "anti-deceit clause" commonly contained in the oaths of classical treaties.[22] Unlike the previous alliance, this one is designed to last "forever" (*aeidion*), which will also become standard in classical alliances. Again, evidently, the opinion of the signatories at the time inclined more towards the expectation of a working relationship that extended beyond any immediate goals. The text closes with an implicit mention of a religious

16 Henri van Effenterre, "La fondation de Paestum," *La Parola del Passato* 192 (1980): 161–175; Giangiulio, "La φιλότης tra Sibariti e Serdaioi," 33–35.

17 Giangiulio, 33. The treaty calls the agreement a *philotēs*, not a *symmachia*.

18 Greco, "Serdaioi."

19 Jean Taillardat, "Φιλότης, πίστις et foedus," *Revue des Études Grecques* 95 (1982): 1–14; Mary Scott, "Philos, Philotēs and Xenia," *Acta Classica* 25 (1982): 1–19; Panessa, *Philiai*, 23–30.

20 Peter Karavites, *Promise-Giving and Treaty-Making: Homer and the Near East* (Leiden: Brill, 1992), 49–52.

21 Kurt Raaflaub, "Politics and Interstate Relations in the World of Early Greek Poleis: Homer and Beyond," *Antichthon* 31 (1997): 25.

22 Edward Wheeler, "Sophistic Interpretations and Greek Treaties," *Greek, Roman and Byzantine Studies* 25 (1984): 254–255; Edward Wheeler, "Anti-Deceit Clauses in Greek Treaties: An Apologia," *Electrum* 14 (2008): 57–84.

punishment from the *proxenoi* gods (and nearby Poseidonia) for any violation of the treaty.

2.c *Anaitoi and Metapioi*

Finally, the third treaty, from the beginning of the fifth century, is between the Anaitoi and Metapioi. Nothing else is known about either of these groups. Since the treaty is written in the Elean dialect of the Greek language, it is likely that they were located somewhere in the region of Elis, though their status vis-à-vis Elis is not clear.[23] They inscribed a copy of their treaty on a bronze plaque measuring 6.5 cm high x 19 cm wide x 0.2–0.4 cm deep. It reads as follows:

> Ἀ ϝράτρα τὸς Ἀναίτο[ς] καὶ τὸ[ς] Μεταπίος. φιλίαν πεντάκοντα ϝέτεα. κ' ὀπόπαροι μὲνπεδέοιαν ἀπὸ τῶ βομῶ ἀποϝελέοιάν κα τοὶ πρόξενοι καὶ τοὶ μάντιερ· αἰ τὸ[ν] ὅρκον παρβαίνοιαν, γνῶμαν τὸρ ἰα[ρ]ομάορ τ' Ὀλυνπίαι.
>
> The agreement between the Anaitoi and the Metapioi: friendship for fifty years. And if either side violates the compact, let both the protectors and the priests expel them from the altar. If they transgress the oath, judgment shall belong to the priest at Olympia.[24]

The preamble contains the same elements as the previous ones. It is also called a *fratra* (ϝράτρα). As mentioned above, scholars often interpret *fratra* as an arrangement that formalizes exploitation. Jim Capreedy, for example, argues that because the treaty was displayed at Olympia, then under the control of Elis, both parties must have been members of the Elean League, and were therefore subordinate and subservient to Elis.[25] However the preamble continues with more information that complicates this scenario. It also describes the new relationship of the two communities as a *philia*. Robert Bauslaugh opines that a *philia*, unlike a *symmachia*, was an agreement of neutrality: "as 'friends' the parties will not cause injury to one another."[26] Ernst Baltrusch, however, comments that "in Greek interstate law the friendship

23 Bauslaugh, *The Concept of Neutrality in Classical Greece*, 58–59; Roy, "Elis," 494, 500. Massimo Nafissi, "Elei e Pisati. Geografia, storia e instituzioni politiche della regione di Olimpia," *Geographia Antiqua* 12 (2003): 42–43 and Kõiv, "Early History of Elis and Pisa," 329–330 think that both were located near Olympia but may not have been members of the Elean League. Minon, *Les inscriptions éléennes dialectales*, 99–100 places the Metapioi elsewhere in the Peloponnese or in Aetolia.

24 *IvO* 10. For commentary on the text, see Biagio Virgilio, "A proposito della ϝράτρα tra Aneti e Metapi e su alcuni uffici pubblici e religiosi ad Olympia," *Athenaeum* 50 (1972): 68–77; Panessa, *Philiai*, 102–107; Minon, *Les inscriptions éléennes dialectales*, 97–103; Julián Méndez Dosuna, "La clause finale de l'accord entre les Anaitiens et les Métapiens (*IvO* 10 = *IÉD* 14, L. 5–7)," *Zeitschrift für Papyrologie und Epigraphik* 184 (2013): 147–155.

25 Jim Capreedy, "A League within a League: The Preservation of the Elean Symmachy," *The Classical World* 101 (2008): 490; cf. Virgilio, "A proposito della ϝράτρα tra Aneti e Metapi."

26 Bauslaugh, *The Concept of Neutrality in Classical Greece*, 60–64.

treaty was, conversely, a prerequisite for an alliance treaty."[27] Sarah Bolmarcich also believes that in the archaic period, the use of *philia* "may suggest a growing interest in establishing affective relationships with other states that would support and strengthen purely legal relationships like *summakhiai* or peace treaties."[28] It is difficult to uncover a comprehensive definition for all cases, but it seems that *philia* indicates a new relationship between two peoples. If this is indeed what is meant in this treaty, then precisely how it worked within the context of the Elean League is not obvious. Although the Anaitoi and Metapioi were members of that league, it is clear that they were not kept from entering a bilateral friendship of their own, a relationship that, as indicated in the word *philia*, had a social character as much as a political or military one.

Following *philia* in the preamble is the phrase *pentakonta fetea* (πεντακοντα ϝετεα), fifty years. This refers to the duration of this *philia*. It is not quite as long as the previous treaties, but it would have extended beyond any of the immediate goals that the two parties had. The articles following the preamble include a casuistic clause specifying the punishment of religious exclusion for any transgression of the (unrecorded) terms.[29] Though this treaty is brief and simple in its articulation, one can detect in its preamble conventional diplomatic language. Each of these three treaties opens with an announcement of the socially charged designation—*symmachia*, *philotēs*, or *philia*—and the lengthy duration of the agreements. The form and the vocabulary of these preambles circulated throughout Greece and were picked up by more and more communities for their own treaties. The hub for this circulation of diplomatic language was Olympia.

3 Proliferation

Even before the three treaties at Olympia, the Greeks recorded their official documents on perishable material, such as papyrus, waxed tablets, or wooden boards. In the late seventh century and early sixth century, for example, the Athenians carved onto wood the respective laws of Dracon and Solon, but these have long since deteriorated. In the sixth century, the Greeks began to display their documents on more durable materials. The so-called "Constitution of Chios"—the oldest known *rhetra*, a word that appears in the preambles of the Olympia treaties—was inscribed on four sides of a freestanding stone and erected in a public space.[30] The earliest public inscriptions, therefore, were displayed in highly visible locations, indicating that they were meant to be

27 "*im griechischen Völkerrecht der Freundschaftsvertrag umgekehrt Voraussetzung eines Bündnisvertrages war*" (Baltrusch, *Symmachie und Spondai*, 7).
28 Bolmarcich, "Communal Values in Ancient Diplomacy and Culture," 125; cf. Jean-Christophe Couvenhes, *La symmachia comme pratique du droit international dans le monde grec: d'Homère à l'époque hellénistique* (Besançon: Presses universitaires de Franche-Comté, 2016), 38–39.
29 Dosuna, "La clause finale" comments on the final line of the treaty.
30 ML 8.

seen, read, and talked about. The same is the case for the public exhibition of the three treaties at Olympia.

Although the later Greek inscriptions were commonly made in stone, the material on which the Olympia treaties were inscribed was bronze, a new medium for public inscriptions that began in the sixth century. The local stone at Olympia was not suitable for inscribed pillars and other monumental architecture. Even many of the buildings at Olympia were made from imported stone.[31] With the large number of dedications at Olympia, it would have been too crowded to accommodate them if they were all made in stone.[32] Therefore, the parties to these three alliances inscribed their treaties into *pinakes* (bronze plaques). Lilian Jeffrey even suggested that this particular medium began at Olympia and then spread to other areas, a notion that complements this essay's assertion that the language of the preambles of the Olympia treaties spread to other areas.[33] For example, also in the sixth century, there were bronze inscriptions for a dedication to Athena placed on the acropolis in Athens, a law code set in the Heraion at Argos, and the text for land regulations displayed in Naupactus, perhaps in the temple of Apollo.[34] Some had holes in the upper corners so that they could be hung on a wall and turned over if one wanted to read the other side—the same style as the three bronze plaques at Olympia.

Although the size of each plaque was not enormous, they were displayed in conspicuous positions of the Altis, Olympia's sacred precinct. They were either on or nearby the treasuries, small temple-like buildings that served as repositories for dedications from around the Greek world. The treaty between the Eleans and the Ewaoioi was affixed to the outer wall of the Sybarite Treasury, the one between the Sybarites and the Serdaioi hung on the same treasury, and the Anaitoi and Metapioi's inscription was displayed somewhere in the Altis. One reason for exhibiting them here was that it was a place of great visibility. At Olympia, the treasuries were arranged in an orderly line on an elevated platform along the Sacred Way, between the sanctuary of Hera to the west and the athletic stadium to the east. The treasuries have been characterized variously as

31 Michael Scott, *Delphi and Olympia: The Spatial Politics of Panhellenism in the Archaic and Classical Periods* (Cambridge: Cambridge University Press, 2010), 165; Nancy Klein, "'Internationalism' in Architecture: Olympia," in *A Companion to Greek Architecture*, ed. Margaret M. Miles (Malden, MA: Wiley Blackwell, 2016), 121–134.

32 On the early dedications at Olympia, see Catherine Morgan, *Athletes and Oracles: The Transformation of Olympia and Delphi in the Eighth Century B.C.* (Cambridge: Cambridge University Press, 1990), 57–105; Scott, *Delphi and Olympia*, 146–180; Komar, "Epigraphic Culture in Olympia."

33 Lilian Hamilton Jeffery, *The Local Scripts of Archaic Greece* (Oxford: Clarendon Press, 1961), 55.

34 *IG* I^2 393 (Athens); *IG* IV 506 (Argos); ML 13 (Naupactus); cf. Jeffery, *The Local Scripts of Archaic Greece*, 55–56; Ronald Stroud, "A Fragment of an Inscribed Bronze Stele from Athens," *Hesperia* 32 (1963): 138 n.1; Elizabeth A Meyer, "Posts, Kurbeis, Metopes: The Origins of the Athenian 'Documentary' Stele," *Hesperia* 85 (2016): 360–361 n. 142.

offerings, venues for elite display and for architectural display, "club houses" for visitors from the donating communities, expressions of civic pride, and the means by which the treasury donors played out their rivalries.[35] There is no doubt that this was a prominent place for the spectators at Olympia to view the treasuries and their dedications, including the bronze plaques.[36]

The specific display location suggests that the inscriptions were meant to be not only seen but also read.[37] The language contained in these inscriptions exemplifies the origins of the common vocabulary of diplomacy used in the archaic and classical periods. Every four years, when visitors from all around the Greek world saw the plaques, the first thing that they would have read was the preambles. They would adopt the same media and formulae in their own interstate agreements. Eventually, more followed suit until there was a standard practice of recording interstate alliance treaties.

When compared to the elements of treaties from later in Greek history, the preambles of the three archaic treaties are rudimentary. Afterwards, as more and more Greek communities interacted, there emerged a standard form for preambles. An example of a typical preamble comes from the first ten lines of the fragmentary inscription recording the *symmachia* between the Athenians and the Rhegians in 433.

> [θεοί. πρέσβες ἐκ Ῥεγίο *h*]οὶ τὲν χσυμμαχίαν [ἐποέσαντο καὶ τὸν *h*όρκ]ον Κλέανδρος Χσεν- [.................]τίνο, Σιλενὸς Φόκο, [............ ἐπ' Ἀφ]σεύδος ἄρχοντος κ[αὶ τε͂ς βολε͂ς *h*ε͂ι Κριτιά]δες προ͂τος ἐγραμμ[άτευε vv ἔδοχσεν τε͂ι βο]λε͂ι καὶ τοῖ δέμοι. Ἀ[καμαντὶς ἐπρυτάνευε, Χ]αρίας ἐγραμμάτευ[ε, Τιμόχσενος ἐπεστάτ]ε, Καλλί[ας εἶπε. χσυμμαχίαν εἶν]αι Ἀθεναίοις καὶ [Ῥεγίνοις.]
>
> Gods. Envoys from Rhegion who made the alliance and the oath, Kleandros son of Xen—son of—tinos, Silenos son of Phokos,[—son of—]. In the archonship of Apseudes and under the council for which Kritiades was first secretary. The council and the assembly decided. Akamantis was the prytany. Charias was secretary. Timoxenos was chairman.

35 Georges Roux, *Temples et sanctuaries: Séminaire de recherche 1981–1983 sous la direction de G. Roux* (Paris: GIS-Maison de l'Orient, 1984), 154; Morgan, *Athletes and Oracles*; Panos Valavanis, *Games and Sanctuaries in Ancient Greece: Olympia, Delphi, Isthmia, Nemea, Athens* (Los Angeles: J. Paul Getty Museum, 2004), 63; Richard Neer, "Delphi, Olympia, and the Art of Politics," in *Cambridge Companion to Archaic Greece*, ed. H. Alan Shapiro (Cambridge: Cambridge University Press, 2007), 225–264; Nigel Spivey, *The Ancient Olympics* (Oxford: Oxford University Press, 2012), 187; Klein, "'Internationalism'," 132. Paus. 6.19 describes the inventories of the treasuries.

36 On the spatial aspects of the treasuries, see Scott, *Delphi and Olympia*, 163–169.

37 Scholars continue to debate whether public inscriptions were meant to be read (Chiara Lasagni, "'For Anyone Who Wishes to Read up Close . . .' A Few Thoughts Revolving around the Formula σκοπειν τωι βουλουμενοι in Attic Inscriptions," *Rivista di Filologia e di Istruzione Classica* 146 (2018): 334–380) or just seen (Rosalind Thomas, *Oral Tradition and Written Record in Classical Athens* (Cambridge: Cambridge University Press, 1989), 60–68; Charles Hedrick, "For Anyone Who Wishes to See," *Ancient World* 31 (2000): 127–135).

> Kallias proposed: there shall be an alliance between the Athenians and the Rhegians.[38]

This preamble contains the title for the alliance: *symmachia* (spelled here with an initial chi: χσυμμαχία), the same title for the alliance between the Eleans and the Ewaoioi. More elements have been added than were in the earlier ones at Olympia, but one can see how it builds on these earlier examples.

Outside of Athens, the Spartans and the Erxadieis, an otherwise unknown Aetolian community, made an alliance at some point in the late fifth century. Its preamble also adopts the conventions set by the earlier treaties at Olympia. In this case, there is the familiar alliance titles of *philia* and *symmachia* and an eternal duration clause:

> [συνθε͂κ]αι Αἰτολοῖς. κ̣[αττάδε?φιλία]ν̣ καὶ hιράναν ||[——ποτ' Αἰτο]λ̣ὸς καὶ συνμαχ[ίαν?ἀίδιον——]
>
> Alliance with the Aetolians. On the following terms [friendship?] and peace [shall be?] made with the Aetolians, and alliance [for all time?——].[39]

The treaty for the alliance among the Athenians, Argives, Mantineans, and Eleans in 420 instructed that the stone inscriptions be set up on the Athenian acropolis; the temple of Apollo in the Argive agora; and at the temple of Zeus in Mantinea; with an additional bronze copy, erected collectively by all parties, at Olympia. It was this latter copy that Thucydides recorded in his *History of the Peloponnesian War*.[40] One of the allies was Elis, whose inscribed treaty with the Ewaioi was also at Olympia. It is no surprise, therefore, that the preamble to this 420 treaty would follow in line with what went before by including the alliance title (*spondas*, σπονδὰς), a duration clause, and an anti-deceit clause:

> [Ἀργείον. Μαντινέον. Ἐλ]ε[ί]ον. [σπονδὰς ἐποιέσαντο *h*εκατὸν Ἀθεναίοι ἔτε καὶ Ἀργεῖοι καὶ Μαντινε͂ς καὶ Ἐλεῖο]ι πρὸς ἀλλέλος *h*-[υπὲρ σφο͂ν αὐτο͂ν καὶ το͂ν χσυμμάχον *h*ο͂ν ἄρχοσι *h*εκάτεροι ἀδόλος καὶ ἀβλαβε͂ς καὶ] κατὰ γε͂ν καὶ κα[τὰ θάλατταν.]
>
> [Of the Argives, Mantineans], Eleans. A treaty was made for a hundred years by the Athenians and by the Argives, Mantineans and Eleans with one another, on behalf of themselves and the allies whom they rule on each side, without deceit or damage, by land and by sea.[41]

38 *IG* I³ 53. A treaty for a contemporary Athenian alliance with the Leontinians (*IG* I³ 54) is nearly identical, which permits the reconstruction of the fragmentary inscriptions.

39 *SEG* 26.461; OR 128.

40 *IG* I³ 83; Thuc. 5.47; Paus. 5.12.8; cf. Michael Clark, "Thucydides in Olympia," in *Text and Tradition: Studies in Greek History and Historiography in Honor of Mortimer Chambers*, eds. Ronald Mellor and Lawrence Tritle (Claremont, CA: Regina Books, 1999), 115–134.

41 *IG* I³ 83; Thuc. 5.47.1.

Likewise, the preamble to the treaty for an alliance between the Athenians and Argives in 416 contains the same elements:

> [..]όδορος Πολυχάρος Ἀ[μφιτροπε͂θεν(?) ἐγραμμάτευεν. ἔδοχσεν τε͂ι] βολε͂ι καὶ τοῖ δέμοι. Αἰαν[τὶς ἐπρυτάνευε, ... όδορος ἐγραμμάτευε, ... ἐπεσ] τάτε, Εὔφεμος ἐ͂ρχε. χσυ[μμαχίαν καὶ χσυνθέκας ἀδόλος καὶ ἀβλαβε͂ς ἐ͂ναι Ἀθεναίοις καὶ Ἀργείοις πε]ντέκοντα ἔτε·
>
> In the secretaryship of—odoros Polycharos of Amphitrope. The council and the assembly decided. Aiantis was the prytany.—odorus was secretary,—was chairman, and Euphemos was archon. There is an alliance and agreement without deceit or damage between the Athenians and Argives for fifty years.[42]

According to Thucydides, even the Persians adopted similar language in their treaty with the Spartans in the closing decade of the Peloponnesian War.

> 'ξυνθῆκαι Λακεδαιμονίων καὶ τῶν ξυμμάχων πρὸς βασιλέα Δαρεῖον καὶ τοὺς παῖδας τοὺς βασιλέως καὶ Τισσαφέρνην, σπονδὰς εἶναι καὶ φιλίαν κατὰ τάδε.
>
> The agreement of the Spartans and the allies with King Darius and the sons of the King, and with Tissaphernes, for a treaty and friendship, as follows.[43]

This trend continued into the fourth century with the many Athenian alliances with the Boeotians in 395; Locrians in 395; Chians in 384; Olynthians in 383; Byzantines in the late 380s; Methymneans in the late 380s; Corcyraeans in 375; the Arcadians, Achaeans, Eleans, and Phliasians in 362; the Thessalians in 361; and three northern kings (Ketriporis the Thracian, Lyppeios the Paionian, and Grabos the Illyrian) in 356.[44] The examples can be multiplied but what is noticeable is that they all contain verbal elements that were introduced to the practice of treaty-making in the sixth century at Olympia.

4 Conclusion

This portrait of the design and diffusion of alliance language in the preambles of the Olympia treaties has wider implications about the generation of norms and identity construction in antiquity. Traditionally, scholars of political science have interpreted the interstate relations of the ancient Greeks through the lens of realism, which stresses the influences of endemic conflict and

42 *IG* I³ 86.

43 Thuc. 8.37.1.

44 Boeotians (*IG* II² 14; Xen. *Hell.* 3.5.7–16); Locrians (*IG* II² 15); Chians (*IG* II² 34); Olynthians (*IG* II² 36); Byzantines (*IG* II² 41); Methymneans (*IG* II² 42); Corcyraeans (*IG* II² 97); Arcadians, Achaeans, Eleans, and Phliasians (*IG* II² 112); Thessalians (*IG* II² 116); and three northern kings (*IG* II² 127).

competition on interstate behavior. In this view, states make and maintain alliances for purposes of national security or to maximize geopolitical standing. This can be seen previously in how some scholars have interpreted the treaties at Olympia. But more recently, another school has emerged with an emphasis on the representation of interstate activity: constructivism.[45] When constructivists talk about the relations between states, it is not in the realist terms of structural determinism or rationalism but of social interactions, the manifestations of those interactions in language, and how participants in the alliances think about and identify with their interstate relationships.

To constructivists, the way that states interact is both socially and linguistically constructed. Intersubjective discourse—the way that parties speak, write, and represent their thoughts—forms the shape of international relations. Nicholas Onuf, who coined the term "constructivism," was the first to apply this work on language to the modern study of international relations. As he puts it in his seminal work *World of Our Making*, world and words constitute each other.[46] Elsewhere, he spells out how words develop into and constitute the rules of international behavior:

> Whether speech acts accomplish anything depends on whether others respond to what they hear. . . . Constantly repeated, the same old speech acts turn into convention as everyone comes to believe that the words themselves, and not the speakers mouthing them, are responsible for what happen. . . . Conventions come close to being rules. . . . Formality strengthens a rule by making its normative character clearer.[47]

Language, therefore, is a fundamental part of the constructivists' view that the world is protean and can be constructed according to how it is represented conceptually, such as in the treaties that were displayed at Olympia. Rather than imposing an external perspective that does not correspond with the evidence, this approach seeks to uncover how the participants identify with their alliances. As Michael Barnett notes, "constructivists attempt to recover the meanings that actors give to their practices and the objects that they construct."[48] In sum, the constructivist viewpoint prioritizes the social interactions that form the bases of alliances, how those alliances are represented in

45 Nicholas Onuf, *World of Our Making: Rules and Rule in Social Theory and International Relations* (Columbia, SC: South Carolina Press, 1989); Alexander Wendt, "Anarchy Is what States Make of It: The Social Construction of Power Politics," *International Organization* 46 (1992): 391–425.

46 Onuf, *World of Our Making*, 78–95.

47 Nicholas Onuf, "Constructivism: A User's Manual," In *International Relations in a Constructed World*, eds. Vendulka Kubálková, Nicholas Onuf, and Paul Kowert (London: Routledge, 1998), 66–67.

48 Michael Barnett, "Constructivism," in *The Oxford Handbook of International Security*, eds. Alexandra Gheciu and William C. Wohlforth (Oxford: Oxford University Press, 2018), 89.

verbal and non-verbal language, and what the participants to alliances thought about their interstate relations.

The preambles to the three archaic treaties substantiate this view. They reveal only the bare outlines of what would rapidly become formulaic in the Greek world throughout the fifth century—what Karl-Joachim Hölkeskamp calls "the monumentalisation of norms."[49] The parties to the earlier treaties were from around the Greek world, in the Peloponnesus and in southern Italy. They saw fit to display their treaties at Olympia, a privileged center of Greek international consciousness at the time, on the treasuries, a privileged position within Olympia. Visitors from all around the Greek world would take note of the treaties—their language, their material, and their display site—and adopt the same media in their own interstate agreements. One might imagine that after the Eleans and Ewaoioi posted their inscription at Olympia, the Sybarites and Serdaioi might have observed that inscription and adopted some of its language in their treaty, and the same is true afterwards for the Anaitoi and Metapioi. Eventually, more communities followed suit until by the end of the middle of the fifth century, there was a standard diplomatic vocabulary throughout the Greek world.

Figure 2.1 Bronze Inscription of the Treaty between the Eleans and Ewaoioi, ca. 500 BCE (British Museum).

49 Karl-Joachim Hölkeskamp, "Written Law in Archaic Greece," *Proceedings of the Cambridge Philological Society* 38 (1992): 100.

Abbreviations

IG = *Inscriptiones Graecae*. Kirchner, Johannes, ed. 1913–1940 Berlin: Jules Delamarre. 1913–1940.

IvO = *Die Inschriften von Olympia*. Dittenberger, Wilhelm and Karl Purgold. 1896. Berlin: Asher, 1986.

ML = *A Selection of Greek Historical Inscriptions to the End of the Fifth Century BC*. Meiggs, Russell and David M. Lewis, eds. Oxford: Oxford University Press, 1988.

OR = Osborne, Robin and Peter J. Rhodes, eds. *Greek Historical Inscriptions 478–404 BC*. Oxford: Oxford University Press, 2018.

SdA = Bengtson, Hermann. ed. *Die Staatsverträge des Altertums*. München: C. H. Beck. 1962.

SEG = Pleket, Henk W. and Ronald S. Stroud. Eds. *Supplementum Epigraphicum Graecum*. Leiden: Brill, 1913–present.

References

Baltrusch, Ernst. *Symmachie und Spondai: Untersuchungen zum griechischen Völkerrecht der archaischen und klassischen Zeit*. Berlin: de Gruyter, 1994.

Barnett, Michael. "Constructivism." In *The Oxford Handbook of International Security*, edited by Alexandra Gheciu and William C. Wohlforth, 86–99. Oxford: Oxford University Press, 2018.

Bauslaugh, Robert A. *The Concept of Neutrality in Classical Greece*. Berkeley: University of California Press, 1991.

Bengtson, Hermann (ed.). *Die Staatsverträge des Altertums*. München: C.H. Beck. 1962.

Bolmarcich, Sarah. "Communal Values in Ancient Diplomacy and Culture." In *Valuing Others in Classical Antiquity*, edited by Ralph M. Rosen and Ineke Sluiter, 113–136. Leiden: Brill, 2010.

Capreedy, Jim. "A League within a League: The Preservation of the Elean Symmachy." *The Classical World* 101 (2008): 485–503.

Clark, Michael. "Thucydides in Olympia." In *Text and Tradition: Studies in Greek History and Historiography in Honor of Mortimer Chambers*, edited by Ronald Mellor and Lawrence Tritle, 115–134. Claremont, CA: Regina Books, 1999.

Couvenhes, Jean-Christophe. *La symmachia comme pratique du droit international dans le monde grec: d'Homère à l'époque hellénistique*. Besançon: Presses universitaires de Franche-Comté, 2016.

Cross, Nicholas D. *The Roots of Cooperation: Constructing Interstate Alliances in Ancient Greece*, Forthcoming.

Dittenberger, Wilhelm and Karl Purgold. 1896. *Die Inschriften von Olympia*. Berlin: Asher, 1986.

Dosuna, Julián Méndez. "La clause finale de l'accord entre les Anaitiens et les Métapiens (*IvO* 10 = *IÉD* 14, L. 5–7)." *Zeitschrift für Papyrologie und Epigraphik* 184 (2013): 147–155.

Effenterre, Henri van. "La fondation de Paestum." *La Parola del Passato* 192 (1980): 161–175.

Fischer-Hansen, Tobias, Thomas Heine Nielsen, and Carmine Ampolo. "Italia and Kampania." In *An Inventory of Archaic and Classical Poleis*, edited by Mogens Herman Hansen and Thomas Heine Nielsen, 249–320. Oxford: Oxford University Press, 2004.

Giangiulio, Maurizio. "La φιλότης tra Sibariti e Serdaioi (Meiggs-Lewis, 10)." *Zeitschrift für Papyrologie und Epigraphik* 93 (1992): 31–44.

Greco, Emanuele. "Serdaioi." *Annali di archeologia e storia antica* 12 (1990): 39–57.

Guarducci, Margherita. *Epigrafi di carattere pubblico*. Roma: Istituto poligrafico dello Stato, 1969.

Hall, Jonathan M. "International Relations." In *The Cambridge History of Greek and Roman Warfare*, vol. 1, edited by Philip Sabin, Hans van Wees, and Michael Whitby, 85–107. Cambridge: Cambridge University Press, 2007.

Hansen, Ove. "The Coins with the Legend MEP and the Origin of the Etruscans." *Parola del Passato* 45 (1990): 447–448.

Hedrick, Charles. "For Anyone Who Wishes to See." *Ancient World* 31 (2000): 127–135.

Henry, Alan S. *The Prescripts of Athenian Decrees*. Leiden: Brill, 1977.

Hölkeskamp, Karl-Joachim. "Written Law in Archaic Greece." *Proceedings of the Cambridge Philological Society* 38 (1992): 87–117.

Jeffery, Lilian Hamilton. *The Local Scripts of Archaic Greece*. Oxford: Clarendon Press, 1961.

Karavites, Peter. *Promise-Giving and Treaty-Making: Homer and the Near East*. Leiden: Brill, 1992.

Kirchner, Johannes (ed.). *Inscriptiones Graecae*. Berlin: Jules Delamarre, 1913–1940.

Klein, Nancy. "'Internationalism' in Architecture: Olympia." In *A Companion to Greek Architecture*, edited by Margaret M. Miles, 121–134. Malden, MA: Wiley Blackwell, 2016.

Kõiv, Matt. "Early History of Elis and Pisa: Invented or Evolving Traditions?" *Klio* 95 (2013): 315–368.

Komar, Paulina. "Epigraphic Culture in Olympia." In *Epigraphic Culture in the Eastern Mediterranean in Antiquity*, edited by Krzysztof Nawotka, 68–80. New York: Routledge, 2021.

Lasagni, Chiara. "'For Anyone Who Wishes to Read up Close . . .' a Few Thoughts Revolving Around the Formula σκοπειν τωι βουλουμενοι in Attic Inscriptions." *Rivista di Filologia e di Istruzione Classica* 146 (2018): 334–380.

Lombardo, Mario. "Il trattato tra i Sibariti e i Serdaioi: problemi di cronologia e inquadramento storico." *Studi di Antichità* 12 (2008): 49–60.

Meiggs, Russell and David M. Lewis (eds.). *A Selection of Greek Historical Inscriptions to the End of the Fifth Century BC*. Oxford: Oxford University Press, 1988.

Mello, Francesca. "Ἀ ϝράτρα τοῖς ϝαλείοις. Rhetra e le wratrai olimpiche." *Zeitschrift für Papyrologie und Epigraphik* 167 (2008): 50–66.

Meyer, Elizabeth A. "Posts, Kurbeis, Metopes: The Origins of the Athenian 'Documentary' Stele." *Hesperia* 85 (2016): 323–383.

Minon, Sophie. *Les inscriptions éléennes dialectales (VIe-IIe siècle avant J.-C.)*, vol. 1. Geneva: Droz, 2007.

Morgan, Catherine. *Athletes and Oracles: The Transformation of Olympia and Delphi in the Eighth Century B.C.* Cambridge: Cambridge University Press, 1990.

Nafissi, Massimo. "Elei e Pisati. Geografia, storia e instituzioni politiche della regione di Olimpia." *Geographia Antiqua* 12 (2003): 23–55.

Neer, Richard. "Delphi, Olympia, and the Art of Politics." In *Cambridge Companion to Archaic Greece*, edited by H. Alan Shapiro, 225–264. Cambridge: Cambridge University Press, 2007.

Onuf, Nicholas. *World of Our Making: Rules and Rule in Social Theory and International Relations*. Columbia, SC: South Carolina Press, 1989.

Onuf, Nicholas. "Constructivism: A User's Manual." In *International Relations in a Constructed World*, edited by Vendulka Kubálková, Nicholas Onuf, and Paul Kowert, 58–78. London: Routledge, 1998.

Osborne, Robin and Peter J. Rhodes (eds.). *Greek Historical Inscriptions 478–404 BC.* Oxford: Oxford University Press, 2018.
Panessa, Giangiacomo. *Philiai: l'amicizia nelle relazioni interstatali dei greci.* Pisa: Scuola Normale Superiore, 1999.
Pausanias. *Description of Greece*, Translated by William Henry Samuel Jones. Cambridge, MA: Harvard University Press, 1918.
Pleket, Henk W. and Ronald S. Stroud (eds.). *Supplementum Epigraphicum Graecum.* Leiden: Brill, 1913–present.
Raaflaub, Kurt. "Politics and Interstate Relations in the World of Early Greek Poleis: Homer and Beyond." *Antichthon* 31 (1997): 1–27.
Rhodes, Peter J. *The Athenian Boule.* Oxford: Clarendon Press, 1972.
Rhodes, Peter J. and David M. Lewis. *The Decrees of the Greek States.* Oxford: Clarendon Press, 1997.
Roux, Georges. *Temples et sanctuaries: Séminaire de recherche 1981–1983 sous la direction de G. Roux.* Paris: GIS-Maison de l'Orient, 1984.
Roy, James. "The *Perioikoi of Elis.*" In *The Polis as an Urban Centre and as a Political Community*, edited by Mogens H. Hansen, 282–320. Stuttgart: Franz Steiner Verlag, 1997.
Roy, James. "Elis." In *An Inventory of Archaic and Classical Poleis*, edited by Mogens Herman Hansen and Thomas Heine Nielsen, 489–504. Oxford: Oxford University Press, 2004.
Roy, James and Damian Schofield. "*IvO* 9. A New Approach." *Horos* 13 (1999): 155–165.
Rutter, N. Keith. *Historia Numorum: Italy.* London: British Museum Press, 2001.
Scott, Mary. "Philos, Philotēs and Xenia." *Acta Classica* 25 (1982): 1–19.
Scott, Michael. *Delphi and Olympia: The Spatial Politics of Panhellenism in the Archaic and Classical Periods.* Cambridge: Cambridge University Press, 2010.
Spivey, Nigel. *The Ancient Olympics.* Oxford: Oxford University Press, 2012.
Strabo. *Geography*, Translated by Horace Leonard Jones. Cambridge, MA: Harvard University Press. 1923–present (1924).
Stroud, Ronald S. "A Fragment of an Inscribed Bronze Stele from Athens." *Hesperia* 32 (1963): 138–143.
Taillardat, Jean."Φιλότης, πίστις et foedus." *Revue des Études Grecques* 95 (1982): 1–14.
Thomas, Rosalind. *Oral Tradition and Written Record in Classical Athens.* Cambridge: Cambridge University Press, 1989.
Thucydides. *History of the Peloponnesian War*, Translated by Benjamin Jowett. Oxford: Clarendon, 1881.
Troncoso, V. Alonso. "Olimpie et la publication des traités internationaux." *Rivista di diritto ellenico* 2 (2012): 3–26.
Valavanis, Panos. *Games and Sanctuaries in Ancient Greece: Olympia, Delphi, Isthmia, Nemea, Athens.* Los Angeles: J. Paul Getty Museum, 2004.
Virgilio, Biagio. "A proposito della ϝράτρα tra Aneti e Metapi e su alcuni uffici pubblici e religiosi ad Olympia." *Athenaeum* 50 (1972): 68–77.
Wendt, Alexander. "Anarchy Is What States Make of It: The Social Construction of Power Politics." *International Organization* 46 (1992): 391–425.
Wheeler, Edward. "Sophistic Interpretations and Greek Treaties." *Greek, Roman and Byzantine Studies* 25 (1984): 253–274.
Wheeler, Edward. "Anti-Deceit Clauses in Greek Treaties: An Apologia." *Electrum* 14 (2008): 57–84.
Xenophon. *Hellenica*, Translated by Carleton L. Brownson. Cambridge, MA: Harvard University Press, 1918.

3 Prefaces of legal documents in Late Imperial China

Frédéric Constant

1 Introduction

Prefaces are a fundamental part of Chinese book culture, dating back to the Han Dynasty (206 BCE–220),[1] through which authors attested to their authorship and hope to achieve posterity. Thus, prefaces usually contained biographical information about the author, a description of his lineage, the context in which the work was written, and the principles that guided the composition. The prefaces were originally placed at the end of the book and could also serve as a table of contents, indicating both the title of the chapters and the number of characters contained. This was a way to preserve the work from possible alterations and to guarantee the authenticity of the copies. The preface was the author's last words and as such, was placed in the last bundle or scroll. But with the development of printing under the Song Dynasty (960–1279) and the resulting change in the format of books, the practice of placing it at the beginning of the text was adopted.[2] Prefaces are generally used by modern historiography to document the context in which a work was written, to collect information about an author, or to study the professional and social environment of the writers, whose existence is apparent through the inclusion of prefaces written by acquaintances. Prefaces are therefore often valuable for the bibliographic information that they contain and the insight into the social context that they provide. The prefaces to legal works follow this general pattern, especially when they were written on the initiative of individuals, and were used under the same conditions and with the same objectives as those that we have mentioned.

Nevertheless, it is necessary to consider some of the specific features of legal works. As a matter of fact, there was a great variety of legal works in China, whose prefaces could be of different forms or pursue various objectives. We first present these different categories of publications and describe for each of

1 All dates are Common Era unless specified as BCE.

2 Wang Guoqiang 王國強, *Zhongguo guji xuba shi* 中國古籍序跋史 [History of the Preface of Chinese Ancient Books] (Wuhan: Wuhan daxue chubanshe, 2015).

DOI: 10.4324/9781003534815-4

them the characteristics and the usual contents of their prefaces. It is important to consider that the codes were official works, whose formalism was somehow specific. In a second step, we analyze the information prefaces contain, their usefulness for legal historians, and what they tell us about Chinese law. Beyond the bibliographical information already mentioned, the prefaces of legal works often describe the conception that jurists had of the law. In them, one finds a coherent thought that addresses central questions, such as authority in law, the evolution of codes, or the definition of justice.

Our study presents in a synthetic way the main ideas developed in the prefaces. It spans several centuries, from the third century to the end of the nineteenth century, covering the entire period for which we have available legal documents with prologues or prefaces. This period also corresponds to the history of Chinese codified law, that is, the time period during which jurists presented the law in a systematic way.

2 A variety of legal works

An important distinction must first be made between official works, produced by the administration, and works of private initiative. In addition to the undisputed normative value of official works, their prefaces had a particular formalism that distinguished them from those of private works. Private works also contain works of different natures, but their prefaces present a greater uniformity. We can classify under the category of official texts all of the documents promulgated by the administration, especially the central administration. These include not only the codes but also the regulations issued by administrative offices and even compilations of laws that did not have normative value in themselves but served to diffuse already existing rules.

First, it should be recalled that China has a very old tradition of codification of law, which dates to at least the third century.[3] These works were not simple compilations of rules already in force but constituted a systematic presentation of the legal order, considered as one of the manifestations of the natural order that it was to reflect. Chinese codes contained mainly penal rules, played a strong symbolic role of the state's will to preserve social order, and had a political dimension of primary importance: the promulgation of a code represented a core element of sovereignty at the time of a dynasty change. A new ruler, or one of his immediate successors, could thus order his ministers to revise the law of the previous dynasty to promulgate a new dynastic code. Once the work was done, the officials submitted a "memorial" (*biao* 表) to the emperor that explained the principles that had motivated the codemakers. These memorials were to serve as a preface to the codes. The surviving editions of the codes of

3 Geoffrey MacCormack, "The Transmission of Penal Law (lü) from the Han to the T'ang: A Contribution to the Study of the Early History of Codification in China," *Revue internationale des droits de l'Antiquité*, 51 (2004): 47–86.

the Ming (1368–1644) and Qing (1644–1911), the last two reigning dynasties, also contain prefaces written by the emperor (*xu* 序). In the case of a new edition—there were a total of three successive editions of the statutes under the Qing—the old prefaces were included in the new versions of the code. The memorials written by the commissions charged with amending the code were also recorded and can be read as prefaces as well.

Under the Qing, the process of code revision was highly regulated: from the mid-eighteenth century onwards, the codification bureau was responsible for implementing two types of revision: a general revision every ten years and a more limited revision every five years. Usually, a "memorial" (*zoushu* 奏疏) that described the process and the major revisions made and contained the list of the officials who participated in the draft of the code was also included at the beginning of these works. In the introduction to the codes, we also find sometimes the "directions to the reader" (*fanli* 凡例), indicating the table of contents and the guidelines of the book. For example, the directions of the Yongzheng edition of the Qing code (1725) specify the changes in the number of articles since the previous edition, that the content of 130 laws or their commentaries was amended, and that the "substatutes" (*li* 例) were placed after the corresponding "statutes" (*lü* 律).[4] The Chinese codes were based on a distinction between two sources, namely, the statutes that represented a pole of stability and were normally fixed—even if in practice their content could change—and the substatutes that were by definition ad hoc measures that adapted the content of the statutes to the circumstances.[5]

The Chinese administration also produced numerous compilations of administrative regulations (*zeli* 則例), and many of those promulgated under the Qing have been preserved. Usually, the prefaces to these books comprise the memorials in which the officials of the office concerned had asked for a compilation of all of the rules that they had to apply. The preface functions here mainly to preserve the memory of the history of the constitution of the work since its first edition by following the course of its later modifications. The content is generally similar, with officials indicating in their memorials that many regulations have been enacted since the last compilation and that knowledge of the law and greater efficiency in administrative work required the collection of new regulations.[6] In addition to the details of the process leading to the writing of the codes, the prefaces provide us with a great deal of information about the structure of the codes and Chinese thinking on codification.

This information is particularly valuable for the earliest periods, whose codes have not reached us. Thus, we have a better knowledge of the conditions of

4 *Da Qing lüli jijie fuli* 大清律集解附例 [The Great Qing Code with Commentaries and Substatutes], 19b/20a.

5 Derk Bodde and Clarence Morris, *Law in Imperial China: Exemplified by 190 Ch'ing Dynasty Cases* (Cambridge, MA: Harvard University Press, 1967), 63–67.

6 See, for instance, *Qingding libu zeli* 欽定禮部則例 [Regulations of the Board of Rites], 1a/2a.

emergence of the codification of law in China mainly through the prefaces of the first codes, some of which have been preserved, whereas the codes of this period are all inaccessible. For instance, the preface of the code of the Wei (220–265), dating from 229, and the memorials of Zhang Fei presenting his commentary of the code to the sovereign of the Jin (265–420), promulgated in 267, have been preserved. The original documents have since disappeared, but fragments of these texts were reproduced by historians of the Tang Dynasty (618–907), who were responsible for writing the official histories of these dynasties.[7] The structure of these codes is known to us largely through the historiographic works written at that time. These prefaces not only summarized the codes but also developed the legal thinking of their author. We discuss the lessons that can be drawn from them in the second part of this article.

The works that we now present have in common that they were written on the initiative of private individuals, and they therefore have no particular normative value, even if their influence on legal practice was often great. The purpose of these works, beyond their particularities, was to clarify the law and to serve as a guide to its application. They can be described as manuals in the broadest sense of the word, that is, practical works offering instructions to officials on how to apply the law. They are part of a larger genre of literature, the handbooks for officials, and their content was specifically concerned with the study of the code and the application of administrative rules to justice.[8] Among the genres represented in this category, we first mention the commentaries of the codes. The authors had often worked in the ministries and glossed in their work the terms that were difficult to understand. Private commentaries could have been very authoritative, both because they influenced the understanding of the law by officials and because these books could also be given an authoritative status by the emperor. Thus, commentaries written by Ming jurists were incorporated into the Qing code and became de facto rules of law. Case collections are also an important part of Chinese legal treaties. They contained either important judgments rendered by the central administration, which made it possible to disseminate knowledge of them, or judgments pronounced by a local magistrate who might desire to demonstrate to a large audience his competence as administrator.[9]

7 There are 24 official histories in total, composed by commissions of historians appointed by the throne. The history of a dynasty was usually written after its fall, from the preserved archives. See "Standard Histories," in *Chinese History: A New Manual*, ed. Endymion Wilkinson (Cambridge, MA: Harvard University Press, 2012), 501–515.

8 Pierre-Étienne Will, *Handbooks and Anthologies for Officials in Imperial China: A Descriptive and Critical Bibliography*, 2 vols. (Leiden: Brill, 2020).

9 On the importance of these publications in the promotion of careers during the Ming period, see Tam Kai-chai, *Justice in Print: Discovering Prefectural Judges and Their Judicial Consistency in Late-Ming Casebooks* (Leiden: Brill, 2020).

A final category of legal works includes handbooks of all types written for officials and their clerks charged with applying the law. There is some continuity between handbooks and case collections, some of which were published to provide models for officials. Books in this category may be collections of administrative documents, contain explanations of how to carry out legal proceedings, and provide all kinds of advice on the administration of justice, especially for the local magistrate in charge of the administration of the lower unit of the Chinese bureaucracy, the district. Their prefaces could again present the biography of the author or the reasons for the publication of the work. Thus, one often finds general considerations on the importance of rendering justice properly to maintain public order in a district or on the correct way to fulfill one's office.

These handbooks addressed a fundamental problem faced by local magistrates in charge of a district, the lowest administrative level, in direct contact with the population. Magistrates received only a very general education based on the study of the Classics to develop their moral aptitudes, a benchmark for access to the bureaucracy, but they never obtained any training in the specific areas of knowledge that they needed to actually administer a district. The term Classics refers to a corpus of books written in antiquity that formed the common basis of the education of the literati. This corpus formed an official doctrine sanctioned by the State and was associated with Confucius (551-479 BCE), who was supposed to have himself written or ensured the transmission of several of these texts. Candidates for the imperial examinations that allowed access to the bureaucracy were tested on their knowledge of this corpus.[10] Local magistrates had to therefore rely on the expertise of private secretaries specialized in specific areas of the administration, including that of justice.[11] The prefacers thus sometimes recalled the importance for magistrates to learn on the job, particularly by reading the books that they were introducing.[12] There were also personal ethical implications for the judges, as their decisions could decide the life or death of individuals or aggrieve a victim's soul if they did not punish appropriately.[13]

折獄致刑，出生入死，一不中而人非鬼責隨其後。

When trying criminal cases and giving punishment, one determines who can escape to live and who enters death. Whenever one has not aimed at the right decision, men and spirits blame him and pursue him.

10 For a presentation of these texts, see Michael Nylan, *The Five "Confucian" Classics* (New Haven: Yale University Press, 2001).

11 On the traditional legal education in China, see Chang Wejen, "Legal Education in Ch'ing China," in *Education and Society in Late Imperial China, 1600–1900*, eds. Benjamin A. Elman and Alexander Woodside (Berkeley: University of California Press, 1994), 292–339.

12 Bai Ruzhen 白如珍, *Xingming yide* 刑名一得 [*Notions Acquired from Legal Practice*], Jueluo Yuzheng 覺羅玉正's preface.

13 Yan Junyan 顏俊彥, *Mengshui zhai cundu* 盟水齋存牘 [Official Documents Kept at Meng River Studio], Lu Ao 陸鏊's preface (1632).

The belief in retribution for deeds was widespread in China, so some judges were particularly careful not to commit injustice.

In total, prefaces to the private legal books follow the model described in our introduction, and their main purpose was to highlight the merits of the author. Many of these authors worked or had worked as officials or private secretaries, and they relied on their knowledge or private archives to transmit their experience, reflecting their personal achievements. This is particularly the case for collections of judgments, which were intended to provide models for readers and thus testify to their author's virtues as a judge. Finally, we underline that there were sometimes commercial motivations for writing a preface, which is also related to the search for fame associated with the publication of these works. In both cases, the addition of a preface written by a reputed person or a superior was supposed to widen the audience for the book.[14] Regardless of the category of legal work of which we have just presented a simplified typology, the prefaces regularly recalled the general principles on which the Chinese legal order was based. We now review the salient elements that forged a common awareness of Chinese law.

3 Chinese law seen through the prefaces

In this section, we describe the recurring themes that appear in prefaces, regardless of the genre of the legal work, which were central to the definition of codes in China and to their evolution. The prefaces were firstly based on numerous extracts from classical texts, a common principle of argumentation of the Chinese literati. The Classics played a major role in the organization of the administration and more generally in the intellectual life of China. The Chinese considered that the true knowledge had been held by the ancient sages, whose content had to be reconstructed with the help of the few fragments divulged in the Classics. The Classics could thus serve as arguments in support of a thesis or as models for legislators and officials to follow. The authors of the prefaces of the legal works referred to several questions frequently debated by Chinese jurists by using quotations from the Classics. The *Book of Documents* is the most frequently cited work, especially the chapter entitled *Punishments of Lü*, which concisely describes the law promulgated at the beginning of the Western Zhou Dynasty (ca. 1046–771 BCE). Although it is only a very fragmentary and indirect description of Zhou law, premodern Chinese scholars considered this text to be one of the earliest records available to them and, thus, a valuable model of governance.[15] Quotations of the *Punishments of Lü* were sometimes used to support the very existence of the codes.

14 Zhang Ting, *Circulating the Code: Print Media and Legal Knowledge in Qing China* (Seattle: University of Washington Press, 2020).

15 We now know that the text is later and probably dates from the early Eastern Zhou, ca. eighth century BCE.

It is known that Confucius presented an ideal of government and society in which the regulation of human relations would be ensured only by the rites, without the necessity of resorting to punishments. The law in China consisted solely of administrative rules and criminal sanctions to regulate the functioning of the state and to guarantee harmony in society. It is only an aspiration, attainable in a society governed by wise men, as the world was in the beginning of its history. In the world as it is now, punishments are necessary, as shown by the example of the early Zhou, who despite their antiquity, already epitomized a decayed form of government. For instance, an anonymous preface to the *Required Reading for the Zither Hall* (*Qintang bidu* 琴堂必讀) asks rhetorically why so much emphasis is placed on settling lawsuits when it is agreed that the most essential task of government is to enable agriculture to thrive. However, in the time of Yao and Shun, which corresponded to a kind of golden age that the origin of mankind knew, there were already criminals, and this is why the rulers had to resort to punishments. If the criminals are not punished, then the people cannot live in peace and be fully dedicated to agriculture.[16]

The question of the origins of law often emerges in the prefaces, and one of the paradoxes is to explain why the sages came to establish punishments against the principle of ruling through morality. The most common explanation was that of a progressive decadence of the state of society. The responsibility for the troubles was sometimes attributed to Chiyou, ruler of a barbarian people in conflict with the Chinese kings in early antiquity. It was also argued that the punishments then established were not implemented but were only figurative and used as a means to educate the people.[17] Another preface suggests that the sages established punishments in anticipation of the needs of future generations: it was better for those with knowledge to make them clear than to leave humanity in the dark afterwards. In his preface to Wang Mingde's *Dulü peixi*, Zhan Weisheng 詹惟聖, who once served as a vice director for a bureau of the Board of Punishments, purports that the ancients promulgated a code only as a guideline for future generations, fearing that they would not be able to clearly articulate the law and would misunderstand the correctness of the punishment.[18]

> 固知聖王未嘗不用刑，特恐後之人不明夫立法之心，或敢以意為重輕。於是乎原本協中之旨，制為一定之律。
>
> It is known that the ancient sages never renounced the use of punishments, because they feared above all that people in later generations

16 Bai Ruzhen 白如珍, *Qintang bidu* 琴堂必讀, 1841.

17 Zhu Jingxun 朱敬循, *Da Ming lüli zhijun qishu* 大明律例致君奇術 [The Penal Code of the Great Ming: A Marvelous Method to Assist the Ruler], Luo Dong 羅棟's preface.

18 Wang Mingde 王明德 *Dulü peixi* 讀律佩觿 [A Belt Bodkin Worn to Untangle the Code], Zhan Weisheng 詹惟聖's preface.

would not understand the intention of establishing law, or dare to decide on the lightness or severity at will. Thus, they enacted as immutable laws the formerly guiding principles that determine what is appropriate.

None of these arguments are specific to the prefaces of legal works, as the authors draw on a common fund of ideas about the emergence of law already discussed in early Chinese historians' works written under the Han.

The prefaces also outline the framework within which justice was to be exercised according to the tenets laid down by the ancients. Since the Sui Dynasty (581–618), Chinese law has been organized according to a scale of twenty degrees of punishment, allowing for a fair balance between the seriousness of the acts and the severity of the punishment. This attention to the balance between facts and punishments is older than the Sui code and can be traced back at least to the Qin (221–206 BCE), even if it was not formalized in such a systematic way. The excerpts from classical works cited by the authors of the prefaces did not contain specific references to institutions that indicate how this balance was achieved in ancient times, but they served as a guide on how to implement the rules using the major principles that structured the law.

First, several authors of prefaces insisted on the secondary place of law in relation to morality, pointing out that punishments were ultimately only a tool to support education (*bi jiao* 弼教).[19] Expressed differently, government was based on the complementarity of rites and punishments, with rites preventing the occurrence of crimes, and punishments repressing those nevertheless committed.[20] This understanding of the relationship between punishments and rites was underpinned by a cosmological edifice that interpreted social events in relation to natural phenomena. The world was divided into classes, one of the most structuring being the binary opposition between *yin*, associated with death and Autumn, and *yang*, the principle of vitality generated alongside with Spring. A virtuous government had to guarantee the harmony between social and cosmic phenomena, a principle that structured the functioning of the administration.[21] Thus, it was necessary to avoid executing criminals in the spring or summer or to at least to make sure that those who were executed really deserved to die. This attention to the fate of criminals was materialized by the institution of the Autumn Assizes, which was in charge of reviewing a large part of the capital judgments executed, if required, in the autumn.[22] In

19 For instance, Zhang Kai 張楷, *Lütiao shuyi* 律條疏議 [Comments and Explanations to the Penal Code], Ni Qian 倪謙's preface.

20 Cishan shiye zi 此山貰冶子, Wang Yuanliang 王元亮 (reprint), *Tang lü shi wen* 唐律釋文 [Comments to the Tang Code], in *Zhongguo lüxue wenxian* 中國律學文獻, ser. 2, vol. 1 (Heilongjiang renmin chubanshe, 2005).

21 Anon., *Minggong shupan qingming ji* 名公書判清明集 [A Collection of Enlightened Judgments by Famous Officials], Sheng Shixuan 盛時選's postface (1569).

22 On this institution, see Marinus Meijer, "The Autumn Assizes in Ch'ing Law," *T'oung Pao* 70 (1984): 1–17.

general, emperors were advised to promote life and to therefore use punishment sparingly, which could conflict with the duty to severely punish acts that undermined the foundations of society. The author of the preface to the *Comments to the Tang Code* expresses the dilemma in the following way:

> 從輕則惠姦何益，加重則反善猶難
> As once we judge with clemency, we grant a favor to the brigands without justification; as once we judge too severely, we oppose goodness. All this is very difficult.[23]

Another preface outlines the path to striking a balance between severity and benevolence:

> 固以律例為根本，而準情酌理，或嚴以懲刁健之風，或寬以養善良之氣
> Although the code remains the foundation, it is necessary to decide, according to the circumstances, whether to punish with great rigor in order to repress the flourishing of scoundrels, or to exempt from punishment in order to promote the vigor of good habits.[24]

Justice was a matter of impartiality, of being able to "harmonize and strike the right balance" (*ke xie jue zhong* 克協厥中).[25] No excesses in either regard were acceptable, as the rules of the judicial system were designed to ensure that officials had the least possible power of interpretation. The legislation promulgated by the rulers at the beginning of a dynasty took these balances into account perfectly. The legislation of Ming, for example, "is strict in appearance, but its intention is in clemency" (*lifa yan er yongyi shu* 立法嚴而用意恕).[26] The law was already lenient, and only the emperor could have exceptionally decided to go beyond it (*fa wai zhi ren* 法外之仁), but officials sometimes bent the law to save lives. However, if officials separate what is related or make connections of dissimilar things in an attempt to apply their own sense of mercy, this can only lead to going against human feelings.[27]

We touch here on a major theoretical question that was discussed at length by Chinese jurists and was at the heart of their thinking on the codification of law. The problem can be posed as follows: how can a code anticipate the full range of possible circumstances while being as concise as possible? This quest for a code that was both succinct and complete is described in the *Legal*

23 Cishan shiye zi, *Tang lü shi wen*.
24 Li Jun 李鈞, *Panyu lucun* 判語錄存 [Preserved Records of Judgments], Bian Fenghui 邊鳳翽's preface (1831).
25 *Minggong shupan qingming ji*.
26 Wang Mingde 王明德, *Dulü peixi* 讀律佩觽 [A Belt Bodkin Worn to Untangle the Code], Peng Shidu 彭師度's preface (1674).
27 Ding Xiangjin 丁湘錦, *Xingbu bo'an huichao* 刑部駁案彙鈔 [Anthology of Cases Rejected by the Ministry of Justice], Suldei 蘇爾德's preface (1764).

Treatise of the *Book of the Sui*. The treatise describes the evolution of the law of five successive dynasties between 502 and 618, during a period in which China was fragmented into kingdoms, none of which was able to extend its authority over all of China. This political situation favored the repeated replacement of dynasties over a relatively short period of time and, thus, the promulgation of different codes. The merits of the various codes were therefore judged by their ability to capture the essential without getting lost in the details. The metaphor of a net was often used: the nets of the law should not be too loose so as not to let crimes go unpunished but without being too narrow either, at the risk of overloading justice otherwise.[28]

This question first addresses a practical concern related to the administration of justice in China. The officials had to strictly apply the law and could pronounce a punishment only if the facts were specified in the law. The judges did not have the power to interpret the law, and if the law was silent, they had to refer to the emperor, who could decide to enact a new rule corresponding to the facts at stake. These institutional mechanisms tended to inflate the number of laws, as judges were faced with the choice of either letting behaviors that they considered unlawful go unpunished or requiring the promulgation of a new statute to fill in the loopholes in the law. The interest in these issues also relates to the central role assigned by Chinese thinkers to change in understanding the world. The law obeyed the same principles as those animating all phenomena, and understanding its mutations and how to adapt it to situations that were by nature changing was thus an important task for jurists. We now examine how these issues were addressed in the prefaces.

Several prefaces first present a classification of the sources of law, contrasting the intangible sources with the others. According to Su You 蘇祐 (1492–1573), author of the preface of *A Collection for the Legalist*, a handbook for legal practitioners, “A punishment is a complete form, it is therefore achieved and once it is achieved, it can no longer change” (刑，成也，一成而不可變).[29] In the institutional context of the Ming and Qing, the opposition between stable and changing norms was materialized by the distinction between statutes and substatutes. Statutes, once constituted, were not to change, while substatutes were enacted according to actual circumstances (*yin shi yi zhi yi* 因時以制宜). The way to judgment was to exhaust these two sources.[30] The difficulty came from the impossibility for the law to anticipate “the multitude of variations of the true and false” (*qingwei baibian* 情偽百變), an expression that often appears in the prefaces. If the law was silent, then it was possible to refer to cases already judged, specifically, those qualified as leading cases (*cheng’an*

28 Wei Zheng 魏徵; Linghu Defen 令狐德棻, *Sui shu* 隋書 [The Book of Jin], Beijing, Zhonghua shuju, 1973, volume 25, 702 and 712.

29 Anon. *Fajia pouji* 法家裒集 [A Collection for the Legalist], Su You 蘇祐’s preface (1548).

30 Quan Shichao 全士潮, *Bo’an xinbian* 駁案新編 [A New Collection of Rejected Cases], Ruan Kuisheng 阮葵生’s preface (1781).

成案), whose circumstances were close to those of the case in question. As the substatutes were consolidated in the code, they became as fixed as the statutes, and the leading cases became the flexible element of the law.[31]

Leading cases should not be equated with the common law precedents from which they differ, particularly in one important respect: they were not a creation of the judges per se but rather the ratification, nominally by the emperor, of a proposed decision made by officials. A leading case was an *ad hoc* decision taken for a particular factual situation and could be cited only under a very restricted procedure. If the new case to be tried did not correspond exactly, the punishment had to be adapted again. Sometimes, in order to avoid these burdensome procedures, the officials preferred to adapt the facts to fit exactly the existing laws, a phenomenon described in a preface as "altering the facts" (*yi qing* 移情).[32]

The art of judging thus involved the ability to match facts and punishment, either by applying the appropriate law in the case of a perfect fit between a law and a case or by adjusting a legal punishment to the seriousness of the facts; the key was to preserve the "balance between facts and law" (*qing fa zhi ping* 情法之平).[33]

If the law was a matter of balance, then this was because it was possible to measure it, and the term "weight" (*quan* 權) appeared regularly in the prefaces. As we have seen, Chinese punishments were organized around a scale of five punishments and twenty degrees, which provided a standard for measuring the severity of punishment. The compass and the square were sometimes used to represent the exactitude and objectivity of the law.[34] Justice thus resided in the ability to perceive the infinitesimal variations, as several prefaces indicate.[35]

4 Conclusion

The prefaces to Chinese legal works served a number of functions that we have identified in this chapter. In China, prefaces usually permitted the identification of the authorship of a work, a characteristic found in legal works, especially those written based on the initiative of individuals. The authors described their aims, including the diffusion of a better knowledge of the law. The intended audience of both the codes and the legal commentaries was not the general population but the officials and specialists

31 Ilibu 伊里布, *Xue'an chumo* 學案初模 [Elementary Models for the Study of Cases] (1834).
32 Quan Shichao, *Bo'an xinbian*.
33 Bao Shuyun 鮑書芸, *Xing'an huilan* 刑案匯覽 [A Conspectus of Judicial Cases] (1834).
34 Meng Kui 孟奎, *Cujie Xingtong fu* 粗解刑統賦 [Prose-Poem on the Song Penal Code, with Unskilled Explanations].
35 For instance, Ding Xiangjin, *Xingbu bo'an huichao*, or Shen Xintian 沈辛田, *Mingfa zhizhang zengding* 名法指掌增訂 [A Guide to Penal Law, Revised and Enlarged], Tang Suizu 唐綏祖's preface.

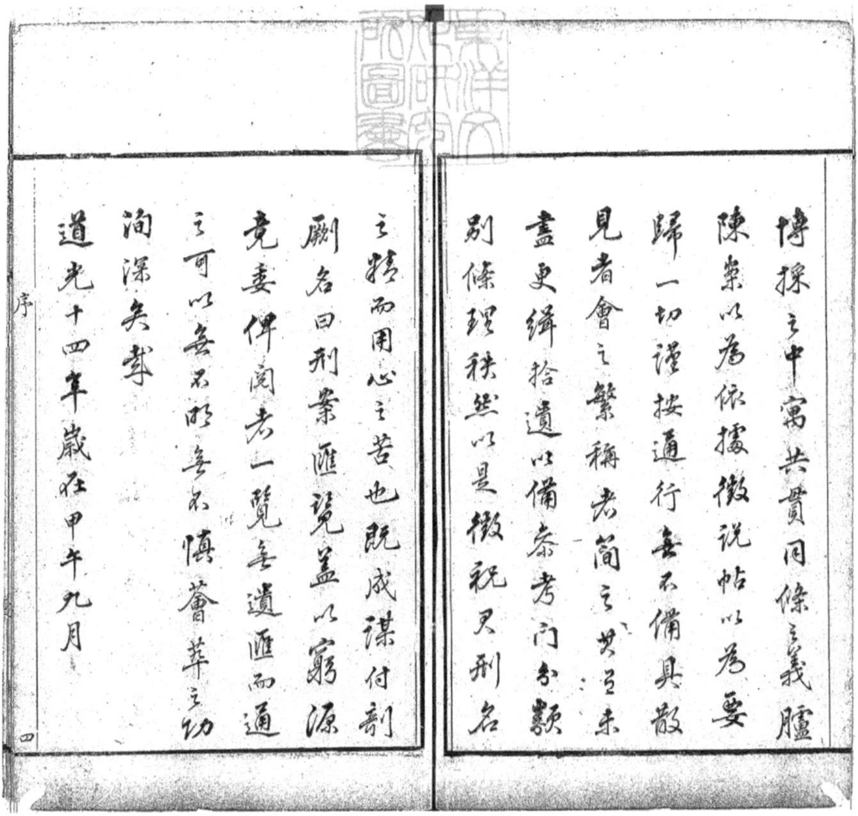

Figure 3.1 Preface of "A Conspectus of Judicial Cases" (Xing'an huilan 刑案匯覽), 1834, Tōyō Bunka Kenkyūjo

who gravitated around the administration of justice. Biographical elements are sometimes found in the prefaces, which shed light on the social context in which these works were written. In addition, the question of authority was central, whether it was the question of the authors of the works, of the discussions of the authority of the different sources of law, or more generally of the legitimacy of law. This question was in fact related to that of the origins of law, as authority is associated with tradition in China. Thus, many prefaces, especially those of the codes, contained historical developments that traced the genealogy of the law. The prefaces to legal works are valuable for their exposition of the intellectual frameworks on which Chinese law was based. In the various prefaces, a coherent picture emerges that depicts fundamental issues such as the relationship between law and morality, the evolution of law, and the definition of justice. The entire system, rooted in cosmological representations and a shared education among all officials, maintained a high degree of coherence.

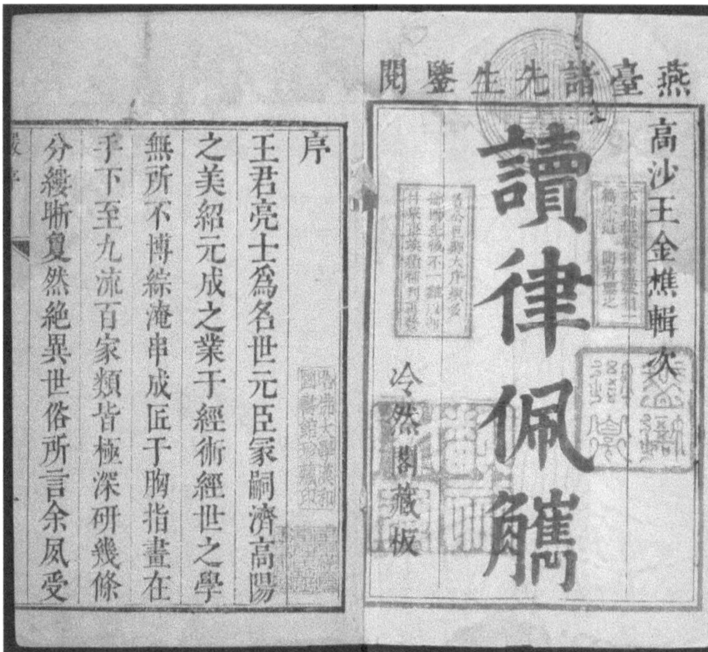

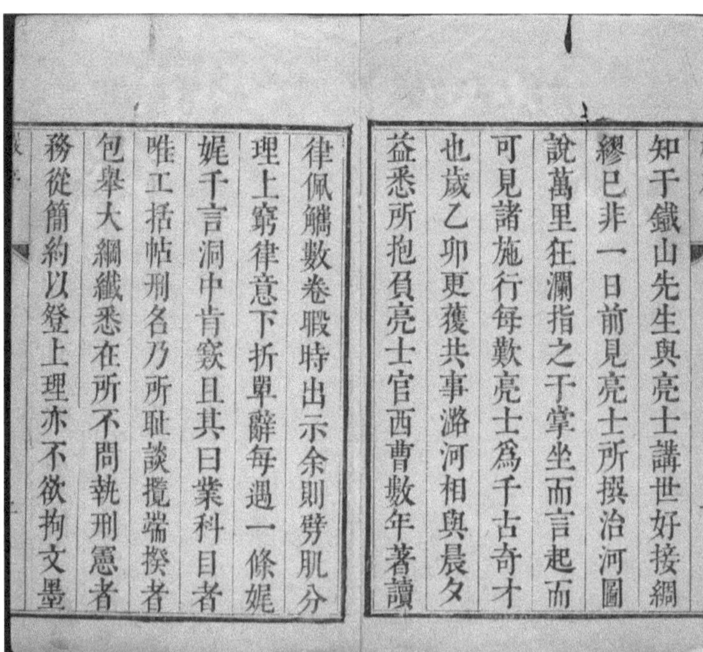

Figure 3.2 Preface of "A Belt Bodkin Worn to Untangle the Code" (Duli peixi 讀律佩觿), 1674, Harvard-Yenching Library

References

Anon. *Fajia pouji* 法家裒集 [A Collection for the Legalist], Su You 蘇祐's Preface (1548).

Anon. *Minggong shupan qingming ji* 名公書判清明集 [A Collection of Enlightened Judgments by Famous Officials], Sheng Shixuan 盛時選's Postface (1569).

Bai, Ruzhen 白如珍. *Qintang bidu* 琴堂必讀, 1841 (edition kept at the Institute for Legal History of the Chinese Academy of Social Sciences).

Bai, Ruzhen 白如珍. *Xingming yide* 刑名一得 [Notions Acquired from Legal Practice], Jueluo Yuzheng 覺羅玉正's Preface, 1784.

Bao, Shuyun 鮑書芸. *Xing'an huilan* 刑案匯覽 [A Conspectus of Judicial Cases] (1834).

Bodde, Derk and Morris Clarence. *Law in Imperial China: Exemplified by 190 Ch'ing Dynasty Cases.* Cambridge, MA: Harvard University Press, 1967.

Chang, Wejen. "Legal Education in Ch'ing China." In *Education and Society in Late Imperial China, 1600–1900*, edited by Benjamin A. Elman and Alexander Woodside, 292–339. Berkeley: University of California Press, 1994.

Cishan shiye zi 此山貰冶子 and Wang Yuanliang 王元亮 (reprint). *Tang lü shi wen* 唐律釋文 [Comments to the Tang Code], in *Zhongguo lüxue wenxian* 中國律學文獻, ser. 2, vol. 1, Heilongjiang renmin chubanshe, 2005.

Da Qing lüli jijie fuli 大清律集解附例 [The Great Qing Code with Commentaries and Substatutes].

Ding, Xiangjin 丁湘錦, *Xingbu bo'an huichao* 刑部駁案彙鈔 [Anthology of Cases Rejected by the Ministry of Justice], Suldei 蘇爾德's Preface (1764).

Ilibu 伊里布. *Xue'an chumo* 學案初模 [Elementary Models for the Study of Cases] (1834).

Li, Jun 李鈞. *Panyu lucun* 判語錄存 [Preserved Records of Judgments], Bian Fenghui 邊鳳翽's Preface (1831).

MacCormack, Geoffrey. "The Transmission of Penal Law (lü) from the Han to the T'ang: A Contribution to the Study of the Early History of Codification in China." *Revue internationale des droits de l'antiquité* 51 (2004): 47–86.

Meijer, Marinus. "The Autumn Assizes in Ch'ing Law." *T'oung Pao* 70 (1984): 1–17.

Meng, Kui 孟奎. *Cujie Xingtong fu* 粗解刑統賦 [Prose-Poem on the Song Penal Code, with Unskilled Explanations].

Nylan, Michael. *The Five 'Confucian' Classics.* New Haven, CT: Yale University Press, 2001.

Qingding libu zeli 欽定禮部則例 [Regulations of the Board of Rites].

Quan, Shichao 全士潮. *Bo'an xinbian* 駁案新編 [A New Collection of Rejected Cases], Ruan Kuisheng 阮葵生's Preface (1781).

Shen, Xintian 沈辛田. *Mingfa zhizhang zengding* 名法指掌增訂 [A Guide to Penal Law, Revised and Enlarged], Tang Suizu 唐綏祖's Preface.

Tam, Kai-chai. *Justice in Print: Discovering Prefectural Judges and Their Judicial Consistency in Late-Ming Casebooks.* Leiden: Brill, 2020.

Wang, Guoqiang 王國強. *Zhongguo guji xuba shi* 中國古籍序跋史 [History of the Preface of Chinese Ancient Books], Wuhan: Wuhan daxue chubanshe, 2015.

Wang, Mingde 王明德. *Dulü peixi* 讀律佩觿 [A Belt Bodkin Worn to Untangle the Code], Zhan Weisheng 詹惟聖's Preface.

Wei, Zheng 魏徵 and Linghu Defen 令狐德棻. *Sui shu* 隋書 [The Book of Jin], Beijing: Zhonghua shuju, 1973.

Wilkinson, Endymion. *Chinese History: A New Manual.* Cambridge, MA: Harvard University Press, 2012.

Will, Pierre-Étienne. *Handbooks and Anthologies for Officials in Imperial China. A Descriptive and Critical Bibliography*, 2 vols. Leiden: Brill, 2020.

Yan, Junyan 顏俊彥. *Mengshui zhai cundu* 盟水齋存牘 [Official Documents Kept at Meng River Studio], Lu Ao 陸鏊's Preface (1632).
Zhang, Kai 張楷. *Lütiao shuyi* 律條疏議 [Comments and Explanations to the Penal Code], Ni Qian 倪謙's Preface.
Zhang, Ting. *Circulating the Code: Print Media and Legal Knowledge in Qing China*. Seattle, WA: University of Washington Press, 2020.

4 The conservative case for warrior law

Legal change in medieval Japan

Christoffer Bovbjerg

1 Introduction

The List of Precedents on Judgment, *Goseibai shikimoku*, revolutionized law in premodern Japan. Promulgated in 1232, the List of fifty-one articles outlined the legal philosophy and guiding principles of the Kamakura shogunate, the administration of the country's top military official, the shogun. This legal framework expounded both general and specific provisions, including strict limitations on warrior authority. These binding precedents and guidelines would govern the samurai, who wielded increasing power across the archipelago and remained a foundational touchstone for legal thought in Japan for the following 600 years.[1]

The List of Precedents represented the first legal standard for issues specifically related to samurai—or warriors, as they called themselves—who had not been addressed in Japan's classical law (*ritsuryō*) and its amendments. Remarkably, the shogunate—an organization of warriors recently victorious on the field of battle—chose to specifically limit the power of its own officials. The List reflected this impulse and made clear that Kamakura's legislation and limits would apply across the country.[2] For the first time, warriors would be held legally accountable for their actions according to a universal standard, including provisions that promised due process and impartial judgment. Critically, these principles were disseminated in writing—in the vernacular, no less—and distributed widely. Finally, through the List, those outside of the capital could share a common understanding of the law.

1 Special thanks to the University of Tokyo's Historical Glossary Project for their help with translation, especially Endo Motoo, Joan Piggott, and Dan Sherer. I am also immensely grateful to Beth Berry, Luke Roberts, Randy and Barbara Bovbjerg, and Giuliana Perrone for their patience and insightful suggestions.

2 There are, of course, exceptions to the authority of Kamakura over warriors, most notably over those both outside the ranks of its housemen and in more remote areas, especially the island of Kyushu. But even there, Kamakura housemen drafted their own laws in the spirit of the List of Precedents, as the Ōtomo family did in Bungo Province with the New Articles on Judgment (*shin goseibaijō*) in the 1240s. Takahashi Jun'ichirō, ***Bushi no okite*** (Tōkyō: Shin Jinbutsu Ōraisha, 2012), 92–93.

DOI: 10.4324/9781003534815-5

Table 4.1 Major Events of the Kamakura Shogunate.

Major Events of the Kamakura Shogunate	
Minamoto no Yoritomo appointed shogun	1192
Jōkyū Disturbance	1221
Hōjō Yasutoki became shogunal regent	1224
Kangi Famine	c.1229–c.1232
The List of Precedents on Judgment promulgated	1232
Kamakura Shogunate overthrown	1333

From its inception, the List of Precedents has been recognized as an epochal marker in Japanese legal history. Contemporaries cited the text with lofty language, especially as the Kamakura shogunate came to be known for its impartial justice. Petitioners submitted claims from across the country hoping for judgments on an expanding number of issues, with some even journeying hundreds of miles to plead their case in person.[3] Legal manuals proliferated to assist new litigants through the intricacies of the system.[4]

The List of Precedents remained the ultimate guide for shogunal judges until the fall of the Kamakura shogunate in 1333, when all Kamakura law was nullified. Yet the List continued to be an essential text and legal influence. It became the explicit basis for the laws of the succeeding Muromachi shogunate and was lauded by later medieval jurists as the foundation of warrior legal and governing philosophy.[5] In the early modern period, the List remained an important part of educating the governing (warrior) elite, serving as a mainstay in schools.[6]

Modern historians see the List of Precedents as the beginning of a formal "warrior law," "a founding document of Japan's medieval society," and "the representative of medieval law." Many interpret it as the capstone of a transition from the classical to medieval legal systems and the beginning of the

3 Perhaps most famously, the poet Abutsu-ni traveled roughly 250 miles from Kyoto to Kamakura to make her case in shogunal courts in the late thirteenth century, chronicling her journey in *Izayoi nikki*. For translation, see Edwin O. Reischauer, "The Izayoi Nikki (1277–1280)," *The Harvard Journal of Asiatic Studies* 10 no. 3/4 (December 1947): 255–387. Many other would-be litigants tailored the terms of their petitions to the shogunate in response to the List of Precedents by highlighting specific concerns, especially bandit (*akutō*) activity, in the hopes of a trial and a favorable ruling. See Morten Oxenboell, *Akutō and Rural Conflict in Medieval Japan* (Honolulu: University of Hawai'i Press, 2018), 7.

4 See Carl Steenstrup, "Sata Mirensho: A Fourteenth-Century Law Primer," *Monumenta Nipponica* 35 no. 4 (Winter 1980): 405–435.

5 Kenneth Grossberg, *The Laws of the Muromachi Bakufu* (Tokyo: Monumenta Nipponica, Sophia University, 1981), 7.

6 Yoshinaga Koizumi, "Learning to Read and Write—A Study of Tenaraibon" and Machi Senjurō, "The Evolution of 'Learning' in Early Modern Japanese Medicine," in *Listen, Copy, Read*, eds. Matthias Hayek and Annick Horiuchi (Leiden: Brill, 2014), 102, 167. Murakami Kazuhiro et al., *Shiryō de yomu Nihon hōshi* (Kyoto: Hōritsu Bunkasha, 2016), 45.

ascendancy of warrior law, which would last until its replacement in 1868.[7] Guided by the List, shogunal courts boasted what one scholar describes as "astonishingly 'modern'" procedures, including an adversarial system in which the court was a neutral arbiter, the litigants set the object of litigation, and both sides could access and contest evidence and appeal the judgment. Under the Kamakura shogunate, Japan developed a civil litigation system "more just and careful than that found in Western Europe at the time." Shogunal courts handled cases "to such a level of quality that even the loser could leave the court convinced that it had heard him carefully, weighed all arguments, and decided his case impartially."[8] While this assessment may overstate the case, it nevertheless indicates how scholars have appreciated the novelty and importance of the List of Precedents and its revolutionary results. Still, they often neglect to appreciate the context in which the List was conceived and the process undertaken to derive the changes that it wrought. To approach the List without this broader framing both undersells its accomplishments and misunderstands the deliberative, pluralist, and strategic transition to warrior law.

Essential to understanding these articles and their place in history are two letters written by their compiler, Hōjō Yasutoki, the shogunal regent who exercised power in the name of the imperially appointed military leader. These notes, written to his brother Shigetoki in Kyoto, provided the contemporary framing for this legal transformation and offer not only important insights into the arguments and justifications for this intervention but also the legal philosophy underpinning it. Yasutoki made his case for formalizing the customary practices and precedents of warriors and incorporating warrior law into the broader body of written law, including aristocratic law (*kuge hō*), which regulated the imperial court and (non-military) public administration, and estate law (*honjo hō*), a diverse collection of rules and policies set by proprietors and guarantors for their private estates. Yasutoki needed to convince the elites in and around Kyoto, the imperial capital, who structured and benefited from these laws and had the most to lose from their disruption or replacement, to accept the formal addition of warrior law. He sought to alleviate the concerns of these elite aristocrats and religious institutions by emphasizing continuity. Yasutoki framed the List of Precedents as a necessary update to existing classical law, a supplement that would add to rather than alter what had come before, and downplayed any potential breaks from the past. These rather revolutionary ideas were then, in Yasutoki's telling, not a rethinking

7 Murakami et al., *Shiryō de yomu Nihon hōshi*, 44–45. Hiroshi Oda, *Japanese Law* (Oxford: Oxford University Press, 1999), 16; Ishimoda Shō, "Japan's Medieval World," in *Capital and Countryside in Japan, 300–1180*, ed. Joan R. Piggott, trans. Joan R. Piggott (Ithaca, NY: East Asia Program, Cornell University, 2006), 337; Ishii Ryōsuke, *Hōseishi* (Tōkyō: Yamakawa Shuppansha, 1964), 123.

8 Carl Steenstrup, "New Knowledge Concerning Japan's Legal System before 1868, Acquired from Japanese Sources by Western Writers since 1963," in *Law in Japan: A Turning Point*, ed. Daniel H. Foote (Seattle: University of Washington Press, 2007), 12–16.

of the foundations of Japanese law but merely minor, necessary adjustments, much as aristocratic law and estate law had been. The shogunate was simply incorporating warriors into Japan's legal corpus, formalizing existing customary practices and crafting new legislation only when necessary and consistent with *dōri*, the universalizing concept of "reason" or "morality."

This savvy approach allowed Yasutoki to present well-reasoned justifications and assurances that his administration would preserve the status quo. It enabled the shogunate to govern powerfully but predictably, maintain order, and bolster its own authority, all while laying the foundation for a more durable yet nimble administrative and legal system. Furthermore, this framing of a shogunate committed to justice and good governance became a cornerstone for a narrative—both real and exaggerated—of Kamakura generally and of Yasutoki in particular as icons of just rule. Ultimately, the choice to work within the existing legal system and to emphasize this conservatism allowed the shogunate to achieve remarkable reforms that changed the rule of law in Japan forever.

2 The need for warrior law

The 1220s presented existential challenges for the Kamakura shogunate. Within a decade, the warrior regime endured a military attack from imperial forces, confusion and lingering violence in its aftermath, and a historic famine. Hōjō Yasutoki was at the forefront of each struggle. As a field general, he led the shogunal invasion of Kyoto. As shogunal regent, he issued rulings and orders to stem disorder. As a governor, he enacted humanitarian relief policies to ease widespread hunger. These experiences informed Yasutoki's decision to compile the List of Precedents and his strategy for shaping the formalization of warrior law.

The Kamakura shogunate was the first enduring organization of its kind. Around the time of Yasutoki's birth in 1183, the germ of the shogunate formed in eastern Japan as a private regional network of warriors under Minamoto no Yoritomo, who became the first Kamakura shogun in 1192.[9] The nascent shogunate was incorporated into the imperial state as its military and police arm and granted permanent military and legal authority over its followers. These warriors swore themselves as housemen to the shogun and expected rewards, specifically, income rights, in return. The shogun fulfilled this obligation by appointing housemen as local law enforcement officials (*jitō*, "land head"). These appointments provided both income rights and security of tenure.

9 Officially, Yoritomo was made *seii tai shogun*, "barbarian-subduing generalissimo," a designation first used in the eighth century in the context of wars against the Ezo in northeastern Japan. Until Yoritomo's appointment, *seii tai shogun* was a temporary position. Satō Shin'ichi, *Nihon no chūsei kokka* (Tokyo: Iwanami Shoten, 1983), 97–99. Masuda Takashi, "Kamakura bakufu," in *Kokushi daijiten*, vol. 3, ed. Kokushi daijiten henshū iinkai (Tokyo: Yoshikawa Kōbunkan, 1983), 549–553.

Unlike previous positions held by warriors, which were under the authority of aristocratic or estate regulations, shogunal appointments lay outside existing forms of written law. As military appointments by the shogun, they could be rescinded only by the shogunate.

This delegation of authority to the shogunate posed a grave threat to the continued primacy of the capital aristocracy and major religious institutions. These "gates of power" boasted extensive connections and political sway, diversified portfolios of income rights in landholdings, and their own military forces and allies. The shogunate's emergence presented a direct challenge to their status by threatening to disrupt or discontinue the steady payment of rents and taxes. Still, the capital elites were content to manage the shogunate at first and were satisfied that its unprecedented autonomy was possible only through imperial edict.[10]

Yasutoki's family changed that calculation. In the years following the death of the first shogun in 1199, the Hōjō, the late Minamoto no Yoritomo's in-laws, consolidated their power in Kamakura and maneuvered their way through coups, counter-coups, and intrigue into ruling in the name of Yoritomo's sons. But when the last Minamoto shogun died in 1219, the Hōjō ruled without a shogun at all. Seeking to eliminate these upstarts and reassert imperial control over the shogunate and its officials, a coalition of retired emperors and other capital elites orchestrated an attack on the shogunate in 1221, known as the Jōkyū Disturbance. Yasutoki took the field as a general, led the shogunate's rout of the imperial forces, and occupied Kyoto. There, he led Kamakura's effort to remake the imperial court by exiling the belligerent retired emperors and placing a new emperor on the throne. Despite undertaking these unprecedented punishments, shogunal leaders largely preserved the status quo and chose to reaffirm the imperial institution and the shogunate's role nominally beneath it. However, the balance of power had quite clearly shifted: the shogunate had become the dominant force in Japan.

Yasutoki oversaw the expansion of shogunal power from Kyoto, serving as the shogunate's new deputy in the capital. There, he administered the expansion of shogunal officials, as housemen were granted appointments as rewards for their service. Nominally appointed to keep the peace, their presence did little to restore order. New officials were frequently bad matches for their appointments: they often came from across the country and were ignorant of local history and customs while many locals had no experience with this sort of official and their new shogunal authority. Many warrior officials exploited

10 When Minamoto no Yoritomo died suddenly in 1199, the imperial court was presented with an opportunity to attempt to revoke or amend shogunal powers, but it did not. Quite the opposite, an imperial proclamation was made that Yoritomo's son, Yoriie, was "to inherit the legacy of the former *seii tai* shogun Minamoto [Yoritomo] *ason* and command his housemen and followers and administer the military governors of the various provinces as before." *Azuma kagami* vol. 2, comp. Kuroita Katsumi and Kokushi taikei henshūkai (Tokyo: Yoshikawa Kōbunkan, 1989), 554.

and exacerbated this confusion with aggression and avarice, working to wring the most out of their new appointments. Others were simply clueless to local conditions and fell prey themselves to dispossession.

These difficulties were compounded by the limits of the legal system. Under the existing, pluralist body of medieval law, warrior officials operated in a liminal space: under shogunal authority, they were beyond the reach of aristocratic courts and estate proprietors, even as they served on lands otherwise within those jurisdictions. To the extent that warriors were regulated, it was largely through custom and precedent alone. This led to confusion, frequent appeals to the shogunate, and inconsistent judgments both from Kamakura and its deputies in Kyoto. Warrior officials all too often underlined these weaknesses by robbing, extorting, and otherwise terrorizing the locals who they were supposed to protect. Yasutoki fielded numerous complaints from capital elites who pleaded for the shogunate to force its warriors to respect their legal rights as public officials and private proprietors. The shogunate was receptive to these appeals, typically issuing judgments in favor of civilian petitioners.[11] First as deputy, and then as regent, Yasutoki himself also gave blanket orders to curtail such unlawful behavior.

Disputes between warriors added to the burden on Kamakura's courts. In the absence of written law, warriors had for centuries relied on customary practices and precedents for some of their most important issues, including managing the relationships and obligations between lord and retainer, handling the succession of duties and rights, and overseeing networks and alliances.[12] But this was necessarily limiting: unwritten custom had no predictability and no standard interpretation, application, or recognized enforcement mechanism. As an administrator, Yasutoki found that existing warrior justice was not enough. Petitions and disputes multiplied, and the courts simply could not keep up. Judgments were slow, inconsistent, and influenced by personal connection and political power. Taking advantage of these circumstances, warriors pressed the limits of their power on the ground and took more cases to court. The growing burden of adjudication meant that the shogunate struggled to effectively govern its police and resolve complaints against and disputes among them.

Yasutoki became the shogunal regent in 1224, inheriting the growing concerns of persistent violence and overwhelmed shogunal courts from his late father. The situation quickly grew much worse. Unseasonable and inclement weather led to repeated failed harvests; thus, hunger spread. Yasutoki himself

11 Of the extant rulings prior to the List of Precedents, the shogunate ruled overwhelmingly in favor of estate guarantors against Kamakura housemen by a margin of forty-seven to one. Murai Shōsuke, "Jūsan-jūyon seiki no Nihon: Kyoto, Kamakura," in *Iwanami kōza Nihon tsūshi*, vol. 8, ed. Asao Naohiro et al. (Tokyo: Iwanami Shoten, 1994), 8.

12 Carl Steenstrup, *A History of Law in Japan Until 1868* (Leiden: E.J. Brill, 1996), 78.

observed, "the world is in famine and people will die of starvation."[13] Indeed, the resulting Kangi Famine was perhaps the worst in Japanese history. The dead clogged streets and waterways, armed gangs attempted brazen robberies, and the desperate sold their children, spouses, and even themselves into slavery to escape starvation.[14] In areas around the capital, pending lawsuits were "canceled as there [was] nothing remaining after these losses."[15]

In response, Yasutoki pursued a variety of reforms, including issuing regulations for Kamakura housemen, dispensing judgments and punishments against those who disobeyed, and providing food and debt relief. But these ad hoc measures were not enough. They not only routinely failed to prevent warrior predation or alleviate general suffering but also did little to address their underlying causes. They also did not stem the rising tide of complaints and lawsuits that threatened to finally sink the shogunate's courts. While the weather remained beyond the grasp of men or governing institutions, Yasutoki controlled what he could. He made the law the cornerstone of his reform efforts.

3 A new law

Within the context of disorder, Yasutoki seized the opportunity to effect change within the existing legal system. Yasutoki commissioned a team of legal specialists to study written law and warrior customary practices and precedents and to then compile a set of basic guidelines for judging suits involving warriors. In 1232, Yasutoki unveiled the result: the List of Precedents on Judgment, fifty-one articles that laid out shogunal legal philosophy, policy, and procedure.[16] In two letters written to his brother Shigetoki, who represented the shogunate in Kyoto, Yasutoki outlined the main points that he hoped would convince the old guard in the capital to accept reforms. By emphasizing the need for a legal update, the List of Precedents' complementary relationship to existing law, its applicability to warriors alone, and his vision for improving justice and moral governance, Yasutoki was able to enact these major reforms without significant opposition or additional disruption.

In his letters, Yasutoki anticipated and attempted to address the concerns of the imperial court, aristocracy, and major religious institutions. First, he

13 "Kamakura bakufu hō #20," in *Chūsei hōsei shiryōshū*, vol. 1, comp. Satō Shin'ichi et al. (Tokyo: Iwanami Shoten, 2001), 70.

14 William Wayne Farris, *Japan's Medieval Population: Famine, Fertility, and Warfare in a Transformative Age* (Honolulu: University of Hawai'i Press, 2009), 33–42.

15 Fujiwara Sadaie, *Meigetsuki*, vol. 3. (Tokyo: Kokusho Kankōkai, 1969), 238.

16 Uwayokote Masataka, *Hōjō Yasutoki* (Tokyo: Yoshikawa Kōbunkan, 1981), 84–87. John Carey Hall, "Japanese Feudal Law: The Institutes of the Judicature," *Transactions of the Asiatic Society of Japan* 34, part 1 (1906): 17–45. For full treatment, see Christoffer R. Bovbjerg, "The United State in Kamakura Law," Ph.D. diss. (University of California, Berkeley, 2018).

needed to explain why legal change was necessary. Yasutoki did this by framing the reforms as essential to justice and peace. As it stood, the judicial system was unpredictable in its decisions; these decisions could only be consistently counted on to favor the powerful. Those with connections and clout could demand hearings, while the claims of those without advantages went ignored. Moreover, when courts did accept lawsuits, judges often issued their rulings based on the relative power of the litigants, ignoring the evidentiary merits of the cases before them. Furthermore, judges relitigated the same issues again and again, which clogged the courts and muddied the jurisprudence with contradictory verdicts. The courts themselves were out of order—it was clear that something had to be done to standardize judgments. "These articles were drafted," Yasutoki explained, "so that . . . the severity [of judgments] will not be dependent on [the social power or political influence of] the parties." The List would also serve as a guide for future rulings so that they are "rendered impartially, without discrimination between high and low."[17]

Yasutoki's audience was the rich and powerful, so his message needed to appeal beyond an idealistic "justice for all" talking point. He needed to convince them that standardizing warrior justice could provide ample rewards for the capital elites, who had themselves been through a number of crises and understood that their power depended on stability and, since 1221, the support of the shogunate. For one, a more predictable process would benefit (almost) everyone involved. Predictability in shogunal courts would inspire trust in the process—that litigants there would be heard and treated uniformly. In addition, creating standards for judgments offered enticing returns for the elites who so often found themselves dealing with overly assertive and aggressive warrior officials. Finally, warriors would be held accountable.

As things stood, Yasutoki argued, the law's inaccessibility led to poor outcomes for all involved. He was careful to respect classical law, but explained that for those outside the halls of power in the capital, its specifics were all but unknown. Yasutoki observed that the texts of older forms of law, laudable as they were, were written in Sino-Japanese and incredibly difficult to understand. "Such matters *should* be based and judged solely on the provisions of [existing] law," but among warriors and the common people, "there is not even one in a thousand or ten thousand . . . who understand this way."[18] Even those literate in Chinese characters could not make sense of the formal and complex provisions. Moreover, "for those who only know the Japanese syllabary, when they are confronted with Chinese characters, it is as though their eyes have gone blind." When an incident occurred—even if it clearly merited legal action—few involved knew the correct procedure. Litigants were

17 All translations of Hōjō Yasutoki's letters are by the author, based on "Hōjō Yasutoki shōsoku," *Chūsei hōsei shiryōshū*, vol. 1, comp. Satō Shin'ichi et al. (Tokyo: Iwanami Shoten, 2001), 56–59.

18 Emphasis added.

ignorant of what rules applied to them. When they encountered legal opinions citing classical law, they stumbled as though "wandering into a mountain full of deer traps and unknowingly fall into them."

Litigants were not alone. Officials tasked with investigating claims and crimes, researching precedents, and issuing rulings struggled too. The clerks of the imperial courts inconsistently cited texts, leading to uneven judgments and punishments. Kamakura's own legal specialists found conflicting precedents and varied customs. This heterogeneity only further exacerbated the problem. "We hear that the people are confused," Yasutoki opined. Change was needed to make the law understandable and effective.

The List of Precedents would address these shortcomings, Yasutoki assured his audience. It was written in the Japanese syllabary and in simpler language designed "to be easily understood by the people far and wide." Its concepts would be comprehensible even to "those who cannot read," including not only the warriors whom it regulated but also the populace who were policed by them. Furthermore, the List of Precedents would bring uniformity to judgment; by expressing the principles of law in plain language, its compilers sought to ensure that "judgments do not deviate" from this new standard.

Crucially, the List was distributed widely. Yasutoki instructed his brother to make copies and send them to the top warrior official in each province, where they were to "clearly explain" its contents to all of the housemen in their jurisdiction. Although Yasutoki did not order the List to be shared directly with the elites of the capital, aristocratic families, temples, and shrines soon added copies to their libraries—it was their concerns regarding its provisions that served as the impetus for Yasutoki's letters in the first place.

Farther afield, commoners quickly became familiar with the shogunate's legal principles, utilizing them in numerous suits against shogunal officials. Indeed, the List of Precedents became the best and most widely known legal text in medieval Japan. Both the use of the vernacular and a wide distribution signaled dramatic departures. The List was the first major legal document to be written in the Japanese syllabary and stood out among medieval legal texts as particularly widely and well known—it was referenced and understood at a level unsurpassed until the early modern era. This unprecedented expansion of access to written law, however, was framed by Yasutoki as merely a necessary reform.

Yasutoki sought to create a standard for shogunal housemen that would bring the existing legal system up to date. The nature of classical law and its amendments had led to warriors falling outside of its orbit, and the List would correct that. This new law was explicitly "only for the management of warriors." The shogunate would operate under a principle of non-interference: it would in no way "alter the authority of Kyoto's courts or the rules of classical law." The List and warrior law more broadly, then, should be understood more as amendments to classical law than as any sort of foundational break with it.

In fact, Yasutoki went to great lengths to prevent any perception that his efforts would undercut classical law. He articulated this fear in both letters, drawing on similar language to emphasize this point to his brother: "I am apprehensive and embarrassed that there will surely be those around the capital who will scorn it, scoffing that it was compiled by ignorant country bumpkins" and "ask what is its textual authority." This last point—the textual basis for the List of Precedents and warrior law as a whole—was paramount. Yasutoki conceded that these principles deviated from classical law, though only "in some minor ways." The List would be "a body of judgments" that highlighted important precedents to help guide judges in future rulings. As such, it would merely systematize existing practices—the customary practices and procedures of warriors—rather than institute drastic breaks from classical law and contemporary rulings. Some scholars suggest that its name itself invoked this connection; the word chosen for "precedent" (*shiki*) was the same used as a category of amendments within classical and aristocratic law. This choice would not only underline a complementary relationship with classical law but also reinforce the claim that these were regulations meant to update it.[19]

Ultimately, Yasutoki reasoned in his letters, these new guidelines should be understood as fulfilling an old role: updating the law to be consistent with new practical circumstances. The drastic expansion of warrior influence and the sudden imposition of new warrior officials operating outside of existing laws demanded action. Abuse by warrior officials threatened the established elites and the common people, not to mention the greater stability of the state. Established law had legislated updates to the structures of the imperial court and higher-level governance, whereas the List of Precedents would incorporate warriors into the legal body. It would apply only to warriors and respect the pre-existing authorities and jurisdictions of law that already existed.

In practice, the List of Precedents did formalize longstanding warrior customs, set clear limits on shogunal authority, and respected the rights of non-warrior actors. However, Yasutoki naturally neglected to highlight the articles of the List of Precedents that directly opposed principles of classical law. On issues from statutes of limitations to slavery, inheritance, and family law, the List formalized customary practices not previously recognized in law and legislated entirely new standards.[20] For example, Article Twenty-Three affirmed the right of childless women to adopt heirs. Even though this was "not allowed by [classical] law," it had long been a warrior custom, and there was substantial "evidence of this practice in [the] capital and countryside."[21]

The List of Precedents also did not rely entirely on precedent. On this point, Yasutoki came clean: "In truth, it does not rely on any original text; it

19 Nagamata Takao, "Goseibai shikimoku seiritsu no haikei," *Kokugakuin daigaku Nihon bunka kenkyūsho kiyō* no. 95 (March 2005): 139–140.

20 Nagamata Takao, "Goseibai shikimoku seiritsu no haikei," 121–124.

21 "Goseibai shikimoku," *Chūsei hōsei shiryōshū*, vol. 1, comp. Satō Shin'ichi et al. (Tokyo: Iwanami Shoten, 2001), 45.

was written only in keeping with reason (*dōri*)."[22] Reason—*dōri*—thus played an important role in warrior law and society. It was not a new idea or term. *Dōri* appeared in commentaries on aristocratic law as early as the ninth century, in which it was used to describe written decisions based on classical law.[23] It was also referenced elsewhere within Yasutoki's lifetime. Dōgen, the founder of the Sōtō sect of Zen Buddhism in Japan, considered *dōri* in his writings as the norms and values that were reasonable, virtuous, and natural—a sort of moral compass.[24] In *Gukanshō*, a history written in the 1220s, an aristocratic abbot interpreted *dōri* as a form of historical consciousness.[25] For the abbot, *dōri* represented the unseen principles that drive history, which were tied to Buddhist conceptions of the inevitable decline in "the age of Final Law."[26] For Yasutoki, however, *dōri* signified something more immediate: a combination of morality, justice, and lived experience of the law (as opposed to its written definition). This included the traditional practices of warriors—the customs and conventions that united warrior groups and had been observed in some cases for centuries—and the philosophical principles drawn from the Confucian and Buddhist traditions. "Reason" would help to explain and justify deviations from older bodies of law. Although the List modified Japan's written legal tradition, the reliance on *dōri* suggested that the addition of warrior law was entirely consistent with existing jurisprudence; it simply incorporated custom in order to produce a more unified legal body.

Furthermore, these principles and their emphasis aligned with a broader moral philosophy, traditions of just governance, and the use of law to improve society. Yasutoki envisioned greater unity and a more universal system of justice with its incorporation. "If followers devote their loyalty to their masters, children have filial devotion for their parents, and wives obey their husbands," he wrote, "then those with crooked hearts will be rejected and the upright will be rewarded, and the people naturally will be at peace." These conditions represent three of the five fundamental Confucian relationships. Yasutoki also invoked the legacy of Prince Shōtoku (574–622), the semi-legendary prince, statesman, and purported author of Japan's first legal text, the Seventeen Article Constitution. Indeed, the very structure of the List of Precedents was likely

22 *Dōri* is a notoriously difficult term to define, let alone translate. It has also been rendered in English as "reasonableness," "principle of things," "precedent," "moderation," "pattern in the way of things," "state of affairs," and "public-spiritedness," among others.

23 Ishimoda, "Japan's Medieval World," 336.

24 Hee-Jin Kim, *Dōgen on Meditation and Thinking: A Reflection on His View of Zen* (Albany: State University of New York Press, 2007), 103–104.

25 *Dōri* featured in the abbot Jien's thinking so prominently that early readers referred to his text as "The Tale of Dōri" (*Dōri no monogatari*). *The Future and the Past: A Translation and Study of Gukanshō*, Translated by Delmer Myers Brown and Ichirō Ishida (Berkeley: University of California Press, 1979), 4.

26 In Japan, this period was known as *mappō* and was thought to have begun in 1052. Brown and Ishida, *The Future and the Past*, 3–4.

a nod to this seminal text.[27] Yasutoki sought to revive Shōtoku's mission to use law to improve society, but instead of appealing only to abstract principles, Yasutoki intended to combine them with the customary practices of warriors, building a more universal standard for law and good governance.[28]

The presentation of the List of Precedents and warrior law not only framed legal change in the best possible light but also ultimately enhanced the reputation of its compiler. By the mid-thirteenth century—only years after Yasutoki's death—the shogunal regent was already cast as a paragon of good government and morality, and the shogunate was famous for its impartial justice. These reputations were no doubt earned—Yasutoki's administration was a high-water mark for the shogunate, and the systematization of shogunal justice was an unequivocal success—but the creation and reinforcement of this narrative ensured that it stuck. The initial framing of the List set the story, which was then reinforced by shogunal histories and the ultimately unquestionable competence of Kamakura's courts. This helped solidify the place of the shogunate and the primary role of warriors in society, but it mattered especially for Yasutoki and the members of the Hōjō family. As the in-laws to the first shogun, they had no legitimate claim to rule and did so only through the unofficial position of shogunal regent. Along with the continued backing of the warriors, the support of the aristocracy and religious institutions was central, if not essential, to their continued leadership. Hōjō leaders, Yasutoki foremost among them, estimated that safeguarding order and preserving (most of) the establishment's traditional rights offered the surest avenue to a long, stable reign. This foundation of standards, predictability, and law ensured the survival of the Hōjō family for a century and warrior law for many more centuries to come.

4 Conclusion

The List of Precedents on Judgment was an important early step in the formalization and standardization of warrior law. Its reforms were by no means perfect, and in some areas, the List represented ideals that did not always translate into practical guidelines. Some problems persisted; for instance, legal records reveal many attempts from warriors and civilians alike to exert undue influence on the system, and abuse by warrior officials remained a problem until warriors were finally removed from the land in the 1590s. But despite its limitations, the List of Precedents brought a marked improvement to the

27 The number fifty-one was considered significant as a representation of seventeen, in honor of Prince Shōtoku's Seventeen Article Constitution, multiplied by three. Scholars speculate that the original List of Precedents, however, did not contain the entirety of the articles in the extant iteration but was reorganized to absorb later additions while maintaining fifty-one articles. Satō Shin'ichi, *Nihon no chūsei kokka* (Tokyo: Iwanami Shoten, 1983), 112–113.

28 Carl Steenstrup, *Hōjō Shigetoki (1198–1261) and His Role in the History of Political and Ethical Ideas in Japan* (London: Curzon Press, 1979), 29.

adjudication of disputes and created the foundations for a stable state and durable legal authority that outlasted Yasutoki's own regime. Yasutoki's framing of his intervention was critical to this success. By employing the rhetoric of conservatism and reason, Yasutoki was able to secure broad support for warrior law from across society. He mobilized that support to make incremental but very meaningful reforms that fundamentally restructured Japanese law and planted the seeds for the growth of warrior authority.

The legal system that grew out of the List of Precedents was remarkably sophisticated. The List formalized customary warrior practices in the vernacular (not unlike what Blackstone did for English common law) and created clear precedents and principles that complemented these customary practices to inform future rulings. It located these standards not only in warrior precedent but also in classical law and *dōri*—reason and practical morality, akin to Western notions of natural law. Shogunal courts prioritized civil procedure, allowing anyone to file suit and expect an unbiased hearing. Those dissatisfied with the process could file appeals. New rulings would create further precedents and be circulated as necessary, building a common law. With these reforms, shogunal courts proved popular, drawing more litigants and paving the way for the eventual predominance of warrior law over the coming centuries.

To put the List of Precedents into a fuller context, consider England's Magna Carta, executed in 1215. Like the List of Precedents, it imposed limits on the authority of an executive power. But the Magna Carta was the work of rebel barons who forced King John to accept restrictions on his own authority and guarantee them certain rights. The List of Precedents, meanwhile, was the centerpiece of the shogunate's agenda. In England, barons had to fight to limit monarchical power; in Japan, recently victorious warriors limited their own power and systematized the law by choice. Furthermore, they were able to incorporate warrior law into the existing legislative body without the use of (additional) violence. As Yasutoki's letters demonstrate, this was no simple transformation; it involved compromise, plural authorities, and a great deal of steady, evolutionary change to eventually achieve revolutionary ends. By framing the List of Precedents as non-revolutionary and non-threatening, Yasutoki and the Kamakura shogunate were able to achieve more much faster and more effectively than was likely possible through confrontation or conquest.

References

Adolphson, Mikael. *The Gates of Power: Monks, Courtiers, and Warriors in Premodern Japan*. Honolulu: University of Hawai'i Press, 2000.

Bovbjerg, Christoffer R. "The United State in Kamakura Law." Ph.D. diss., University of California, Berkeley, 2018.

Brown, Delmer Myers and Ichirō Ishida (trans.). *The Future and the Past: A Translation and Study of Gukanshō, an Interpretive History of Japan Written in 1221*. Berkeley: University of California Press, 1979.

Farris, William Wayne. *Japan's Medieval Population: Famine, Fertility, and Warfare in a Transformative Age*. Honolulu: University of Hawai'i Press, 2009.

Fujiwara, Sadaie. *Meigetsuki*, vol. 3. Tokyo: Kokusho Kankōkai, 1969.
Grossberg, Kenneth A. (ed.). *The Laws of the Muromachi Bakufu: Kemmu Shikimoku (1336) and Muromachi Bakufu Tsuikahō*. Tokyo: Monumenta Nipponica, 1981.
Hall, John Carey. "Japanese Feudal Law: The Institutes of the Judicature." *Transactions of the Asiatic Society of Japan* 34, part 1 (1906): 17–45.
Ishii, Ryōsuke. *Hōseishi*. Tokyo: Yamakawa Shuppansha, 1964.
Ishimoda, Shō. "Japan's Medieval World." In *Capital and Countryside in Japan, 300–1180*, edited by Joan R. Piggott, translated by Joan R. Piggott, 326–361. Ithaca, NY: East Asia Program, Cornell University, 2006.
Kim, Hee-Jin. *Dōgen on Meditation and Thinking: A Reflection on His View of Zen*. Albany: State University of New York Press, 2007.
Koizumi, Yoshinaga. "Learning to Read and Write—a Study of *Tenaraibon*." In *Listen, Copy, Read: Popular Learning in Early Modern Japan*, edited by Matthias Hayek and Annick Horiuchi, 91–138. Leiden: Brill Press, 2014.
Kuroita, Katsumi and Kokushi taikei henshūkai (comp.). *Azuma kagami*, vol. 1–4, rev. ed. Tokyo: Yoshikawa Kōbunkan, 1988–1989.
Machi, Senjurō. "The Evolution of 'Learning' in Early Modern Japanese Medicine." In *Listen, Copy, Read: Popular Learning in Early Modern Japan*, edited by Matthias Hayek and Annick Horiuchi, 163–204. Leiden: Brill Press, 2014.
Masuda, Takashi. "Kamakura bakufu." In *Kokushi daijiten*, vol. 3, edited by Kokushi daijiten henshū iinkai, 549–553. Tokyo: Yoshikawa Kōbunkan, 1983.
Murai, Shōsuke. "Jūsan-jūyon seiki no Nihon: Kyoto, Kamakura." In *Iwanami kōza Nihon tsūshi*, vol. 8, edited by Asao Naohiro, Ishii Susumu, Hayakawa Shōhachi, Amino Yoshihiko, Kano Masanao, and Yasumaru Yoshio, 1–68. Tokyo: Iwanami Shoten, 1994.
Murakami, Kazuhiro, Nishimura Yasuhiro, Hatakeyama Ryō, and Kita Yasuhiro. *Shiryō de yomu nihon hōshi*. Kyoto: Hōritsu bunkasha, 2016.
Nagamata, Takao. "Goseibai shikimoku seiritsu no haikei." *Kokugakuin daigaku Nihon bunka kenkyūsho kiyō* no. 95 (March 2005), 115–151.
Oda, Hiroshi. *Japanese Law*. Oxford: Oxford University Press, 1999.
Oxenboell, Morten. *Akutō and Rural Conflict in Medieval Japan*. Honolulu: University of Hawai'i Press, 2018.
Reischauer, Edwin O. "The Izayoi Nikki (1277–1280)." *The Harvard Journal of Asiatic Studies* 10, no. 3/4 (December 1947): 255–387.
Satō, Shin'ichi. *Nihon no chūsei kokka*, 8th ed. Tokyo: Iwanami Shoten, 1983.
Satō, Shin'ichi, Ikeuchi Yoshisuke, and Maki Kenji (comp.). *Chūsei hōsei shiryōshū*, vol. 1, 15th ed. Tokyo: Iwanami Shoten, 2001.
Steenstrup, Carl. *Hōjō Shigetoki (1198–1261) and His Role in the History of Political and Ethical Ideas in Japan*. London: Curzon Press, 1979.
Steenstrup, Carl. "Sata Mirensho: A Fourteenth-Century Law Primer." *Monumenta Nipponica* 35, no. 4 (Winter 1980): 405–435.
Steenstrup, Carl. *A History of Law in Japan Until 1868*. Leiden: E.J. Brill, 1996.
Steenstrup, Carl. "New Knowledge Concerning Japan's Legal System before 1868, Acquired from Japanese Sources by Western Writers since 1963." In *Law in Japan: A Turning Point*, edited by Daniel H. Foote. Seattle: University of Washington Press, 2007.
Takahashi Shin'ichirō. *Bushi no okite: "michi" wo meguru Kamakura, sengoku bushitachi no mou hitotsu no tatakai*. Tokyo: Shinjinbutsu Ōraisha, 2012.
Uwayokote, Masataka. *Hōjō Yasutoki*. Tokyo: Yoshikawa Kōbunkan, 1981.

5 Bodies of law in early medieval England and Scotland

Andrew Rabin

1 Introduction

In the abrupt and inconclusive final chapter of the *Vita Alfredi regis*, the text's author, Asser, describes the supervisory role taken by King Alfred in matters of law and the administration of justice. Asser writes (somewhat implausibly) that Alfred reviewed all judgments handed down in his kingdom to ensure that none were tainted by evil (*iniquitas*) or ignorance (*ignorantia*). In the case of the latter, the king,

> reprimanding their inexperience and lack of knowledge with discretion and moderation, would say, 'I am exceedingly amazed at your insolence, since through God's gift and my own you have assumed the office and status of wise men, yet you have ignored the study and application of wisdom. For that reason, I command you either to relinquish immediately the positions of worldly power you hold, or else to devote yourselves much more conscientiously to the study and application of wisdom.'[1]

For Asser, this portrait of royal engagement allows him to characterize the king as an interventionist—if a benevolent one—monarch and lawgiver in the Solomonic mode, a depiction that Alfred himself exploited when issuing

1 *Discrete et moderantur illorum imperitiam et insipientam redarguens, aibat inquiens: 'Nimium admirer vestram hanc insolentiam, eo quod, Dei dono et meo, sapientium ministerium et gradus usurpastis, sapientiae autem stadium et operam neglexistis. Quapropter aut terrenarum potestatum ministeria, quae habetis, illico dimittatis, aut sapientiae studiis multo devotius docere ut studiatis impero.'* Asser, *De rebus gestis Alfredi*, cap. 106, in William Henry Stevenson, *Asser's Life of King Alfred, Together with the Annals of Saint Neot's Erroneously Ascribed to Asser* (Oxford: Clarendon Press, 1959), 93. Here and elsewhere, all translations are my own. On this chapter in Asser, see Stefan Jurasinski and Lisi Oliver, *The Laws of Alfred: The Domboc and the Making of Anglo-Saxon Law* (Cambridge: Cambridge University Press, 2021), 54–55; David Pratt, *The Political Thought of King Alfred the Great*, Cambridge Studies in Medieval Life and Thought, (Cambridge: Cambridge University Press, 2007), 121–122; Patrick Wormald, *The Making of English Law: King Alfred to the Twelfth Century* (Malden: Blackwell Publishers, 1999), 118–125.

DOI: 10.4324/9781003534815-6

his legislative compendium several years later.[2] Yet this anecdote is as much about legal knowledge as it is about royal power. Alfred's interrogation of ignorant judges positions the king as the source not merely of legal authority but also of jurisprudential expertise: the prerogative to exercise judicial review rests upon Alfred's superior knowledge of the law, as does his right to dismiss judges ignorant of its precepts. Implicitly, judgments must conform to the king's notion of law and legal reasoning, leaving the judiciary little room for independent decision or interpretation.

Asser's emphasis on Alfred's legal expertise represents a salvo in a debate that shaped much of the early development of Germanic law. Although legal authority derived from the king in his role as the Lord's anointed, it remained a frequent matter of dispute whether the expertise necessary to administer that law in the form of legal judgments lay primarily with judges and legislators (*iudices*) or with the sovereign.[3] The stakes in this debate were not trivial: for the various secular and ecclesiastical bodies grappling for power in the fluid political world of post-Roman Europe, superiority in legal knowledge provided a foundation for the assertion of greater authority in practical matters of interpretation, judgment, and enforcement. Over the course of the fifth and sixth centuries, the transformation of former imperial colonies into independent kingdoms, the consolidation of legal authority by regional rulers, and the evolution of standalone post-Roman legal cultures led to increasingly aggressive attempts by emergent royal dynasties to claim a monopoly on legal knowledge for themselves.[4] Central to the royal argument was the production of written legislation, particularly lengthy and detailed injury schedules setting out specific penalties for injuries to different parts of the body.[5] Injury sched-

2 Pratt, *The Political Thought of King Alfred the Great*, 163.

3 Andrew Rabin, *Crime and Punishment in Anglo-Saxon England*, England in the Early Medieval World (Cambridge: Cambridge University Press, 2020), 54. In a specifically Scottish context, see Alice Taylor, *The Shape of the State in Medieval Scotland* (Oxford: Oxford University Press, 2016), 114–175.

4 Rabin, *Crime and Punishment*, 51; Alice Rio, *Legal Practice and the Written Word in the Early Middle Ages*, Cambridge Studies in Medieval Life and Thought (Cambridge: Cambridge University Press, 2009), 11–20; Sarah Foot, "Reading Anglo-Saxon Charters: Memory, Record, or Story?," in *Narrative and History in the Early Medieval West*, eds. Elizabeth M. Tyler and Ross Balzaretti (Turnhout: Brepols, 2006), 39–67; Herwig Wolfram, "Political Theory and Narrative in Charters," *Viator* 26 (1995): 39–51; James Q. Whitman, "At the Origins of Law and the State: Monopolization of Violence, Mutilation of Bodies, or Setting of Prices?," *Chicago-Kent Law Review* 71 (1995): 41–84.

5 Taylor, *Shape of the State*, 135–136; Alice Taylor, "Lex Scripta and the Problem of Enforcement: Anglo-Saxon, Welsh, and Scottish Law Compared," in *Legalism: Community and Justice*, eds. Fernanda Pirie and Judith Scheele (Oxford: Oxford University Press, 2014), 47–75; M. T. Clanchy, *From Memory to Written Record, England 1066–1307*, 3rd ed. (Cambridge: Blackwell, 2013); Andrew Rabin, "Witnessing Kingship: Royal Power and the Legal Subject in the Old English Laws," in *Kingship, Legislation and Power in Anglo-Saxon England*, eds. Gale R. Owen-Crocker and Brian Schneider (Woodbridge: Boydell and Brewer, 2013), 219–136, at 23–24; Patrick Wormald, "*Lex Scripta* and *Verbum Regis*: Legislation and Germanic Kingship,

ules not only portrayed the punishment of wrong-doing as an exclusively royal prerogative (even if carried out vicariously by his agents) but also asserted the king's right to judge the bodies of his subjects and assess their value according to his own standard. As components of royal legislation, they exerted a normative force on legal behavior, and, in the words of Patrick Wormald, as "repositories of ancient traditions," they may even have served as "ethnic marker[s]."[6] Perhaps most importantly, injury schedules arrogated to the king the right to determine the parameters according to which disputes involving bodily harm may be settled: judges were to act only in accordance with the king's criteria rather than exercise judgment themselves. Injury schedules occur in nearly every compendium of Germanic legislation between the first issuance of Salic Law in the early sixth century to their final appearance in the late ninth-century *domboc* of Alfred the Great, after which they fell out of use. Although little evidence survives to suggest that they ever played much role in the practical exercise of law, for their compositors, application was less important than the ideology of kingship that they represented.[7]

Yet despite their seeming disappearance following the reign of Alfred, a short injury schedule of the Germanic type survives, unexpectedly, in a Scottish legal compilation of the twelfth century, known to modern scholars as the *Leges inter Brettos et Scottos* (*LBS*).[8] The *Leges* appears to have originated as a compilation and distillation of various sources dealing with compensation, injury payments, and social status, possibly for judicial use, grafted onto the

from Euric to Cnut," in *Early Medieval Kingship*, eds. P. H. Sawyer and I. N. Wood (Leeds: Leeds University Press, 1977), 105–138. There is an extensive body of scholarship on early medieval injury schedules, but see especially Lukas Bothe, Stefan Esders, and Han Nijdam, eds., *Wergild, Compensation and Penance: The Monetary Logic of Early Medieval Dispute Resolution* (Leiden: Brill, 2021); Przemyslaw Tyszka, *The Human Body in Barbarian Laws, c. 500–800: Corpus Hominis as Cultural Category* (Frankfurt am Main: Peter Lang GmbH, 2014); Lisi Oliver, *The Body Legal in Barbarian Law*, Toronto Anglo-Saxon Series (Toronto: University of Toronto Press, 2011). William Ian Miller, *Eye for an Eye* (Cambridge: Cambridge University Press, 2006). Patrick Wormald, "The *Leges Barbarorum*: Law and Ethnicity in the Post-Roman West," in *Regna and Gentes: The Relationship between Late Antique and Early Medieval Peoples and Kingdoms in the Transformation of the Roman World*, eds. Hans-Werner Goetz, Jörg Jarnut, and Walter Pohl (Leiden: Brill, 2003), 21–55; Whitman, "Origins of Law," 41–84.

6 Wormald, "*Leges Barbarorum*," 41, 46.

7 See Taylor, *Shape of the State*, 151–152; Wormald, "*Lex Scripta* and *Verbum Regis*," 105–138.

8 The standard edition of the *Leges inter Brettos et Scottos* can be found in Alice Taylor, *The Laws of Medieval Scotland* (Edinburgh: The Stair Society, 2019), 427–444. The injury schedule occurs as cap. 212; see Taylor, *Laws*, 441–443. For detailed discussions of the text and its history, see Taylor, *Laws*, 243–264; Taylor, *Shape of the State*, 123–132; Robert Black, "A Historical Survey of Delictual Liability in Scotland for Personal Injuries and Death," *The Comparative and International Law Journal of Southern Africa* 8 no. 1 (1975): 46–70, at 48–56. On early Scottish law, see especially Andrew R. C. Simpson and Adelyn L. M. Wilson, *Scottish Legal History: Volume One, 1000–1707* (Edinburgh: Edinburgh University Press, 2017); Taylor, *Shape of the State*; Cynthia Neville, *Land, Law, and People in Medieval Scotland* (Edinburgh: Edinburgh University Press, 2010); Hector L. MacQueen, *Common Law and Feudal Society in Medieval Scotland* (Edinburgh: Edinburgh University Press, 1993).

great compilation of early Scottish law, the *Regiam maiestatem*.[9] Although multiple versions of the text survive, even the earliest postdates its composition by several centuries. The version that is the focus of this chapter is that found in MS. Edinburgh, National Library of Scotland, Advocates 25.5.6, compiled by the scribe James Monynet *ca.* 1488—the most complete witness to the *Leges*.[10] Surprisingly, the injury schedule, which forms this version's final chapter, has failed to attract much scholarly attention, but its anomalous presence in a fifteenth-century recension of the *Leges* provides a valuable case study in the ways that early law was transmitted across periods of time and cultural borders.

However, it is not simply the inclusion of the schedule in the *Leges* that lends it significance. Unlike the more formal injury schedules of the earlier Middle Ages, this version of the *Leges* schedule, despite being the longest and most detailed, is contradictory, incomplete, and in many places, largely incoherent. These aspects of the text attest to a history of revision and intervention, shedding light on both its reception and the many influences that led to its current form. This history is a matter not only of changing legal practice, however, but also of changing notions of legal knowledge. In its earliest manifestations, the purpose of an injury schedule was to allow its royal issuer to claim knowledge of—and, by extension, power over—the bodies of his subjects. Yet even after such texts ceased to be issued as formal legislation, their subsequent preservation and adaptation, often over the course of centuries, illustrates how a knowledge of legal history could become an instrument in later political disputes over national and cultural identity. This history of use and appropriation can be seen in the evolution of the *LBS* injury schedule from its earliest manuscript witness to its incorporation into Sir John Skene's 1609 edition of the great Scottish legal compendium, the *Regiam maiestatem*. In this way, the history of the *Leges* schedule, particularly when viewed alongside that of earlier examples of the genre, provides a useful case study that illustrates evolving notions of what it meant to "know" law and to whom that knowledge rightly belongs.

2 Costing an arm and a leg

To understand the idiosyncrasies of the *Leges* schedule, it is necessary to consider personal injury schedules as a genre—both their history and their generic features. Fifteen such texts survive from the period between the sixth and ninth centuries. These include the schedules found in the laws of the Visigoths (*ca.* 480 and 654), the Burgundians (*ca.* 500), the Salian Franks (*ca.* 500),

9 On the *Leges*' place in the *Regiam*, see MacQueen, *Common Law*, 85; Taylor, *Laws*, 245–251.

10 On Advocates 25.5.6, see Taylor, *Laws*, 117–130 and the manuscript descriptions at https://manuscripts.nls.uk/repositories/2/resources/15606 and https://cotr.ac.uk/guidelines/model-dynamic-regiam/description-manuscripts/.

Anglo-Saxon Kent (*ca.* 610), the Alamannian Franks (*ca.* 620 and 730), the Ripuarian Franks (*ca.* 630), the Lombards (643), the Bavarians (*ca.* 745), the Frisians (*ca.* 785), the Thuringians (*ca.* 802–3), the Saxons (803), the Chamavan Franks (*ca.* 813), and Anglo-Saxon Wessex (*ca.* 890).[11] In addition, injury schedules are found in the early laws of Sweden, Norway, Iceland, and Denmark, which, though not written down until *ca.* 1200–1300, may contain passages first developed as early as the eighth century. Although the influence of the *Corpus iuris civilis* or the *Codex Theodosianus* can often be found in the law codes containing the injury schedules, the schedules themselves exhibit few signs of Roman influence.[12] It has been argued—particularly by legal historians of the nineteenth and early twentieth centuries—that the schedules' non-Roman character indicates that they are little more than vestigial remainders of a pre-textual pan-Germanic legal culture, but this is inaccurate.[13] Rather, they originate, evolve, and change in response to conquest, cultural interaction, the needs of the juridical community, and other external pressures. Thus, the injury schedule occurring in the laws of the Ripuarian Franks reflects the influence of both Salic and Burgundian law; the Bavarian injury schedule echoes the Lombard *Edictus Rothari*; the schedule in the laws of the Chamavan Franks is derived from that of the Ripuarians; and Alfred's West Saxon injury schedule was influenced by Frisian law and the Kentish laws of Æthelberht. In the case of the Ripuarian Franks and Alamannian Franks, the use of injury schedules likely derives, not from some native practice, but from the influence of Salic law when these communities were conquered by the Merovingians. Something similar may be the case in Kent which, though not conquered by the Merovingians, had a Merovingian queen.[14] These patterns of influence, revision, and intertextual connection suggest that the injury schedules were understood as living law to be imposed, altered, expanded or shortened, depending on need or circumstance.

Insofar as the early medieval injury schedules were living texts, they provide both insight into the priorities of the legal system that produced them and a valuable set of comparanda for our Scottish example. The first point to be made is that, despite their differences, the early Germanic injury schedules were secular in nature. Although the advent of written law frequently coincided with the arrival of Christian missionaries and many of the law-codes in which injury schedules are found include special provisions for the Church, no reference to canon law occurs in the schedules themselves. Second, the organization of

11 See Thomas Faulkner, *Law and Authority in the Early Middle Ages: The Frankish leges in the Carolingian World* (Cambridge: Cambridge University Press, 2016); Oliver, *The Body Legal in Barbarian Law*, 14–17.

12 Oliver, *The Body Legal in Barbarian Law*, 13.

13 See, for instance, Sir Frederick Pollock and Frederic William Maitland, *The History of English Law Before the Time of Edward I*, 2nd ed., 2 vols. (Cambridge: Cambridge University Press, 1911), 42–43.

14 This summary is based on Oliver, *The Body Legal in Barbarian Law*, 17 and 235–236.

injury schedules is typically top down, starting with the head and ending with the feet.[15] This organization is not necessarily followed in the same way in each instance, but the broader point stands, namely, that the injury schedules show evidence of self-conscious construction and that the model for this construction is the body itself. This might seem an obvious point, but the wide range of legal priorities informing injury schedules opens the possibility of multiple organizational models designed to highlight one or more bodily functions or physical capacities. Third, the injury schedules demonstrate a nuanced understanding of human anatomy. The seventh-century *Lex Alamannorum*, for instance, distinguishes between damage to the eye resulting in loss of the vitrium and damage to the eye in which the vitrium remains.[16] Likewise, the Kentish laws recognize the difference in severity of wounds to the outer and inner tabulum of the skull.[17] Finally, in assessing penalties, the injury schedules prioritize functionality and aesthetics.[18] The *Lex Ripuaria* penalizes the loss of a nose resulting in an inability to hold mucous greater than it does the loss of a nose following which the victim can hold his mucous.[19] The Lombard laws assess a special penalty for the loss of a tooth that "appears in a smile."[20] The laws of the Bavarian Franks require a relatively high degree of compensation for the loss of a little finger, as its loss would make it impossible to properly balance a sword.[21] The little toe is equally important, because its loss makes it impossible to walk without a limp.[22] Of particular importance in all of the Germanic laws was reproductive capacity: the penalty for damaging genitals to such a degree that a man cannot impregnate a woman can be can be as much as that for murder, as it is a "person" who is lost if a man cannot participate in sexual reproduction.[23]

15 Oliver, *The Body Legal in Barbarian Law*, 74. Tom Lambert, "Compensation, Honour and Idealism in the Laws of Æthelberht," in *Wergild, Compensation and Penance*, eds. Lukas Bothe, Stefan Esders, and Han Nijdam, 133–160.

16 *Pactus Alamannorum, fragmentum secundum* §1, ed. in Johann Merkel, *Leges Alamannorum*, in *Monumenta Germaniae Historica: Legum* (Hannover: Hahn, 1898), 34.

17 *Æthelberht* 36–37, ed. in Felix Liebermann, *Die Gesetze der Angelsachsen*, 3 vols. (Halle: Max Niemeyer, 1903–1916), I.1–8, at 5. On this clause, see Lisi Oliver, "Æthelberht's and Alfred's Two Skulls," *The Heroic Age* no. 14 (2010).

18 Oliver, *The Body Legal in Barbarian Law*, 240.

19 *Lex Ripuaria* 5.2, eds. in Franz Beyerle and Rudolf Buchner, *Lex Ribuaria*, vol. 3.2, *Monumenta Germaniae Historica: Leges nationum* (Hannover: Hahn 1964), 74.

20 *qui in risu apparit. Edictum Rothari* 51, ed. in Friedrich Bluhme, *Edictum Rothari*, in *Leges Langobardorum*, *Monumenta Germaniae Historica: Legum* (Hannover: Hahn, 1868), 1–225, at 21.

21 *Leges Baiuwariorum* IV.11 ed. in Johann Merkel, *Leges Baiuwariorum*, in *Monumenta Germaniae Historica: Legum* (Hannover: Hahn, 1898), 183–496, at 291.

22 *Leges Baiuwariorum* IV.22 ed. in Merkel, *Leges Baiuwariorum*, 293. See also Wormald, "*Lex Scripta* and *Verbum Regis*," 114–115 and 36.

23 Oliver, *The Body Legal in Barbarian Law*, 128–129.

Bearing these features in mind, it is notable that no evidence survives of an injury schedule actually being used to settle a dispute.[24] This should not be surprising. Although early medieval disputation records are certainly not short of instances of grievous bodily harm, as I and others have argued elsewhere, the image of centralized legal administration found in these texts was more aspirational than actual.[25] Without the bureaucratic structures and enforcement capabilities of a modern nation-state, regional customs, local norms, and communal priorities all played a far greater role in the resolution of disputes than did the seemingly arbitrary pronouncements of a distant monarch. In this sense, they have been described as ideological, but it may be just as accurate to think of them as epistemological. That is, they establish a legislative structure that not only asserts the king's prerogative as the *source* of legal authority but also monopolizes legal knowledge such that diverging perspectives can be dismissed as irrelevant at best and at worst, treasonous.

Understanding the injury schedules in this way helps clarify their relationship to the concept of wergild[26]: unlike wergild, the injury tariffs are not differentiated by class. A wound to the eye of an aristocrat appears to be worth the same as a wound to the eye of a peasant. This apparent equity has led scholars to suggest that the compensation payments in such schedules are meant to be understood as ratios rather than absolutes.[27] That is, a specified penalty of, for example, 10 shillings, should be treated as a percentage of a standardized wergild, to be adjusted up or down as the situation requires. Since 10 shillings is 10% of a model wergild of 100 shillings, then an aristocrat with a wergild of 200 shillings would be owed 20 shillings, and a peasant with a wergild of 50 shillings would receive only 5 shillings in compensation. If this was indeed the case, then it means that the assessed compensation for a body part was not set according to an objective standard; rather, it reflected the king's determination of the relative value of an individual in society.

24 Harald Siems, "Observations Concerning the 'Wergild System': Explanatory Approaches, Effectiveness and Structural Deficits," in *Wergild, Compensation and Penance*, eds. Lukas Bothe, Stefan Esders, and Han Nijdam, 38–64, at 53; Taylor, *Shape of the State*, 151–152.

25 Tom Lambert, *Law and Order in Anglo-Saxon England* (Oxford: Oxford University Press, 2017), 1–26; Andrew Rabin, "Capital Punishment and the Anglo-Saxon Judicial Apparatus: A Maximum View?," in *Capital and Corporal Punishment in Anglo-Saxon England*, eds. Jay Paul Gates and Nicole Marafioti (Woodbridge: The Boydell Press, 2014), 181–200; Paul R. Hyams, "Feud and the State in Late Anglo-Saxon England," *Journal of British Studies* 40 (2001): 1–43. On this point, see also the chapter by Culbertson in this volume.

26 Lit. "man-price," wergild was the amount of compensation owed to a person or their family as recompense for an injury. The amount of one's wergild depended on factors such as social class, gender, and ethnicity.

27 Siems, "Observations," 54. Lisi Oliver, "*Wergild*, *Mund*, and *Manbot* in Early Anglo-Saxon Law," in *Wergild, Compensation and Penance*, eds. Lukas Bothe, Stefan Esders, and Han Nijdam, 113–133, at 121–122; Han Nijdam, "Wergild and Honour: Using the Case of Frisia to Build a Model," in *Wergild, Compensation and Penance*, eds. Lukas Bothe, Stefan Esders, and Han Nijdam, 161–182, at 168.

3 "*L'usage de Scot' et de Bret*'"

Possibly compiled as early as *ca.* 1100, the *Leges inter Brettos et Scottos* is among the earliest surviving Scottish legal tracts, yet its transmission history is perhaps the most complex. The text survives in two recensions: the first (and likely earliest) survives in the late thirteenth-century manuscript Edinburgh, National Records of Scotland, PA5/1, in which—translated into French—it forms the final chapter of the *Leges Scocie*.[28] This iteration of the text lacks the injury schedule. The second recension occurs as part of the early fourteenth-century compilation *Regiam maiestatem*, which grew in length as more material came to be grafted on to the *Regiam* in subsequent iterations.[29] This recension includes the earliest manuscript of the *Leges* to contain the injury schedule: Edinburgh, National Library of Scotland, Advocates 25.5.6, compiled by the scribe James Monynet in 1488, possibly at the behest of a Royal assize court. It is this version that is discussed in detail in the following. Although Advocates 25.5.6 provides the first instance of the injury schedule occurring as part of the *Leges*, versions of the schedule itself, separated from the *Leges*, survive in several earlier legal tracts, including the *Statuta Gilde* (*ca.* 1249), the fourteenth-century *Liber de iudicibus*, the *Assise Regis Dauid* (1318–9), the compilation *Omne Gaderum* (1425), and later fifteenth-century versions of the *Leges Burgorum*.[30] Two conclusions may be drawn from this: first, the *Leges* itself, though of an early date, largely survived as a component of later legal compilations, with its shape and content determined by the interests of the compilers; second, the injury schedule had a long independent life before finally being added to the *Leges*. Consequently, not only the version of the *Leges* preserved in Advocates 25.5.6 but also its injury schedule are the result of a lengthy process of revision and adaptation. As a result, by the time that it came to be attached to the *Leges*, the schedule may have been obsolete as a mode of dispute resolution, but its evolution reflects more than just the typical vagaries of manuscript transmission; it also reveals changing notions of legal expertise and juridical authority.

Evidence of these changes can be found in the significant variations between the texts' various witnesses. As Alice Taylor has shown, neither the *Leges* nor the injury schedule had ever been stable, unified texts with consistent content.[31] The chapters of the *Leges* survive not only in multiple versions but also in various configurations and as components of different texts, including not just the *Leges Scocie* and the *Regiam maiestatem* but other early Scottish legal

28 Taylor, *Laws*, 250–251; Richard Oram, *Domination and Lordship: Scotland, 1070–1230*, The New Edinburgh History of Scotland (Edinburgh: Edinburgh University Press, 2011), 221. MacQueen, *Common Law*, 85.

29 Taylor, *Laws*, 260, 428–431; Taylor, *Shape of the State*, 123–126; MacQueen, *Common Law*, 85.

30 Taylor, *Laws*, 251.

31 Taylor, *Laws*, 252–253.

tracts as well. From this, she deduces that the components of the *Leges* and schedule are only selections from larger collections of chapters available for use by the manuscripts' compilers and readers.[32] Given the range of material included in just those witnesses that survive witnesses, it well may be the case that a distinct text with the title *Leges inter Brettos et Scottos* never existed at all but was instead the result of scribes assembling otherwise semi-independent *capitula* into portable compilations.[33] Indeed, the title itself appears nowhere in the text's many manuscripts but instead occurs in a 1305 decree by Edward I that "it is decreed that the custom of the Scots and the British (*l'usage de Scot' et de Bret'*) is henceforth banned, so that it cannot be applied."[34] The text comes to be unified only at the moment when it is declared obsolete. Edward's language is telling, however: consolidating the disparate chapters into what he calls *l'usage de Scot' et de Bret'* stabilizes the text's contents in a way that makes it easier for them to be summarily dismissed. This marks a significant departure from the chapters' probable origin: the disparate nature of the *Leges* chapters and the appearance of various excerpts in such texts as the *Leges Scocie* and the *Liber de iudicibus* suggests that they may have originated as reference handbooks of varying content, whose organization reflected the individual needs of the itinerant or regional judges responsible for their compilation.[35] That is, they represent the knowledge that any given judge felt was necessary in order to claim the authority that accompanies legal expertise. Their diversity points to the essentially decentralized nature of early Scottish judicial practice.[36] Unifying the chapters under a single rubric enabled Edward to assert his own centralizing authority over their contents. The unification (and subsequent dismissal) of the *Leges* chapters thus reflected Edward's ongoing attempts to solidify his control over Scotland.[37] Yet by the time that the *Leges* and schedule came to be transcribed in Advocates 25.5.6 in 1488, they had ceased to be law and had become instead simply records of past practice. Instead, the

32 Taylor, *Laws*, 258–259.

33 Taylor, *Laws*, 247–249; Simpson and Wilson, *Scottish Legal History*, 10–11; Simpson and Wilson also note that judges were frequently accused of ignorance of the law, making handbooks of this sort highly desirable. See Simpson and Wilson, *Scottish Legal History*, 103.

34 *Ordiné est que l'usage de Scot' et de Bret' desorendroit soit defendu, si que mes ne soit usez. A decree issued by the king for the pacification of Scotland* [*Ordinacio facta per dominum regem super stabilitate terre Scocie*] in E. L. G. Stones, *Anglo-Scottish Relations, 1174–1328: Some Selected Documents*, Oxford Medieval Texts (Oxford: The Clarendon Press, 1965), 240–259, at 51. See also Alice Taylor, "What Does *Regiam Maiestatem* Actually Say (and What Does It Mean)?," in *Common Law, Civil Law, and Colonial Law*, ed. William Eaves et al. (Cambridge: Cambridge University Press, 2021), 47–85, at 55n. 30; Taylor, *Laws*, 245–246.

35 Simpson and Wilson, *Scottish Legal History*, 10–11; Taylor, *Laws*, 251, 258; MacQueen, *Common Law*, 82–84.

36 Taylor, *Shape of the State*, 152; Simpson and Wilson, *Scottish Legal History*, 19, 111–112; MacQueen, *Common Law*, 75–82.

37 Taylor, "What Does Regiam Maiestatem Actually Say?," 55, 75; Taylor, *Shape of the State*, 135–136, 173.

compilation of the manuscript at the order of a royal assize called by James III therefore represented an assertion of *Scottish* royal control over Scotland's legal past. Implicitly, the king's authority as a maker of laws rested in part in his knowledge of and control over the legal history of his kingdom. In short, the *Leges* and schedule appear to have served as necessary sources of expertise, not just for the purpose of judicial practice but also for the colonizing agenda of an English king and the reclamation of royal legal authority by a Scottish one.

This tangled history of reception, use, and appropriation helps explain the eclectic nature of the Advocates 25.5.6 injury schedule. The schedule opens with a reference to Biblical *Lex talionis*, particularly as found in *Exodus* 21: 23–5. Recalling *Exodus*, the text reads, "according to divine law, a head for a head, a hand for a hand, eyes for an eye."[38] This is followed by the specification that "according to human law, for a man's life, 180 cows."[39] It then continues in a both general and haphazard manner:

> [3] For a foot 1 mark, the same for a hand. [4] For an eye, half a mark; the same for an ear. [5] For a tooth, 12 *denarii*. [6] 12 *denarii* also for each thumbs-length[40] of a wound. [7] 12 *denarii* also for each thumbs-length of width of a wound. [8] For a blow below the ear, 16 *denarii*. [9] For a blow with a staff, 8 *denarii*, and if he was knocked over by the blow, 16 *denarii*. [10] For a wound to the face, he shall give a gold image. [11] And [according to] human law, for broken bones, 2 ores. [12] *Item*, if someone is wounded under his garment, 12 *denarii*. [13] Moreover, if he has sleeves, 15 *denarii*. [14] For any visible wound, except on the face, 15 *denarii*. [15] *Item*, for a man's life, 12 marks; 5 shillings above the neck, and 40 *denarii* below the neck. [16] For a blow with a foot, 40 *denarii*. [17] For the shedding of blood, 25 shillings or, across the sea, 6 cows.[41]

Although the text contains resemblances to more traditional injury schedules found in early medieval Germanic legislation—particularly in the distinction between visible and invisible wounds, the emphasis on aesthetics, the

38 [§1] *Per legem diuinam caput pro capite manus pro manu oculos pro oculo.* I have added the clause numbers for ease of reference, though they do not appear in either the manuscript or Taylor's edition.

39 [§2] *Per legum humanam pro uita hominis ix*^{xx} *uacce.*

40 This is also one inch.

41 [3] *Pro pede unam arca; pro manu tantum.* [4] *Pro oculo dimidia marca; pro aure tantum.* [5] *Pro dente xii.d.* [6] *Pro quolibet policce longitudinis plage xii d.* [7] *Pro quolibet policce latitudines plage xii d.* [8] *Pro ictu sub aure xvi d.* [9] *Pro ictu cum baculo viii d. et si cecideret cum ictu illo xvi d.* [10] *Pro wlnere in facie dabi ymagenem auri.* [11] *Et lex humana pro fracura ossium ii oras.* [12] *Item si sub tegimento wlneratus fuerit quis xii d.* [13] *Si autem habeat manicam xv d.* [14] *Pro qualibet uisibili plaga excepta facie xv d.* [15] *Item pro uita hominis xii marce supra anelitum v.s. sub anelitu xld.* [16] *Pro ictu cum pede xl d.* [17] *Pro extracione sanguinis xxv.s. ultra mare vi uacce.* See also appendix.

equivalence of hands and feet, and the privileging of use—these parallels do not imply that the *Leges* schedule served a similarly practical function. Indeed, from a legal perspective, the *Leges* schedule is virtually useless. First, the penalties assessed for different sorts of injuries are too vague to be enforceable: the identical fine for a hand and a foot, for instance, or an eye and an ear reflect typical anatomical associations, but they fail to specify the context, intention, or severity of the wound. Other clauses seem almost arbitrary, such as the specification of penalties for a blow with a staff or stick but not with other types of weapons. It is unusual to find penalties assessed in different currencies: livestock, specie in the form of marks-shillings-*denarii*, and the "golden image" [*ymagenem aurum*], a particular form of gold coinage not used in the British Isles before the early fourteenth century. Finally, several of the clauses simply make little sense, such as those assigning different degrees of compensation for the taking of an individual's life, assessing a special penalty if the victim is wearing sleeves, or using the mysterious phrase "over the sea, six cows" [*ultra mari vi uacce*]. With such vagaries, it is difficult to see how these tariffs could have been much assistance in the settlement of legal disputes or personal injury claims.

Significantly, the features that contribute to the text's impracticality shed light on the text's reception history. It is impossible to reconstruct the original form of the *Leges* schedule, though earlier versions do provide some hints. The earliest clauses are likely those shared both with other versions of the text and with the Germanic schedules of the early Middle Ages, namely, the stipulations concerning the loss of feet and teeth, damage to sensory organs, wounds under an inch, wounds to the face, broken bones, and wounds under the clothes (§§ 3, 4, 5, 8, 11, and 12). Although these clauses calculate compensation payments in traditional currency—marks, ores, shillings, and pennies (*denarii*)—§10 is notable for its mention of a "gold image" as the penalty for wounds to the face. "Gold image" coinage (gold coins featuring the ruler's face) was introduced into Scotland by Robert III sometime between 1390 and 1400, indicating a late intervention, possibly intended to align the wounded face with the face on the coin.[42] This intervention is surprising given that the *Leges* had lost their legal status in 1305, indicating that a scribe still saw the text as worthy of intervention more than eighty-five years after it had been declared obsolete. Clauses in §9 (concerning a blow with a staff) and §17 (concerning bloodshed) may have been added as late as the mid-thirteenth century, as their wording closely resembles that of c. ix of the *Statuta gilde* (post-1249), though in the latter case, the penalty is left up to the guild alderman.[43] Alternatively, given the frequency with which wounds caused by rods, sticks, or staffs are penalized in the Germanic schedules, it may be that the

42 Philip Grierson, *Coins of Medieval Europe* (London: Seaby, 1991), 157–158.

43 *Statuta gilde* cap. ix, ed. in Cosmo Innes, *Ancient Laws and Customs of the Burghs of Scotland: A. D. 1124–1424* (Edinburgh: John Greig and Son, 1868), 64–88, at 68.

Statuta gilde was instead borrowing from the *Leges* schedule. In either case, however, the similarities of wording suggest some degree of crossover between the two texts. The penalty of two ores for the breaking of a bone appears to have been somewhat controversial, as the version of the schedule in the fourteenth-century *Liber de iudicibus* raises the penalty to five ores (possibly because two ores was considered too low), and the *Omne gaderum* of 1425 somewhat indecisively states that the penalty is "five ores but other books say two ores" (*quinque oras alii libri dicunt duas oras*), a phrase also found in the later *Leges Burgorum*.[44] The *Omne gaderum* also includes stipulations specifying that certain penalties are drawn from *lex humana*, perhaps indicating that the opening Biblical reference and implied distinction between earthly and spiritual law were among the latest additions to the text.[45] Unfortunately, such indications of scribal intervention are not substantial enough to enable us to set forth in detail the degrees by which the *Leges* schedule developed into the form transcribed in Advocates 25.5.6 in 1488. Nonetheless, they do testify to a history of readership and revision that continued uninterrupted despite the text's 1305 demotion. Accordingly, the value of the text for its preservers seems to lie somewhere other than in its potential application.

Yet if the injury schedule fails as applied law, it still sheds light on the expectations and norms that shaped early Scottish legal practice. These expectations and norms are not merely echoed in the text; rather, the text itself plays an active role in establishing and reinforcing them. This normative function underlies the text's unusual opening clauses: "[1] According to divine law, a head for a head, a hand for a hand, eyes for an eye. [2] According to human law, for a man's life, 180 cows."[46] The allusion to *Exodus*' *lex talionis* in §1 is the only Biblical reference to occur in either the *LBS* or its related text, the *Leges Scocie*. The valuation of a person's life at 180 cows, however, is a commonly found component of early Scottish legal texts. In the *Leges Scocie*, a murder committed under the king's peace is to be compensated with the value of 180 cows, a penalty also found in the *Capitula* of King David for murder committed in the king's hall.[47] Likewise, in the *Statuta regis Alexandri*, the penalty for failure in a trial by combat is 180 cows.[48] In effect, the distinction in §1 and §2 between divine and human law serves as the schedule's framing device, but it is deemed unnecessary in its predecessors or elsewhere in the *LBS*. Here, however, pairing human law—and especially *Scottish* human law—with divine law invests *lex humana* with a heightened degree of authority as the worldly counterpart to *lex divina*. As such, its assessments assume

44 Taylor, *Laws*, 252 and n.

45 Athol L. Murray, "The Town Clerk of Perth's *Liber Omne Gaderum*, 1425," *Scottish Archives: The Journal of the Scottish Records Association* 5 (1999): 63–66, at 63.

46 [1] *Per legem diuinam caput pro capite manus pro manu oculos [sic] pro oculo.* [2] *Per legem humanam pro uita hominis ix*^{xx} *uacce.*

47 *Leges Scocie* 21§2, in Taylor, *Laws*, 407–26 at 423; and *Capitula assisarum et statutorum domini Dauid* §31, in Taylor, *Laws*, 483–546, at 519.

48 *Statuta regis Alexandri* §11, in Taylor, *Laws*, 571–624 at 519. See also Taylor, *Shape of the State*, 146.

a divine *imprimatur* and normative force that supersedes the appearance of arbitrariness or caprice. One might be forgiven for observing that the need to establish the text's authority in this fashion suggests a degree of defensiveness and a fear that the text might not be as authoritative as its compositor might hope, but this in itself is revealing. The injury schedule is a foreign genre with few precursors in either Roman law or earlier Scottish legal texts. The insertion of divine authority provides a normative standard that compensates for the absence of legal precedent.

Equally telling are the injury clauses themselves. Especially unusual in these clauses is the limited criteria to determine the severity of injuries, a degree of specificity particularly characteristic of the *Leges* schedule's earlier Germanic analogues. In part, the relative lack of such criteria limits the usefulness of the *Leges* in resolving injury-based disputes as it is difficult to assess whether the decreed compensation accurately reflects the harm caused by the wound. However, the absence of criteria may indicate that the clauses initially had been drafted to function cumulatively rather than individually so that a blow by a weapon (§9) that broke the skin (§6) but only under the clothes (§12) could result in a total compensation of thirty-two *denarii*. When understood this way, the clauses provide their own criteria, but—unlike the objective standards of earlier injury schedules—the questions of which clauses to apply and how to apply them leave judges considerable leeway in assessing an injury and using such an assessment to negotiate a settlement. Yet insofar as the *Leges* by this time had lost any force as law, it is unlikely that readers of the text were seeking guidance for the adjudication of real disputes. Even so, the reduction of each injury to its barest form still encodes within the text the relative seriousness of different forms of bodily injury. Thus, injuries caused by weapons (§9) demand lower compensation than those caused by the body of the attacker (§16), a distinction that suggests that the text was more concerned with the severity of violence than the severity of the injury. Similarly, the 180-cow penalty for taking a person's life (§2) is identical to that listed elsewhere in the *Leges* for violating the king's peace. A similar justification may underlie the different penalties for wounds breaking the skin (§6) and bloodshed more generally (§17), that is, the nature of the injury is of less importance than the violence that caused it. Accordingly, the *Leges* schedule appears to reflect concerns about the act of initiating violence rather than the consequences of such violence for the individual victim. If Advocates 25.5.6 had been compiled as part of a fifteenth-century initiative to centralize Scottish law, then a focus on society rather than the individual would be very much in keeping with such an effort. That the *Leges* schedule had been understood in this way is suggested by its place in the text itself. Excluding the injury schedule, the body of the *Leges* consists of lists of *cro*—that is, wergild—and *kelchin*, that is, class-based (rather than injury-based) compensation for insults or injury.[49] The injury schedule

49 *Leges* caps. 187 and 190 in Taylor, *Laws*, 432–435, 437–439. See also Taylor, *Shape of the State*, 148–150; Alasdair Ross, *The Kings of Alba, c. 1000-c. 1130* (Edinburgh: John Donald, 2011), 53–54.

thus functions in much the same way as it did in its early medieval predecessors: as an extension of the reach of a centralized legal authority to encompass the body as a means of monopolizing legal knowledge and its exercise.

It remains to be asked whether the idiosyncrasies in the *Leges* schedule can provide any clues to the schedule's origin and primary influences. Despite Scotland's close relationship with Scandinavia during the early Middle Ages, the injury schedule offers little indication of Scandinavian influence, though perhaps this should not be surprising. Scandinavian schedules tend to assign penalties in the form of percentages of the victim's wergild rather than specified monetary amounts. Moreover, even the Scandinavian texts that include injury schedules focus more on courtroom procedures and the means of adjudication than on the simple assignment of penalties.[50] A closer connection can be found between the *Leges* schedule and those of Wessex and Kent. Particularly relevant are the clauses that distinguish between wounds that can be concealed by clothing and those that cannot and the clauses that assesses the severity of a wound by length. All injury schedules penalize wounds that cannot be hidden more harshly than those that can, but the laws of Æthelberht of Kent and Alfred of Wessex are the only ones to explicitly cite clothing as a criterion to determine visibility.[51] Æthelberht's and Alfred's laws are also the only injury schedules to assess the severity of a wound by its length and to measure this length in inches (or its equivalent, "thumbs").[52] Moreover, later iterations of the puzzling clause in the *Leges* that assesses a specific fine "if the victim has sleeves" instead penalize wounds "below the sleeve" (i.e., the wrist), a phrase found elsewhere only in *Alfred*, suggesting that the wording of the earlier clause is a scribal error.[53] The fact that these two clauses appear only in pre-Conquest English law suggests that the *LBS* injury schedule is based on an insular source. This is not to say that the source necessarily was the laws of either Æthelberht or Alfred—the surviving record is spotty enough to make it difficult to determine how many legal issuances have been lost, though this list almost certainly includes the laws of the Northumbrian kings, the laws of Mercia, and possibly the laws issued by Eorcenberht of Kent[54]—but it suggests that the source was likely English in origin. A number of scholars have

50 See, for instance, *Erik's Law of Zealand* 33–39, eds. Ditlev Tamm and Helen Vogt, *The Danish Medieval Laws*, Routledge Medieval Translations (London: Routledge, 2016), 156–232, at 176–178.

51 *Æthelberht* 60, ed. in Liebermann, *Gesetze*, I.3–8, at 7. and *Alfred* 66.1, ed. in Liebermann, *Gesetze*, I.16–88, at 84.

52 *Æthelberht* 67.1 and *Alfred* 45–45.1 in Liebermann, *Gesetze*, I.7 and I.78. On the relationship between inch and thumb, see Guus Kroonen, *The Proto-Germanic* n*-Stems: A Study in Diachronic Morphophonology*, Leiden Studies in Indo-European (Amsterdam: Rodopi, 2011), 287–288.

53 *Alfred* 66.1. See the Appendix to this volume.

54 See Liebermann, *Gesetze*, I.9 and III.17; Patrick Wormald, "In Search of King Offa's 'Law-Code'," in *Legal Culture in the Early Medieval West: Law as Text, Image and Experience* (London: The Hambledon Press, 1999), 201–224.

noted the likelihood that the author of the *Leges* was familiar with pre-Conquest law, so its use here would hardly be out of character.[55] Though there is much to suggest that the *LBS* injury schedule was composed all or in part well after 1066, the use of early English legal texts appears to have provided both authoritative precedent and a history of use.

Although the idiosyncrasies in the schedule shed light on its history and purpose, the reason for their presence in the first place remains a mystery. That is, given the freedom with which previous scribes edited or revised the schedule over the previous three centuries, it is unclear why the manuscript's scribe chose not to regularize the text and smooth over any inconsistencies. We can only speculate, but part of the reason may lie in the inherent conservatism of legal composition. The authority of precedent—even if, as in this case, the precedent has ceased to be relevant—may have made the scribe reluctant to revise the text to such an extent. Equally, the manuscript's purpose as a compilation of historical documents may also have affected the scribe's decision. Insofar as the text was not being transcribed for use in legal dispute resolution, revision may have seemed unnecessary. Yet what seems clear is that for the scribe and his readers, the authority of the injury schedule as law—however obsolete—lay in its structure as much as, if not more so, its content. That is, the schedule needed to *look* like law, whether its clauses were truly functional or not. The scribe preserves the form of a Germanic injury schedule but neglects the consistency and specificity that gave such texts at least the potential for use as applied law. If the text's form preserves its previous function as enforceable law, then its peculiarities provide both proof of and justification for its obsolescence. In short, the schedule may not have been regularized simply because its contemporary readers did not need or expect it to be so.

Evidence for this suggestion may lie in the fact that the schedule was eventually regularized once a more "authoritative" version came to be required. The *editio princeps* of the *Regiam maiestatem* was published by Sir John Skene in 1609 with funds provided by the Parliament of Scotland.[56] With the

55 Taylor, "What Does Regiam Maiestatem Actually Say?," 50–51; Taylor, *Shape of the State*, 126; Patrick Wormald, "Anglo-Saxon Law and Scots Law," *The Scottish Historical Review* 88 no. 2 (2009): 192–206; Jenny Wormald, "Bloodfeud, Kindred and Government in Early Modern Scotland," *Past & Present* 87 (1980): 63–64.

56 Sir John Skene, *Regiam Majestatem. The Auld Laues and Constitutions of Scotland, Faithfully Collected Furth of the Register, and Other Auld Authentic Books* (Edinburgh: Thomas Finlayson, 1609). On this edition, see Taylor, "What Does Regiam Maiestatem Actually Say?," 47–85, at 47–49. Skene's text was later reused in the Stair Society edition by Lord Thomas Cooper: Thomas Mackay Cooper, *Regiam Majestatem and Quoniam Attachiamenta*, Stair Society (Edinburgh: J. Skinner and Co., 1947). On the *Regiam maiestatem*, see John Reuben Davies and Alice Taylor, *Regiam Maiestatem: The Earliest Known Version* (Edinburgh: The Stair Society, 2022), 1–168; Taylor, "What Does Regiam Maiestatem Actually Say?," 47–85; Hector L. MacQueen, "*Regiam Majestatem*, Scots Law, and National Identity," *The Scottish Historical Review* 74 no. 197 (1995): 1–25; MacQueen, *Common Law*, 5, 89–98; Cooper, *Regiam Majestatem*, 1–54.

destruction of so many early legal documents by the English King Edward I and the dissolution of monastic *scriptoria* during the Reformation of the previous century, it was decided that an official ("record") edition of medieval law was required, not merely as historical documentation, but as evidence for the continuity of Scottish institutions and national identity.[57] Tasked with publishing such an edition, Skene began compiling his text with an eye towards modern political value as much as historical accuracy. The result was an edition that, though unreliable by scholarly standards, nonetheless satisfactorily fulfilled the parliament's nationalist agenda.[58] In order to produce a document that would provide precedent for contemporary Scottish law and illustrate the authority and sophistication of its origins, Skene introduced revisions into his texts to ensure that they conformed to the desired historical narrative. Perhaps not surprisingly, Skene's interventions are especially visible in the *Leges* injury schedule. To begin with, Skene erases the schedule's first clause with its Biblical allusion to the *lex talionis*, a concept viewed as both primitive and contrary to the Reformation's Calvinist theology.[59] In addition, ambiguous clauses, such as the increased penalty for harming those who wear sleeves, have been clarified. The clause now refers to wounds *before* the sleeve—that is, to the wrist.[60] Likewise, the mysterious clause, "for bloodshed 25 shillings, or over the sea 6 cows" has been revised so that it now differentiates between shedding blood on the south side of the Firth of Forth and shedding blood on the north side, thus drawing a comprehensible distinction between the economies and local customs of the Scottish Highlands and Lowlands.[61] Moreover, in a clause added at the end, the reader is instructed to consider context and custom [*usus et consuetudo*] when applying these penalties.[62] Accordingly, the text has now gained the appearance of usability. Though still out of step with contemporary legal practice, the revised *Leges* schedule better approximates early modern legal practice and, in doing so, provides evidence (albeit somewhat manufactured) for the essential modernity of even the oldest Scottish laws. Implicitly, the schedule—along with the *Regiam* itself—remains a repository of legal knowledge but of a different type: it now provides a necessary originary narrative that authorizes both contemporary Scottish law and contemporary Scottish identity.

57 Simpson and Wilson, *Scottish Legal History*, 119–120; Oram, *Domination*, 272; Cooper, *Regiam Majestatem*, 23.
58 Oram, *Domination*, 272.
59 Wormald, "Bloodfeud, Kindred and Government," 93.
60 §10 in *Regiam Maiestatem* cap. 40, in Cooper, *Regiam Majestatem*, 279.
61 §17 in *Regiam Maiestatem* cap. 40, in Cooper, *Regiam Majestatem*, 279. On the regional differences between these two legal cultures, see Simpson and Wilson, *Scottish Legal History*, 10; Wormald, "Bloodfeud, Kindred and Government," 60–61.
62 §18 in *Regiam Maiestatem* cap. 40, in Cooper, *Regiam Majestatem*, 279.

4 Conclusion

The emergence of royal authority in post-Roman Europe was not a steady march towards centralization; rather, it took the form of ongoing disputes over the power to make and enforce law. Within these disputes, debates over legal knowledge—who possessed it and who had the right to instrumentalize it—became a proxy battle for political authority. Yet if the Germanic injury schedules of the early Middle Ages represented a direct assertion of the king's control over the bodies of his subjects, then the complex history of the *Leges* schedule illustrates the ways in which such texts could be adapted, usurped, dismissed, and reclaimed in service to a wide variety of legal uses and political ideologies. Initially composed for use by regional *iudices*, the schedule came to be appropriated by the English as part of the repression of Scottish law, recuperated as part of a reassertion of Scottish royal autonomy, and finally preserved as a symbol of Scottish national identity. Though it lost its status as law in 1305, the schedule remained a repository of legal knowledge and by extension, an emblem of legal authority. Indeed, as both the Germanic and *Leges* schedules illustrate, even despite radical changes in historical and cultural circumstances, it nonetheless remained true that control of the kingdom ultimately belonged to those controlling knowledge of its laws.

References

Beyerle, Franz and Rudolf Buchner. *Lex Ribuaria. Monumenta Germaniae Historica: Leges Nationum*, vol. 3.2. Hannover: Hahn, 1964.

Black, Robert. "A Historical Survey of Delictual Liability in Scotland for Personal Injuries and Death." *The Comparative and International Law Journal of Southern Africa* 8, no. 1 (1975): 46–70.

Bluhme, Friedrich. "Edictum Rothari." In *Leges Langobardorum. Monumenta Germaniae Historica: Legum*, 1–225. Hannover: Hahn, 1868.

Bothe, Lukas, Stefan Esders, and Han Nijdam (eds.). *Wergild, Compensation and Penance: The Monetary Logic of Early Medieval Dispute Resolution*. Leiden: Brill, 2021.

Clanchy, M. T. *From Memory to Written Record, England 1066–1307*, 3rd ed. Cambridge: Blackwell, 2013.

Cooper, Thomas Mackay. *Regiam Majestatem and Quoniam Attachiamenta*. Stair Society. Edinburgh: J. Skinner and Co., 1947.

Davies, John Reuben and Alice Taylor. *Regiam Maiestatem: The Earliest Known Version*. Edinburgh: The Stair Society, 2022.

Faulkner, Thomas. *Law and Authority in the Early Middle Ages: The Frankish Leges in the Carolingian World*. Cambridge: Cambridge University Press, 2016.

Foot, Sarah. "Reading Anglo-Saxon Charters: Memory, Record, or Story?" In *Narrative and History in the Early Medieval West*, edited by Elizabeth M. Tyler and Ross Balzaretti, 39–67. Turnhout: Brepols, 2006.

Grierson, Philip. *Coins of Medieval Europe*. London: Seaby, 1991.

Hyams, Paul R. "Feud and the State in Late Anglo-Saxon England." *Journal of British Studies* 40 (2001): 1–43.

Innes, Cosmo. *Ancient Laws and Customs of the Burghs of Scotland: A. D. 1124–1424*. Edinburgh: John Greig and Son, 1868.

Jurasinski, Stefan and Lisi Oliver. *The Laws of Alfred: The Domboc and the Making of Anglo-Saxon Law*. Cambridge: Cambridge University Press, 2021.

Lambert, Tom. *Law and Order in Anglo-Saxon England*. Oxford: Oxford University Press, 2017.
Lambert, Tom. "Compensation, Honour and Idealism in the Laws of Æthelberht." In *Wergild, Compensation and Penance: The Monetary Logic of Early Medieval Dispute Resolution*, edited by Lukas Bothe, Stefan Esders, and Han Nijdam, 133–160. Leiden: Brill, 2021.
Liebermann, Felix. *Die Gesetze Der Angelsachsen*, 3 vols. Halle: Max Niemeyer, 1903–1916.
MacQueen, Hector L. *Common Law and Feudal Society in Medieval Scotland*. Edinburgh: Edinburgh University Press, 1993.
MacQueen, Hector L. "*Regiam Majestatem*, Scots Law, and National Identity." *The Scottish Historical Review* 74, no. 197 (1995): 1–25.
Merkel, Johann. "Leges Alamannorum." In *Monumenta Germaniae Historica: Legum*, 1–182. Hannover: Hahn, 1898.
Merkel, Johann. "Leges Baiuwariorum." In *Monumenta Germaniae Historica: Legum*, 183–496. Hannover: Hahn, 1898.
Miller, William Ian. *Eye for an Eye*. Cambridge: Cambridge University Press, 2006.
Murray, Athol L. "The Town Clerk of Perth's *Liber Omne Gaderum*, 1425." *Scottish Archives: The Journal of the Scottish Records Association* 5 (1999): 63–66.
Neville, Cynthia. *Land, Law, and People in Medieval Scotland*. Edinburgh: Edinburgh University Press, 2010.
Nijdam, Han. "Wergild and Honour: Using the Case of Frisia to Build a Model." In *Wergild, Compensation and Penance: The Monetary Logic of Early Medieval Dispute Resolution*, edited by Lukas Bothe, Stefan Esders, and Han Nijdam, 161–182. Leiden: Brill, 2021.
Oliver, Lisi. "Æthelberht's and Alfred's Two Skulls." *The Heroic Age* no. 14 (2010): n.p.
Oliver, Lisi. *The Body Legal in Barbarian Law*. Toronto Anglo-Saxon Series. Toronto: University of Toronto Press, 2011.
Oliver, Lisi. "*Wergild*, *Mund*, and *Manbot* in Early Anglo-Saxon Law." In *Wergild, Compensation and Penance: The Monetary Logic of Early Medieval Dispute Resolution*, edited by Lukas Bothe, Stefan Esders, and Han Nijdam, 113–133. Leiden: Brill, 2021.
Oram, Richard. *Domination and Lordship: Scotland, 1070–1230*. The New Edinburgh History of Scotland. Edinburgh: Edinburgh University Press, 2011.
Pollock, Sir Frederick and Frederic William Maitland. *The History of English Law before the Time of Edward I*, 2nd ed., 2 vols. Cambridge: Cambridge University Press, 1911.
Pratt, David. *The Political Thought of King Alfred the Great*. Cambridge Studies in Medieval Life and Thought. Cambridge: Cambridge University Press, 2007.
Rabin, Andrew. "Witnessing Kingship: Royal Power and the Legal Subject in the Old English Laws." In *Kingship, Legislation and Power in Anglo-Saxon England*, edited by Gale R. Owen-Crocker and Brian Schneider, 219–236. Woodbridge: Boydell and Brewer, 2013.
Rabin, Andrew. "Capital Punishment and the Anglo-Saxon Judicial Apparatus: A Maximum View?" In *Capital and Corporal Punishment in Anglo-Saxon England*, edited by Jay Paul Gates and Nicole Marafioti, 181–200. Woodbridge: The Boydell Press, 2014.
Rabin, Andrew. *Crime and Punishment in Anglo-Saxon England*. England in the Early Medieval World. Cambridge: Cambridge University Press, 2020.
Rio, Alice. *Legal Practice and the Written Word in the Early Middle Ages*. Cambridge Studies in Medieval Life and Thought. Cambridge: Cambridge University Press, 2009.

Ross, Alasdair. *The Kings of Alba, C. 1000–C. 1130.* Edinburgh: John Donald, 2011.

Siems, Harald. "Observations Concerning the 'Wergild System': Explanatory Approaches, Effectiveness and Structural Deficits." In *Wergild, Compensation and Penance: The Monetary Logic of Early Medieval Dispute Resolution*, edited by Lukas Bothe, Stefan Esders, and Han Nijdam, 38–64. Leiden: Brill, 2021.

Simpson, Andrew R. C. and Adelyn L. M. Wilson. *Scottish Legal History: Volume One, 1000–1707.* Edinburgh: Edinburgh University Press, 2017.

Skene, Sir John. *Regiam Majestatem. The Auld Laues and Constitutions of Scotland, Faithfully Collected Furth of the Register, and Other Auld Authentic Books.* Edinburgh: Thomas Finlayson, 1609.

Stevenson, William Henry. *Asser's Life of King Alfred, Together with the Annals of Saint Neot's Erroneously Ascribed to Asser.* Oxford: Clarendon Press, 1959.

Stones, E. L. G. *Anglo-Scottish Relations, 1174–1328: Some Selected Documents.* Oxford Medieval Texts. Oxford: The Clarendon Press, 1965.

Tamm, Ditlev and Helen Vogt. *The Danish Medieval Laws.* Routledge Medieval Translations. London: Routledge, 2016.

Taylor, Alice. "Lex Scripta and the Problem of Enforcement: Anglo-Saxon, Welsh, and Scottish Law Compared." In *Legalism: Community and Justice*, edited by Fernanda Pirie and Judith Scheele, 47–75. Oxford: Oxford University Press, 2014.

Taylor, Alice. *The Shape of the State in Medieval Scotland.* Oxford: Oxford University Press, 2016.

Taylor, Alice. *The Laws of Medieval Scotland.* Edinburgh: The Stair Societ, 2019.

Taylor, Alice. "What Does *Regiam Maiestatem* Actually Say (and What Does It Mean)?" In *Common Law, Civil Law, and Colonial Law*, edited by William Eaves, John Hudson, Ingrid Ivarsen, and Sarah White, 47–85. Cambridge: Cambridge University Press, 2021.

Tyszka, Przemyslaw. *The Human Body in Barbarian Laws, C. 500–800: Corpus Hominis as Cultural Category.* Frankfurt am Main: Peter Lang GmbH, 2014.

Whitman, James Q. "At the Origins of Law and the State: Monopolization of Violence, Mutilation of Bodies, or Setting of Prices?" *Chicago-Kent Law Review* 71 (1995): 41–84.

Wolfram, Herwig. "Political Theory and Narrative in Charters." *Viator* 26 (1995): 39–51.

Wormald, Jenny. "Bloodfeud, Kindred and Government in Early Modern Scotland." *Past & Present* 87 (1980): 54–97.

Wormald, Patrick. "*Lex Scripta* and *Verbum Regis*: Legislation and Germanic Kingship, from Euric to Cnut." In *Early Medieval Kingship*, edited by P. H. Sawyer and I. N. Wood, 105–138. Leeds: Leeds University Press, 1977.

Wormald, Patrick. "In Search of King Offa's 'Law-Code'." In *Legal Culture in the Early Medieval West: Law as Text, Image and Experience*, 201–224. London: The Hambledon Press, 1999.

Wormald, Patrick. *The Making of English Law: King Alfred to the Twelfth Century.* Malden: Blackwell Publishers, 1999.

Wormald, Patrick. "The *Leges Barbarorum*: Law and Ethnicity in the Post-Roman West." In *Regna and Gentes: The Relationship between Late Antique and Early Medieval Peoples and Kingdoms in the Transformation of the Roman World*, edited by Hans-Werner Goetz, Jörg Jarnut, and Walter Pohl, 21–55. Leiden: Brill, 2003.

Wormald, Patrick. "Anglo-Saxon Law and Scots Law." *The Scottish Historical Review* 88, no. 2 (2009): 192–206.

6 Promises and Perils of Macaulay's Preface to the Indian Penal Code

Elizabeth Lhost

1 Introduction

For a century and a half, the Indian Penal Code (IPC) has remained an influential legal text.[1] It not only is the basis for criminal law in postcolonial India, Pakistan, and Bangladesh today but also continues to provide legal scholars and practitioners with fodder for study, analysis, and discussion.[2] The code's success says a great deal about the ingenuity and intent of its framers, the members of the first Indian Law Commission, led by Thomas Babington Macaulay.[3] Its success also speaks to the enthusiasm with which Indian lawyers, editors, publishers, and princely rulers accepted the code and its principles of uniformity, consistency, and clarity and embraced them for their own purposes. Taking the law commissioner's preface to the original draft code as a point of departure, this essay considers what happens when interest in the code

1 Stanley M. H. Yeo, "Lessons on Provocation from the Indian Penal Code," *The International Comparative Law Quarterly* 41 no. 3 (1992): 615. The code also became (and remains today) the basis for the penal law in Singapore, Sudan, Sri Lanka, Brunei, Nigeria, and the Straits Settlements. Stanley Yeo and Barry Wright, "Revitalising Macaulay's Indian Penal Code," in *Codification, Macaulay and the Indian Penal Code: The Legacies and Modern Challenges of Criminal Law Reform*, eds. Wing-Cheong Chan, Barry Wright, and Stanley Yeo (Farnham: Ashgate Publishing Ltd., 2011), 3–17.

2 See, for example, Renisa Mawani and Iza Hussin, "The Travels of Law: Indian Ocean Itineraries," *Law and History Review* 32 no. 4 (2014): 733–747; Raminder Kaur, "Specters of Macaulay: Blasphemy, the Indian Penal Code, and Pakistan's Postcolonial Predicament," in *Censorship in South Asia: Cultural Regulation from Sedition to Seduction*, ed. William Mazzarella (Bloomington: Indiana University Press, 2009), 175–205; and David Skuy, "Macaulay and the Indian Penal Code of 1862: The myth of the inherent superiority and modernity of the English legal system compared to India's Legal System in the Nineteenth Century," *Modern Asian Studies* 32, no. 3 (1998): 513–557.

3 The code's long-lasting influence has not been entirely positive, however. As Yeo and Wright write, "the IPC has left many unintended problems of interpretation for the courts which have had the unenviable task of finding ways, not always successful, of applying the nineteenth-century attitudes and approaches embodied in the Code to social and moral situations in the twentieth and twenty-first centuries." Their solution is not to dismiss the code but to instead "revitalize" its "original technical attributes." Yeo and Wright, "Revitalising," 3–4.

DOI: 10.4324/9781003534815-7

inspires multiple approaches to the code and when the codifiers' insistence on making the code public leads to multiple publications of the code.

The law commissioners could hardly anticipate the success of their code when they set out to draft it. Noting that there was nothing like it yet in India and that what they encountered on the ground was wholly inadequate, the commissioners cataloged their accomplishments and touted the code's benefits, and in the preface, they addressed Governor-General George Lord Auckland.[4] As a statement of the code's objectives and a formal report on the commissioners' work, this preface summarized key arguments about the codifiers' approach to reforming criminal law and positioned their code as the vanguard of future legal reforms. The commissioners saw their code (which they submitted in October 1837, though it did not become law until 1860)[5] not only as a remedy for the inconsistencies and uncertainties plaguing the British East India Company's existing regulations but also as emblematic of a new approach that would place the reins of lawmaking into the hands of the diligent legislator rather than leaving it under the control of the undisciplined jurist. Their code, in turn, would lay the foundation for further legislator-driven reforms in substantive civil and procedural law.[6]

However, for all of its accomplishments, the code was far from flawless, and its success required more than perfection on paper. Indeed, scholars have highlighted how subsequent and supplementary codes of procedural law undermined the code's principles of uniformity and consistency—especially when it came to the equal application of the law to Indians and Europeans.[7] Uniformity in the application of the law across all territories and to all classes of persons was a key component of the drafters' work but one that even they feared might remain out of reach if the law exempted royal families and Indian princes.[8] Likewise, the law commissioners' emphasis on translating, publishing, and disseminating the code not only spurred the government of India to commission official translations and affordable publications of the text but

4 T. B. Macaulay et al., preface to "A Penal Code, Prepared by the Indian Law Commissioners, and published by Command of the Governor-General of India in Council. Addressed to the Right Honourable George Lord Auckland, C.G.C.B., Governor-General of India in Council," October 14, 1837. Reprinted in T.B. Macaulay et al., *The Indian Penal Code as Originally Framed in 1837 with Notes. A Verbatim Reprint* (Madras: Higginbotham and Co., 1888), vii–xxii, hereafter, "Prefatory Address." Although the letter was co-signed by the other commissioners, Macaulay is credited with authoring the text, and it was subsequently reprinted in compilations of his writings and speeches. See, for example, Macaulay, "Introductory Report upon the Indian Penal Code," in *The Miscellaneous Writings Speeches and Poems of Lord Macaulay, in Four Volumes*, Vol. IV (London: Longmans, Green, and Co., 1880), 3–22.

5 The Indian Penal Code (IPC) was Act XLV of 1860. Though adopted in 1860, it did not go into effect until January 1, 1862.

6 The second and third law commissions addressed these areas.

7 Elizabeth Kolsky, "Codification and the Rule of Colonial Difference: Criminal Procedure in British India," *Law and History Review* 23 no. 3 (2005): 631–684.

8 Macaulay, "Prefatory Address," xx.

also inspired the production and publication of countless guidebooks, manuals, analyses, digests, and abridgments of the code.[9] Although the editors of these works framed them as supplements and complements to the actual code, their circulation nonetheless raises doubts about whose version was authoritative and which interpretation was authentic. Moreover, by the second decade of the twentieth century, another type of penal code began to circulate in British India, as the rulers of princely states issued and introduced their own penal codes. By this point, many of the princely states were too small or too weak to support entirely separate judicial systems, but some states, such as Hyderabad and Indore, introduced their own codes in an effort to retain sovereign authority and resist British hegemony.[10] The promulgation of these spin-off codes, which embraced the idea of codification but challenged the IPC's paramount authority, thus undermined the law commissioners' objectives in other ways.

Bringing these subsequent codes into conversation with the principles that Macaulay outlined in the preface to the original draft provides an opportunity not only to reconsider the legacy of the first Indian Law Commission but also to address how the circulation of law shaped the history of codification and colonial rule more broadly.[11] So long as princely state penal codes disrupted the uniformity, consistency, and clarity of Macaulay's imagined legal order, that order remained tenuous. If there could be multiple penal codes in British India well into the twentieth century, then had the penal code really achieved its aims? Had the code created a more uniform system of penal law or merely provided cover for a multiplicity of laws to persist? Had the code placed law in the hands of capable legislators or simply outsourced lawmaking to anyone with a law degree and a printing press? Lingering questions about the code's accomplishments in relation to the preface's stated aims point to inescapable tensions between the framers' intent and the law's effects, especially since that intent included publishing and publicizing the law and making it public.

9 The government commissioned Urdu author, novelist, and civil servant Nazir Ahmad to translate the IPC into Urdu. Allan Octavian Hume (who later founded the Indian National Congress) and Deputy Magistrate Kour Luchmun Singh published a translation into Hindi. These translations were completed and published in 1861, before the law went into effect.

10 There were hundreds of so-called "princely states" in British India. Of these, only a dozen or so of the largest states introduced separate penal codes. The IPC applied in most states that did not have their own codes. On the history of Shahjahan Begum of Bhopal's administrative reforms—including the introduction of the *Tanẓīmāt-i Shāhjahānī* (*Shahjahani Code*)—see Barbara Metcalf, "Islam and Power in Colonial India: The Making and Unmaking of a Muslim Princess," *The American Historical Review* 116 no. 1 (2011): 1–30.

11 My thinking about circulation here draws from Iza Hussin, "Circulations of Law: Cosmopolitan Elites, Global Repertoires, Local Vernaculars," *Law and History Review* 32 no. 4 (November 2014): 773–795; and Ting Zhang, *Circulating the Code: Print Media and Legal Knowledge in Qing China* (Seattle: University of Washington Press, 2020).

2 Codification: uniformity, consistency, clarity

The first law commission's assignment—to draft a code of penal law that would support British rule in South Asia—was part of a broader effort in the early nineteenth century to regularize and standardize the law through codes. Yet although codification was taking off around the world, namely, across continental Europe (Germany and France), North America (New York and Louisiana), and the Ottoman Empire, it received little support in England, where judge-made common law reigned supreme.[12] Despite their impassioned speeches and reasoned pleas in parliament, English Utilitarians such as Jeremy Bentham and his followers struggled to get their proposals off the ground.[13] As a result, the colonies became, by default or by design, an opportunity for Utilitarian statesmen and legislators to enact abroad the legal reforms that remained impossible at home.[14]

For Macaulay, codification was a "benefit" that the British could bring to India and something that they could graciously "bestow" upon their "Indian subjects," as he made clear in a speech before parliament in 1833, not long before the commission began its work.[15] Codification, Macaulay asserted, was the only way to rid India of the "evil" arising from the bifurcated structure of British rule in India. The Supreme Court (in Kolkata), which "was originally instituted for the protection of natives against Europeans," had deteriorated into "pedantry, cruelty, and corruption," and the only check on the court's power was "a Legislature fifteen thousand miles off" (in London).[16] As he imagined it, once the government of India had been established as the

12 Macaulay cites the "French Code" and the "Code of Louisiana, prepared by the late Mr. Livingston," as sources of "valuable assistance." Macaulay, "Prefatory Address," xiv. For additional background on the "codification debate" in England, see Lindsay Farmer, "Reconstructing the English Codification Debate: The Criminal Law Commissioners, 1833–45," *Law and History Review* 18 no. 2 (2000): 397–425; and on its broader entanglements with British colonialism, see Karuna Mantena, *Alibis of Empire: Henry Maine and the Ends of Liberal Imperialism* (Princeton, NJ: Princeton University Press, 2010), esp. chapter 3, 89–118; and Kolsky, "Codification and the Rule of Colonial Difference." On codification in the Ottoman Empire, see Avi Rubin, "Modernity as a Code: The Ottoman Empire and the Global Movement of Codification," *Journal of the Economic and Social History of the Orient* 59 (2016): 828–856.

13 Farmer, "Reconstructing," 404.

14 Kolsky, "Codification," 633–634. On Utilitarianism and imperialism more broadly, see, for example, Eric Stokes, *The English Utilitarians and India* (Oxford: Oxford University Press, 1989); and Bart Shultz and Georgios Varouxakis (eds.), *Utilitarianism and Empire* (Lanham: Lexington Books, 2005).

15 [Thomas] Macaulay, "A Speech Delivered in the House of Commons on the 10th of July 1833," *Hansard Parliamentary Debates*, H.C. Deb. (July 10, 1833), § 504–537; reprinted in *The Miscellaneous Writings and Speeches of Thomas Macaulay. Popular Edition* (London: Longmans, Green, and Co., 1889), 551–572. He made the speech during debates surrounding the renewal of the East India Company's charter. The law commission was created during this process.

16 Macaulay, "A Speech Delivered," 567–568.

"supreme legislative power" in the land, the law commission could then, "as soon as possible," form the country's scattered laws "into a Code" to address this urgent need. Lacking the "freedom and civilisation" that would limit the potential benefits of codification in Britain, the need for law codes arose in India both from internal shortcomings and from external threats of European corruption and excess.[17] A proper code would justify imperial rule by fulfilling Britain's civilizing mission while at the same time demonstrating the broader utility of codification by bringing unruly Europeans into line.

Macaulay's speech before parliament was a prelude to his work on the law commission, and many of the arguments that he made there also found their way into the penal code's preface. With the draft in hand, however, Macaulay's general arguments about codification also became an opportunity to extol the commissioners' accomplishments. Where India lacked a code, the law commissioners supplied one. Where existing regulations were variable and irregular, they brought uniformity. Where crimes were haphazardly classified and punishments inconsistent, they brought regularity and consistency. And where confusion and disorder reigned, they brought certainty and clarity. Furthermore, the commissioners were justified in proposing an entirely new code because, as Macaulay explained,

> if we had found India in possession of a system of criminal law which the people regarded with partiality, we should have been inclined rather to ascertain it, to digest it, and moderately to correct it, than to propose a system fundamentally different.[18]

If the people were partial to no code in particular, then the law commissioners were free to supply something new.

In addition to these general criticisms, history and circumstances were also part Macaulay's rationale.[19] Successive phases of conquest and assimilation

17 Macaulay, "A Speech Delivered," 568.

18 Macaulay, "Prefatory Address," viii–ix.

19 To be clear, the "history" here is of Macaulay's making. Few academic historians would accept the claims that he makes as representative of past historical processes. For more nuanced understandings of the law in pre-colonial India under Muslim rule, see, for example, Nandini Chatterjee, *Negotiating Mughal Law: A Family of Landlords across Three Indian Empires* (Cambridge: Cambridge University Press, 2020); Farhat Hasan, *State and Locality in Mughal India: Power Relations in Western India, c. 1572–1730* (Cambridge: Cambridge University Press, 2004); and Elizabeth Thelen, *Urban Histories of Rajasthan: Religion, Politics and Society (1550–1800)* (London: Gingko Library, 2022). For detailed analyses of Company encounters with "Mughal" and "Muslim" law, see Jörg Fisch, *Cheap Lives and Dear Limbs: The British Transformation of the Bengal Criminal Law, 1769–1817*, Beiträge Zur Südasienforschung, Bd. 79 (Wiesbaden: F. Steiner, 1983); Robert Travers, *Ideology and Empire in Eighteenth Century India: The British in Bengal* (New York: Cambridge University Press, 2007); Travers, *Empires of Complaints: Mughal Law and the Making of British India, 1765–1793* (New York: Cambridge University Press, 2022); and Radhika Singha, *A Despotism of Law: Crime and Justice in Early Colonial India* (New Delhi: Oxford University Press, 1998).

meant that "none of the systems of penal law" in British India were indigenous. "All those systems are foreign" and had been "introduced by conquerors differing in race, manners, language and religion from the great mass of the people," he argued.[20] Replicating British imperialist tendencies to divide Indian society into two monolithic religious groups with separate and distinct legal traditions—"Hindoo" and "Mahomedan"—Macaulay added that Hindu criminal law had been "long ago superseded" by Muslim criminal law and that Muslim criminal law was "the last system of criminal law which an enlightened and humane Government would be disposed to revive."[21] Macaulay's comments about India's earlier legal traditions were, of course, more straw-man arguments than analytical engagements with pre-colonial legal history, but such arguments gave the law commissioners license to overhaul the criminal law system. Removing local traditions from consideration allowed the law commissioners to advocate for a new system of their design.

Ill-conceived pre-colonial "codes" were not the only problematic inheritances that Macaulay encountered. He also faulted company regulations, which had "altogether discarded" the criminal law of the Hindus and the Muslims, for their variability, inconsistency, and irregularity. Across the three presidencies of Bengal, Bombay, and Madras, punishments for similar crimes were highly irregular. In Bengal, he explained, "serious forgeries" were punished with a prison sentence that was twice as long as the sentence imposed for perjury. In Bombay, the situation was reversed: "perjury is punishable with imprisonment for a term double the term fixed for" forgeries. In Madras, the prescribed punishment was equal for both crimes.[22] Not only did the criminal regulations vary across the Company's territories, but variation in the assigned punishments failed to order crime and punishment in any meaningful way. What was considered heinous in one territory was a misdemeanor in another, and vice versa. The commissioners' draft code would no doubt fix these problems.

If creating a uniform code that would apply equally across Britain's Indian territories was one of the law commissioners' chief aims, then inconsistency within those codes was the reason that none could serve as a model. Of the three presidencies' regulations, Bombay's were the most likely to serve, but they were still faulty.[23] "The Government of that Presidency," Macaulay explained,

> appears to have been fully sensible to the great advantage which must arise from placing the whole law in a written form before those who are

20 Macaulay, "Prefatory Address," ix.

21 Macaulay, "Prefatory Address," ix. Incidentally, Fisch suggests that the British made the enforcement of criminal law more severe by making it easier to convict and punish offenders. Fisch, *Cheap Lives*, 82.

22 Macaulay, "Prefatory Address," ix.

23 The Bombay Code (or the Elphinstone Code as it was also known, in honor of Mountstuart Elphinstone who was then the governor of the presidency) was a set of twenty-six regulations enacted in 1827. Within that set of regulations, which covered everything from

> to administer and those who are to obey it; and, whatever may be the imperfections of the execution, high praise is due to the design.[24]

Though he did not agree with the code's specific contents, he nonetheless praised the project. It not only demonstrated that the British could enact a new system of law without "the smallest sign of discontent among the people" but also encapsulated the codifiers' preference for written statutes over unwritten judicial sentiments.[25]

Nonetheless, the Bombay Code was far from ideal. Its crimes and punishments were scattered and disordered. Five years' imprisonment was the penalty for destroying property, even though the property may be of little value. Conspiracies of all kinds were classified under the same heading such that one accused of a conspiracy "as atrocious as the gunpowder plot" and as harmless as "putting off an unsound horse on a purchaser" faced the same potential punishment. Planning to commit petty theft (and then subsequently abandoning the plan and confessing to the plot) would result in a punishment "twenty times" as severe as the punishment for committing the theft. In short, "the principles according to which crimes ought to be classified and punishments apportioned have been less regarded [in the Bombay regulations] than in the legislation of Bengal and Madras," Macaulay concluded.[26]

Bombay's written code also failed to observe one of the "first principles of penal law:" that the punishment for merely concealing a crime after the fact should be less than the punishment for committing the crime directly. In Bombay, however, concealing a murder was "punishable as murder," and concealing a gang-robbery was "punishable as gang-robbery," though this was not the case for all crimes.[27] The code also failed to recognize a distinction between deliberate acts and incidental effects. Keen legislators, Macaulay averred, should "bear constantly in mind . . . the distinction between harm voluntarily caused and harm involuntarily caused."[28] The Bombay Code upheld the inverse, allowing judges to punish the "unintentional commission" of a crime "according to the Court's judgment," with the punishment not to exceed "that prescribed for the offence committed."[29] Macaulay's critique supported the reformers' conviction that well-reasoned laws should account for intent.

the organization of the judiciary to the appointment of qazis, Regulation XIV ("crimes and punishments") contained much of the code's penal content, though it was supplemented by regulations relating to criminal jurisdiction, the police, criminal justice, and the employment of landholders as police authorities.

24 Macaulay, "Prefatory Address," xi.
25 Macaulay, "Prefatory Address," xi.
26 Macaulay, "Prefatory Address," xi.
27 Macaulay, "Prefatory Address," xii.
28 Macaulay, "Prefatory Address," xii–xiii.
29 Macaulay, "Prefatory Address," xiii.

Despite these important and necessary criticisms, Macaulay's main argument against using the Bombay Code as a potential model for penal law was its "omission" of "many important classes of offences" that were not directly enumerated but instead swept under a broad morality clause.[30] This clause undermined not only the law's clarity and opened the door to wide-ranging judicial discretion but also undermined the law's uniformity. As he explained, "this clause does not apply to people who profess a religion with which a system of penal jurisprudence is not inseparably connected." Muslims who commit adultery, for instance, would be "punishable for adultery," but Christians who commit the same act would be free to do so with impunity.[31] In other words, if the perpetrator's religious code did not prescribe a punishment for the offense, then the courts had no way to convict. Such inconsistencies in the definition and application of the law went against Macaulay's arguments for codification.

3 The draft code

If a desire to make penal law uniform across the East India Company's territories was the code's primary motivation and enumerating criminal acts (and their punishments) consistently and completely was the code's main objective, then clarity and certainty were its intended outcomes. As such, the commissioners drafted the text to be "precise" and "easily understood," for the code could not function if there were questions about its meaning or interpretation.[32] As Macaulay asserted, "a loosely-worded law is no law, and to whatever extent a legislature uses vague expressions, to that extent it abdicates its functions, and resigns the power of making law to the Courts of Justice."[33] That is, if legislators were to have an impact on the interpretation of the law, then they needed to make laws that were clear and easy to interpret.

No doubt the commissioners' emphasis on clarifying the law's meaning fit with the codification movement's larger interests in making the law comprehensible. After all, penal law could only "provide for public safety by the restraint of offenders."[34] As such, the law commissioners' project was not simply to perfect the penal law on the books but also to improve society through the creation of a just, rational, and reliable legal system. Disseminating accessible information about which acts were criminal and forbidden (and which remained permissible) was thus a necessary part of the legislators' project to improve public morality. Like the criminal law commissioners in England,

30 Macaulay, "Prefatory Address," xiii. He describes this clause as one granting the courts "almost unlimited power to punish as they think fit offences against morality, or against the peace and good order of society, if those offences are penal by the religious law of the offender."

31 Macaulay, "Prefatory Address," xiii. For a discussion of how criminal law reform blurred the lines between morality and legality, see Singha, *A Despotism of Law*, esp. ch. 4.

32 Macaulay, "Prefatory Address," xv.

33 Macaulay, "Prefatory Address," xv–xvi.

34 Farmer, "Reconstructing," 411.

Macaulay and his co-authors were committed to these goals in India, and authoring a successful code that not only categorized and classified the law but also explained and interpreted it was part of their mission.

Yet clarity, comprehension, and concision were often at odds with one another. Where other legislators embraced simpler language and shied away from technical terms, the Indian law commissioners took the opposite tack. Rather than rely on common sense definitions and well-known understandings, the law commissioners reveled in minutiae and in some cases, excessive explanation. Their interest in making the text precise resulted in wordiness and repetition, and their desire to make it comprehensible contributed to the inclusion of excessive examples, which in numerous cases, far exceeded the main text of the law.[35] Chapter XIX, "Of Offences Against Property," for example, opened with a brief definition of theft:

> Whosoever, intending to take fraudulently any thing which is property, and which is not attached to the earth, out of the possession of any person, without that person's consent, moves that thing in order to such taking, is said to commit 'theft.'[36]

Seven explanations followed this definition, each addressing one or more of the text's terms to exorcise any possible confusion about what, for instance, it meant to be fastened to the ground (explanations 1–3), to move (or to remove an obstacle to movement) or to induce or entice to move (explanations 4–5), to give consent for a thing to be moved (explanation 6), or to move, even if one intends to later restore (explanation 7). Twenty-six illustrations followed these explanations, one for each letter of the alphabet. While some of these examples mapped onto the preceding explanations directly (e.g., C and D involved enticing animals to move), others verged on the absurd. In illustration P, Person A becomes "exasperated at a passage in a book" that happens to be lying on the counter in Person Z's bookshop. Unable to resist the urge, A tears the book to pieces and destroys Z's property. Although A may have committed criminal trespass or mischief, he has not committed "theft," as there was nothing fraudulent in his actions. He destroyed Z's property in plain sight. In illustration Q, "A" and "Z" are gardeners. Z grows an amazing pineapple that A takes and places before judges who award it the best pineapple prize. A then returns the pineapple to Z but has, according to the law commissioners, committed theft: he not only stole Z's pineapple prize but also fraudulently presented the pineapple before the judges as his own.[37]

35 See, for example, the twenty or so lines of illustrations under the five lines of text for Section 399 "Of Mischief," in Macaulay et al., *The Indian Penal Code as Originally Framed*, 74–75; or the five examples included under the section on "Criminal Breach of Trust" (Section 386), Macaulay et al., *The Indian Penal Code as Originally Framed*, 70–71.

36 Macaulay et al., *The Indian Penal Code as Originally Framed*, 64–65.

37 Macaulay et al., *The Indian Penal Code as Originally Framed*, 64–67.

The chapter on theft was one of several that offered detailed and imaginative explanations such as these.

The law commissioners were not blind to the potential ill-effects that their "copious" explanations, illustrations, and examples might have on the law's receipt. Indeed, Macaulay framed this feature as one of "peculiarity," which set their code apart from others. He also acknowledged that the commissioners had, at times, sacrificed "neatness and perspicuity" in favor of "precision."[38] As he explained, they had decided to privilege preciseness over conciseness, even if it made their text more difficult to read:

> A legislator may, if he thinks fit, avoid such definitions, and by avoiding them he will give a smoother and more attractive appearance to his workmanship; but in that case he flinches from a duty which he ought to perform, and which somebody must perform.[39]

As his explanation made clear, judges would be the ones to perform the legislator's duty, if he did not perform it himself. Thus, to keep law-making out of the hands of judges, the law commissioners included in their draft "these unpleasing but indispensible [*sic*] parts of a Code," wordy though they may be.[40] It was a hard task, but somebody had to do it.

Beyond the inclusion of copious examples and illustrations, the commissioners also offered suggestions on how to fix any problems that might arise later, after the draft code became law. Should judges have doubts about a section's interpretation or application, they should not attempt to revise the law from the bench but should instead submit their questions to a legislative commission for subsequent revision and clarification. "Such questions will certainly arise, and, unless proper precautions taken, the decisions on such questions will accumulate till they form a body of law of far greater bulk than that which has been adopted by the legislature."[41] This body of judge-made law would be not only "bulky" and unwieldy but also "uncertain and contradictory," and the government should not allow it to come into being.[42] Thus, reaching beyond the subject of the code itself, Macaulay proposed a mechanism for transmitting judicial questions to the legislators for future review.

> Every judge of every rank whose duty it is to administer the law as contained in the Code should be enjoined to report to his official superiors every doubt which he may entertain as to any question of construction which may have arisen in his Court,

38 Macaulay, "Prefatory Address," xiv.
39 Macaulay, "Prefatory Address," xv.
40 Macaulay, "Prefatory Address," xv.
41 Macaulay, "Prefatory Address," xvii.
42 Macaulay, "Prefatory Address," xvii.

and "all the questions" should then be reported to whatever permanent legislative body the government might create.[43] If the government were to follow such a procedure, then with each successive edition of the code, the law would become better, clearer, and more precise.[44]

Finally, Macaulay acknowledged the need to make the code public. The commissioners' work would be worthless if publications and translations of the code into the languages spoken and written by the people of India were not circulated widely and publicly. "The native population should, with as little delay as possible, be furnished with good versions of [the code] in their own languages."[45] Such translations, which would be difficult to produce and would require the joint efforts of "enlightened Europeans and natives" working together, were necessary for the code to have its intended effects. The law commissioners thus concluded their prefatory address with a statement that they were "confident that [his] Lordship in Council [would] not grudge any thing that may be necessary for enabling the people who are placed under [his] care to know what that law is according to which they are to live."[46] In substance, the law was to be uniform, consistent, and clear, and in practice, it should be translated, published, and circulated.

4 Multiple printings/multiple prefaces

It is clear from reading the preface that the law commissioners not only considered the code to be part of the larger movement for codification at the time but also saw the preface as a necessary framing device. Higginbotham and Company, the publisher of the 1888 "verbatim reprint" that included the prefatory address, also considered these introductory materials essential to the subsequent interpretation and application of the code and included both the first and the second report on the code in this reprint. These writings were "exceedingly rare" and "frequently sought for as helps to the elucidation of the law as it at present exists," and they explained and lamented their inability to secure additional documents relating to the code's progression from proposed draft to official law.[47] Fifty years after the commissioners first framed the code and almost thirty years after the code was adopted in British India, Higginbotham, a successful and well-known publisher of law books, offered the original draft and the commissioners' prefatory address as important documents for publication and circulation.

They were, however, a bit late to the party. By the time Higginbotham published this reprint of the original draft, dozens of translations, analyses, and reproductions of the penal code were already in circulation. Few (if any)

43 Macaulay, "Prefatory Address," xviii.
44 Macaulay, "Prefatory Address," xix.
45 Macaulay, "Prefatory Address," xxi.
46 Macaulay, "Prefatory Address," xxii.
47 H[igginbotham] & Co[mpany], preface to Macaulay et al., *The Indian Penal Code as Originally Framed in 1837 with Notes* (Madras: Higginbotham & Company, 1888), iii.

of these reproductions included the commissioners' original preface. Instead, these editions included a range of meta- and para-textual explanations to support different approaches to reading and interpreting the code. Generally aimed at students, aspiring civil servants, legal practitioners, and "the public," these publications adopted different approaches to making the text accessible and comprehensible, and while many of them shared the law commissioners' aims in disseminating information about the penal code, their publication also raised questions about whether the law commissioners were themselves successful at producing a code that was uniform, consistent, and clear.

One of the earliest of these publications was R. Ragoonath Row's *Alphabetical Index of the Penal Code* (1862). Ragoonath Row was a deputy collector in the Madras Presidency who, according to his introductory note, realized as soon as the code was published that "an alphabetical Statement of crimes" was "absolutely called for." Even though the intervening introduction of the criminal procedure code, which included an organized schedule of crimes, almost rendered the proposed publication of his index unnecessary, he nonetheless proceeded to publish his work "in the hope that it may be found useful . . . to the public."[48] His index, which converted the text of the penal code into a tabulated list of offenses, punishments, and references that directed readers to the relevant section of the code, was no doubt intended to supplement—not to replace—the original code by making it easier to search.

Angelo Lewis's version of the penal code, which was published as volume one of the Indian Law Manuals series, took this interest in utility one step further. Recognizing that "so many able and elaborate treatises on the Indian Penal Code" were already circulating, Lewis proposed to offer something different. His edition was designed as a manual and was "intended to fulfil [*sic*] . . . the purpose of *instruction*."[49] To achieve this aim, Lewis converted each section of the text into a question. The section on "offences against property" thus opened with the question "When is a person said to commit 'theft'?" to which the correct answer was the language of Section 378 "of theft."[50] For Lewis, works of reference and works of instruction had contradictory motivations, and he aimed his edition at teaching. Although "copiousness and minuteness of detail" were "valuable qualities" for works of reference, those same qualities were "positive disadvantages to the student, who approaches a subject for the first time, and whose chief desiderata are clearness and conciseness."[51] Even

48 R. Ragoonath Row, "Introduction," *Alphabetical Index of the Indian Penal Code, (Act XLV of 1860)* (Madras: The Hindu Press, 1862), np.

49 Angelo J. Lewis, "Preface," in *The Indian Penal Code*, India Law Manuals, No. 1 (London: Wm. H. Allen & Co., 1870), v (emphasis in the original).

50 Lewis, *The Indian Penal Code*, 113.

51 Lewis, "Preface," v. Interestingly, Lewis concludes his preface by noting that "the original language of the Code has been preserved so far as practicable, consistently with conciseness, the alternations being mainly restricted to grammatical compression." Lewis, *The Indian Penal Code*, vi.

though it is difficult to see the pedagogical ingenuity of Lewis's approach, by which he rephrased statements as questions that still required students to memorize the code in order to provide the correct answer, he was not the only commentator to adopt a student-centered approach.

John Cutler and Edmund Fuller Griffin also underscored the need for brevity in their preface to *An Analysis of the Indian Penal Code* (1871). Their rendition aimed to "present [the code's] provisions in as succinct a form as possible for reference by the Student of Indian Law as well as by the [legal] Practitioner."[52] They not only truncated and abbreviated the main text but also synthesized and summarized the law commissioners' copious explanations and illustrations, reducing the explanatory material under theft, for instance, to a handful of short sentences.[53] Likewise, a metrical version of the penal code that was published in Urdu around 1898 described the text as offering many benefits to the public (*ba'ẓ fā'ida-yi 'awāmm*), under which it listed administrators, lawyers (*vakīls*), agents and representatives (*mukh̲tārān*), civil service exam candidates (*umīdwārān*), and police officials (*ahl-karān-i pōlīs*).[54]

By 1933, K. P. Upadhyaya, a retired government employee, had taken the task of digesting the code into easy to remember segments to the next level. The preface to his *Mnemonics or the Sutras of the Indian Penal Code* described his work as a "novel and interesting method of studying the most abstruse subject of Law by means of Memoria Technica [memory techniques]" and framed the system that he created as one modeled on Panini's Sutras (a complex work of Sanskrit grammar composed in the fourth century BCE).[55] To introduce students to the substance of the code, Upadhyaya, for instance, offered the mnemonic "Mir abets Chap 'D'," a phrase that, if deconstructed according to his technique, captured the principal subjects of the code's twenty-three substantive chapters, as shown in Figure 6.1. (He excluded the first and second chapters for being of a general nature.)[56] By a similar token, the mnemonic "WAFerS" was the key to understanding what was excluded from the code: warship, ambassador, alien enemies, foreign sovereign, foreign army, sovereign.[57] Even if the law

52 John Cutler and Edmund Fuller Griffin, *An Analysis of the Indian Penal Code; Including the Indian Penal Code Amendment Act, 1870, with Notes* (London: Butterworths, 1871), np.

53 John Cutler and Edmund Fuller Griffin, *An Analysis of the Indian Penal Code; Including the Indian Penal Code Amendment Act, 1870, with Notes* (London: Butterworths, 1871), 60. The code itself reduced the draft's seven explanations to five and twenty-six illustrations to sixteen. Government of India, Legislative Department, *The Indian Penal Code, as Modified Up to the 1st August, 1890* (Calcutta: Office of the Superintendent of Government Printing, 1890), 153–155.

54 Tēk Chand, *Ta'zīrāt-i Hind Manẓūm* (Meerut: Faiz-i 'Am Press, [1898]).

55 K. P. Upadhyaya, "Preface" to *The Mnemonics or the Sutras of the Indian Penal Code* (Ahmedabad: Gujarat Printing Press, 1931), 3.

56 K. P. Upadhyaya, "Preface" to *The Mnemonics or the Sutras of the Indian Penal Code* (Ahmedabad: Gujarat Printing Press, 1931), 5–6.

57 K. P. Upadhyaya, "Preface" to *The Mnemonics or the Sutras of the Indian Penal Code* (Ahmedabad: Gujarat Printing Press, 1931), 6.

2 1 1 3 1 3 1 2 4 1 2 2
M I R A B E T S C Ha P D = 23 = Mir abets Chap 'D'

1 M_1 – Measures - offences against Weights.
2 M_2 – Marriage - offences relating to Marriage.
3 I_1 – Intimidation - offences of criminal Intimidation
4 R_1 – Religion - offences against Religion.
5 A_1 – Abetment - offences against Abetment
6 A_2 – Army - offences against Army, Navy &c.
7 A_3 – Attempts - to commit offences.
8 B_1 – Body - offences against human Body.
9 E_1 – Exceptions - General.
10 E_2 – Elections - offences against Elections.
11 E_3 – Evidence - offences against false Evidence.
12 T_1 – Tranquility - offences against Tranquility.
13 S_1 – State - offences against State.
14 S_2 – Servants - offences by or relating to public Servants.

Figure 6.1 Illustration showing K. P. Upadhyaya's "Mir abets Chap 'D'" mnemonic. Upadhyaya, *Mnemonics*, 5.

commissioners had yearned for a systematic and comprehensible code, it is hard to imagine that they had in mind a system like Upadhyaya's mnemonics when they set out to make the code publicly accessible.

Whether the subsequent publication of different editions and approaches to understanding the code was due to widespread acceptance of the code's principles of clarity and public education or to the growth of the lucrative exam preparation and textbook business, the proliferation of these penal codes necessarily challenged the authority and uniformity of the original version. Indeed, Higginbotham's publication of the law commissioners' original draft, along with Macaulay's preface, both responded and contributed to the expansion of approaches, adding an additional framework to consider when interpreting and applying the law. After all, if legal practitioners, retired civil servants, police inspectors, and barristers published their own "analyses," "commentaries," "manuals," and "mnemonics" to help students and would-be civil servants make sense of the code, then the law commissioners' preface to the original draft code must be equally relevant for these quests to clarify its meaning.

5 "But in all cases certainty"[58]

Even though a generous reading of the multiple explanatory and analytical versions of the penal code could still support the argument that the law commissioners had succeeded in their task and had created a law that was uniform, consistent, and clear, it is hard to maintain this view in light of the penal codes that were

58 Macaulay, "A Speech Delivered," 570.

introduced across several of British India's princely states.[59] In theory, these codes, which drew from the law commissioners' model to varying degrees, embraced the principles of codification: they synthesized and streamlined existing laws into coherent and comprehensive codes, introduced and published the law so that the public would be aware of its contents, and in many cases, supplemented the introduction of a penal code with reforms to legal procedure and the judiciary. Yet despite these parallels with the law commissioners' motivations, the princely penal codes also challenged the codifiers' ultimate aims. Even if the application of these codes was limited to small principalities and their substance was in some cases nearly identical to that of the Indian Penal Code, their very promulgation challenged the IPC's authority, more directly in some cases than in others.

For instance, while questions of "sovereignty" were omitted from the original IPC, the penal code for the princely state of Hyderabad, the *Majmūʿa-yi Taʿzīrāt-i Mamālik-i Maḥrūsa-yi Sarkār-yi ʿĀliya* (*Compendium of the penal laws of the well-protected dominions of the exalted government*) opened with a statement of sovereign authority:

> For every person and every act or failure to act that is deserving of punishment in the aforementioned code, that act [or failure to act] will be punished when committed within the territories of the *Sarkār-i ʿĀliya* [exalted government, namely, Hyderabad state] and will be punished according to the punishments prescribed in this code, not on any other basis.[60]

The next section also supported princely sovereignty by asserting that in some cases, crimes committed outside the state's territories could be brought under investigation according to the code.[61] Although the IPC contained similar statements of jurisdiction and extent, their presence within a princely code—asserting uniformity without respect to individual status (every person, *har shak̲h̲ṣ*) and acknowledging that the provisions of the code could be extended to crimes committed beyond the state's borders—undermined the authority of British Indian penal law, symbolically, if not practically.

To understand how these codes differed in substance from India's penal code requires more systematic analysis than can be provided here, but even a simple analysis of their preambles provides interesting evidence for discussion,

59 For an introduction to the princely states, see Barbara N. Ramusack, *The Indian Princes and Their States* (Cambridge: Cambridge University Press, 2004); see also Lauren A. Benton, *A Search for Sovereignty: Law and Geography in European Empires, 1400–1900* (Cambridge: Cambridge University Press, 2010), 222–278 for a discussion of their status as sovereign entities.

60 *Majmūʿa-yi Taʿzīrāt-i Mamālik-i Maḥrūsa-yi Sarkār-yi ʿĀliya*, Act 5 of 1324 F. [1914], 1. Note that the Hyderabad penal code, like the official Urdu translations of the IPC, uses the word "*taʿzīrāt*" to refer to the code of penal law. This term, which means punishing or censuring, refers, in Islamic law, to punishments given at the judge's discretion (i.e., to punishments that were not specified in the Qurʾan).

61 *Majmūʿa-yi Taʿzīrāt-i Mamālik-i Maḥrūsa-yi Sarkār-yi ʿĀliya*, Act 5 of 1324 F. [1914], 1.

in part because their preambles remained perfunctory and brief. Macaulay's preface extended to sixteen pages, and editors of subsequent editions offered a few paragraphs, whereas princely penal codes included little more than a single-sentence preamble. The preambles to the Cochin Penal Code of 1883 and the Marwar Penal Code of 1913/4 were nearly identical,[62] save for a difference in the state name ("Whereas it is expedient to provide a general Penal Code for Marwar/Cochin"). Hyderabad's read simply as follows: "Whereas it is expedient [*maṣlaḥat*] that the penal laws of the territories of the exalted government [i.e., of Hyderabad state] should be explicated and arranged, therefore the order [*ḥukm*] is given as follows [*ḥasb-i ẕail*]." The Marathi-language penal code for Baroda state, the "Gaikwad Government's Penal Code" (*Gāyakwāḍ Sarkārano̅ Pho̅jdārī Nibandh*) of 1926, also followed this pattern, except for the addition (and acknowledgment) of the ruling Gaikwad's name.[63]

Compared to these examples, the Bhopal judicial code, the *Tanẓīmāt-i Shāhjahānī* (*The Shahjahani Code*) of 1294 Hijri (1897 CE) and the Indore Penal Code (Act No. II of Fuslee 1288 [1915]) were outliers. The two-page introduction to the *Tanẓīmāt-i Shāhjahānī*, which admittedly focused more on the judicial system than on penal law, identified the code as one of the ruling begum's several reforms, praised the code's principles, and provided a brief overview of its contents.[64] Like the others, the Indore penal code's preamble also mentioned the need for a general penal law but used the opportunity to simultaneously praise the perfection of Hindu law (and thereby question the need for a written code) and indicate that the code's creation was the product of political necessity:

> Whereas substantive and adjective penal laws are absolutely necessary for the well-being of the public; and whereas, although the Hindu Law is perfect and complete in itself . . . yet in the present state of India, its operation must be restricted and modified, the following rules, not inconsistent with the Hindu Law, are hereby promulgated with the sanction of His Highness Shreemunth Maharajadhiraj Raja Rajeswar Savai Takojee Rao Holkar Bahadoor.[65]

62 There is some inconsistency with the date. The first page of the code identifies it as "The Marwar Penal Code, 1913." The title page of the publication, however, refers to it as "The Marwar Penal Code. 1914."

63 A. D. C. Barr, "Preamble," in *Marwar Penal Code of 1914* (Bombay: Shri Venkateshwar Steam Press, 1915), 1; "Preamble," The Cochin Penal Code (I of 1059), in *The Acts and Proclamations of Cochin*, vol. II (Ernakulam: The Cochin Government Press, 1938), 1; and [Preamble], *Gāyakwāḍ Sarkārano̅ Pho̅jdārī Nibandh*, 1. A rough translation of the preamble for the Gaikwad's penal code is "[Whereas] it is desirable to consolidate and amend the laws, rules, circular orders, and orders on criminal offences [the Gaikwad ruler] defines them as follows."

64 Maulvi Muḥammad Majīd Ḵẖān (ed.), *Tanẓīmāt-i Shāhjahānī* (*The Shahjahani Code*) (Bhopal: Maṭba'-yi Sikandarī, 1294 AH [1897]), 2–3.

65 "Preamble," in *Indore Penal Code, Act no. II of Fuslee 1288: Passed with Sanction of . . . Tukojee Rao Holkar Bahadur, Maharajah of Indore* (Madras: C. Foster, [1882?]), 1. For further analysis, see A. C. Lyall, "A Modern Hindu Code," *Law Quarterly Review* 6 no. 1 (1890): 86–89.

The code was necessary on account of "the present state of India," but in remaining consistent with Hindu law, it rejected the legislator's authority to remake the law, and the extracts from the law codes of Manu that followed this introduction supported this claim. Indore would have a penal code but one that begrudged its own need to exist.

The expediency that these codes acknowledged was twofold. First, it was an acceptance of the general need to codify the penal law and to synthesize existing rules, orders, and statutes into a single text. Second, it was a recognition of the princely rulers' precarious position. As studies of the princely states have shown, initiating reforms (judicial, economic, and governmental) from within was one way to prevent British interventions from without.[66] Introducing their own penal codes thus allowed these rulers to maintain their nominal independence and authority.[67] If reformers such as Macaulay could not point to an inferior system that needed replacing, then imperial intervention would remain difficult to justify, and the princely rulers were more likely to retain control over their judicial affairs—even if those affairs increasingly resembled judicial business in British India. Given these countervailing effects, the fact that Macaulay's push for legal uniformity sparked such a wide range of translations, interpretations, and princely recreations justifies the attention given to his preface here. Without understanding the law commissioners' original objectives and motivations, it would be difficult to understand the disruptions and disturbances that the publication of these multiple penal codes caused. While the princely penal codes are themselves worthy of additional attention, their promulgation and publication nonetheless satisfied and challenged the law commission's broader aim at penal law reform.

6 Conclusion

As these examples show, after it went into effect, the Indian Penal Code was published, translated, disseminated, and circulated across British India. The adopted code also became the basis for penal law in several of Britain's other overseas territories, where in many cases, its influence continues to this day. Yet with the publication of new editions, interpretations, analyses, and abridgments, the language of the code drifted further away from the law commissioners' original meaning and ventured into the territory of inconsistency and uncertainty that they feared. Instructional editions aimed at students, aspiring civil servants, and policemen raise questions about who was learning the law and how carefully they were learning it: if students required extensive mnemonics or assistance from rhyming metrical abridgments, then were they capable of mastering the code? Was the code clear enough for their comprehension? Likewise, summarizing and paraphrasing raised doubts about whether these editions conveyed the code's full meaning: if extensive explanations and

66 For a general discussion of these patterns, see Ramusack, *Indian Princes*, esp. ch. 6.
67 Other states, such as Mysore, adopted the IPC with local modifications.

illustrations were part of the original text, then did the code retain sufficient specificity when reduced to simple statements or question and answer formats? Finally, if the code was meant to create a system of penal law where such systems were lacking, then what did it mean to have spin-off codes enacted in India's princely states? If one code was necessary, then did the presence of multiple codes undermine its broader objectives?

Macaulay's prefatory address provided context and framing for the penal code, explaining the drafters' rationale and their approach to the project. It justified their interventions and clarified their intent. What the preface did not provide, however, was a key to understanding the role of law for a society in which individuals accessed and interacted with the law not only in different languages but also at different levels. If the code was to be a model of moral behavior for common criminals, then it was also a series of answers to be mastered by students and civil servants. If the code was to define the limits of acceptable and permissible behavior within British India, then it also represented a model of enlightened governance and a guidebook for reforming and refining penal law among sovereign princes. In other words, while the preface presented the code in one way, once it became public, it took off in multiple directions and gained multiple meanings.

References

Barr, A. D. C., Esquire (compiler). *The Marwar Penal Code, 1914.* Bombay: Shri Venkateshwar Steam Press, 1915.

Benton, Lauren A. *A Search for Sovereignty: Law and Geography in European Empires, 1400–1900.* Cambridge: Cambridge University Press, 2010.

Chan, Wing-Cheong, Barry Wright, and Stanley Yeo (eds.). *Codification, Macaulay and the Indian Penal Code: The Legacies and Modern Challenges of Criminal Law Reform.* Farnham: Ashgate Publishing Ltd., 2011.

Chatterjee, Nandini. *Negotiating Mughal Law: A Family of Landlords across Three Indian Empires.* Cambridge: Cambridge University Press, 2020.

Cutler, John and Edmund Fuller Griffin. *An Analysis of the Indian Penal Code; Including the Indian Penal Code Amendment Act, 1870, with Notes.* London: Butterworths, 1871.

Farmer, Lindsay. "Reconstructing the English Codification Debate: The Criminal Law Commissioners, 1833–45." *Law and History Review* 18, no. 2 (2000): 397–425. https://doi.org/10.2307/744300.

Fisch, Jörg. *Cheap Lives and Dear Limbs: The British Transformation of the Bengal Criminal Law, 1769–1817.* Beiträge Zur Südasienforschung, Bd. 79. Wiesbaden: F. Steiner, 1983.

Gāyakwāḍ Sarkārana̱ Rājyāmāñ [Gaikwad Government]. *Phōjdārī Nibandh [Penal Code].* Vadodara: Āryā Sudhārak Chhāp Khanā, 1926.

Government of Cochin. "The Cochin Penal Code (I of 1059)." In *The Acts and Proclamations of Cochin*, vol. 2, 1–184. Ernakulam: The Cochin Government Press, 1938.

Government of India, Legislative Department. *The Indian Penal Code, as Modified up to the 1st August, 1890.* Calcutta: Office of the Superintendent of Government Printing, 1890.

Hasan, Farhat. *State and Locality in Mughal India: Power Relations in Western India, c. 1572–1730.* Cambridge: Cambridge University Press, 2004.

Hussin, Iza. "Circulations of Law: Cosmopolitan Elites, Global Repertoires, Local Vernaculars." *Law and History Review* 32, no. 4 (2014): 773–795. https://doi.org/10.1017/S0738248014000479.

Indore Penal Code, Act No. II of Fuslee 1288: Passed with Sanction of . . . Tukojee Rao Holkar Bahadur, Maharajah of Indore. Madras: C. Foster, 1882?

Kaur, Raminder. "Specters of Macaulay: Blasphemy, the Indian Penal Code, and Pakistan's Postcolonial Predicament." In *Censorship in South Asia: Cultural Regulation from Sedition to Seduction*, edited by William Mazzarella, 175–205. Bloomington: Indiana University Press, 2009.

Ḵẖān, Maulvi Muḥammad Majīd (ed.). *Tanẓīmāt-i Shāhjahānī* (*The Shahjahani Code*). Bhopal: Maṭbaʿ-yi Sikandarī, 1294 AH [1897].

Kolsky, Elizabeth. "Codification and the Rule of Colonial Difference: Criminal Procedure in British India." *Law and History Review* 23, no. 3 (2005): 631–684. https://doi.org/10.1017/S0738248000000596.

Lewis, Angelo J. *The Indian Penal Code*. India Law Manuals, No. 1. London: Wm. H. Allen & Co., 1870.

Lyall, A. C. "A Modern Hindu Code." *Law Quarterly Review* 6, no. 1 (1890): 86–89.

Macaulay, T. B. *The Miscellaneous Writings Speeches and Poems of Lord Macaulay, in Four Volumes*, vol. 4. London: Longmans, Green, and Co., 1880.

Macaulay, T. B., J. M. Macleod, G. W. Anderson, and F. Millett. *The Indian Penal Code as Originally Framed in 1837 with Notes. A Verbatim Reprint*. Madras: Higginbotham and Co., 1888.

Macaulay, T. B. "A Speech Delivered in the House of Commons on the 10th of July 1833." In *The Miscellaneous Writings and Speeches of Thomas Macaulay. Popular Edition*, 551–572. London: Longmans, Green, and Co., 1889.

Mantena, Karuna. *Alibis of Empire: Henry Maine and the Ends of Liberal Imperialism*. Princeton, NJ: Princeton University Press, 2010.

Mawani, Renisa and Iza Hussin. "Travels of Law: Indian Ocean Itineraries." *Law and History Review* 32, no. 4 (2014): 733–747.

Metcalf, Barbara. "Islam and Power in Colonial India: The Making and Unmaking of a Muslim Princess." *The American Historical Review* 116, no. 1 (2011): 1–30. https://doi.org/10.1086/ahr.116.1.1.

Ramusack, Barbara N. *The Indian Princes and Their States*. Cambridge, UK: Cambridge University Press, 2004.

Row, R. Ragoonath. *Alphabetical Index of the Indian Penal Code, (Act XLV of 1860)*. Madras: The Hindu Press, 1862.

Rubin, Avi. "Modernity as a Code: The Ottoman Empire and the Global Movement of Codification." *Journal of the Economic and Social History of the Orient* 59, no. 5 (2016): 828–856. https://doi.org/10.1163/15685209-12341415.

Shultz, Bart and Georgios Varouxakis (eds.). *Utilitarianism and Empire*. Lanham: Lexington Books, 2005.

Singha, Radhika. *A Despotism of Law: Crime and Justice in Early Colonial India*. Delhi: Oxford University Press, 1998.

Stokes, Eric. *The English Utilitarians and India*. Oxford: Oxford University Press, 1989.

Tēk Chand. *Taʿzīrāt-i Hind Manẓūm*. Meerut: Faiẓ-i ʿĀm Press, 1898.

Thelen, Elizabeth. *Urban Histories of Rajasthan: Religion, Politics and Society (1550–1800)*. London: Gingko Library, 2022.

Travers, Robert. *Ideology and Empire in Eighteenth Century India: The British in Bengal*. New York: Cambridge University Press, 2007.

Travers, Robert. *Empires of Complaints: Mughal Law and the Making of British India, 1765–1793*. New York: Cambridge University Press, 2022.

Upadhyaya, K. P. *The Mnemonics or the Sutras of the Indian Penal Code*. Ahmedabad: Gujarat Printing Press, 1931.

Yeo, Stanley and Barry Wright. "Revitalising Macaulay's Indian Penal Code." In *Codification, Macaulay and the Indian Penal Code: The Legacies and Modern Challenges of Criminal Law Reform*, edited by Wing-Cheong Chan, Barry Wright, and Stanley Yeo, 3–17. Farnham: Ashgate Publishing Ltd., 2011.
Zhang, Ting. *Circulating the Code: Print Media and Legal Knowledge in Qing China*. Seattle: University of Washington Press, 2020.

Part II

Breaking apart

7 (Re-)framing Hammurabi's laws

Worldbuilding with prologues and epilogues in the Ancient Near East

Laura Culbertson

1 Introduction

Scribes of the Ancient Near East (ANE) created the earliest written examples of law collections in human history, the most famous of which is the "Code of Hammurabi" (ca. 1750 BCE).[1] This composition is described as consisting of three components: a prologue, a collection of laws (approaching 300 individual entries), and an epilogue. Today, this law collection makes frequent cameos in all kinds of intellectual histories and legal studies. It has been positioned as an incipient stage in the history of law and a "precursor"[2] representing "a very early phase in the evolution of law,"[3] and it is recognized for serving as "a significant advance toward a legal system" and concept of rule of law.[4] Despite the deeply entrenched social and political inequalities of Hammurabi's time—inequalities affirmed in Hammurabi's laws—the Code's prologue and epilogue have also been recruited as evidence for the roots of modern ideas such as human rights[5] and mentioned among the origins of "humanitarian

1 An authoritative translation is Martha T. Roth, *Law Collections from Mesopotamia and Asia Minor* (Atlanta: Scholars Press, 1995a); an open-access version of Roth's translation is "Laws of Hammurabi," *Open Educational Resources for the Ancient Near East* (2022), 134. https://stars.library.ucf.edu/ancientneareast/134, last revised May 2023. Another digital version of the laws are provided here: https://ehammurabi.org/.

2 Wim Voermans, *The Story of Constitutions, Discovering the We in Us* (Cambridge University Press, 2023).

3 W. Voermans, M. Stremler, and P. Cliteur, *Constitutional Preambles: A Comparative Analysis* (Edward Elgar Publishing, 2017), 6.

4 Simon Chesterman, "An International Rule of Law?" *The American Journal of Comparative Law* 56 no. 2 (2008): 331–361. See also Paul Gordon Lauren, *The Evolution of International Human Rights: Visions Seen*, 3rd ed. (PA: University of Pennsylvania Press, 2011), 12.

5 For example, see Paul Gordon Lauren, "The Foundations of Justice and Human Rights in Early Legal Texts and Thought," in *The Oxford Handbook of International Human Rights Law*, ed. Dinah Shelton (Oxford University Press, 2013), 12; and Micheline Ishay, *The History of Human Rights: From Ancient Times to the Globalization Era* (CA: University of California Press, 2008).

DOI: 10.4324/9781003534815-9

trends."[6] These characterizations arise from broad visions of history—and scholars know that there is no linear string of ideas across millennia—but we encounter a limitation. Although such depictions extol the Code of Hammurabi for its contributions, they define its value and achievements in terms of later, foreign traditions instead of its own.

How does it look from the other direction? Hammurabi's law collection was drafted by specialized scribes who self-consciously engaged with the cuneiform traditions that preceded them. These scribes inventively leveraged older compositions for legitimacy and authority, culling ideas from different royal genres.[7] Specialists of ANE history and law have long described the Code as a "milestone rather than a starting point in the social history of the ancient Near East,"[8] with emphasis on the text as the "end result of a cumulative process"[9] with a "sense of achievement" coming at the end of Hammurabi's thirty-eight-year career and conquests.[10] It is "the culmination of one stream of tradition and a witness to the start of another."[11] Scholars note how the composition exudes the heroism and hyperbole of a royal inscription—how it is "infused with inventiveness" that we can only grasp by looking into the native legal-literary traditions that precede it.[12] These depictions reflect engagement with a lineage of royal compositions such as cuneiform decrees, edicts, and law collections and analysis of the laws, as well as the so-called prologue and epilogue—the framing texts.

Scholars of many fields have pointed to the significance of the prologue and epilogue, cautioning against segmenting the text because these portions are "not farfetched or superfluous pieces."[13] Despite apparent consensus on such importance—and plenty of studies noting the mutually necessary relationship between the components of these codes—the laws have received far more attention and analysis in modern scholarship. Over a century of debate persists

6 Emilio J. Buis. *Taming Ares: War, Interstate Law, and Humanitarian Discourse in Classical Greece* (Leiden: Brill, 2018), 16, note 60.

7 See Gerhard Reis, *Prolog und Epilog in Gesetzen des Altertums* (Munich: C.H. Beck), 18–30; Dominique Charpin, *Writing Law, and Kingship in Old Babylonian Mesopotamia,* Translated by Marie Todd (IL: University of Chicago Press, 2010), 72; Marc Van De Mieroop, *King Hammurabi of Babylon: A Biography* (Oxford: Blackwell, 2005), 109.

8 Francis Rue Steele, "The Lipit-Ishtar Law Code," *American Journal of Archaeology* 52 no. 3 (1947): 164.

9 Dominique Charpin, *Writing, Law, and Kingship,* 72.

10 Marc Van De Mieroop, *King Hammurabi of Babylon,* 100–101.

11 Pamela Barmash, *The Laws of Hammurabi: At the Confluence of Royal and Scribal Traditions* (Oxford University Press, 2021), 3.

12 Barmash, *The Laws of Hammurabi,* 87–88.

13 Jean Bottéro, *Mesopotamia: Writing, Reasoning, and the Gods,* Translated by Zainab Bahrani and Marc Van De Mieroop (IL: University of Chicago Press, 1992), 158; see also Barmash, *The Laws of Hammurabi,* 89–91; M. T. Roth, "Mesopotamian Legal Traditions and the Laws of Hammurabi," *Chicago-Kent Law Review* 70 no. 1 (1995b): 13–39; M. T. Roth, "Hammurabi's Wronged Man," *Journal of the American Oriental Society* 122 no. 1 (2002): 38–45.

about whether the laws comprise non-legislative royal apologia[14] and the degree to which they held any practical applications or were simply a compilation of case laws—or could even be considered legal statutes at all.[15] Sometimes, prologues and epilogues are invoked to make arguments about the functions of the laws and their judicial agency.[16] Of course, these texts were not drafted in the service of modern historiographical and legal questions. Their authors may never have imagined the potential for such confusion about where the laws stand; they situated the entries within carefully crafted frameworks, after all.

Rather than solving long-standing questions about the practical uses of ANE laws—and rather than arguing for one method of positioning the codes in legal history over others—this chapter explores how ANE prologues and epilogues reflect dynamic and intentional framing processes. Drawing from modern media studies, "framing" is here taken as a constructive process involving sense-making, naming, mapping, context construction, categorizing, and narrative or storytelling to historicize law and power.[17] Framing is a communicative process that creates channels of meaning between text and audience.[18] The communicative process may be coercive as much as familiar, aiming to persuade the audience to adopt a distorted view of reality to encourage their acceptance of a new authority. For the ANE scribes, framing involved a strategic effort to draw upon and reorganize known "frames," such as familiar literary and legal tropes, stacking them into innovative new structures.[19] These framing processes had revolutionary, rhetorical worldbuilding capacities, which formed entirely new spaces for ideas about law and justice to reside. The resulting media—prologues and epilogues—had multidimensional roles. They advanced claims about the king's divine sanction, positioned the law and king in a renovated narrative of history, and effectively remapped both the territorial state and the cosmos. This chapter examines how their authors

14 J. J. Finkelstein, "Ammisaduqa's Edict and the Babylonian 'Law Codes,'" *Journal of Cuneiform Studies* 15 no. 3 (1961): 103.

15 For an overview of important 20th-century contributions to this debate, see Russ VerSteeg, *Early Mesopotamian Law* (NC: Carolina Academic Press, 2000), 13–18; see also Raymond Westbrook, "Cuneiform Law Codes and the Origins of Legislation," *Zeitschrift für Assyriologie* 79 (1989): 201–222.

16 For example, the curse formulae in Hammurabi's epilogue has been cited as proof that Hammurabi expected the laws to be followed, making the whole text binding; see the citations in Westbrook "Cuneiform Law Codes and the Origins of Legislation," 75.

17 This understanding of "framing" is adapted from the scholarship synthesized by Merlijn van Hulst and Dvora Yanow, "From Policy 'Frames' to 'Framing': Theorizing a More Dynamic Political Approach," *American Review of Public Administration* 46 no. 1 (2016): 92–112. The concepts have been deployed to so many different fields that a comprehensive synopsis cannot fit here, but see Michael J. Carter, "The Hermeneutics of Frames and Framing: An Examination of the Media's Construction of Reality," *SAGE Open* (April–June 2013): 1–12.

18 R. M. Entman, "Framing: Towards a Clarification of a Fractured Paradigm," *Journal of Communication* 43 no. 4 (1993): 51–58.

19 Here, "frame" is an object, a fixed thing that one can point to, and "framing" is a process.

employed framing techniques to advance a new understanding of the world: one in which conquests and the violent reordering of politics was painted in claims of continuity, inevitability, and restoration. Prologues and epilogues drew on familiar frames to fortify these radical claims in sense, legitimacy, and geography, even if the corresponding reality was far from stable. These are aspects of the sources that we miss if we presume that the ANE sources are precursors of modern Western streams of ideas—or if we reduce the codes to fixed material monuments instead of seeing them as instantiations of framing processes.

2 Law collections: their contexts and roles[20]

Before diving into the matter of frames and framing, a sketch of the historical context and an overview of the sources are needed. The compositions in question originated in the southern lowland regions of ancient Mesopotamia (modern-day Iraq). In the third and beginning of the second millennia BCE, southern Mesopotamia consisted of a constellation of powerful and competitive city-states. Between ca. 2300 and 1750 BCE, the political history of this area was characterized as a sequence of attempts to unify the mini polities under the power of one dynasty seated in just one city. Sargon, who came from Akkad (an obscure city north of the area just described) was the first warlord to achieve this unification, followed by Ur-Namma of Ur, followed by Hammurabi of Babylon, who was an outsider like Sargon, in this case, an Amorite. Other warlords rambled into politics, claiming kingship, and faded away; some like Sargon were venerated into the first millennium BCE as the archetypes of conquerors. The experimental polities of these short-lived dynasties inevitably fragmented and re-localized.

Despite a high degree of linguistic, cultural, and ethnic diversity in southern Mesopotamia, kingship over its peoples involved self-conscious conformity to the Babylonian culture of the local urban elites and their trappings, traditions, and performances to the extent that scholars today describe such phenomena as "assimilative powers."[21] For example, Hammurabi utilized cuneiform and local Akkadian as the administrative language of his state, just as Sargon had, even though Hammurabi had an Amorite background.[22] Each dynasty drew upon the works, tropes, and trappings of previous kings when designing their visual and written programs. The result of these efforts to "Mesopotamianize" leaves us with an impression of impressive unity, conformity, and continuity,

20 The term "collection" is preferred to "code" by many specialists of ancient Near Eastern history and law because of the aforementioned doubts about legislative function in the sense of a modern law code. The term "collection" puts emphasis on the scribal context of the text. The designation "code" was first applied to this text by Friedrich Delitzsch (1899), using *Code Hammourabi* as a reference to *Code Napoleon*, a comparison with many limitations.

21 Gwendolyn Leick, *The Babylonian World* (Routledge, 2007), 2.

22 Van De Mieroop, *King Hammurabi of Babylon*, 2–3.

but "Mesopotamia" itself is a construct encouraged by this veneer of coherence. Generations of scribes and administrators maintained this impression, what A. Leo Oppenheim dubbed "a stream of tradition."[23]

We can also understand these assimilative efforts as confessions of intrusion. In the context of diversity and fragmentation, anyone not at home was foreign. Dynasties were founded by warlords, usurpers, and invaders—interlopers from the view of any local city-state—who immediately confronted the challenge of how to justify and legitimize their military actions to diverse populations in a region with strong centrifugal political tendencies.

Toward the end of the third millennium BCE, the promulgation of cuneiform law collections and edicts had become central to legitimizing kingship to both gods and the newly subjugated humankind. Prologues and epilogues helped cast and frame new claims to "naturalize" the dynasts. The best-known surviving examples of law collections to emerge from this context are as follows:

- Ur-Namma of Ur (ca. 2100 BCE), Sumerian language, rediscovered in fragments (copies of an unknown monument on cuneiform tablets) throughout the nineteenth century through the twenty-first century
- Lipit-Ishtar of Isin (ca. 1930 BCE), Sumerian, rediscovered the 1890s and after
- Dadusha of Eshnunna (ca. 1770 BCE), Akkadian language, rediscovered in the 1940s
- Laws of Hammurabi (ca. 1750 BCE), Akkadian, stele discovered in 1901, other fragments are known

These texts were drafted at the culmination of conquest activities, once the new territorial state had been staked and power consolidated. In fact, the Laws of Ur-Namma of Ur were very likely drafted by Ur-Namma's son and successor Shulgi after the conquest phase was over and the work of building the state administration was underway.[24] In this case, the laws were retroactively attributed to Ur-Namma as if part of the grand design and justification for conquest all along. As we will see, the prologue implausibly describes Ur-Namma's conquest as a liberation and "restoration" of order and justice.

Scribes composed new legal-literary prologues and epilogues for the laws by curating and reformulating content from older compositions, including a variety of types of royal inscriptions.[25] The prologues and epilogues are highly

23 Leo Oppenheim, "Assyriology: Why and How?," *Current Anthropology* 1 (1960): 410f.

24 D. Frayne, *Ur III Period (2112–2004 BC), The Royal Inscriptions of Mesopotamia* (Toronto University Press, 1997), 44.

25 Barmash, *The Laws of Hammurabi*, 90–100 compares Hammurabi's prologue to his literary and poetic royal inscriptions, calling the latter "models" for the Code while building from the important works of Reis, *Prolog und Epilog* and Victor Avigdor Hurowitz, *Inu Anum ṣirum: Literary Structures in the Non-Juridical Sections of Codex Hammurabi* (Philadelphia, PA: University Museum, 1994).

literary. For example, Hammurabi's prologue employs poetic language, replete with "stylistic elements commonly found in [contemporary] Old Babylonian hymns and epics."[26] The tone contrasts with the rigid and formulaic structure of the laws, which has led to speculations about different authors who spliced the works together, even though the composition is one synthesized treatise.

The texts were originally inscribed on stone monuments—writing on stone was a strictly royal prerogative, a hallmark of kingship—and displayed in semi-public spaces. We have little of these stone monuments today (only fragments), except for the stele of Hammurabi, an inscribed, seven-foot slab of diorite originally displayed in the city of Sippar (see Figure 7.1). None of the other inscriptions survived the numerous political upheavals and rebellions that followed the successive dynastic collapses described previously. We therefore know of the other monuments mostly from scribal curricular exercises, in which learners of cuneiform writing copied monumental inscriptions onto small clay tablets.

Figure 7.1 The Stele of Hammurabi in the Musée du Louvre

26 Barmash, *The Laws of Hammurabi*, 100.

Scribes illustrated knowledge of older texts and applied great skill and inventiveness in redrafting them.[27] This approach to cuneiform pedagogy advanced knowledge of cuneiform writing while helping to inculcate the scribal elite and bureaucratic class with the stories and morals enshrined in the "stream of tradition." Because the existing record of these curricula is woefully incomplete, the law collections are consequently piecemeal and laconic, reconstructed from different and sometimes overlapping copies. Much like the term "Mesopotamia," the notions of "Mesopotamian law" or "Ancient Near Eastern law" are also constructs postulated by modern academics rather than references to a systematized or fully recovered body of materials from ancient times.[28]

As noted, doubts persist about the degree to which the law compositions either guided or reflected judicial decisions, a matter that calls the entire purpose of law collections into question. Most scholars today do not think that the laws of stelae were binding in practice, but the degree to which they informed or reflected the living legal culture is unclear. The laws undoubtedly reflected real social and economic concerns and informed the ways that scribes conceptualized society and justice, but the dynamics of communication between society and law are difficult to reconstruct. We have hundreds of thousands of cuneiform documents on clay tablets—including lawsuits, contracts, receipts, and personal letters about legal conflicts and all kinds of matters of "civil law"—but none of them directly refer to their contemporary law collections or appeal to these laws on judicial matters in an explicit way.[29] The law collections are neither explicitly cited in procedural texts nor recorded as having informed judicial panels, lending to the argument that compositions such as Hammurabi's code are part of an "elaborate royal inscription."[30] To some scholars, the laws are therefore a collection of cases or curated examples to inspire ideas to address new disputes. It has also been suggested that the laws were aspirational while also reflecting society[31] or that the laws

27 For example, see Barmash, *The Laws of Hammurabi*, 141–146.

28 On this, see Laura Culbertson, "Theorizing Legal Pluralism for Early Mesopotamian States and Cities," in *Dieux, rois et capitales dans le Proche-Orient ancien. Compte rendu de la LXVe Rencontre Assyriologique Internationale (Paris, 8–12 juillet 2019)*, eds. Marine Berengér, Francesca Nebiolo, and Nele Ziegler (Leuven: Peeters, 2023), 69.

29 Raymond Westbrook, "Codification and Canonization," in *Ex Oriente Lex: Near Eastern Influences on Ancient Greek and Roman Law*, eds. Raymond Westbrook, Deborah Lyons, and Kurt Raaflaub (MD: Johns Hopkins University Press, 2015), delved into the reasons for this disconnect, questioning whether we should expect a "code" to be cited in the same way then as now. He noted the argument of negative evidence; the fact that the texts do not mention the laws does not mean that they had no influence in how judges and other officials made decisions and thought about justice.

30 P. Michalowski, "The Presence of the Past in Early Mesopotamian Writings," in *Thinking, Recording, and Writing History in the Ancient World*, ed. Kurt A. Raaflaub (Wiley Blackwell, 2014), 153.

31 And see discussion in Martha Roth, "Women and Law," in *Women in the Ancient Near East: A Sourcebook*, ed. Mark Chavalas (London: Routledge), 144.

were enumerated to present "an ideal of justice that was in the purview of the great monarch."[32] Many scholars regard the law collections as works of royal ideology, propaganda, or simply didactic tools whose *Sitz im Leben* was the scribal school curriculum rather than judicial contexts.[33] Martha T. Roth also emphasized the physical and material context of the laws, noting that the medium of Hammurabi's laws—a towering stele—is itself a form of "military muscle-flexing."[34] To that point, it is important to note that most residents of southern Mesopotamia would not be able to read any of the legal monuments, even if they could admire the archaic style of cuneiform on stone. This quick survey of functions indicates the complexity of these so-called codes, both as sources on law and politics and as physical assertions of power in an environment with a history of resisting unification.

A final note here concerns the legacies of these inscriptions. For most of Western civilization and indeed world history, these sources were lost and unknown. To be sure, fragments of the "early" law collections were transmitted through the cuneiform school curriculum well into the first millennium BCE, and the law codes of the Hebrew Bible clearly reflect engagement with ANE legal treatises in structure, phrasing devices, and even specific laws. Nevertheless, there are many temporal disconnections between the time of promulgation and modern translation into Western languages. The stele of Hammurabi itself was plundered when Sippar was sacked by the Elamites around 1100 BCE, who toted it off to Susa (in modern Iran) as a trophy that nobody could read. There, it was partially defaced, displayed, and eventually forgotten until rediscovery by excavation in 1901–2, after which time it was shipped to the Musée du Louvre where it remains on display. Before its rediscovery, a few fragmentary school copies from successive periods were identified. These captivated nineteenth-century scholars, who could only postulate the existence of a complete collection of laws before they were proven correct. The stele inscription was first translated by

32 Michalowski, "The Presence of the Past," 153.

33 E. Otto. 1994. "Aspects of Legal Reforms and Reformulations in Ancient Cuneiform and Israelite Law," in *Theory and Method in Biblical and Cuneiform Law*, ed. Bernard M. Levinson, 160–196. Sheffield Academic Press (1994), 161. To be sure, Hammurabi himself does not argue that the laws should serve as a state-wide legislative code, but they simply offer a passive resource of council for those seeking help. The epilogue states this quite clearly: "Let any wronged man who has a lawsuit come before the statue of me, the king of justice, and let him have my inscribed stela read aloud to him, thus may he hear my precious pronouncements and let my stela reveal the lawsuit for him; may he examine his case, may he calm his (troubled) heart, (and may he praise me), saying: 'Hammurabi, the lord, who is like a father and begetter to his people, submitted himself to the command of the god Marduk, his lord, and achieved victory for the god Marduk everywhere'" (translation after Roth, "Mesopotamian Legal Traditions," 17–18). On this epilogue, see Roth, "Hammurabi's Wronged Man."

34 Roth, "Mesopotamian Legal Traditions," 24.

V. Scheil in 1902,[35] some years after Henry Maine's 1861 *Ancient Law*,[36] and we thus should not overstate the influence of this law code in the modern development of ideas about "ancient law codes" and "ancient law." All of this is to remind us that there is no postulating an unbroken "evolution" of laws, preambles, or prologues, even if we can trace specific facets of the tradition into the West via biblical sources.

3 Innovative framing in ANE law collections

In the context of upheavals, usurpations, and transition across a diverse region, prologues and epilogues served as critical infrastructures for grounding and communicating assertions of power and new claims of authority about justice. Without them, a collection of laws has no meaning or legitimacy, no connection to a specific king, and no basis for presuming supremacy over other claims of justice. These mechanisms are essential in moments of transitional justice, establishing links between content and context. Additionally, drafting prologues and epilogues was itself a constructive framing process that helped scribes participate in a new regime and distribute ideas—or frames—about law and justice beyond a localized setting.

To understand how scribes crafted these mechanisms, we can draw from established theories of frames and framing, with limitations and cautions.[37] Modern media studies, from which our definitions are adapted, deal with an entirely different media environment and a wider scope of audience than our ancient settings. Thus, the terms are adapted only for use here, not in the studies of how frames and framing processes work. Generally, a "frame" can refer to a stable idea, for example, a concept, image, symbol, or metaphor. As organizing principles and points of reference for an audience, frames link and chart information, structuring depictions of the world in a coherent even if distortive way. "Framing" here refers to a process: the communication

35 V. Scheil, *Code des lois de Hammurabi (Droit Privé), roi de Babylone, vers l'an 2000 av. J.-C. In Mémoires de la Délégation en Perse*, vol. IV, Textes élamites et sémitiques 2 (Paris, 1902).

36 Henry Sumner Maine, *Ancient Law: Its Connection to the History of Early Society* (London: J.M. Dent & Sons, 1861).

37 These concepts have been worked over many times for many different fields, always pertaining to contexts very different from ANE societies, but we can adapt core ideas with limitations. Many understandings emanate from the works of Erving Goffman (see volume introduction) and inherit ideas from George Lakoff's works, such as *Don't Think About the Elephant: Know Your Values and Frame the Debate* (Chelsea Green Publishing Co., 2004) and George Lakoff and Mark Johnson, *Philosophy in the Flesh: The Embodied Mind and Its Challenge to Western Thought* (New York: Basic Books, 1999). Studies of framing today often pertain to linguistics, modern media studies, policy-making, and social movement studies—all in contexts that vary substantially from the ANE and would entail different relationships between media and audiences. Thus, here, we adopt core ideas and not assumptions about audience and the scope of accessibility to the media under discussion (royal law collections).

strategies that involve selecting and employing frames and promoting these recognized and salient points of reference to encourage a particular interpretation or perception of the world.[38] This is a dynamic and political process laden with distortions and misleading depictions of objective reality.[39] An effective and persuasive framing process must recruit familiar, socially-shared frames to stake relevance, resonate with the audience, and influence their perception or acceptance of the world depicted. An audience is more likely to accept a distorted framing reality when frames are effective and culturally resonant. Whether or not an audience accepts the message, the framing process can still direct perceptions of future events and messages. Frames establish power in this way, directing how an audience will process ensuing information.[40]

Scribes employed several methods of framing in composing their prologues and epilogues: sense-making, naming (selecting and categorizing), mapping, and narrative.[41] These strategies culminate in new depictions of the world, its political structure, and its history—an entirely new context for law. Thus, the framing devices not only introduced the laws but also constructed and reordered the world that they were meant to inhabit. But before we examine how the scribes employed these strategies, we must consider the audience. Law collections on monuments targeted multiple gazes. Erected in temples, they were directed at divine audiences, but they were undeniably meant to impress contemporary audiences too, conveying power and statements about the kings' role in upholding justice. The epilogues also direct curses at future kings, warning them not to efface or change the inscriptions. Whether or not we believe that all subjects were able to freely access stelae inscribed with laws, it is clear from a number of cues that these compositions were meant to be "decipherable." For example, the image atop the stele of Hammurabi is loaded with visual frames, incorporating "elements of performativity and memorialization that would have resonated in its Mesopotamian cultural setting."[42]

The image shows Shamash (right), the Mesopotamian sun god associated with law and justice, clad in the traditional icons of divinity, facing Hammurabi

38 Robert M. Entman, "Framing: Towards Clarification of a Fractured Paradigm," *Journal of Communication* 43 no. 4 (1993): 52. Entman sees culture as a stock of frames, 52–53.

39 van Hulst and Yanow, "From Policy 'Frames' to 'Framing'," Michael J. Carter, "The Hermeneutics of Frames and Framing: An Examination of the Media's Construction of Reality," *SAGE Open* (April–June 2013): 6.

40 These understandings are synthesized from Entman "Framing," van Hulst and Yanow, "From Policy 'Frames' to 'Framing';" Carter, "The Hermeneutics of Frames and Framing" and M. Edelman, "Contestable Categories in Public Opinion," *Political Communication* 10 (1993): 231–242.

41 This takes inspiration from van Hulst and Yanow, who argued that framing in policy communications today involves three actions: sense-making, naming, and storytelling, "From Policy 'Frames' to 'Framing.'"

42 Kathryn E. Slanski, "The Law of Hammurabi and Its Audience," *Yale Journal of Law and the Humanities* 24 no. 97 (2012): 97. Slanski discusses the case for a "public dimension" aimed at conveying the "state's commitment to justice," 98.

(left) clad in the traditional icons of kingship.[43] Hammurabi receives the rod and ring (or coil and rope) representing surveyor's tools, symbols for setting things right and making things straight, that is, justice. This example of visual propaganda conveys that Shamash is authorizing and equipping Hammurabi to lay the foundations for justice. The use of familiar icons situates this new claim of authority in a familiar, graspable vernacular—even while making a stunning new claim.

Hammurabi's prologue, like those before it, is also steeped in strategies for sense-making, drawing on all kinds of old frames, including tropes of "a non-legal character,"[44] to convey new claims of authority and legitimacy. These literary casings contain resynthesized tropes, poetic devices, and metaphors from royal inscriptions of kings who preceded them.[45] Meshing the new narratives into long-standing, grandiose literary traditions helped to normalize the new king—an outsider and interloper—using the traditional lexicon and frames of kingship, even if this vernacular was as much invented as inherited or pilfered. Some tropes and thematic resemblances are so pronounced and overstated that they lose potency to modern readers ("I established justice in the land," "I restored order," "I did not deliver the orphan to the oppressor," etc.).

A prevailing theme of these tropes is an imperative to *restore* an imagined order, to return the land to a state of justice, and to free the people who were oppressed—a poetic reframing of events for subjects who just experienced a conquest and subjugation. To illustrate, Ur-Namma's inscription reads as follows:

> The orphan was not handed over to the rich man. The widow was not handed over to the mighty man. The man of one shekel was not handed over to the man of one mina. The man of one sheep was not handed over to the man of one ox (Text: the man of one ox was not handed over to the man of one sheep).[46]

Hammurabi's scribes, too, deployed the frame of reversing oppression:

> At that time the gods . . . name me by my name: Hammurabi, the pious prince, who venerates the gods, to make justice prevail in the land, to abolish the wicked and the evil, to prevent the strong from oppressing the weak, to rise like the sun-god Shamash over all humankind . . .

43 See Slanski, "The Law of Hammurabi and Its Audience," 105–106 for a dissection of the imagery.

44 Samuel Greengus, "Some Issues Relating to the Comparability of Laws and the Coherence of the Legal Tradition," In *Theory and Method in Biblical and Cuneiform Law: Revision, Interpolation, and Development*, ed. Bernard Levinson (Sheffield Academic Press, 1994), 74.

45 Barmash, *The Laws of Hammurabi*, 90–100.

46 Adapted from Frayne, *The Royal Inscriptions of Mesopotamia*, 49.

> When Marduk (god of Babylon) commanded me to provide just ways for the people of the land (in order to attain) appropriate behavior, I established truth and justice as the declaration of the land, I enhanced the well-being of the people.[47]

Similarly, part of the prologue of the Laws of Lipit-Ishtar states,

> At that time, I liberated the sons and daughters . . . of the lands of Sumer and Akkad, who were subjugated by the yoke, and I restored order.[48]

Metaphors serve as a type of frame to emphasize this portrayal of events. In line with the above themes, law collections and royal edits alike exhibit a rich lexicon of metaphors for restoration to freedom and protection of the weak. For example,

- **níg-si-sá** (Sumerian) literally means "thing made straight" and is translated as "justice" or "rightness." The component **si-sá** ("to make straight" or "render just") serves as the term for conducting a lawsuit in the earliest periods, in the sense that a legal proceeding has the purpose of straightening things out—bringing order into balance. It is adapted as a term for promulgating a royal legal reform and expanded to mean "justice" and "equity."
- ***mīšarum*** (Akkadian) is a related term in Akkadian, the successor language of Sumerian in royal inscriptions. It refers to a royal decree aimed at redressing social and economic disharmony or restoring a malfunction to the proper order. We find it in the legal formula "Because the king established *mīšarum* in the land," which precedes an executive order, so to speak.
- **ama-ar-gi$_4$** (Sumerian) means "freedom" or a return to freedom/native status (ama=mother, gi$_4$=return). The term is used for making a person equivalent to native status, and by extension, it means manumission. It also possibly referred to the annulment of taxes by royal decree.
- ***andurārum*** (Akkadian equivalent of the former) is usually linked with "freedom." It refers to the remission of debts or taxes, manumission of slaves, and canceling of obligatory services. (The root word [d r r] relates to freedom of movement.) Relatedly, it could also refer to an edict whereupon a king, upon ascension, declared all debts canceled (or claimed to have done so).

Taking all of these framing concepts and metaphors together, it is clear that the Mesopotamian conception of oppression meant bondage, enslavement, and exploitation through debt and other means. In cultures that had normalized

47 From Roth, *Law Collections*, 76 (column i 27 of the stele) and 80–81 (column v 14–24 of the stele).
48 Roth, *Law Collections*, 25.

debt slavery, all of these problems intersected. By contrast, justice meant the peace that ensued from a restoration of people to non-slave status or release from debt. The metaphors of restoration and liberation would presumably hold resonance to the (human) audience and please the gods. Scribes and presumably other elites from all of these periods would find such frames familiar and even expect them. In short, these deeply established packages of liberation and restoration frames were organized into new narratives to make sense of radical claims of kingship. They gave new collections of laws weight and purpose.

Next, framing the laws entailed naming or, more specifically, selecting and categorizing frames. This is a dynamic political activity, as it entails strategically selecting the ideas, actors, and categories that support the framers' agenda. Prologues and epilogues manifest the results of this strategic selection process. These texts name the divine actors who conferred power and judicial authority to the kings, for example. The purpose of divine sanction is not only to establish the king's moral and legal authority but also to emphasize their political legitimacy and supremacy. Ur-Namma is appointed by Nanna, a god of Ur, the political capital of Ur-Namma's dynasty. Hammurabi is pictured receiving royal attributes from the god Shamash, as we have seen, but the prologue also emphasizes that Hammurabi is mandated by Marduk, god of Babylon, Hammurabi's political capital. They also name the king as the primary actor in providing justice despite these texts being most likely composed by scribes writing in the king's voice (I am Hammurabi, the shepherd . . . the capable king . . . the seed of royalty . . . the discerning king").[49]

Mapping is closely related to naming in these texts. The first four columns of Hammurabi's prologue meticulously and boastfully convey his restoration and fulfillment of local rituals across numerous conquered cities. Specific temples and cultural institutions are named as having been repaired, improved, or cleansed by Hammurabi. This portion reads as both a catalog of achievements or pious deeds and as a tour of the newly unified state.[50] As an example of the political nature of this catalog, the major god Ea is omitted from mention, with only his city named (Eridu).

> The omission of Ea may be to strengthen the naming of Marduk, the city-god of Babylon, Hammurabi's capital . . . it may be speculated that Eridu is diminished by the omission of the god's name in favor of the ascension of Babylon.[51]

Following this section, the prologue weaves through the territories and cities of central Mesopotamia, integrating them into a coherent "map" of

49 Roth, *Law Collections*, 77.

50 Barmash, *The Laws of Hammurabi*, 103, argued that this segment does not read so much as a narrative but is phrased with a tone of timelessness, as the deeds have eternal success.

51 Barmash, *The Laws of Hammurabi*, 105.

Hammurabi's state. Place, power, and history are interwoven in this construct. In the Ancient Near East, cities were "anchors of time."[52] In written traditions, cities comprised the organizing principle of political chronologies as much as space. *The Sumerian Kinglist*, a composition from the second millennium BCE, presents a succession of different city dynasties who ruled since the beginning of creation, with the implication that kingship was a moveable institution that leapt from city to city in succession. With this view of time and space in mind, we can see how the scribes aimed to establish a new locus of hegemony and a new "spatial imaginary"[53] based at the conquering king's city. Thus, Ur-Namma's prologue states, "When the gods An and Enlil turned over the kingship of the city of Ur to the god Nanna." Hammurabi's prologue similarly venerates Babylon. The overall implication is clear: these kings are the supreme rulers over other spaces. In Hammurabi's case, he is the custodian of the institutions most important to divine overseers and human subjects.[54]

As each Mesopotamian city has a patron deity, any mention of gods or temples is a reference not just to geopolitical hierarchies but also to the economic structure of the region. City-gods resided in temples, massive complexes that dominated the cityscape. Temple institutions served both as the "houses" of the gods and as centers of economic redistribution, namely, sites of bureaucratic offices where the economic activities of the city and hinterland were coordinated; sometimes, they functioned as the sites of conflict adjudication. To this point, the law collections usually name weights and measures, standardizing them, and some describe the implementation of labor conscription systems, both of which reflect the economic roles of the temples.

To claim that a territorial state had integrated the sundry independent cities under the hegemony of *one* city also amounted to an upheaval in cosmic geography. This claim of a new topography of divine power is clear in Hammurabi's prologue, in which Marduk, the god of Hammurabi's Babylon, is referenced in the opening:

> When the august god Anu, king of the Anunnaki deities, and the god Enlil, lord of heaven and earth, who determines the destinies of the land, allotted supreme power over all peoples to the god Marduk.[55]

52 Eva von Dassow, "Temporality and Periodization in Ancient Near Eastern History," *Social Science History* 36 no. 1 (2012): 122.

53 After A. Smith, *The Political Landscape: Constellations of Authority in Early Complex Polities* (University of California Press, 2003), 210.

54 Ur-Namma's prologue states, "At that time, by the might of Nanna, my lord, I liberated Akshak, Marad, Girkal, Kazallu, and their settlements, and for Usarum, whatever (territories) were under the subjugation of Anshan." The subjugation of places is couched in the language of liberation and restoration as usual. In a longer-winded fashion, Hammurabi announces the subjugation of all great powers and gods of the region, including Nippur, Eridu, Ur, Sippar, Larsa, Uruk, Isin, Kish, Kutfi, Borsippa, Dilbat, Kesh, Lagash, Girsu, Zabala, Karkara, Adab, Mashkan-shapir, Malgium, Mar, Tuttul, Babylon, Akkad, Assur, and Nineveh (which is the definition of "universal" for his time).

55 After Roth, *Law Collections*, 76.

Thus, the city-enumerating strategies rechart the economic, political, and religious landscape up to a cosmic level. Moreover, these techniques advance a concept that would have been unfathomable to people of the Ancient Near East before the end of the third millennium: universal dominion.[56] The prologues reimagine the landscape as coherent and integrated under the hegemony of just one king. Such claims of centrality contended with the political norms that had prevailed for a millennium, that is, the preexisting systems of political and legal plurality. The implications for law suggest a new territorial coherence of law and justice even if a degree of sovereignty is acknowledged for the other metropolises.[57]

The implication of these mapping strategies is that disorder, oppression, and injustice permeated the land. This kind of context construction helped to establish why a law collection was needed and created the space within which the kings could promulgate their laws. In fact, the laws serve to support the claims of past disorder established in the framing texts: whether enacted in society or not, their presence cemented the possibility of eradicating conflict and plurality by postulating a harmonized set of norms that could transcend local judicial traditions and idiosyncrasies under the jurisdiction and protection of one king. Of course, contemporary legal documents (trial records, lawsuits, and contracts) do not show this harmonization to be a reality from one archive to another, and the kings were not necessarily claiming the eradication of local norms but simply the elevation of their role above all local norms. Regional variations in judicial authorities and practices persisted in all periods.

Finally, we come to the strategy of narrative and how scribes historicized these claims and the law itself. Counter to what we might assume, writing was not used to depict history and past events in early ANE sources but only to inform present and future events; "historical issues never stood alone, but were always embedded in a multifaceted discursive matrix that is not always easy to disentangle."[58] In the case of the prologues, the past is bound by very recent events, and the catalyzing event was the decision of the gods to install kingship and universal dominion in a specific god, place, and king. Taking an example from Hammurabi, the prologue opens by citing primordial gods and their selection of destinies for the land.

> They allotted to Marduk, firstborn son of Ea, lordship over all people.
> They exalted him among the Igigi-gods, gave Babylon its august name,

56 This term is taken from Piotr Michalowski, "The Presence of the Past in Early Mesopotamian Writings," in *Thinking, Recording, and Writing History in the Ancient World*, ed. Kurt A. Raaflaub (Wiley Blackwell, 2014), 144–168. This concept of "universal" is not to be conflated with Western uses of the term in the sense of "universal human rights."

57 On this topic, see S. Démaire-Lafont, "Villes et Capitales dans la culture juridique," in *Dieux, rois et capitales dans le Proche-Orient ancien. Compte rendu de la LXVe Rencontre Assyriologique Internationale (Paris, 8–12 juillet 2019)*, eds. Marine Berengér, Francesca Nebiolo, and Nele Ziegler (Leuven: Peeters, 2021), 11–12.

58 Michalowski, "The Presence of the Past," 146.

> made it preeminent among the regions of the world; they established for him within it an eternal reign, whose foundations are as secure as heaven and earth.[59]

That is, Babylon is introduced as the predestined center of the world and kingship, despite whether anyone had experienced, heard, or read otherwise. Correspondingly, Hammurabi is elevated: "At that time, Anum and Enlil to improve the welfare of the people ordained Hammurabi the pious prince who fears the gods."[60]

The future orientation of the texts is most evident in the epilogues. These included summaries of the kings' achievements in establishing justice, eliminating oppression, and restoring order and justice, followed by literary-style curses. The curses are warnings to any future person who would dare alter the law, try to take credit for it, or interfere or efface it in any way under penalty of total eradication from existence and memory. Ur-Namma's epilogue concludes as follows:

> As for the one who erases this inscription and writes his own name there, or who because of its curse incites another to do so, or who erases its inscription and writes his own name, that man whether he be king, lord, or governor . . . May his city be torn down from its summit shrine. May his city not find favor with the god Enlil. May the gates of his city be flung open. May the . . . young men of his city become blind. May the young women of his city not fall asleep.[61]

Lipit-Ishtar similarly states,

> When I established justice in the lands of Sumer, and Akkad, I erected this stela. He who will not do anything evil to it, who will not damage my work, who will not efface my inscription and write his own name on it—may he be granted life and breath of long days; may he raise his neck to heaven in the Ekur temple; may the god Enlil' s brilliant countenance be turned upon him from above.
>
> But he who does anything evil to it, who damages my work, who enters the treasure room, who alters its pedestal, who effaces this inscription and writes his own name (in place of mine), or, because of this curse, induces an outsider to remove it—that man, whether he is a king, a lord, or an ensi-ruler . . . may he be completely obliterated.[62]

59 After Barmash, *The Laws of Hammurabi*, 101.
60 Barmash, *The Laws of Hammurabi*, 101.
61 After Frayne, *Royal Inscriptions of Mesopotamia*, 49.
62 Adapted from Roth, *Law Collections*, 34.

Hammurabi concludes his epilogue by explicitly stating the ambitions of memory:

> In order that the mighty not wrong the weak, to provide just ways for the orphan and the widow, I have inscribed my precious pronouncements upon my stele and set [them] before my image, the just king, in the city of Babylon. . . . By the order of [the god] Marduk, my lord, may my engraved design not be confronted by someone who would remove it. May my name always be remembered faithfully in the Esagil temple (in Babylon) which I love.[63]

Then come the curses to any man whosoever tampers with the stele or the laws; he will face "total obliteration," along with "the obliteration of his city, the dispersion of his people, the supplanting of his dynasty, and the blotting out of his name and his memory from the land," among numerous other afflictions and punishments.[64] The epilogues are thus more concerned with the memory of the king than the integrity of the laws over time, implying that the laws are inextricable from the king and his ability to guarantee them.[65]

4 Conclusion: law as worldbuilding and reordering

The prologues and epilogues belonged in a continuum of ideas and frames, including tropes, literary devices, and potent metaphors. Instead of depicting them as "early" examples of prologues, we can see how scribes made sophisticated use of framing strategies to chart entirely new worlds. These strategies advance the law collections as ideological charters, tools of education and indoctrination, and conduits of literary traditions. The framing process itself would have inculcated scribes in these traditions and ideologies while enabling their participation in new regimes.

The complete texts—prologue, laws, and epilogue—did not seem to have a clear or explicit impact on legal praxis itself but rather presented a political platform for claims about new and tenuous polities.[66] Their appearance primarily in records of scribal education and absence from legal and economic records indicates this imbalance and emphasizes the importance of the whole text to a literary tradition over the laws alone to a legal tradition. Here, the

63 Slanski, "The Law of Hammurabi and Its Audience," 107.

64 Roth, *Law Collections*, 136–137.

65 The curses have been misunderstood as Hammurabi's failure to grasp that laws will change, see Max Hamburger, "Equitable Law: New Reflections on Old Conceptions," *Social Research* 17 no. 4 (1950): 444.

66 It is not expected that the state should have a monopoly on law to exert power; "but it was imperative for the monarchy to be perceived to exert overall power. The state did not have a monopoly on law, but it utilized royal ideology to give the appearance of paramount control," according to Barmash, *The Laws of Hammurabi*, 50–51.

emphasis falls upon the reordering of society, both human and divine, under a single king and single tradition, a novel concept that remained an aberration in Mesopotamian third- and second-millennium history.

Through the prologue and epilogue, Hammurabi frames not just his law code but also his rule in a language that speaks to the stream of tradition familiar to the scribal elites who he must convince in order to maintain his rule. Hammurabi (or the team working on his behalf) attempts to make sense of his new role as a universal king uniting the lands of Mesopotamia through a divine mandate. He names himself as the sole source of authority and the divine powers that bestowed on him such a mandate. He creates a new map of Mesopotamia centered on Babylon and containing all of the major cities of the region under his, Babylon's, and Marduk's authority. All of this is set in a literary context that would be familiar to people who may be uneasy with the political context that they were living through, portraying Hammurabi as a bringer of justice by straightening out a chaotic land and creating order where there was disorder, despite what empirical evidence may tell his audience. And he places all of this within a story that connects back to both political and divine narratives that would be familiar to his audience, providing justifications for his actions that would appear to be outside normally accepted behavior. The literary nature of the prologue and epilogue further inserts the foreigner, Hammurabi, into the Mesopotamian stream of tradition, with the success of this endeavor seen in the continued presence of his code in the curriculum of the scribal elites. By using the concept of frames and framing, we can see the techniques by which scribes accomplished all of this and how they built an entire world and history from the works that preceded them. This helps us understand the law collections in the way that the scribes saw them, not simply as monuments, but as constructions developed from interactive processes, which helped them convey royal claims and ideas about law beyond their circles to elites of the state.

References

Barmash, Pamela. *The Laws of Hammurabi: At the Confluence of Royal and Scribal Traditions*. Oxford: Oxford University Press, 2021.

Bottéro, Jean. *Mesopotamia: Writing, Reasoning, and the Gods*, Translated by Zainab Bahrani and Marc Van De Mieroop. IL: University of Chicago Press, 1992.

Buis, Emilio J. *Taming Ares: War, Interstate Law, and Humanitarian Discourse in Classical Greece*. Leiden: Brill, 2018.

Carter, Michael J. "The Hermeneutics of Frames and Framing: An Examination of the Media's Construction of Reality." *SAGE Open* (April–June 2013): 1–12.

Charpin, Dominique. *Writing, Law, and Kingship in Old Babylonian Mesopotamia*, Translated by Marie Todd. Chicago and London: University of Chicago Press, 2010.

Charpin, Dominique. *Hammurabi of Babylon*. New York: I.B. Taurus, 2012.

Civil, M. "The Law Collection of Ur-Namma." *CUSAS* 17 (2011): 221–286.

Culbertson, L. "Theorizing Legal Pluralism for Early Mesopotamian States and Cities." In *Dieux, rois et capitales dans le Proche-Orient ancien. Compte rendu de la LXVe Rencontre Assyriologique Internationale (Paris, 8–12 juillet 2019)*, edited by Marine Berengér, Francesca Nebiolo, and Nele Ziegler. Publications de l'Institut du Proche-Orient Ancien du Collège de France, vol. 5, 61–82. Leuven: Peeters, 2023.

Démaire-Lafont, Sophie. "Villes et Capitales dans la culture juridique." In *Dieux, rois et capitales dans le Proche-Orient ancien. Compte rendu de la LXVe Rencontre Assyriologique Internationale (Paris, 8–12 juillet 2019)*, edited by Marine Berengér, Francesca Nebiolo, and Nele Ziegler. Publications de l'Institut du Proche-Orient Ancien du Collège de France, vol. 5, 3–24. Leuven: Peeters, 2023.

Edelman, M. "Contestable Categories in Public Opinion." *Political Communication* 10 (1993): 231–242.

Entman, R. M. "Framing: Towards a Clarification of a Fractured Paradigm." *Journal of Communication* 43, no. 4 (1993): 51–58.

Finkelstein, J. J. "Ammisaduqa's Edict and the Babylonian 'Law Codes.'" *Journal of Cuneiform Studies* 15, no. 3 (1961): 91–104.

Frayne, D. *Ur III Period (2112-2004 BC). The Royal Inscriptions of Mesopotamia (RIM), Early Periods*, vol. 3/2. Toronto: University of Toronto Press, 1997.

Greengus, S. "Some Issues Relating to the Comparability of Laws and the Coherence of the Legal Tradition." In *Theory and Method in Biblical and Cuneiform Law: Revision, Interpolation, and Development*, edited by Bernard Levinson, 60–87. Sheffield Academic Press, 1994.

Hurowitz, Victor Avigdor. *Inu Anum ṣirum: Literary Structures in the Non-Juridical Sections of Codex Hammurabi*. Occasional Publications of the Samuel Noah Kramer Fund 15. Philadelphia, PA: University Museum, 1994.

Ishay, Micheline. *The History of Human Rights: From Ancient Times to the Globalization Era*. CA: University of California Press, 2008.

Lakoff, George. *Don't Think about the Elephant: Know Your Values and Frame the Debate*. Chelsea Green Publishing Co., 2004.

Lakoff, George and Mark Johnson. *Philosophy in the Flesh: The Embodied Mind and Its Challenge to Western Thought*. New York: Basic Books, 1999.

Lauren, Paul Gordon. *The Evolution of International Human Rights: Visions Seen*, 3rd ed. PA: University of Pennsylvania Press, 2011.

Lauren, Paul Gordon. "The Foundations of Justice and Human Rights in Early Legal Texts and Thought." In *The Oxford Handbook of International Human Rights Law*, edited by Dinah Shelton. Oxford University Press, 2013.

"Laws of Hammurabi." *Open Educational Resources for the Ancient Near East* (2022), 134. https://stars.library.ucf.edu/ancientneareast/134, last revised May 2023.

Leick, Gwendolyn. *The Babylonian World*. London: Routledge, 2007.

Maine, Henry Sumner. *Ancient Law: Its Connection to the History of Early Society*. London: J. M. Dent & Sons, 1861.

Max, Hamburger. "Equitable Law: New Reflections on Old Conceptions." *Social Research* 17, no. 4 (1950): 441–460.

May, Larry. *Ancient Legal Thought: Equity, Justice, and Humaneness from Hammurabi and the Pharaohs to Justinian and the Talmud*. Cambridge University Press, 2019.

Michalowski, P. "The Presence of the Past in Early Mesopotamian Writings." In *Thinking, Recording, and Writing History in the Ancient World*, edited by Kurt A. Raaflaub, 144–168. Wiley Blackwell, 2014.

Reis, G. *Prolog und Epilog in Gesetzen des Altertums*. München: C.H. Beck, 1984.

Roth, M. T. *Law Collections from Mesopotamia and Asia Minor*. Atlanta, GA: Scholars Press, 1995a.

Roth, M. T. "Mesopotamian Legal Traditions and the Laws of Hammurabi." *Chicago-Kent Law Review* 71, no. 1 (1995b): 13–39.

Roth, M. T. "Hammurabi's Wronged Man." *Journal of the American Oriental Society* 122, no. 1 (2002): 38–45.

Roth, M. T. "Women and Law." In *Women in the Ancient Near East: A Sourcebook*, edited by Mark W. Chavalas, 144–174. London: Routledge, 2014.

Oppenheim, A. L. "Assyriology: Why and How?" *Current Anthropology* 1 (1960): 409–423.

Otto, E. "Aspects of Legal Reforms and Reformulations in Ancient Cuneiform and Israelite Law." In *Theory and Method in Biblical and Cuneiform Law*, edited by Bernard M. Levinson, 160–196. Sheffield Academic Press, 1994.

Scheil, V. "Code des lois de Hammurabi (Droit Privé), roi de Babylone, vers l'an 2000 av. J.-C." In *Mémoires de la Délégation en Perse*, vol. 4. Textes élamites et sémitiques 2. 111–162. Paris, 1902.

Slanski, Kathryn E. "The Law of Hammurabi and Its Audience." *Yale Journal of Law and the Humanities* 24, no. 97 (2012): 97–110.

Smith, A. *The Political Landscape: Constellations of Authority in Early Complex Polities.* University of California Press, 2003.

Steele, Francis Rue. "The Lipit-Ishtar Law Code." *American Journal of Archaeology* 52, no. 3 (1947): 158–164.

van Hulst, Merlijn and Dvora Yanow. "From Policy 'Frames' to 'Framing': Theorizing a More Dynamic Political Approach." *American Review of Public Administration* 46, no. 1 (2016): 92–112.

Van De Mieroop, Marc. *King Hammurabi of Babylon: A Biography.* Oxford: Blackwell Publishing, 2005.

VerSteeg, Russ. *Early Mesopotamian Law.* NC: Carolina Academic Press, 2000.

Voermans, W., M. Stremler, and P. Cliteur. *Constitutional Preambles: A Comparative Analysis.* Edward Elgar Publishing, 2017.

von Dassow, E. "Temporality and Periodization in Ancient Near Eastern History." *Social Science History* 36, no. 1 (2012): 122.

Westbrook, Raymond. "Cuneiform Law Codes and the Origins of Legislation." *Zeitschrift für Assyriologie* 79 (1989): 201–222.

Westbrook, Raymond. "Codification and Canonization." In *Ex Oriente Lex: Near Eastern Influences on Ancient Greek and Roman Law*, edited by Raymond Westbrook, Deborah Lyons, and Kurt Raaflaub, 181–193. MD: Johns Hopkins University Press, 2015.

8 Prefaces in the legal texts of the crusader Kingdoms of Jerusalem and Cyprus

Adam M. Bishop

1 Introduction to the crusades and crusader law

The crusaders who established the Kingdoms of Jerusalem and Cyprus and the other crusader states in the eastern Mediterranean were very interested in the law. They sought to give a legal framework to their conquests, to clearly define the relationships between themselves and the populations that already lived there, and to distinguish themselves from new crusaders who arrived later from Europe. The inhabitants of Jerusalem and Cyprus were "amateurs" in the sense that they had not studied law in universities back in Europe, but they enjoyed discussing and arguing about law, and some were prolific writers. They wrote many legal treatises, some of which were only a few pages long, while others were many hundreds of pages long. Most of these treatises contain some sort of preface or introduction to explain the purpose and content of the work. To better understand these treatises and the information found in their prefaces, we first briefly examine the complex politics involved in the crusades and the crusader states in the twelfth and thirteenth centuries.

The First Crusade was called by Pope Urban II at the Council of Clermont in November 1095. The origins of the crusade are still debated today, but the most immediate cause was a request for help from the Byzantine emperor in Constantinople. The Byzantine Empire was the eastern half of the ancient Roman Empire, and although its inhabitants now mostly spoke Greek, they still rightfully considered themselves the continuation of Rome. By this time in the eleventh century, the eastern empire was largely reduced to the Balkans and Anatolia. Meanwhile, the western half of the empire had been replaced by smaller kingdoms, some of which spoke languages derived from Latin, while others spoke Germanic languages. A new empire centered on Germany and Italy, the so-called Holy Roman Empire, also claimed to be the successor of the Romans in the west.

This was the situation in Europe in 1071 when the Byzantine Empire was defeated at the Battle of Manzikert by the Seljuk Turks, who were nomads from central Asia. The Seljuks, who had recently converted to Islam, then began to settle in Anatolia. By 1095, the Byzantines felt obliged to ask for help from their compatriots in western Europe. The crusade that was organized

DOI: 10.4324/9781003534815-10

after the Council of Clermont was initially meant to help the Byzantines recover their lost territory. At some point, however, the crusaders were convinced that they could continue all the way to Jerusalem, which had once been a significant Christian city in the Roman/Byzantine Empire but had now been under Muslim control for over 400 years, since the seventh century.

A first wave of enthusiastic but poorly prepared crusaders set off toward Constantinople early in 1096. They crossed over into Anatolia and were destroyed by the Seljuks almost immediately. The second, better-organized wave left in August 1096. The expedition lasted almost three years, but the crusaders managed to succeed in their goal of capturing Jerusalem on July 15, 1099. Along the way, the crusaders had also conquered Edessa in Mesopotamia and Antioch in northern Syria.[1]

This success was never repeated by subsequent crusades from Europe, but those who remained in Jerusalem after 1099 carved out a Latin Christian kingdom between the Mediterranean coast and the Jordan River. "Jerusalem" is thus used here to refer to both the city and the crusader kingdom. Because the crusaders adhered to the Latin Catholic rite, they and their kingdom are often called "Latin." Because they usually came from France, or more precisely from the territory of the earlier medieval Germanic people known as the "Franks," they often referred to themselves as Franks and Frankish. These terms were also used by the Muslims and Greeks whom the crusaders encountered in the east, and modern historians also now use them as synonyms for "crusader."

One of the leaders of the First Crusade, Godfrey of Bouillon, was elected as the first ruler of the kingdom at the end of the crusade in 1099. He died the next year in 1100, but despite his short reign, later generations remembered him as a legendary hero who, among other things, established the kingdom's legal system and first set of laws. Godfrey was succeeded by his brother Baldwin of Boulogne, or Baldwin I.[2]

Baldwin I brought other important sites under crusader rule, including the cities of Acre, Tripoli, and Beirut on the coast and the trade routes in the desert to the east. The kingdom eventually encompassed roughly modern Israel, Palestine, and Lebanon and parts of Syria, Jordan, and Egypt. Baldwin

1 An excellent recent overview of the First Crusade is Thomas Asbridge, *The First Crusade: A New History* (Oxford, UK: Oxford University Press, 2004). Other recent histories of the crusades in general include Jonathan Riley-Smith, *The Crusades: A History*, 3rd ed. (New Haven, CT: Yale University Press, 2014), Christopher Tyerman, *God's War: A New History of the Crusades* (New York, NY: Penguin, 2006), and Jonathan Phillips, *Holy Warriors: A Modern History of the Crusades* (New York, NY: Random House, 2009).

2 The biographies of Godfrey and Baldwin I have recently been published in the "Rulers of the Latin East" series. See Simon John, *Godfrey of Bouillon: Duke of Lower Lotharingia, Ruler of Latin Jerusalem, c. 1060–1100* (New York, NY: Routledge, 2017), and Susan B. Edgington, *Baldwin I of Jerusalem, 1100–1118* (New York, NY: Routledge, 2020).

I died in 1118 and was succeeded by his cousin Baldwin of Bourcq (Baldwin II).[3] Under Baldwin II, a short legal code was established at the Council of Nablus in 1120, and in 1123, a treaty was signed with the Italian city-state of Venice, which helped capture the important port of Tyre.

As the strength of the Latin kingdom grew throughout the twelfth century, so too did the response of its Muslim neighbours. By the 1170s, Syria and Egypt were united for the first time under the leadership of one man: Saladin, the sultan of Egypt and Damascus. Saladin invaded the kingdom in 1187, and Jerusalem fell to Saladin later that year. The Third Crusade, led by Richard I of England and Philip II of France, took back most of the Mediterranean coast but not Jerusalem itself, and the kingdom was re-established in Acre in 1191. This kingdom is sometimes known as the "second kingdom" or the "Kingdom of Acre," although the Franks continued to abstractly call it "Jerusalem." Another crusader kingdom was also established on the island of Cyprus, which was conquered by Richard of England during the crusade.

In 1225, the queen of Jerusalem, Isabella II, married the Holy Roman Emperor, Frederick II, but Isabella died in 1228 giving birth to their son, Conrad. In 1229, Frederick arrived in person and claimed to be regent for the infant Conrad both in Cyprus and in Jerusalem. Frederick also managed to regain the city of Jerusalem, not by force, but rather through a treaty with the sultan of Egypt. Some of the local crusader nobility supported him, but he was opposed by the powerful Ibelin family, whose members and allies were also the ones who were writing treatises on the kingdoms' laws.

The Franks lost Jerusalem to Egypt once again in 1244, and in response, a new crusade arrived from Europe led by King Louis IX of France. Louis' crusade failed, but the pressure of the crusade caused the sultan of Egypt to be overthrown by his Mamluk slave-soldiers, who established their own dynasty in Egypt in 1250. It was the Mamluks who finally conquered the Kingdom of Jerusalem's remaining territory until only Acre remained in Frankish hands. Acre was destroyed in 1291, ending the crusader presence on the mainland. Cyprus, however, continued to be ruled by its Frankish kings until it fell under Venetian control at the end of the fifteenth century.

This second period of the Kingdom of Jerusalem is the most important period for the subject of this chapter. Most of the surviving Frankish legal texts were written in the mid-thirteenth century when the Latins looked back to 1187 and earlier in the twelfth century as a kind of mythological age of glory. This was, in part, a way to counter the growing influence of newly arrived European crusaders, particularly Emperor Frederick and his representatives.

The Kingdoms of Jerusalem and Cyprus in the thirteenth century were ruled by a relatively small group of Franks who came from many different parts

3 Baldwin II is also the subject of a new biography in the same series: Alan V. Murray, *Baldwin of Bourcq: Count of Edessa and King of Jerusalem (1100–1131)* (New York, NY: Routledge, 2021).

of Europe, including France, Italy, Germany, and England.[4] Below the Franks in the social hierarchy were native eastern Christians, who were often referred to collectively as "Syrians" by the crusaders. For the most part, they were Greek, Armenian, and Syriac Orthodox Christians, but there may also have been some Copts from Egypt, Georgians, Ethiopians, and adherents of the Church of the East in Persia (known to the Franks as "Nestorians"). In Lebanon, there were also Maronite Christians, who, by the thirteenth century, had united with the crusaders' Latin-rite church. There were also Jewish residents and a small number of Samaritans.[5] The Muslim population was divided into Sunnis, whose spiritual head was the Abbasid caliph in Baghdad, and Shi'ites, who followed the Fatimid caliph in Cairo until the Fatimids were overthrown by Saladin in 1171.[6] However, the crusaders were not very interested in the non-Christian population. While they were happy to distinguish between different groups of eastern Christians, most Franks probably had no idea about the divisions and sects within Judaism and Islam.

2 Influences on crusader law

Into this environment, the Franks introduced their own legal system, which, at least according to their own traditions, was meant to treat all of the different ethnic and religious groups equally. Crusader laws were based on the different kinds of law that the Franks already knew in Europe, specifically, ancient Roman law, the laws of the Germanic peoples who had replaced the Roman Empire in western Europe, and the law of the Roman church, known as canon law.

Canon law began to be collected in the eleventh and twelfth centuries, around the same time as the crusades, from many separate older documents. One of the earliest standard compilations was the *Decretum*, collected by the jurist Gratian in the first half of the twelfth century. Since it was derived from so many different sources from many different parts of the Latin Catholic world over many centuries, canon law was often inconsistent or contradictory, and Gratian's task was to harmonize all of these sources into a coherent text. Canon law was meant to apply to all Catholics, no matter their social status or where they lived, from Iceland to Jerusalem and beyond.[7]

4 Joshua Prawer, "Social classes in the Latin Kingdom: The Franks," in Kenneth M. Setton, ed., *A History of the Crusades, vol. V: The Impact of the Crusades on the Near East*, eds. Norman P. Zacour and Harry W. Hazard (Madison, WI: The University of Wisconsin Press, 1985), pp. 171–192.

5 Joshua Prawer, "Social classes in the Crusader States: The 'Minorities'," in *A History of the Crusades, vol. V*, pp. 65–70.

6 Prawer, "Social classes: The 'Minorities'," pp. 62–65.

7 For an introduction to canon law, see James A. Brundage, *Medieval Canon Law* (London: Longman, 1995).

Roman law also existed in discordant, inconsistent texts, and the same effort was made to develop a coherent legal code but much earlier in the sixth century during the reign of the eastern Roman emperor Justinian. The various parts of this compilation, perhaps most notably the section called the *Digest*, remained in use in the eastern empire, but since the western half of the empire had already disappeared by that point, Justinian's code was largely forgotten there. In the eleventh and twelfth centuries, again coincidentally around the time of the crusades, Justinian's code was rediscovered and was subject to academic study, especially at the University of Bologna in Italy.[8]

Starting in the fifth century, the western half of the Roman Empire was replaced by Germanic kingdoms ruled by the Germanic tribes that had settled in or conquered different parts of the empire, namely, the Lombards, Visigoths, Vandals, and original Franks, among numerous others. The Germanic rulers used their own legal customs, while the surviving Roman inhabitants of their kingdoms continued to use Roman law. Due to the influence of written Roman law, the originally unwritten Germanic customs began to be written down as well.[9]

Now that the Roman law compilations of Justinian and the canon law compilations of the church were being formally studied in the schools and universities of western Europe, there was an explosion in new legal codes in the twelfth and thirteenth centuries. Communities throughout Europe were inspired to write down their own laws and customs. For example, in France, the customs of the royal domain around Paris were written down in the mid-thirteenth century (often known as the *Établissements de Saint Louis*), and those of Normandy, Toulouse, Champagne, and Brittany, among others, were compiled in the thirteenth and fourteenth centuries. The longest legal text from France was the customs of Clermont-en-Beauvais, recorded by Philippe de Beaumanoir. All of these customary laws applied only to the areas in which they were written; there was no set of customs for the entire Kingdom of France.[10] Similarly, there was no single set of laws for the Holy Roman Empire, but there were local legal treatises; in southern Italy and Sicily, Holy Roman Emperor Frederick II (who was also king of Sicily) published a legal code known as the *Liber Augustalis*. Meanwhile, in more centralized monarchies such as Spain and England, there were law books that applied to the entire kingdom. In Spain, for example, King Alfonso X of Castile published the *Siete Partidas*, an enormous legal code in six books.

8 Stephan Kuttner, "The Revival of Jurisprudence," in *Renaissance and Renewal in the Twelfth Century*, eds. Robert L. Benson, Giles Constable, and Carol D. Lanham (Cambridge, MA: Harvard University Press, 1982), pp. 301–304.

9 Katherine Fischer Drew (trans.), *The Laws of the Salian Franks* (Philadelphia, PA: University of Pennsylvania Press, 1991), introduction, pp. 29–31.

10 *The* Coutumes de Beauvaisis *of Philippe de Beaumanoir*, Translated by F. R. P. Akehurst (Philadelphia, PA: University of Pennsylvania Press, 1992), introduction, pp. xiii–xiv.

The Frankish nobles in Jerusalem and Cyprus also took part in this trend. The Franks—usually members of the anti-imperial Ibelin family or their supporters—compiled numerous legal treatises to explain the legal system used in Acre and the other crusader cities on the mainland and in the cities of Cyprus. But they also had a secondary motivation: to explain how the laws had been created in the past, back in the early days of the crusades, when Jerusalem was captured in 1099 and before it was lost again in 1187.

Jerusalem and Cyprus had a two-tiered legal system: there was a "high court" for the noble, Latin, aristocratic class and a "burgess court" for the non-noble population, including Latin merchants, settlers from western Europe, and the eastern Christian, Muslim, and Jewish inhabitants. The legal codes used by both courts are collectively known by historians as the "assizes of Jerusalem." For the high court, the major legal texts include the anonymous *Livre au Roi*, the earliest surviving text, probably written around 1200;[11] the lengthy treatise of John of Ibelin, one of the most important crusader nobles in the mid-thirteenth century;[12] the equally important but shorter treatise of Philip of Novara;[13] and the minor works of Geoffrey le Tor[14] and James of Ibelin.[15] The assizes of the burgess court were written by an anonymous author also in the mid-thirteenth century.[16] All of these authors wrote in Old French, the common language of the kingdom.

There were also church courts for religious concerns, which used the canon law collections common to the entire Latin church. However, only a few short legal documents survive that were written specifically for the church in Jerusalem; the most important are the canons of the Council of Nablus, which are actually the earliest example of crusader laws, written in Latin in 1120.[17]

3 Prefaces in ancient and medieval law

Many medieval legal codes are introduced with a preface, whether they are Roman law or Germanic customs, "national" law codes, for example, the *Liber Augustalis* or *Siete Partidas*, or local legal treatises such as those found in France or the crusader kingdoms. Some previous scholarship has been written about prefaces in classical and medieval Latin literature in general, where

11 *Le Livre au roi*, ed. Myriam Greilsammer (Paris: Académie des inscriptions et belles-lettres, 1995).

12 John of Ibelin, *Livre des Assises*, Edited by Peter W. Edbury (Leiden: Brill, 2003).

13 Philip of Novara, *Le Livre de forme de plait*, Edited and Translated by Peter W. Edbury (Nicosia: Cyprus Research Centre, 2009).

14 Geoffrey le Tor, *Livre de Geoffroi le Tor*, in *RHC, Lois*, vol. 1 (Académie royal des inscriptions et belles-lettres, 1841, repr. 1967), pp. 435–450.

15 James of Ibelin, *Livre de Jacques d'Ibelin*, in *RHC, Lois*, vol. 1, pp. 453–468.

16 *Les Livres des Assises et des Usages dou Reaume de Jerusalem sive Leges et Instituta Regni Hierosolymitani*, ed. Édouard H. Kausler (1839).

17 Benjamin Z. Kedar, "On the Origins of the Earliest Laws of Frankish Jerusalem: The Canons of the Council of Nablus, 1120," *Speculum* 74 (1999): 310–335.

introductions are almost always present and follow certain standardized forms. In contrast, not much work has been done on prefaces in law books, especially on legal literature that was not written in Latin.[18] Furthermore, even when prefaces are present in medieval Latin literature, they might not literally be prefaces—introductory material could be placed in the middle as a way to explain what has already been written or as an epilogue at the end to explain the entire work.[19]

Latin books of canon law sometimes do not have a preface or any other sort of introduction at all. Gratian's *Decretum* in the twelfth century, for example, has no preface; it simply begins with the first chapter. To the contrary, for medieval legal treatises that do have introductions, "a prologue gave an author occasion to explain his purpose, his method of working, and anything else he cared to impart to readers."[20] Additionally, a preface might exist in a modern critical edition of a medieval text, even though the prefatory material is not present in every medieval manuscript of the text. In other words, sometimes some medieval readers could have been reading a text with a preface, while others reading the same text would not have seen a preface.

When prefaces do exist, they follow certain rhetorical trends. "A prologue's function was already well-defined in late-antique rhetorical theory: to introduce or explain the intent and content of a work."[21] Prefaces often took the form of a letter to the author's patron, the person who had asked them to write the work or who paid for it. The patron could be a real person, but the author might also have invented one as a rhetorical device. In the sixth century, Justinian's *Codex* opens with a letter to the Roman Senate in Constantinople, explaining the purpose and scope of the work.[22] The preface of Justinian's *Institutes* also explains the purpose of the entire *Corpus*—to provide the empire with a set of coherent laws for the western and eastern halves of the Empire, which Justinian was attempting to restore in the sixth century. There is another opening letter, but this time, it is addressed to young law students.[23]

The *Digest*, perhaps the most influential part of the *Corpus* for later medieval law, appeals to a patron, but in this case, Justinian "desired that God

18 Jacqueline Hamesse, *Les prologues médiévaux: Actes du Colloque international organisé par l'Academia Belgica et l'Ecole française de Rome avec le concours de la F.I.D.E.M. (Rome, 26–28 mars 1998)* (Brepols, 2000), x.

19 Tore Janson, *Latin Prose Prefaces: Studies in Literary Conventions* (Acta Universitatis Stockholmiensis, 1964), xii.

20 Robert Somerville and Bruce Brasington, *Prefaces to Canon Law Books in Latin Christianity: Selected translations, 500–1245* (New Haven, 1998), 15.

21 Bruce C. Brasington, "Prologues to Canonical Collections as a Source for Jurisprudential Change to the Eve of the Investiture Contest," *Frühmittelalterliche Studien* 28 (1994): 228.

22 Bruce W. Frier, *The Codex of Justinian: A New Annotated Translation, with Parallel Latin and Greek Test, based on a translation by Justice Fred H. Blume*, vol. 1 (Cambridge: Cambridge University Press, 2016), 1–13

23 *Justinian's Institutes*, Edited by Paul Krueger, Translated by Peter Birks and Grant McLeod (Ithaca, NY: Cornell University Press, 1987), 33.

should become the author and patron of the whole work."[24] The preface goes on to explain how and why it was written and, as in the *Codex*, how it should be taught to students. Like the *Codex*, it also continues with an abstract discussion of justice, which is listed as the first chapters rather than a continuation of the introduction.[25]

In twelfth-century literature, authors typically no longer used the device of writing to a real or fictional patron and instead used a more direct introduction that explained the purpose and scope of the work, how it was organized, and why it was necessary to write such a work at all. Medieval authors still typically used classical Latin rhetorical devices such as false humility, claiming that they were incompetent to write such a work when older and better books covered the same topic.[26]

But the rhetorical device of claiming God as the patron remained popular in legal literature, as it had been centuries earlier for the books in Justinian's *Corpus*. The work would also typically be placed in a Biblical or otherwise religious context. For example, in the *Liber Augustalis* issued by Emperor Frederick II in 1231, Frederick declared that God had entrusted him, "whom he elevated beyond hope of man to the pinnacle of the Roman Empire and to the sole distinction of the other kingdoms at the right hand of the divine power," with the responsibility of rendering justice to his citizens, at least in the Sicilian part of his empire.[27]

In Spain, the massive *Siete Partidas* issued by Alfonso X has no distinct preface, but introductory material takes up most of what is labelled as *Laws* and *Titles* in the first *Partida*. Alfonso wanted "to make it understood what kind of laws these are, in what manner they are divided, and why they are so named."[28] But the religious element in the first *Partida* is so strong that Alfonso even blurs the line between canon law and secular law—matters such as the appointment of priests and rules for monastic orders usually had no place in secular law books.

The author of the *Customs of Beauvaisis*, Philippe de Beaumanoir, also noted that he was responsible for rendering justice to his people but only in the relatively small local area of the county of Clermont in France. Philippe's patron was a real person, his lord Robert, the Count of Clermont, and a son of the king of France, Louis IX. The Latin Catholic church is similarly not absent from Philippe's work: in his preface, he claimed a Biblical justification for writing, as he noted that "God commanded us to love our neighbour as

24 Alan Watson (trans.), *The Digest of Justinian*, vol. 1 (Philadelphia, PA: University of Pennsylvania Press, 1985), p. xliii.

25 *The Digest of Justinian*, vol. 1, 1–10.

26 Brasington, 230.

27 James M. Powell (trans.), *Liber Augustalis* (Syracuse, NY: Syracuse University Press, 1971), 4–5.

28 Samuel Parsons Scott and Robert I. Burns, *Las Siete Partidas, Volume 1: The Medieval Church: The World of Clerics and Laymen* (Philadelphia, PA: University of Pennsylvania Press, 2001), 1.

ourselves," and he was therefore compelled to ensure that everyone in the county knew the laws that applied to them.[29]

The *Établissements*, compiled by Robert of Clermont's father Louis IX, are relatively short compared to the customs of Beauvaisis or the *Siete Partidas*. They are also rather less religious and more political in nature. The preface states that the *Établissements* were promulgated before Louis left on his crusade against Tunis in 1270 to provide the kingdom (or at least the royal domain in the north) with a standard code of laws. Louis wanted "the people beneath us to be able to live honestly and in peace" while he was away.[30] Louis in fact never returned, as he died of dysentery outside the walls of Tunis.

Meanwhile, in the eastern Roman Empire, the Byzantine Greeks still used Justinian's Latin *Corpus* and continued to write new legal treatises in Greek. The eighth-century *Ecloga*, for example, was issued during the reign of Emperor Leo III and was still in use in the twelfth century when the Franks arrived on crusade; it probably had some influence on the earliest crusader laws. In the preface to the *Ecloga*, Leo noted that the older *Corpus* had become difficult to understand, and he wanted to simplify it—the same reasoning given by Justinian for creating the *Corpus* in the first place. The preface is also heavily religious and Biblical in nature: all justice is attributed to God, who established the Roman empire on Earth and placed Leo III at its head, and there are quotes from the Gospels, Psalms, Proverbs, and from the wisdom of the Israelite king Solomon.[31]

Therefore, from the law codes of the sixth-century Roman emperor Justinian to the legal texts influenced by Justinian in Greek, Latin, and vernacular languages in western Europe, from the eighth to the thirteenth centuries and beyond, there are a few common trends. The authors are heavily indebted to their Christian beliefs, and they quote from the Bible. There is also often a secular or political reason for compiling the laws, for example, to provide a ruler's territories with a written legal code or to give a sense of unity to their lands and the people living in them. Sometimes, these explanations are found in a distinct preface, but sometimes, they are simply treated as the first section of the laws.

The same tendencies are found in the legal treatises written in the crusader states in the twelfth and thirteenth centuries. They were of course imprinted with the Latin Christianity of their western European homeland, and some of them therefore quote from the Bible. Some instead claim to be part of a Roman law tradition, and some refer to a specific event or events that spurred the creation of new law. Additionally, some of the legal texts construct a sort

29 Philippe de Beaumanoir, *The Coutumes de Beauvaisis of Philippe de Beaumanoir*, Edited by F. R. P. Akehurst (Philadelphia, PA: University of Pennsylvania Press, 1992), 3–5.

30 F. R. P. Akehurst (trans.), *The Établissements de Saint Louis: Thirteenth-Century Law Texts from Tours, Orléans, and Paris* (Philadelphia, PA: University of Pennsylvania Press, 1996), 3–4.

31 Edwin Hanson Freshfield, *A Manual of Roman Law: The Ecloga. Published by the Emperors Leo III and Constantine V* (Cambridge: Cambridge University Press, 1926), 66–70.

of mythological past to portray the crusader legal tradition as something that had "always" existed and could not be changed.

4 The Council of Nablus

The earliest legal text from Jerusalem, and the only one written entirely in Latin, is the canons issued at the Council of Nablus, which took place on January 16, 1120. The surviving text of the canons contains a short preface explaining why the council was called: over the previous four years, there had been a famine in the Kingdom of Jerusalem after its crops were destroyed by mice and locusts. The previous year, in 1119, the armies of Jerusalem and Antioch had also been defeated at the Battle of *Ager Sanguinis*—the "field of blood"—by the Seljuks of Syria and Mesopotamia. The king and the patriarch of Jerusalem, along with the other important secular and ecclesiastical leaders of the kingdom, decided that

> there is only one refuge for them: to call upon the mercy of God and, with a certain amount of justice, to impose some restraint on the sins of the people who are sliding into error. Once they have stopped sinning, as we have read happened to the people of Israel, divine vengeance might cease, and the mercy of God, who does not desire the death but rather the correction of the sinner, might rescue his penitent sons from the imminent danger of the enemy.[32]

The council was mainly concerned with ecclesiastical matters, and, as in church law, the twenty-five laws that it produced are known as canons. Most of the canons deal with adultery, prostitution, sodomy, illicit sexual relations with Muslims, bigamy, false accusations, or theft; in other words, matters that were covered by canon law or would later be covered by the assizes of the high court and burgess court in the thirteenth century. The first three canons, however, are quite separate from the issue of crime and punishment: they settle a dispute between the king and the church over the collection of tithes and taxes from royal property, a purely canon law matter.[33]

The canons are somewhat strange compared to the later law books from the thirteenth century, as the punishments are usually some sort of mutilation (of the nose or the tongue, for example, or of the genitals for sexual offenses). The *Novels*, the new laws added to Justinian's *Corpus* back in the sixth century, may be a possible influence on the Nablus canons, since the *Novels* have numerous references to mutilation as a punishment. However, the more direct source

32 Translation by the author, from Kedar, "On the Origins of the Earliest Laws of Frankish Jerusalem," 331–332.

33 Hans Mayer, "The Concordat of Nablus," *Journal of Ecclesiastical History* 33 (1982): 533.

might be the eighth-century *Ecloga*, as mentioned earlier.[34] The Franks might have been aware of the *Ecloga* and other Byzantine legal texts through the Greek population of Antioch or Jerusalem or from the Greeks and Armenians of Edessa, where both Baldwin I and Baldwin II had been counts before becoming kings of Jerusalem.[35]

At this point in the history of the crusader kingdom, there was no mythologizing of Godfrey of Bouillon. Godfrey had died only 20 years earlier, well within the living memory of most people, including his cousin who was now King Baldwin II. But the process of mythologizing the past was clearly already underway: it is implied that a generation earlier during the crusade, the Franks used to be morally upstanding, but they had since fallen into decadence and sin, which caused all of their current misfortunes in 1120.

The Nablus canons occupy a rather odd position among the legal texts from Frankish Jerusalem. They have almost nothing in common with the much more extensive treatises written by the Franks in the thirteenth century. Even when looking only at the preface, there is hardly anything like it in the later law books.

5 The minor thirteenth- and fourteenth-century law books

The earliest of these thirteenth-century legal books is the anonymous *Livre au roi*, or the "Book for the King." It was probably written sometime between 1197 and 1205 when Isabella I was queen of Jerusalem along with her husband, King Aimery of Cyprus; it therefore probably represents the earliest attempt to write down the kingdom's laws or to recreate them after Jerusalem was lost to Saladin in 1187.[36] The earliest surviving version of the *Livre* from the thirteenth century does not have an introduction, but a much later manuscript had introductory material added to it, including the story of the founding of the kingdom and its laws by Godfrey of Bouillon (taken from the treatises of Philip of Novara and John of Ibelin, as is discussed later). Myriam Greilsammer's modern edition of the *Livre* omits this prefatory material.[37]

Aside from the *Livre au Roi*, the majority of the legal treatises were written in the mid-to late-thirteenth century. Most are rather substantial texts, but there are two very short ones attributed to James of Ibelin, the son of John of Ibelin,[38] and another ally of the Ibelin family, Geoffrey le Tor.[39] James was the count of Jaffa after the death of his father in 1266 until the capture of the city by the Egyptian Mamluks in 1268. Afterward, he lived on Cyprus, where

34 Kedar, "On the Origins of the Earliest Laws of Frankish Jerusalem," 313.

35 Kedar, "On the Origins of the Earliest Laws of Frankish Jerusalem," 320–321.

36 Myriam Greilsammer (ed.), *Le Livre au roi* (Paris: Académie des inscriptions et belles-lettres, 1995), introduction, 83–86.

37 Greilsammer, *Le Livre au roi*, 56–59.

38 *Livre de Jacques d'Ibelin*, in *RHC Lois*, vol. 1.

39 *Livre de Geoffroi le Tor*, versions A and B, in *RHC Lois*, vol. 1.

his legal treatise was written in 1276. James' text is always placed after his father John's treatise in the two medieval manuscripts that contain his work and when it is printed in modern editions. The very brief preface to James' work states that since the reader has just finished reading John's text, James is simply explaining a handful of laws with his own interpretation. James himself did not write a preface, but one was added later by copyists. One of the two manuscripts notes that James dictated his work to a scribe on his deathbed in 1276.[40] According to this preface, the assizes are presented "purely," without all of the digressions on court procedure and pleading that are found in John's lengthy treatise and without the personal commentary found in Philip of Novara's work.

The other short thirteenth-century text is by Geoffrey Le Tor, a knight in the Kingdom of Cyprus. Of the various thirteenth-century authors in Jerusalem and Cyprus, only Geoffrey placed his text in a Biblical context, as the authors of the canons of Nablus had done in the twelfth century. Like James of Ibelin's text, Geoffrey's work is found in two medieval manuscripts, but in this case, the two texts attributed to him are quite different, for unknown reasons. One of the manuscripts has a preface, in which Geoffrey says the work is based on two verses from Psalms, namely, Psalms 110 and 51, about the nature of justice and wisdom.[41] Although he does not quote from the same Psalms, Geoffrey's reasoning is similar to the preface of the eighth-century Byzantine *Ecloga*, which (as noted previously) also quoted Psalms on the nature of law and justice. Like James of Ibelin, Geoffrey wanted to write a simpler text, avoiding all the lengthy digressions and commentaries in the longer texts of John of Ibelin and Philip of Novara, but he was much more hostile than James of Ibelin to what he considered to be the subtle trickery found in the longer treatises. According to Geoffrey, these tricksters "have no fear of God, they glorify themselves in their malice."

One of the larger legal treatises from the thirteenth century is the assizes of the burgess court. The burgess assizes were intended for the non-aristocratic and non-Latin population of the Kingdom of Jerusalem, as opposed to the other courts and law books, which were all meant for the Latin aristocratic "high court."

The burgess assizes were probably written in about 1240, but they are anonymous, and the author did not provide a preface, so we do not know exactly when they were written or the circumstances in which they were produced. However, the first several chapters are, in a sense, a preface, as they introduce the concept of law and justice in general, with quotations from both

40 Peter Edbury, "Reading John of Jaffa," in *The Experience of Crusading, vol. 2*, eds. Peter Edbury and Jonathan Philips (Cambridge: Cambridge University Press, 2003), 141.

41 Adam M. Bishop, "'As It Is Said in Scripture and in Law': The Bible in the Crusader Legal System," in *The Uses of the Bible in Crusader Sources*, eds. Elizabeth Lapina and Nicholas Morton (Leiden: Brill, 2017), 445–446.

the Bible and Roman law.[42] However, they are not a preface in the sense that the author described the purpose or contents of the work.

A later text, dating from after the Kingdom of Jerusalem had been destroyed on the mainland, is the *Livre contrefais*. It is also known as the *Livre du plaideant et du plaidoyer* and inaccurately as the *Abrégé du livre des assises de la cour des bourgeois* (as it was once assumed to be a summary of the burgess court assizes).[43] The author is anonymous, and it was written later than the other texts, in fourteenth-century Cyprus. It is also relatively short, although much longer than James' or Geoffrey's texts.

Most importantly for us here, it has a distinct preface that fits with the typical sorts of prefaces described earlier: it is dedicated to a patron, and the author (though anonymous) humbly reminds the reader that he is unfit to write such a work. However, the patron in this case is not a living person and is not the patron said to be God himself but instead "his blessed mother, Our Lady the Virgin Mary," a religious figure but nevertheless a human from whom the author hopes to receive "a small spark, in accordance with my own smallness" so that he may "begin this book, and complete and accomplish it perfectly."[44] This short preface also extends into what is labeled as Chapter 1 of the text, where the author repeats his indebtedness to Mary before briefly explaining the purpose of the work, that is, to name the officers of the court of justice in Cyprus, their duties, and the customs and assizes that govern them. The author's interpretation of the assizes actually begins in what is labeled in the text as Chapter 2.

6 John of Ibelin and Philip of Novara

Returning to the mid-thirteenth century, the two principal legal texts of thirteenth-century Jerusalem and Cyprus were the *Livre des Assises* by John of Ibelin and the *Livre de forme de plait* by Philip of Novara. They both have prefaces. Philip's is a short paragraph, while John's is much lengthier, taking up almost seven pages in Edbury's modern edition.

Philip's prologue is dedicated to "a friend," perhaps another member of the Ibelin family, and explains that the work is meant to teach this friend how to argue cases in court.[45] But there is also material in the middle of the text, in chapters 47 and 48, which are a kind of interlude or as Edbury called them, "hinge chapters,"[46] to explain the current situation of the legal system and what Philip believed the laws had been a hundred years earlier during the first period of the Kingdom of Jerusalem.

42 Joshua Prawer, *Crusader Institutions* (1980, repr. Oxford: Sandpiper Books, 1998), 385–390.

43 *Abrégé du Livre des Asssises de la Cour des Bourgeois*, in *RHC Lois*, vol. 2, 234–352.

44 *Abrégé*, 234.

45 Philip of Novara, prologue, 34, trans. 205.

46 Philip of Novara, ch. 47, 119, trans. 259, note 179.

But these chapters in Philip's book have a hidden agenda. He claimed that the laws had indeed always been written down—but this was the same period when the Holy Roman Emperor Frederick II was attempting to impose his own rule over both kingdoms. Therefore, historians believe that it is likely that Philip was making up a story in order to show that they were independent states with their own laws that took precedence over whatever Frederick wanted to impose.

These written laws were known as the "*Letres dou Sepulcre*", according to Philip, as they were housed in a special box in the Church of the Holy Sepulchre in Jerusalem where they could be consulted only in an elaborate ceremony in the presence of the king and other nobles of the kingdom. The *Letres* were lost when Saladin overran the kingdom in 1187, so a generation later, the thirteenth-century jurists knew them only as oral traditions:

> Things could be done much better and settled far more securely in the kingdom of Jerusalem before the land was lost. For all the *assises*, good *usages* and good customs, that is to say any *usage* of great authority, were written down and kept at the Sepulchre, and they called them the 'Letters of the Sepulchre' because each *assise*, usage and custom was written separately on a large noble parchment. Also there were the usages and the *assises* of the *cour des bourgeois* as well as those of the High Court. Each parchment had the seal and sign manual of the king and also of the patriarch and the viscount of the Jerusalem. All the 'Letters' were in large writing, and the first initial was a large letter illuminated in gold, and all the rubrics were crimson. The *usages* and the customs that were there in writing came into being after much discussion and great deliberation, enquiry and thought.[47]

Despite living many decades after the *Letres* were lost, Philip claimed to have heard this story from much older people who had been alive in 1187 and had seen the *Letres* in person.[48]

John of Ibelin's account of the foundation of the kingdom and its legal system is similar to Philip's, although he does not mention the *Letres* specifically. The earliest medieval manuscripts of John's treatise do not include the story of the creation of the legal system at all; this portion of his preface was added later and was copied from Philip, possibly by John himself or perhaps by another scribe.[49] In John's version of the story, the first ruler of Jerusalem, Godfrey of Bouillon, established the kingdom's high court and burgess court. Godfrey himself presided over the high court, while a royal representative presided over the burgess court. The native eastern Christians (the "Syrians")

47 Philip of Novara, ch. 47, 119, trans. 259.
48 Philip of Novara, ch. 47, 119, trans. 260.
49 Edbury, "Law and custom in the Latin East," 72–73.

came to Godfrey and asked him to establish a third court for them as well. At the same time, the kingdom's laws were first written down.[50]

Modern historians generally agree that the story of the *Letres* is rather suspicious and has clear mythological elements. Israeli historian Joshua Prawer, for example, noted that it was similar to the legendary foundations of the ancient Greek and Roman legal systems.[51] Peter Edbury, the editor and translator of John and Philip's treatises, believed that it was a "legal fiction" invented to solve the dispute between the Franks and Emperor Frederick and his representatives. If they could convince Frederick that they had a long tradition of legal independence going all the way back to the First Crusade in 1099, then perhaps they could weaken the emperor's claims to rule over the two kingdoms.[52]

At first, the legal scholars in Jerusalem and Cyprus were not successful. Emperor Frederick was a fellow scholar of the law and produced his own *Liber Augustalis* for the kingdom of Sicily around the same time, but he and his representatives were not convinced by the legal nitpicking of the jurists in the east. He continued to assert his rights over the two kingdoms and the rights of his infant son Conrad. The local Frankish nobles governed from Acre, while Frederick's lieutenants took control of the kingdom's other major port, Tyre. The imperial representatives were finally expelled from Tyre in 1242, when Conrad was about 15 years old and eligible to rule on his own. But since he remained in Europe and never arrived in the east, the Frankish nobles essentially staged a coup—under their interpretation of the law, they declared that no one could be king if they did not rule in the east in person. In the end, Frederick's lieutenants were removed by military and political force, not by legal arguments. The Frankish nobles invited queen Alice of Cyprus to rule in Conrad's place.[53]

The story of the kingdom's foundation as presented by Philip and John has also been studied as an attempt to create an ideal mythological past.[54] Although Godfrey of Bouillon quickly became famous as the first ruler of Jerusalem, he came from an obscure background. Later generations of Franks in Jerusalem and those back in Europe apparently felt that it was necessary to invent a legendary life and background for him in order to justify the legitimacy of his rule.[55] It did not take long to turn him into a legendary figure: in the first few

50 Edbury, *Livre des Assises*, prologue, 52–54.
51 Prawer, *The Crusaders' Kingdom: European Colonialism in the Middle Ages* (Praeger, 1972, repr. Phoenix Press, 2001), 122.
52 Edbury, "Law and custom in the Latin East," 73.
53 Edbury, *The Kingdom of Cyprus and the Crusades, 1191–1374* (Cambridge: Cambridge University Press 1993), 80–82.
54 Edbury, *Livre des Assises*, introduction, 34.
55 Jérôme Devard, "La 'légendarisation' de Godefroy de Bouillon: Étude d'un processus de mythification (xiie-xiiie siècle)," in *Autour des Assises de Jérusalem*, eds. Jérôme Devard and Bernard Ribemont (Classiques Garnier, 2018), 32.

years after the crusade and after his death in 1100, he was already immortalized as the hero of the "Crusade cycle" of epic poetry, such as the *Chanson d'Antioche* and numerous other poems.[56] He was depicted as a pious Christian, a genius military commander, and a fearsome warrior who could cut down Muslim enemies, their horses, and wild animals with a single blow from his sword. The legal scholars of Jerusalem and Cyprus were also part of this effort. They turned Godfrey into a "founding lawgiver," a figure like Moses from the Bible, or the semi-legendary founders of the Greek and Roman legal systems.[57]

7 Conclusion

The prefaces of the Frankish legal codes have certain elements in common, which they share with other medieval law books and with law books from other periods of history, as seen in the other contributions in this volume. The prefaces of the legal treatises of Jerusalem and Cyprus are typically religious in nature, dedicated to God rather than to a wealthy human patron, and inspired by passages from the Christian Bible. This is not surprising, as the crusades were essentially military expeditions organized by the Latin church. This also fits with some of the themes of this volume—authority and authorship. The author is considered less important than the ultimately divine source and authority of the laws; in some cases, the legal treatises are anonymous, and we do not know the author at all.

Medieval legal prefaces in general might simply describe the layout of the work, but some prefaces explain that the work was written in response to a specific event that required the population to be better acquainted with their laws. This is sometimes the case with the Frankish treatises: something disastrous happened, and the Franks wanted to issue laws to correct the morals and behaviours of themselves and their subjects or they wanted to restore lost laws that had existed (or that they believed had existed) before the disaster. Here, too, we can see the themes present elsewhere in this volume: the Franks wanted to create a legal system or re-create one that they believed they had lost in the past; they wanted to make sure everyone understood the laws, regardless of their ethnicity or language; and above all, they wanted to assert that they had their own coherent set of laws that could not be changed by outside influences from Europe.

The most significant theme is history or a possibly imaginary history that was created and spread through their legal treatises. The Franks sometimes adopted the popular image of Godfrey of Bouillon as a legendary military

56 Devard, "La 'légendarisation' de Godefroy de Bouillon: Étude d'un processus de mythification (xiie-xiiie siècle)," 37.

57 Simon John, *Godfrey of Bouillon: Duke of Lower Lotharingia, Ruler of Latin Jerusalem, c. 1060–1100* (New York, NY: Routledge, 2017), 238.

hero and founder of the kingdom and its legal system, which was meant to prove that there was full continuity between the events of 1099 and the first half of the thirteenth century, even though the city of Jerusalem itself was lost in 1187. If indeed there was complete legal continuity, then, as authors such as Philip of Novara and John of Ibelin would argue, Frederick II's claims over the kingdom would be invalidated. The legal treatises and their prefaces were weaponized as another arm of the political and military forces that were employed against Frederick.

References

Akehurst, F. R. P. (trans.). *The Coutumes de Beauvaisis of Philippe de Beaumanoir*. University of Pennsylvania Press, 1992.

Akehurst, F. R. P. (trans.). *The Établissements de Saint Louis: Thirteenth-Century Law Texts from Tours, Orléans, and Paris*. University of Pennsylvania Press, 1996.

Asbridge, Thomas. *The First Crusade: A New History*. Oxford University Press, 2004.

Beugnot, Auguste-Arthur (ed.). *Livre de Geoffroi le Tor. RHC, Lois*, vol. 1. Académie royal des inscriptions et belles-lettres, 1841.

Beugnot, Auguste-Arthur (ed.). *Abrégé du Livre des Assises de la Cour des Bourgeois. RHC, Lois*, vol. 2. Académie royal des inscriptions et belles-lettres, 1843.

Bishop, Adam M. "'As It Is Said in Scripture and in Law': The Bible in the Crusader Legal System." In *The Uses of the Bible in Crusader Sources*, edited by Elizabeth Lapina and Nicholas Morton. Brill, 2017.

Brasington, Bruce C. "Prologues to Canonical Collections as a Source for Jurisprudential Change to the Eve of the Investiture Contest." *Frühmittelalterliche Studien* 28 (1994).

Brundage, James A. *Medieval Canon Law*. Longman, 1995.

Devard, Jérôme. "La 'légendarisation' de Godefroy de Bouillon: Étude d'un processus de mythification (xiie-xiiie siècle)." In *Autour des Assises de Jérusalem*, edited by Jérôme Devard and Bernard Ribemont. Classiques Garnier, 2018.

Drew, Katherine Fischer (trans.). *The Laws of the Salian Franks*. Philadelphia: University of Pennsylvania Press, 1991.

Edbury, Peter W. *The Kingdom of Cyprus and the Crusades, 1191–1374*. Cambridge University Press, 1993.

Edbury, Peter W. (ed.). *Livre des Assises*. Brill, 2003a.

Edbury, Peter W. "Reading John of Jaffa." In *The Experience of Crusading*, vol. 2, edited by. Peter W. Edbury and Jonathan Philips. Cambridge University Press, 2003b.

Edbury, Peter W. (ed. and trans.). *Le Livre de forme de plait*. Cyprus Research Centre, 2009.

Edgington, Susan B. *Baldwin I of Jerusalem, 1100–1118*. Routledge, 2020.

Freshfield, Edwin Hanson (trans.). *A Manual of Roman Law: The Ecloga: Published by the Emperors Leo III and Constantine V*. Cambridge University Press, 1926.

Frier, Bruce W. (trans.). *The Codex of Justinian: A New Annotated Translation, with Parallel Latin and Greek Test, based on a Translation by Justice Fred H. Blume*, vol. 1. Cambridge University Press, 2016.

Greilsammer, Myriam (ed.). *Le Livre au roi*. Académie des inscriptions et belles-lettres, 1995.

Hamesse, Jacqueline. *Les prologues médiévaux: Actes du Colloque international organisé par l'Academia Belgica et l'Ecole française de Rome avec le concours de la F.I.D.E.M. (Rome, 26–28 mars 1998)*. Brepols, 2000.

Janson, Tore. *Latin Prose Prefaces: Studies in Literary Conventions.* Acta Universitatis Stockholmiensis, 1964.
John, Simon. *Godfrey of Bouillon: Duke of Lower Lotharingia, Ruler of Latin Jerusalem, c. 1060–1100.* Routledge, 2017.
Kausler, Édouard H. (ed.). *Les Livres des Assises et des Usages dou Reaume de Jerusalem sive Leges et Instituta Regni Hierosolymitani.* Adolf Krabbe, 1839.
Kedar, Benjamin Z. "On the Origins of the Earliest Laws of Frankish Jerusalem: The Canons of the Council of Nablus, 1120." *Speculum* 74 (1999).
Kruger, Paul (ed.). *Justinian's Institutes*, Translated by Peter Birks and Grant McLeod. Cornell University Press, 1987.
Kuttner, Stephan. "The Revival of Jurisprudence." In *Renaissance and Renewal in the Twelfth Century*, edited by Robert L. Benson, Giles Constable, and Carol D. Lanham. Harvard University Press, 1982.
Mayer, Hans E. "The Concordat of Nablus." *Journal of Ecclesiastical History* 33 (1982).
Murray, Alan V. *Baldwin of Bourcq: Count of Edessa and King of Jerusalem (1100–1131).* Routledge, 2021.
Phillips, Jonathan. *Holy Warriors: A Modern History of the Crusades.* Random House, 2009.
Powell, James M. (trans.). *Liber Augustalis.* Syracuse University Press, 1971.
Prawer, Joshua. *The Crusaders' Kingdom: European Colonialism in the Middle Ages.* Praeger, 1972.
Prawer, Joshua. *Crusader Institutions.* Oxford University Press, 1980.
Prawer, Joshua. "Social Classes in the Crusader States: The 'Minorities'." In *A History of the Crusades, vol. V: The Impact of the Crusades on the Near East*, edited by Kenneth M. Setton, Norman P. Zacour, and Harry W. Hazard. University of Wisconsin Press, 1985a.
Prawer, Joshua. "Social Classes in the Latin Kingdom: The Franks." In *A History of the Crusades, vol. V: The Impact of the Crusades on the Near East*, edited by Kenneth M. Setton, Norman P. Zacour, and Harry W. Hazard. University of Wisconsin Press, 1985b.
Riley-Smith, Jonathan. *The Crusades: A History*, 3rd ed. Yale University Press, 2014.
Scott, Samuel Parsons and Robert I. Burns. *Las Siete Partidas, Volume 1: The Medieval Church: The World of Clerics and Laymen.* University of Pennsylvania Press, 2001.
Somerville, Robert and Bruce Brasington. *Prefaces to Canon Law Books in Latin Christianity: Selected Translations, 500–1245.* New Haven, 1998.
Tyerman, Christopher. *God's War: A New History of the Crusades.* Penguin, 2006.
Watson, Alan (trans.). *The Digest of Justinian*, vol. 1. University of Pennsylvania Press, 1985.

9 No mere metaphor

The state of nature as a framing device

Susan Longfield Karr

1 Introduction: the power of imagination

The state of nature is among the most ubiquitous metaphors in public discourse and popular culture. At once distant and ever-present, the images that the words conjure up, ranging from peaceful cooperation to bloody conflict, are so familiar that, by sheer repetition, they have constituted a collective memory underpinning (and tying together) Western political and legal thought for more than 500 years. Indeed, the metaphor is so pervasive that modern audiences (and past ones) can quickly render its meaning—or use it to impart their own—with little concern for why and how it came to be so culturally and rhetorically familiar in the first place.

Embedded within the metaphor, however, lurks the question of origins, not least because the state of nature exists everywhere and nowhere, is everlasting and ephemeral, and refers to man's pre-political condition (before state formation) as much as his post-political one (after state fragmentation). Whether used to describe life before the advent of mutual company, to explain the founding moment of a particular society, or to envisage life after its collapse, the invocation of the idea and metaphor stirs up memories in those who have no lived experience of them, not because it is a universal condition, but instead because we imagine it to be. Moreover, those memories are collective and historical—or so it seems.

For example, the 'state of nature' might invite one to imagine a time when humankind toiled and roamed after being expelled from Eden (as told in the Bible). In contrast, another individual might picture a bucolic and empty place where man's morally neutral existence was unencumbered by mutual company beyond brief encounters to satisfy basic needs (as envisioned by Jean Jacques Rousseau).[1] Yet another might picture a slow and gradual process in which humankind, naturally sociable and morally inclined, were drawn to

1 Jean-Jacques Rousseau, *The Discourse on the Origin of Inequality*, Translated by Maurice Cranston (New York: Dover Publications, 2004); and *The Social Contract*, Translated by Maurice Cranston (London: Penguin Books, 2004).

DOI: 10.4324/9781003534815-11

live together and to pursue the common good, founding—by practice rather than decree—villages, towns, cities, and kingdoms (as explained by Ulrich Zasius).[2] For some, a seminal event might also come to mind, namely, when heads of household willingly joined together to establish a civil society governed by civil laws to escape uncertainty and instability and to pursue justice, peace, and security in tandem (as presented by Cicero and Jean Bodin).[3] For others, the metaphor might bring to mind a condition permeated by violence, a war of all against all perpetuated by fear of losing life and limb (as described by Thomas Hobbes).[4] No matter which image (or countless others) our imagination serves up, the impression is so familiar that we might not know (with certainty) whether we acquired the memory through school instruction, public discourse, or independent study.

What we do know, however, is that the arguments or narratives in which the metaphor is employed are calling us to action—to either lament humanity's propensity to transgress the law or pay homage to the tenacity of the human spirit to pursue justice; to despair of the current conditions or to rally against adversity in troubled times; or to defend things as they are or to enact and support fundamental change. Invoking the image of the state of nature not only invites us, in other words, to speculate what the state of nature was and why humankind ultimately left it (to pull resources, to escape tyranny, or to benefit from mutual benevolence?) but also forces us to ponder what might lead us to slide from our current condition back into it (environmental catastrophe, sectarian violence, or weapons of mass destruction?).

Much like visions of the state of nature, the answers to these questions are multiple.[5] Whether in thick outline or breathtaking specificity, both images of and stories about the state of nature can be found in texts stretching from ancient times to the present, expressed in multiple genres ranging from political treatises to science fiction sagas and presented in formats extending from frescos to video games. That the idea of the state of nature extends beyond our imaginations to these other forms, combined with the persistence of our fascination with them, serve as evidence that the obsession with the origins of society (and state-making) runs as deep as the obsession with societal collapse (and failed states). Moreover, we are so accustomed to the state of nature

2 Ulrich Zasius, "In laudem legum oratio," in *Lucubrationes* (Basel: Ioannem Frobenium, 1518); and "De iustitia et iure (Lecture)," in *Opera omnia*, eds. Johann Ulrich Zasius and Joachim Münsinger von Frundeck (Lyon: Sebastianum Gryphium, 1550).

3 Marcus Cicero, *De inventione, de optimo genere oratorum, topica*, Translated by H. M. Hubbell (Cambridge, MA: Harvard University Press, 1949) and Jean Bodin, *Six Books of the Commonwealth (Six livres de la République)* [1576], Edited by Kenneth Douglas McRae (Cambridge, MA: Harvard University Press, 1962).

4 Thomas Hobbes, *De Cive* [1642; 1651] (Cambridge: Cambridge University Press, 1998); and *Leviathan* [1651] (Cambridge: Cambridge University Press, 1991).

5 For an expansive collection of essays that explore the state of nature in political and legal thought, see Mark Somos and Anne Peters (eds.), *The State of Nature* (Leiden: Brill, 2021).

adorning arguments crafted by politicians, pundits, philosophers, and theorists that their absence catches us off guard. We expect it to be used as leverage because its use as leverage is ubiquitous.

Even so, all of these uses tend to distract us from the metaphor's most potent applications. Indeed, the ability to summon quickly and efficaciously imagined, collective, and narrative memories—tied to our greatest hopes and deepest fears—makes it one of the most effective framing devices within the Western legal tradition.[6] This essay aims to illustrate this by focusing on select works by sixteenth-century Renaissance jurists—in Southern and Northern Europe—who invoked images of the state of nature as a preface and warning to call for change in the face of what they regarded as the intractable degradation of law and society in their time.[7]

In this way, Renaissance jurists transliterated legal theory into legal history in various ways and across an expansive range of texts, including lectures, treatises, and dialogues.[8] A common feature among all of these texts that are explored in the second half of this chapter, regardless of form, was their use of the state of nature to ply the historical imagination of their readers to affect a sleight-of-hand, namely, to transform their calls for (sometimes radical) reform into appeals to restore something lost (or even that never was). They did this even though the principles, conditions, and ideas that they aimed to re-establish had no concrete history beyond the collective memory and imagined

6 Here, the term framing device refers to using an overarching and organizing idea such as a preface or, in this case, imagined history to provide meaning to the arguments, critiques, and ideas presented in the text of the Renaissance jurists, that is, legal scholars who, during the fifteenth and sixteenth centuries, integrated humanist methodologies—such as philological analysis and historical contextualization—into the study and interpretation of Roman law under examination. In a broad outline, it also refers to the narrative technique that they used. In the latter case, an author might use it to illuminate aspects of the main story by integrating images or vignettes from a secondary one to make their argument or to conjure a fuzzy background to draw out their criticisms of the world that they lived in more vividly. Or one might briefly invoke the customs and conventions that communities shared in common before the advent of states to emphasize the inter-state relations between states after they were founded. For a robust discussion of frames and framing devices and the scholarship that defines and debates them, see this volume's "Introduction: More than Marginal: The Complex Work of Framing Devices."

7 During the Italian Wars (1494–1559), all of the major powers and significant political entities in central and southern Europe came into conflict—first, over Naples and then, over Milan—in the first half of the sixteenth century. These conflicts were accompanied by socioeconomic crises, peasant revolts, religious reformations, and violent confrontations with non-European empires stretching from the eastern Mediterranean to the Atlantic. All of this prompted—and served as catalyst for—calls for legal reform within states and a reconsideration of the relation between states (especially with regard to the category of just war).

8 The jurists at the center of section three of this chapter, "*The state of nature as a framing device: four case studies in brief*," wherein these texts are central, are German humanist and jurist Ulrich Zasius (1461–1535), English humanist and jurist Thomas More (1478–1535), Spanish (second) scholastic jurist Francesco de Vitoria in Spain (1483–1546), and French humanist jurist Jean Bodin (1530–1596).

scenarios that they summoned to enhance their arguments. Moreover, they appealed to the historical imagination and collective memories of their target audiences so effectively that, five hundred years removed, their narratives and critiques as to why the state exists and the purposes that it was meant to fulfill still resonate and even continue to shape our understanding of states and civil society—and the limits of legal frameworks within and between them—in our present time.

However, before any of this can be shown, it is first necessary to sort out the sense and meaning of some key terms at work within this chapter. For our purposes, the most straightforward definitions to clarify are historical imagination and collective memory. The most complex and unwieldy shorthand term that needs our attention is the Western legal tradition.[9] In exploring the latter, it is also necessary to introduce the Roman legal category *ius gentium*, often rendered in English as the law of nations.[10] Attention to *ius gentium* is essential because, for the Renaissance jurists featured in the second half of this chapter, it was synonymous with the state of nature, insofar as it conjured a time before civil societies were founded, described the realm of interstate relations after such societies were established, and served as a reminder of the condition that humankind might fall back into if the state failed. The history referred to—and communicated by—*ius gentium* also enveloped customs, conventions, rights, and obligations shared among all, regardless of time and place, that Renaissance jurists (and others) could summon to provide evidence that some laws, institutions, and practices had fallen out of association with justice and thus needed immediate adjustment, annulment, or wholesale reform.

9 For accessible and comprehensive accounts of the history and development of the Western legal tradition, see Manlio Bellomo, *The Common Legal Past of Europe, 1000–1800*, 2nd ed., Translated by Lydia G. Cochrane (Washington, DC: The Catholic University of America Press, 1995); Harold Joseph Berman, *Law and Revolution I: The Formation of the Western Legal Tradition* (Cambridge, MA: Harvard University Press, 1983); Berman, *Law and Revolution II: The Impact of the Protestant Reformation on the Western Legal Tradition* (London: Belknap, 2004); Tamar Herzog, *A Short History of European Law: The Last Two and a Half Millennia* (Cambridge, MA: Harvard University Press, 2018); Antonio Padoa-Schioppa, *A History of Law in Europe: From the Early Middle Ages to the Twentieth Century*, Translated by Caterina Fitzgerald (Cambridge: Cambridge University Press, 2017); and Peter Stein, *Roman Law in European History* (Cambridge, MA: Cambridge University Press, 1999).

10 Scholarship that explores the complex and multifaceted history of *ius gentium* includes Chris Covell, *The Law of Nations in Political Thought: A Critical Survey from Vitoria to Hegel* (New York: Palgrave Macmillan, 2009); Dante Fedele, "*Jus gentium: The Metamorphoses of a Legal Concept* (Ancient Rome to Early Modern Europe)," in *Empire and Legal Thought: Ideas and Institutions from Antiquity to Modernity*, ed. Edward Cavanagh (Leiden-Boston: Brill Nijhoff, 2020), 213–250; Martti Koskenniemi, *The Gentle Civilizer of Nations: The Rise and Fall of International Law, 1870–1960* (Cambridge: Cambridge University Press, 2002); Koskenniemi, *To the Uttermost Parts of the Earth: Legal Imagination and International Power 1300–1870* (Oxford: Oxford University Press, 2021); and Susan Longfield Karr, *Jus Gentium in Humanist Jurisprudence: On Justice and Right* (Leiden: Brill, 2023).

2 Preliminaries: shorthand terms, long-standing meanings

In the present context, historical imagination (distinct from conjectural history) refers to the ability to summon a time that never was so that it can anchor a narrative that relies on no empirical evidence. Those who call upon historical imagination tend to use persuasive rhetoric to appeal to the passions or virtues of their audiences, which, in turn, helps them construct a collective memory of what was and, as necessary, what could have been.[11] In its most basic sense, collective memory refers to a shared pool of common knowledge among two or more members of the same social group, whether bound by culture, religion, education, legal framework, or communal identity (or all of the above). In this chapter, the definition is expanded to include a pool of shared knowledge among members of the same professional group, namely, Renaissance jurists and their audiences across early modern Europe, ranging from kings, emperors, and popes to a cadre of professionals engaged in (and scholars fascinated by) lawmaking, statecraft, and the origins and organization of civil society.[12]

Although the jurists—humanist and scholastic—featured here approached questions of law and rights by applying different methods to effect different ends, they shared several features in common. Specifically, they each appealed to historical imagination. They drew from (and contributed to) the collective memory of their target audiences to critique current conditions and suggest, in broad strokes, alternative legal and social frameworks. They also shared an understanding of idioms and concepts that they could draw on, implicitly and explicitly, knowing that their audience, especially those with legal training (gained by attending universities or the Inns of Court), would understand. Together, their political and legal thought helped construct the riggings that ultimately tied many legal traditions into a singular, seemingly systematic one. Today, we refer to the legal artifice that they helped to assemble as the 'Western legal tradition.'[13] We call it this even though such a monolithic tradi-

11 For discussions that emphasize (in multiple ways) the importance of imagination—historical and political—to the development of legal and political thought, see Joseph Canning, "Ideas of Empire in the Thought of the Late Medieval Roman Law Jurists," in *Empire and Legal Thought: Ideas and Institutions from Antiquity to Modernity*, 280–299; Kathleen Davies, *Periodization and Sovereignty: How Ideas of Feudalism and Secularization Govern the Politics of Time* (Philadelphia, PA: University of Pennsylvania Press, 2017); Constantin Fasolt, *The Limits of History* (Chicago: University of Chicago Press, 2004); Koskenniemi, *To the Uttermost Parts of the Earth*; Lauro Martines, *Lawyers and Statecraft in Renaissance Florence* (Princeton, NJ: Princeton University Press, 1968); Martines, *Power and Imagination: City-States in Renaissance Italy* (New York: Vintage Books, 1979); and Anthony Pagden (ed.), *The Languages of Political Theory in Early-Modern Europe* (Cambridge: Cambridge University Press, 1987).

12 This understanding of collective memory and the kind of work that it does in creating common identities is informed by Davies, *Periodization and Sovereignty* and Judith Pollmann, *Memory in Early Modern Europe, 1500–1800* (Oxford: Oxford University Press, 2017).

13 See note nine.

tion never existed in the past and does not exist (as more than a shorthand descriptive term) in the present.

Freed from the burden of details, the term 'Western legal tradition' allows political and legal theorists, jurists, and historians (past and present) to compress disparate and incongruent customs, practices, and institutions within and between cultures—that spanned thousands of years and stretched across vast landmasses and oceans—into a composite whole. The term also serves as a framing device that limits the scope of a common legal past to a millennium or two while simultaneously transforming the messy, haphazard, and disparate histories within it into a seamless narrative anchored in and by an immutable and transcendent conception of justice and right.[14] It is, no doubt, remarkable that one term can accomplish so much. Even so, the term can neither disguise all of the tensions that it is meant to elide nor provide the legal artifice that it describes with stability.

Taken on its own—without the help of historical imagination, collective memory, or burnished narratives to smooth out bumps and fill in cracks—we might assume that the tradition that the shorthand term calls to mind would fall under the weight of its many internal contradictions. It is a distinct product of history, yet its legitimacy relies on being ahistorical. It is the creation of a specific people, but it claims to transcend cultural markers. It draws its authority from being older than memory, yet nearly every legal code embedded within it carries its own unique narrative of its origins.[15] It is regarded as a gift from the gods, but it is considered by many as one of the most significant institutions that humans have ever created. Its structure bears the scars of passion and whim, yet its authority rests on its appeal to universal reason and logic. Seen from afar, it appears to be a splendorous monument to human ingenuity, whereas up close, it reveals itself as a gilded collection of contingencies and fictions (legal and historical).

14 Significant examples include A. P. D'Entreves, *Natural Law: An Introduction to Legal Philosophy* (London: Hutchinson University Library, 1972); Miia Halme and Pamela Slotte (eds.), *Revisiting the Origins of Human Rights* (Cambridge, UK: Cambridge University Press, 2015); Micheline Ishay, *The History of Human Rights: From Ancient Times to the Globalization Era* (CA: University of California Press, 2008); Koskenniemi, *To the Uttermost Parts of the Earth*; Paul Gordon Lauren, *The Evolution of International Human Rights: Visions Seen*, 3rd ed. (Philadelphia, PA: University of Pennsylvania Press, 2011); Quentin Skinner, *The Foundations of Modern Political Thought. Volume I: The Renaissance* (Cambridge: Cambridge University Press, 1978); Skinner, *The Foundations of Modern Political Thought. Volume 2: The Reformation* (Cambridge: Cambridge University Press, 1978); Brian Tierney, *The Idea of Natural Rights: Studies on Natural Rights, Natural Law, and Church Law, 1150–1625* (Atlanta, GA: Scholars Press, 1997); Richard Tuck, Natural *Rights Theories: Their Origin and Development* (Cambridge: Cambridge University Press, 1979); and John Witte, Jr., *"A Short History of Western Rights." In God's Joust, God's Justice: Law and Religion in the Western Tradition*, Edited by John Witte, Jr. (Grand Rapids, MI: Wm. B. Eerdmans Publishing Company, 2006), 31–48.

15 See Bishop and Rabin in this volume to explore this in the context of the crusader state and Medieval English and Scottish legal traditions, respectively.

Given all of its contradictions and tensions, it is fair to ask, what keeps the 'Western legal tradition' from buckling under its weight? What keeps it afloat? As simple as it sounds, one of the devices that has provided a semblance of stability and durability to the 'Western legal tradition' for more than 500 years is the idea of the state of nature. Jurists, theorists, scholars, and statesmen have invoked it not only to explain the necessity for specific legal practices and procedures but also to invite audiences to consider whether it would even be possible to live in a world that lacked the institutions and principles that structure the 'Western legal tradition' in the first place. Used to defend and define city-, empire-, or nation-states, the state of nature provided historical and moral authority to the laws that structured them and to those who administered and governed them.[16] Just as important, the state of nature has also been employed as a warning to foretell what lies ahead if laws are permitted to be bent by power or be shattered by influence or to be used to foster fear, division, and hate rather than to serve justice and the common good.[17]

For example, some legal theorists used the state of nature metaphor as the frame and foundation of the rule of law to explain and justify change, especially in the aftermath of war and conquest. In this way, they invoked historical and moral arguments to elide the distance between the new and the old, arguments in which the state of nature and the imagined scenarios and collective memory that it constructed were central. Others tied the state of nature to well-worn narratives (moral, legal, and historical) to establish how far those defeated in war (civil or interstate) had fallen from justice. They also used it to emphasize the proximity between the founders and fathers to the new regime to assure their auditors, readers, and patrons that the victors aimed to restore justice and the rule of law rather than depart from it.[18] Finally, a few invoked the state of nature to compare it with their present conditions. Often idealized as pristine, the metaphor was used to illuminate the corruption of legal structures, cruelty, or the violation of rights (civic and natural) of an ever-changing collection of persons at the hands of unjust rulers and legislators, old and new.

No matter if such theories were grounded in man's propensity towards amity or enmity, the appeal to the greatest hopes and deepest fears of readers served as evidence for why these theories offered viable solutions to the

16 In addition to the essays in *The State of Nature* edited by Somos and Peters, see Annabel S. Brett, *Changes of State: Nature and the Limits of the City in Early Modern Natural Law* (Princeton, NJ: Princeton University Press, 2011); and D. E. Luscombe, "The State of Nature and the Origin of the State," in *The Cambridge History of Later Medieval Philosophy: From the Rediscovery of Aristotle to the Disintegration of Scholasticism, 1100–1600*, eds. Anthony Kenny, Eleonore Stump, Jan Pinborg, and Norman Kretzmann, (Cambridge, UK: Cambridge University Press, 1982), 757–770.

17 The most vivid example of this use of the state of nature, as both prelude and warning, is Hobbes's *Leviathan*.

18 Here, the image of the state of nature used to frame the 1776 American Declaration of Independence comes to mind.

problems that plagued communities before civil society was established, in the wake of political conflict, and for those societies that collapsed under the weight of conquest, tyranny, or discord. All of this was possible because, in each case, lawyers and jurists were able to recast new customs, institutions, and laws as manifestations of principles and norms embedded within a long-established legal tradition—latent principles that either their predecessors were not yet sophisticated enough to grasp or manifest principles that their contemporaries have wholeheartedly transgressed. Accordingly, they set down the blueprints for—and the legitimization of—the modern state as the most rational and stable alternative to injustice, instability, and vulnerability that humankind had ever known.

That the appeal to and the construction of the state of nature and the modern state were coeval and, indeed, entirely dependent on one another enabled jurists and political theorists alike to affect a sleight-of-hand: they anchored their arguments in historical imagination while they presented them as if they were grounded in historical-legal evidence stretching back to a community's founding or drawn from the lived experience of its most recent and current inhabitants. It did not matter that their evidence, arguments, and conclusions were fictions; what mattered was how they simultaneously appealed to and created collective memories that underpinned what we call the 'Western legal tradition' at the very same time that they were helping to construct it. As such, the history of this tradition, or more accurately, *traditions*, and the ideas and narratives invoked by the shorthand term, has constantly been rewritten by those who sought to safeguard it from internal and external threats as much as by those who sought to replace it with something less cumbersome, more systematic, and more just.[19]

One reason that the metaphor of the state of nature was so central to the construction of the modern 'Western legal tradition' and with it, the liberal (i.e., a rights-based) rule of law stems from the fact that it was already so familiar to those Renaissance jurists and theorists who helped to construct it. Descriptions of the state of nature, no less than visions of the ideal state, were so deeply embedded in the works of the ancient (Greek, Roman, and Byzantine) authorities that they studied that sixteenth-century jurists could comfortably use them to provide gravitas to their own ideas—and even to disguise the introduction of new ones. As such, when Renaissance jurists transported their audiences to an altogether different time and place so that they could usher them forward—as slowly or as quickly as their argument required—to their present time, they summoned the dead to help them do so.

19 The Western legal tradition is so pervasive that it has permeated political and legal thought by direct reference or allusion for more than a millennium. Its ubiquity is such that it is more common to find legal and political texts that allude to it than those that do not. Yet, its adaptability and evolution in how it is invoked is a testament to its dynamism. Hence, providing a reader with an array of primary sources to show this beyond the discussion in the second part of this chapter would require a multi-volume appendix.

Appeals to ancient authorities, collective memories, or familiar stories about the value and necessity of legal order imbued the early modern state with historical authority, regardless of whether the history and authorities driving the narrative were misremembered, exaggerated, or fictional. Meanwhile, explanations for why humans deliberately founded civil societies to pursue peace, security, and the common good in tandem ultimately imbued early modern states with moral authority. A seminal category of law that helped affect each explanation framed the Roman *Digest* and the *Institutes*, two foundational texts at the core of the 'Western legal tradition'; *ius gentium* was not only "that law which natural reason has established among all human beings" but also a record of customs shared in common among all humankind, ranging from the advent of private property to the founding of kingdoms.[20] As such, it enabled Renaissance jurists (among others) to summon the Ancients, especially Ulpian and Gaius, to help them flesh out their visions of a world before the establishment of civil societies, which they could use, in turn, to critique laws and practices in their present time.[21]

Together, the historical and moral authority that the idea of the state of nature carried with it made the modern sovereign state a legitimate arbiter of justice and clemency within its territorial boundaries and gave it the moral authority to conduct war and contract peace beyond them. The latter was especially true when states were reconstituted to escape bloody religious, civil, and interstate wars. The state of nature, utilized to defend or critique existing conditions, allowed Renaissance jurists to justify and fortify the emergence of modern sovereignty. Sovereignty was made possible by man's agreement to live by the rule of law and protect and defend the state in its most pure, just, and stable forms against the specter of tyranny, both domestic and foreign. The state, in other words, was founded not only in time but also by choice.

Jean Bodin, for example, emphasized man's inherent sociability, and even love, within and between families as the driving force that led the head of each household to jointly found a commonwealth, in which all would be governed by—and held accountable to—civil authorities and civil laws.[22] Even so, the specter of tyranny (wielded by one or many) permeated his conception of the attributes of sovereignty and his arguments for why it was necessary.[23] Con-

20 For such definitions, see Justinian, *The Digest of Justinian*, Translated by Alan Watson, 2 vols. (Philadelphia: University of Pennsylvania Press, 1998); and Justinian, *Institutes*, Translated by J. A. C. Thomas (Amsterdam: North-Holland Pub. Co., 1975). See also Stein, *Roman Law in European History*.

21 For a detailed discussion of this, see Longfield Karr, *Jus Gentium in Humanist Jurisprudence*.

22 Bodin, *Six Books of the Commonwealth* [1576]. Book I, Chapter VI: What a Citizen is, and how much Citizens differ from Citizens, and how much from strangers: what also is to be understood by the name of a Town, a City, and of a Commonwealth; and Book I, Chapter VII: Of them that are under protection, and the difference betwixt Allies, Strangers, and Subjects.

23 Bodin, *Six Books of the Commonwealth* [1576], *Book I, Chapters 8: Of Sovereignty; Book II, Chapters 4: Of a Tyrannical Monarchy; and Book II, Chapter 5: Whether it be lawful to lay violent hand upon a tyrant's life and to nullify and repeal all his acts, decrees, and laws.*

versely, Thomas Hobbes's infamous state of nature, as a state of war among and against all, was not anchored in love but fear.[24] Indeed, man's fear that his life and liberty were under constant threat led to the founding of civil society in the first place and with it, the establishment of sovereignty. Yet, both agreed that only a commonwealth in which all consented to restrain their rights and submit themselves to the rule of law could serve as a sufficient antidote to the tyranny of unrestrained power and force of a few; both agreed that civil laws and civil authorities that respected the rights and obligations of all were the keys to peace, security, and stability.

In each case, Bodin and Hobbes—and countless others—used the state of nature to construct framing narratives to explain why humans chose to abandon living in an environment without civil law to willingly being part of a society defined by it and further, why society, unencumbered by a particular kind of state (whether monarchy or republic), was always at risk of collapsing into tyranny. History and their present time, they agreed, were littered with examples of the latter. In contrast, their arguments (whether offering a defense or critique of the status quo) were often anchored by ideas of what could have been rather than merely what was. This enabled them to offer visions of stability that could escape the present to suggest a path to a different future.

In this way, the state of nature and its corresponding images and vocabulary set the stage for the origins and failure of certain kinds of society. Such images could also serve as the beacon by which any society could measure its success. The beginning foreshadowed the end, the end explained the middle, and the middle gave meaning to the beginning (which predicted the end). Therefore, the idea of the state of nature, as ubiquitous and circular as it was, did a specific kind of work in political and legal thought precisely because it was so deeply embedded in the imagined histories and collective memories that it required to work as metaphor, allegory, or trope in the first place. The visions that the idea of the state of nature summoned to do this work varied according to the argument that the author hoped to sell to his audience and, thereby, the problem that they aimed to solve.

Given that the category of *ius gentium* encompassed everything from private property (mine and thine) to enslaving captives as a consequence of war, it is not at all surprising that each theorist turned to it—even as they set out to address, critique, or offer solutions to local political, social, and/or religious problems. It was, after all, a category of legal and political thought that existed outside of and beyond the confines of church and state. Inherited from the Romans and used predominantly by medieval jurists to justify institutions and practices that either violated natural law, such as slavery, or to augment various forms of authority as an expression of God's will, Renaissance jurists

24 Hobbes, *Leviathan* [1651]. Part I: Of Man, Chapter XIII: Of The Natural Condition Of Mankind, As Concerning Their Felicity, And Misery, §: Out Of Civil States, There Is Always War Of Everyone Against Everyone.

turned traditional jurisprudence on its head when they redefined and reinterpreted *ius gentium* as a form of natural law and a source of universal rights and obligations shared among all mankind, across time and space, that not only existed before but also transcended civil and political society.

3 The state of nature as a framing device: four case studies in brief

For a variety of reasons that reach well beyond the parameters of the current volume, the jurists considered in the following case studies so thoroughly altered the essential attributes within traditional jurisprudence that they fundamentally transformed it and, in the process, invented conceptual tools—though they would claim that they had merely recovered them—that we tend to identify with the modern 'Western legal tradition' rather than the medieval one.[25] Key to this transformation was their appeal to historical imagination and their use of the state of nature to frame their calls for fundamental reforms or to assert that a specific law or practice was altogether unjust.

In their attempts to account for (and reframe) the understandings of the source and limit of legal and political authority, the Renaissance jurists explored here appealed to their audiences' collective memory to shift their attention away from the *ius commune*, that is, the amalgam of civil and canon law grounded in the authority of emperors, princes, and popes that permeated university-based jurisprudence for nearly four centuries, towards a conceptual interpretation of the foundations of law and society grounded in the attributes and actions of man.[26] In this interpretation, the categories of natural law and *ius gentium* (the law of nations) were central. They did this for multiple reasons, not only to call for the reform of the political and legal frameworks that permeated disputes over power, authority, and jurisdiction among and between rulers, secular and sacred, but also to offer an alternative to civil laws that pitted subjects against one another.

25 See Longfield Karr, *Ius Gentium in Humanist Jurisprudence*, Introduction: "Historical Imagination, Collective Memory, and the Historicization of Roman Law;" and Conclusion: "The Re-formation of Europe and the Turn to *Ius Gentium*."

26 For definitions and discussions of *ius commune* and its relation to Roman law, canon law, and political authority, see especially James A. Brundage, *The Medieval Origins of the Legal Profession: Canonists, Civilians, and Courts* (Chicago: University of Chicago Press, 2008); Berman, *Law and Revolution* I & II; Antony Black, *Political Thought in Europe, 1250–1450* (Cambridge, UK: Cambridge University Press, 1992); Joseph Canning, *Ideas of Power in the Late Middle Ages, 1296–1417* (Cambridge, UK: Cambridge University Press, 2014); Herzog, *A Short History of European Law*; Ernst Kantorowicz, *The King's Two Bodies: A Study in Mediaeval Political Theology* (Princeton, NJ: Princeton University Press, 1967); Kenneth Pennington, *The Prince and the Law 1200–1600: Sovereignty and Rights in the Western Legal Tradition* (Berkeley: University of California Press, 1993); and Peter Stein, "The *Ius Commune* and Its Demise," *The Journal of Legal History* 25 no. 2 (August 2004): 161–167.

In his orations and lectures on Roman law, Ulrich Zasius (1461–1535), who taught at the University of Freiburg, in addition to serving as a city councilor and advisor to Holy Roman Emperor Maximillian I (1459–1519), summoned the ancient past to account for the origins of states and, therefore, the civil and political authority that governed them.[27] Although he appealed to his students' familiarity with Cicero's *De Inventione*, wherein Cicero recounted why and how a wise orator called humankind to give up their rustic and reclusive tendencies to pursue the benefits of peace, security, and the common good, Zasius ultimately offered his students a more complex picture of man's pre-political condition.[28] Drawing on *ius gentium*, which was synonymous with the state of nature for Zasius, he suggested that civil society emerged slowly and organically as communities, bound by respect and affection, which expanded over time. In this way, he set the stage for his theory of universal jurisprudence, wherein rights and obligations were central.[29]

Zasius held that careful attention to *ius gentium* revealed the ubiquity of customs, conventions, and practices shared within all communities before the advent of civil society and those shared among and between states after it was founded. One could access this history embedded in *ius gentium* by observing interactions among persons, communities, and states in their present and by studying the remnants left over from such interactions in legal and political documents from the past. One could also access *ius gentium* through collective memories shaped by oral traditions and devices, such as poetic formulas, adages, or songs that passed on customs from generation to generation.[30] In essence, taking *ius gentium* seriously rather than approaching it as merely a category of Roman law to be discarded once defined made it possible for jurists and lawyers to access the aspects of history that other bodies of law, including *ius commune*, did not reveal.

For example, *ius gentium* served as a record of rights that existed from time immemorial. The most basic was the right to meet force with force when one's life or property was in danger. One also had the right to use force to preserve their family, friends, neighbors, and associates. Such rights had corresponding obligations, including maintaining the peace and pursuing justice. One fulfilled these obligations by obeying God, keeping their promises (*bona fides*), and promoting the common good. These obligations were also preserved within and evidenced by *ius gentium* and were shared among all humankind, regardless of time, place, or condition. Moreover, longstanding rights within communities were sanctioned by *ius gentium*, including the right

27 Zasius, "In laudem legum oratio," 1518.

28 Marcus Cicero, *De inventione, de optimo genere oratorum, topica*, Translated by H. M. Hubbell (Cambridge, MA: Harvard University Press, 1949).

29 Zasius, "Praefatio, de origine legibus;" "De iustitia et iure (Lecture);" and Longfield Karr, *Jus Gentium in Humanist Jurisprudence*.

30 See Rabin in this volume for an in-depth exploration of this process in the Medieval English and Scottish legal traditions.

to own property and engage in trade and commerce. Furthermore, communities had the right to establish kingdoms and boundaries and, if necessary, to use force to protect them against internal (the right to punish) and external (the right to wage war) threats. Finally, *ius gentium* also encompassed the right to enslave captives in war and to contract peace and the duty to allow ambassadors safe passage.[31]

As a cache of all of these practices, usages, rights, and obligations, *ius gentium* effectively served as the common denominator between all peoples and persons for Zasius. As such, it functioned as a collective memory—and an imagined history—as to why man chose to live in civil society in the first place. For Zasius, man founded civil society by practice (rather than decree) to foster peace, security, the common good, and, most importantly, to pursue justice. Pursuing justice, in turn, required civil laws and institutions to respect universal rights and obligations. If civil laws, institutions, and authorities failed to do so, Zasius argued, then lawyers and jurists could call on *ius gentium*—and all that it encompassed—to help them effect legal and institutional reforms. *Ius gentium* could be used to do this work precisely because it embodied and represented man's condition before states existed. Thus, it made it an essential tool to assess whether some laws and institutions violated rather than advanced universal justice.

Juxtaposing the history embedded in and transmitted by *ius gentium* with present conditions allowed Zasius to pinpoint instances in which law and justice had fallen out of joint, to explain what needed to be done to fix it, and to frame his warnings about the turmoil and insecurity that such corruptions, if not corrected, portended for the present and future. One of the most vivid examples that he used to do all of this was slavery—and, by extension, servitude.[32] Traditionally, as a practice and custom that resulted from war, slavery was justified as an institution that provided both peace and security to captives and captors. In contrast, servitude emerged from voluntary agreements—implicit and explicit—to exchange service for security (physical and economic). However, over time, as forms of slavery and servitude became increasingly regulated by civil laws—especially in terms of economic and political subordination—the status of the enslaved or enserfed tended to be diminished as the power of the enslaver or lord was augmented. The latter was especially the case when the laws restricted the ability of those subjected to another's power to engage in common practices, for example, owning property, contracting marriage, and engaging in everyday trade and commerce. By diminishing the legal status of a person in servitude to exercise fundamental rights and obligations (embodied in and sanctioned by *ius gentium*), the power of the enslaver or lord could become absolute.

31 See Rabin in this volume for an in-depth exploration of this process in the Medieval English and Scottish legal traditions.

32 Longfield Karr, *Jus Gentium in Humanist Jurisprudence*, 192–216.

The potential for civil laws and authorities to sanction and justify such extensions of power alarmed Zasius because it had implications for not only persons in various conditions of servitude but also subjects in relation to rulers. The same legal arguments that allowed lords to claim total, unlimited, and unrestricted power over their peasants on their land, for example, could be—and were—mustered to suggest that emperors, kings, princes, and city-states had unlimited jurisdiction and authority over citizens and subjects who resided within their territorial boundaries. Rejecting such practices and arguments, Zasius held that all laws and authorities that attempted to make the conditions of slavery, servitude, and subjection severe required immediate reform precisely because such actions violated *ius gentium*.[33] He went so far as to suggest that no matter if one willingly quit one condition to adopt another (as in the case of Cicero's story) to join civil society, or they were forced to do so (via war and conquest), no persons could be wholly subjected to the power of another (even though claims to the contrary were made by political and legal authorities) as to do so would be to violate universal rights, obligations, and justice in tandem.

Rather than use Cicero to summon an idea of the state of nature, as Zasius had, Francisco de Vitoria (1483–1546), theologian and scholastic jurist who lectured at the University of Salamanca in Spain, invited his audience to consider something comparable. For Vitoria, the idea of people living outside of 'Western' conceptions of civil society, or Latin Christendom in this case, was not something that required an exercise of one's imagination—historical or otherwise—but rather an acknowledgment of the present conditions. Drawing on his audience's familiarity with the ongoing violence between Catholics and Protestants across much of northern and central Europe and their awareness of what was happening in the Atlantic world, Vitoria challenged them to explore the extent to which those who lived within nations, bound by common mores, identities, and customary laws outside *ius commune*, stood as equals to one another in the realm of war and peace. Invoking *ius gentium* and all that it entailed, Vitoria argued that all peoples, regardless of place or time, shared universal rights and obligations, whose violation was a direct affront to dignity and a threat to universal justice.

Writing in the context of the dispossession and enslavement of the Amerinds at the hand of the Spanish, Vitoria understood *ius gentium* in much the same way that Zasius did. Still, he used it to affect a different end. At issue for Vitoria, in his lecture entitled *De Indes* (1539), was whether or not the Spanish had a cause of just war against the natives in the Atlantic world.[34] Against the claim (supported by evidence drawn from *ius commune*) that the Spanish had

33 Zasius, "In laudem legum oratio;" and Longfield Karr, *Jus gentium in Humanist Jurisprudence*, 192–216.

34 Francisco de Vitoria, "De Indis," in *Vitoria: Political Writings*, eds. Anthony Pagden and Jeremy Lawrance (Cambridge, UK: Cambridge University Press, 1991), 231–292.

a right to enslave the natives based on their condition as sinners, heretics, and madmen and their lack of reason, Vitoria offered an in-depth and systematic rebuttal, effectively showing why these claims were fallacious. His refutations boiled down to the argument that if any of these claims stood as a just cause for the Spanish to dispossess and enslave the Amerinds in the new world, then they could also stand as a just cause for the Spanish to be dispossessed and enslaved in the old one—by their newly Protestant neighbors as much as their recently 'discovered' Amerind ones.[35]

After quickly and systematically dismissing all of these claims, Vitoria set out a list of rights that extended from *ius gentium* as a form of universal natural law, which all nations and peoples, across time and space, shared.[36] In the context of this argument, *ius gentium* and the state of nature were synonymous for Vitoria in much the same way as for Zasius. Moreover, each argued that when such rights (and obligations, in the case of Zasius) were violated, those who suffered an injustice or injury as a consequence had the right to resist—to protect themselves, their property, their family, and their community—by meeting force with force. Even so, in the case of individuals, those who used defensive violence had to vindicate their actions after the fact, given that only those within a community can determine whether or not the use of force was warranted and proportional. Once civil laws and civil authorities were established, the community at large was replaced by rulers and jurists.

No such requirement existed among nations in the distant past or in Vitoria's present. Although nations, like individuals, had the right to meet force with force—to protect themselves, their neighbors, and their possessions/property—they were not required to vindicate their actions after the fact, even if they were expected to declare the cause to their adversaries, often by enlisting legal experts within their domains to do so. However, whether they did so or not was immaterial to the right to use violence against their enemies. Indeed, Vitoria went so far as to argue that, faced with violence, dispossession, and enslavement by the Spanish, the Amerinds had the right to defend themselves with force and that their actions were just.[37] The former was the case because *ius gentium*, as a historical record, provided evidence that individuals held a universal right to self-preservation and that nations had the right to wage defensive war.

35 Francisco de Vitoria, "De Indis," in *Vitoria: Political Writings*, eds. Anthony Pagden and Jeremy Lawrance (Cambridge, UK: Cambridge University Press, 1991), 231–292, Question 1: "On the Dominion of the Barbarians, Conclusion," 250–251.

36 Francisco de Vitoria, "De Indis," in *Vitoria: Political Writings*, eds. Anthony Pagden and Jeremy Lawrance (Cambridge, UK: Cambridge University Press, 1991), 231–292, Question 2: "By what unjust titles the Barbarians of the New World passed under the rule of the Spaniards," 251–277.

37 Francisco de Vitoria, "De Indis," in *Vitoria: Political Writings*, eds. Anthony Pagden and Jeremy Lawrance (Cambridge, UK: Cambridge University Press, 1991), 231–292.

In addition to self-defense and defensive war, Vitoria argued that the natives were as entitled as the Spanish to the freedom of movement, trade, emigration, religion, marriage, and free access to the rivers, coasts, and oceans.[38] To prove that the Amerinds held these rights, Vitoria outlined customs that the natives engaged in before the Spanish arrived, including possessing property and establishing boundaries and territories. He also highlighted conventions practiced by Amerinds and Europeans, such as forming alliances in war and contracting peace, long before they first encountered one another. To this, Vitoria added the practice of enslaving captives in war to emphasize that the latter was permitted only as a consequence of war, not for the rejection of faith.[39]

Although Vitoria hoped that exposure to the word of God would eventually bring the natives into Catholic Christendom and thus enable them to adopt the norms and institutions embedded in *ius commune*, he nevertheless emphasized that to try to do so by force not only violated their rights but also robbed them of their dignity. At the same time, he asserted that they had the right to reject the Gospel. If, however, the natives attempted to forbid the Christians from proselytizing—by denying their right to preach or their duty to God to spread the word—the Spaniards would have cause not only to wage war against the Amerinds but also to enslave and conquer them.[40] In much the same way, by implication, Vitoria held that the Spanish had the right to take Iberia back from Muslim kingdoms about a half-century earlier.

Accordingly, for Vitoria and Zasius, attention to the history embedded in *ius gentium* revealed that individuals and nations held universal rights and obligations before the advent of civil societies and that civil societies were founded to secure and protect these rights. Moreover, the history embedded in *ius gentium* revealed that all persons and nations were obligated to

38 Francisco de Vitoria, "De Indis," in *Vitoria: Political Writings*, eds. Anthony Pagden and Jeremy Lawrance (Cambridge, UK: Cambridge University Press, 1991), 231–292.

39 Francisco de Vitoria, "De Indis," in *Vitoria: Political Writings*, eds. Anthony Pagden and Jeremy Lawrance (Cambridge, UK: Cambridge University Press, 1991), 231–292.

40 Francisco de Vitoria, "De Indis," in *Vitoria: Political Writings*, eds. Anthony Pagden and Jeremy Lawrance (Cambridge, UK: Cambridge University Press, 1991), 231–292, Question 3: "The Just Titles by which the Barbarians of the New World passed under the rule of the Spaniards," 277–291. For a discussion of just war in medieval and early modern legal thought, see Jens Bartleson, "Double Binds: Sovereignty and the Just War Tradition," in *Sovereignty in Fragments: The Past, Present and Future of a Contested Concept*, eds. Hent Kalmo and Quentin Skinner (Cambridge, UK: Cambridge University Press, 2010), 81–95; Covell, *The Law of Nations in Political Thought*; James Turner Johnson, "Then and Now: Medieval Conception of Just War versus Recent Portrayals of the Just War Idea," in *Medieval Foundations of International Relations*, ed. William Bain (London: Routledge, 2017), 117–133; Koskenniemi, "Vitoria and Us," *Rechtsgeschichte/Legal History* 22 (2014): 119–138; Koskenniemi, *To the Uttermost Parts of the Earth*; Anthony Pagden, *Lords of All the World: Ideologies of Empire in Spain, Britain, and France c.1500–1800* (New Haven, CT: Yale University Press, 1995); and Frederick H. Russell, *The Just War in the Middle Ages* (Cambridge, UK: Cambridge University Press, 1975).

recognize that others, aside from themselves, also held these rights. As such, appeals to and explanations of *ius gentium* summoned two different images of the state of nature for Vitoria's and Zasius's audiences: a picture of communities bound by kinship and mutual interests in times of peace, from which civil societies emerged, and the realm in which those communities and nations existed vis-a-vis one another as nations or states in times of war. Both visions of the state of nature, through *ius gentium*, served as framing devices for Vitoria's and Zasius's theories of jurisprudence and continue to underpin our modern understanding of the 'Western legal tradition' as a liberal (i.e., rights-based) rule of law that distinguishes it.

Writing twenty years before Vitoria, around the same time as Zasius, Thomas More (1478–1535), an English lawyer and statesman, also gestured to the Atlantic world in his 1516 *Utopia*, although the focal point of his attention was an imagined (and artificial) island state rather than existing nations.[41] Indeed, he invented a fantastical society that chose to live on the margins of European kingdoms and empires yet was distinct from them in nearly every conceivable manner possible. In this way, More offered his readers two corresponding visions of man's natural condition, or pre-political state, amplified by the economy, culture, and laws that characterized sixteenth-century England and its neighbors.[42]

One state of nature—representing the realm in which empire-states operated—was permeated with hostility, conflict, greed, and intolerance. The other—existing on the horizons of the Atlantic world—encompassed peoples who either lived outside of or altogether transcended the corruptions and shortfalls that permeated *ius commune* and with it, the 'Western legal tradition.'[43] Situated between these two extremes was Utopia, a Commonwealth that shunned war but was prepared to win peace by arms when necessary.[44] More's exploration of this imagined community, in which altered legal frameworks and universal conceptions of justice were central, allowed him to offer insightful commentary and sometimes scathing critiques of the world he lived in. It also allowed him to utilize ideas of both an altered state and the state of nature (albeit in a fuzzy outline) as a framing device to warn his readers about the dangers of religious intolerance to civil society.

Although More used historical and critical imagination to a different effect than Zasius and Vitoria, he too invoked *ius gentium*—albeit more implicitly than explicitly—to frame and employ his critique of the customs and conventions that underpin traditional jurisprudence. But instead of a pre-civil society organized by unwritten traditions and customs, Utopia was more

41 Thomas More, *Utopia*, Edited by George M. Logan and Robert. M. Adams. Rev. ed. (Cambridge: Cambridge University Press, 2002). The Utopians severed their connection to a neighboring landmass by digging a wide and deep canal.

42 More, *Utopia*, Book I, 8–41.

43 More, *Utopia*, Book II, 42.

44 More, *Utopia*, Book II, see especially "Warefare," 87–95.

advanced—legally, politically, economically, and socially—than all European states combined.[45] Nevertheless, they practiced the rustic and rudimentary customs embedded in *ius gentium* when they engaged with their unsophisticated European neighbors in matters of war and peace and when they hosted diplomats and other foreign guests, including scholars and missionaries.

Moreover, Utopians only needed to call on or appeal to the universal rights and obligations encompassed by *ius gentium* if their borders were breached or outsiders attempted to change or corrupt their society.[46] After all, all of the laws and institutions that distinguished Utopia as a Commonwealth were perfectly aligned with equity and justice for all.[47] With all necessities satisfied and all aspects of society in precise order, the Utopians had little need for the two things that permeated conventions and fell under and were moderated by *ius gentium*, namely, private property and conquest. There was little need to defend property by force since everything was held in common. Moreover, all resources were distributed equally, all industries were perfected, all farming and fishing were sustainable, and all arts and bodies of knowledge were known. Thus, there was also little need to extend Utopia's claims by offensive war or aggressive trade to feed the existing population or to satisfy the greed of private or public actors.

Nevertheless, no matter how perfect More's imagined society was, those who lived within it were not without human failings. As such, two features traditionally held to extend from *ius gentium* were transformed into aspects regulated by Utopia's civil laws: slavery and punishment.[48] Some of Utopia's enslaved were foreigners who were captured in war and were thus held by the practices of *ius gentium*. A few were Utopians who committed "some heinous offence" that warranted this punishment, whereas most others were foreigners who, having been condemned to death or penal servitude in their own lands, chose to take on the mantle of slavery in Utopia because it was less harsh.[49] In all cases, no matter how one became enslaved, their children were born free.[50] Slavery, as reimagined in Utopia, was limited in terms of the length of servitude and the severity of the condition.[51] Although Utopians enslaved as a result of crime were treated more harshly than foreigners, servitude in

45 More, *Utopia*, Book II, 42.

46 More, *Utopia*, Book II, see especially "The Travels of the Utopians," 60–79; and "Warefare," 87–95.

47 More, *Utopia*, Book II, 42–59.

48 More, *Utopia*, Book II, "Slaves," 80–87.

49 In Utopia, there was no capital punishment. The most severe crimes, therefore, were punished by enslavement. The crimes that warranted this extreme punishment were few, and even then, one would have to commit the crime twice to warrant enslavement.

50 More, *Utopia*, Book II, "Slaves," 80–87.

51 Those enslaved as a punishment for crime could have their sentences lessened or remitted if they showed sufficient remorse to convince the magistrates to pardon them or the public to vote to free them from servitude.

Utopia was less severe than elsewhere. Moreover, if enslaved people wished to leave Utopia altogether, then they did not have to escape but rather leave the state. If one chose to leave, then "no obstacles are put in his way, nor is he sent off empty handed."[52] The latter policy reflected yet another feature of *ius gentium* that all of the Renaissance jurists explored in this chapter recast as a universal right, namely, the freedom of movement.[53] Although this right can be limited and even, in the case of punishment, restrained, it cannot be entirely abrogated.

The Utopians not only allowed those enslaved to leave their state and thereby their servile condition but also did not close their borders to their citizens or to foreign visitors, diplomats, and scholars. Even so, citizens and subjects were required to seek permission to journey within the state and to leave it. It was necessary to do so because the political economy of Utopia was so meticulously balanced that they had to ensure that no part of the island (or her colonies) would suffer a deficit in foodstuffs, industriousness, or materials due to an influx of people from another part or vice versa. Monitoring the movement of its subjects, citizens, and guests also enabled more equitable and frequent travel rather than limiting such experiences and opportunities to a small population of magistrates and dignitaries. Although a closely managed state, the culture of Utopia nevertheless encouraged its inhabitants to travel and to welcome travelers because it facilitated the free exchange of ideas.[54]

Using the example of religion, More illustrated the importance of free exchange by recounting how the Europeans were allowed to introduce Christianity to Utopians.[55] Even after some converted, there remained a liberty of conscience for all. Moreover, anyone who attempted to convert others to their religion by means other than quiet and respectful persuasion would be penalized by exile or slavery.[56] In this respect, the policy of the Utopians was the exact inverse of that found within More's world, wherein force was considered a reasonable and necessary tool to ensure compliance with the word of God. Meanwhile, those in Utopia who tried to use violence and intimidation to force conversion were punished, whereas those who, after hearing the case for conversion, chose not to take on a new faith were not. The latter was the case, More explained because the mythical founder of this imagined society, King Utopus, held, based on his own experience and observation, that the only path to security and peace was tolerance.[57] Thus, the Utopians tolerated Christian-

52 More, *Utopia*, Book II, "Slaves," 80.

53 This freedom was not absolute, however, as government permission was required to travel within and beyond Utopia. Those who violated this law once were severely admonished, whereas those who transgressed the law of second time were enslaved.

54 More, *Utopia*, Book II, "Slaves," 80, Book II.

55 More, *Utopia*, Book II, "Slaves," 80, Book II, see especially "Religions of the Utopians," 95–110.

56 More, *Utopia*, Book II, "Slaves," 80, Book II, 97.

57 More, *Utopia*, Book II, "Slaves," 80, Book II, 97.

ity in the same way that they tolerated every other religion and faith. In the same manner, they tolerated their European neighbors in general.

The liberty of conscience and the policy of toleration set out within More's text before the onset of the Reformation (circa 1517) took a renewed sense of urgency and danger in the wake of the religious violence and war that characterized the world in which the French lawyer and political theorist Jean Bodin (1530–1596) put forth a similar idea 70 years later. In efforts to offer solutions to the problems of religious conflict and turmoil across France, Bodin's exploration of religious toleration can be read as an attempt to uncover underlying universal truths transcending the establishment of civil society, when recognized by civil and political authorities, that could provide a practical alternative to the exclusion, persecution, and violence that had hitherto been justified in the name of God, King, and Country.

Bodin's search for—and investigation of—the belief in God outside of, before, and beyond organized and institutionalized religion can be read as a search for a universal link among all humankind across time and space. This link, in turn, could serve as a means to ensure, from its very foundations, that civil and political societies would respect, at the very least, liberty of conscience. Only if everyone fulfilled their duty to obey God, no matter the religion, would it be possible to exercise and protect universal rights and obligations such as liberty of conscience and promise keeping (*bona fides*) within civil society, thereby enabling all to pursue the common good, peace, and security in tandem. However, exploring this in Bodin's case requires attention to two different expressions of his theory of jurisprudence, wherein the state of nature, illustrated by *ius gentium*, was central. These expressions involve why civil society, and indeed sovereignty, came into being in the first place and his critique of the use of civil laws to limit the religious beliefs of those who lived within modern (i.e., sovereign) states once founded.

In his 1576 *Six Books of the Commonwealth*, Bodin offered readers a sophisticated and sociable image of the state of nature in which families were tied together by friendship, marriage, and commerce.[58] Although seemingly more peaceful and stable than the war-torn states that permeated late-sixteenth-century France, Bodin's state of nature lacked the one thing that he thought necessary to secure peace, justice, and security for all: a sovereign. Convinced that civil society would be mutually beneficial, heads of households agreed to place themselves under the authority of a common legal framework or civil law. Only when they all decided to be equally subject to the rule of law and the institutions that ensure justice, including placing the power of life and death in the hands of the sovereign, could the Commonwealth they founded truly become a fully-fledged state. Mutually bound to one another and to the sovereign—who held the monopoly of violence to punish those under its jurisdiction and wage war against enemies beyond it—engendered mutual trust

58 Bodin, *Six Books of the Commonwealth* [1576].

among subjects that enabled them, in turn, to nurture friendships and love for one another despite fundamental differences in belief. The theory of sovereignty that Bodin offered in this text echoed aspects of Zasius's conception of *ius gentium* as a place and time, as well as a cache of rights and obligations.

Mutual respect and diversity of belief shared among friends rather than communities was at the center of the *Colloquium of the Seven about Secrets of the Sublime*, written as early as 1593 but not published until 1683.[59] This dialogue, attributed to Bodin, among seven interlocutors of different faiths, amplified the same universal rights and obligations embedded in and transmitted by *ius gentium* that informed both Vitoria's acknowledgment and More's defense of liberty of conscience. Although Bodin addressed the question of religious tolerance in his *Six Books*, he did so to emphasize that both commonwealths and sovereignty stemmed from good faith agreements, which, in turn, required faith, some idea of a God, or acknowledgment of some universal and just entity to be meaningful. Such a belief was needed to serve as a check against duplicity, something that he suggested atheists were prone to and persuaded others to adopt. These concerns, although not absent in the *Colloquium*, were pushed to the margins when a Catholic, a Lutheran, a Calvinist, a Jew, a Muslim, a skeptic, and a proponent of natural religion vigorously debated which of their religions constituted the one true faith.

In contrast to Bodin's *Six Books*, which engaged with the necessity to believe in God and the importance of religious toleration within a few paragraphs, the *Colloquium* spans more than 500 pages.[60] Indeed, it takes several meetings, throughout six books, for the interlocutors to reach a consensus to respect one another's piety, regardless of their religious beliefs, and after having gained such an understanding, to agree that they never needed to talk about religion in such depth again. Moreover, such a consensus among friends had direct implications for civic reform, as it suggested tolerance as a policy that could

59 Jean Bodin, *Colloquium of the Seven about Secrets of the Sublime* (*Colloquium Heptaplomeres de Rerum Sublimium Arcanis Abditis*). Translation with Introduction by Marion Leathers Daniels Kuntz (Princeton, NJ: Princeton University Press, 1975). Although there has been some dispute as to whether or not the Colloquium was, indeed, Bodin's text, those who read and circulated the text at the end of the sixteenth-century and after Bodin died believed it to be. Despite the fact that very few of Bodin's works have survived in his hand, analysis of this work in context with his other works suggested that it was indeed his. Kuntz, "The *Colloquium heptaplomeres* and the Sixteenth-Century" and "Manuscripts, Editions, and the Translation," in Bodin, *Colloquium*, xlvii–lxvii.

60 In *The Six Books of the Commonwealth*, Bodin argued for a conception of toleration that enabled all to follow their conscience and thereby practice their faith—at least privately—while at the same time forbidding debates and disputes concerning the veracity of any one religion in the public realm. As long as all those who believed in God, no matter their creed, kept matters of religion to themselves and respected the right of others to do the same, the public goods of peace and security among all was possible. Although positive laws might establish and secure the religion of the sovereign as the state religion, these laws should not attempt to compel men to believe that creed when it is in direct conflict with their conscience. See Book VI.

finally bring religious alienation, strife, and exclusion within commonwealths to an end.

The seven friends established such an equilibrium by addressing fundamental questions in private that they could not address in public. Moreover, they could not have addressed them if bonds of affection and mutual respect had not already tied them. Questions they debated included whether or not there was one, and only one, true religion and whether one could be forced to profess a religion in public that they did not believe in private.[61] If each religion under discussion was equally genuine, then what does this mean for those who insist that only their religion was valid? Furthermore, what implications would such knowledge have for states that place one religion above all others and require all subjects and citizens to swear an oath to it in public?[62] Finally, what about states that forbid the practice of any religion in private in attempts to root out heretics? Would not these policies and practices violate universal rights and obligations, such as liberty of conscience and the duty to obey God, by forcing people to lie about or hide their faith?

In light of these questions, it should come as no surprise that the *Colloquium* is full of hostility and dissonance among the seven when each presents the history and tenets of their religion and in the process, initially tries to convince their peers why theirs is indeed the one true religion. Though never breaking into violence, the discord among these friends mirrors the relationship between equal nations in the realm of *ius gentium* when they come into conflict. After extensive discussions and debate, not one of the seven is convinced to abandon their faith to adopt another's. All remain steadfast in their religious beliefs and suspicious of anyone who might give up their faith so easily (because of mere argument). All realized that everyone's piety transcended church and state. All became aware that piety was a universal requirement shared among their religions because the belief in the divine was common to all humankind. Although this innate knowledge and a corresponding duty to obey God (or nature's God, in the case of the proponent of natural religion) was also shared, the tenets of each religion were simultaneously embedded in long-held customs, practices, and teachings passed on through song, image, word, and action.[63]

By working through the history of each religion under discussion and reaching beyond those histories, whether recorded in texts or passed down by customs, Bodin invoked a time and place wherein all peoples, despite the lack of civil society and religious institutions, shared an innate understanding of God. Moreover, the seven reached their consensus by peeling back the layers that distinguished each religion until they found what they shared: devout respect for and obedience to the divine. Once discovered, this piety could

61 Bodin, *Colloquium of the Seven*, Book III, 143; & Book IV, 163.
62 Bodin, *Colloquium of the Seven*, Book V and VI.
63 Bodin, *Colloquium of the Seven*, Book V & VI.

stand as evidence that all religions should be tolerated within civil society.[64] This revelation arose when they examined whether one could be forcibly converted to another religion. All agreed that to force one to swear affinity to a faith other than their own was not only an injustice but also an affront to God and, thus, an act of tyranny. Civil authorities who attempted to impose religious uniformity violated the liberty of conscience of their subjects.[65] By implication, such laws and authorities transgressed the rights and obligations embedded in and transmitted by *ius gentium*, including one's obligation to obey God, which they were forced to break by swearing an oath that compromised their piety.

Indeed, even as they disagreed on nearly every other topic discussed in the text, they recognized that one's liberty of conscience—as a right that transcends the establishment of church and state—should be respected, mutually and universally, in public and private. After drawing on historical examples from the Ancients, as well as the history, customs, and collective memory embedded in the tenets of their religious traditions, all seven interlocutors also agreed that while religious toleration should be the official position of all states, the sectarian wars tearing France and Europe apart made this difficult in their present time. Nevertheless, by invoking historical examples, real and imagined, the dialogue invited readers to imagine a time in the future when that would no longer be the case, in no small part by conjuring the imaginary time and place in the past when such discord and conflict did not exist.

The technique of appealing to history to draw out problems in the present, utilized by Renaissance jurists, enabled Bodin, More, Vitoria, and Zasius to offer scathing critiques of the world they lived in, albeit from different vantage points and in different tones. Nevertheless, each invoked an image of man's natural condition of living in communities tied by mutual interest, customs, and conventions before states (and religious institutions) were established to frame their discussions of universal rights and obligations among all, which, in turn, framed their calls to reform or change existing practices, laws, and institutions. In essence, they summoned the state of nature as a time and place accessible through and witnessed by the history of *ius gentium* to reinvent or at least recast the 'Western legal tradition' as grounded outside of, and beyond, the existing confines of *ius commune*. To solve the problems created by and entrenched in traditional jurisprudence, in other words, they went in search of the world that existed before it so that they could offer an alternative to it.

By stepping outside of, bypassing, and even dismissing aspects of traditional jurisprudence, Renaissance jurists were able to demarcate the limits of legal and political power vis-à-vis those who were subject to their jurisdictions and in relation to those who were not. They did so in a myriad of ways ranging from offering an explanation as to how and why *ius gentium*—synonymous

64 Book IV & V.

65 Bodin, *Colloquium of the Seven*, Book IV.

with and evidence of man's natural state—was the source of universal rights and obligations (Zasius) to a discussion of the basic rights among all peoples, which, if violated, could stand as a justification of war between nations (Vitoria), and to the necessity of a liberty of conscience among all believers on the basis of piety (More and Bodin).

4 Conclusion

All of the Renaissance jurists explored in this chapter appealed to their audience's collective memory and historical imaginations to frame their critiques of early modern laws, institutions, and practices. Their ability to summon the past to suggest why the state came to be in the first place, whether founded organically or by voluntary compact, enabled them to infuse the state with a moral authority that was anchored outside of traditional jurisprudence (i.e., *ius commune*), and, thus, they could effectively bypass it. Bypassing this jurisprudence was made possible when they implicitly and explicitly equated the customs, conventions, and rights shared among all humankind encompassed within—and communicated through—*ius gentium* with a time and place that existed before civil society (viz., the state of nature or man's pre-political state) was established. In this way, they effectively drew on, reified, and even recast the collective memory and common knowledge shared among their readers to offer a commentary and critique of laws or practices that, in their estimation, directly affronted the universal rights and obligations shared among all humankind, regardless of time or place. Yet, their appeal to distant and imagined pasts infused the picture of man's natural condition with an ersatz nostalgia. This was not a nostalgia for how things were before man entered civil society but rather a nostalgia for what could have been; a nostalgia that they then used to offer a critique and alternative to what was and is.

Reaching beyond recorded history to show how and why a specific law, practice, or claim was no longer connected to—or even directly violated—justice served a fundamental purpose that empirical sources could not. Indeed, appealing to *ius gentium*, explicitly and implicitly, and, therefore, the universal norms of just and right conduct among individuals and communities that permeated it helped them transform civil societies—and the 'Western legal tradition' that structured these societies—from a mere artifice into a work of art. As a result of infusing civil laws and institutions with moral authority, both were deemed as necessary attributes and components of the pursuit of justice, security, and the common good. When and if such civil laws and institutions missed the mark of justice, however, they could be reformed, adjusted, or abolished by referring to what used to be—or at least what was remembered to have been—based on imagined scenarios.

Written sources and recorded history, including discussions of the origin and ends of legal, political, and religious institutions by the ancients and moderns, filled out and even gilded the artifice to be sure, but without the ability to ground these discussions in universal norms that spanned beyond the confines of time and place, the 'Western legal tradition' was a structure without a blueprint, foundation, or buttress that could be called upon to stabilize and protect the rule of law as such. Moreover, focusing on man's informed choice—that is, a choice made from reason and deliberation, not impulse or emotion—to live with civil law and under the jurisdiction of rulers, ranging from councils to emperors, transformed these states and empires into moral persons who stood as equals vis-à-vis one another. There were not only rights and obligations that predated states but also rights and obligations between states.

Even if the moment that specific civil societies, states, and empires were established was lost to recorded memory, the historical fiction of man's prepolitical state was confirmed, for many, by history and experience and thereby, collective memory. Renaissance jurists appealed to this collective memory to move their audiences to action or to convince them that reform was needed. The fact that this imagined history, embodied in *ius gentium*, did not reach back to the origins of man but instead focused on a time when man already lived in mutual company—ranging from families to extended communities—made the pictures that they drew with words more plausible, or at the very least, made them far more helpful than if it these arguments had been rooted in the state of nature at creation, especially given that the latter would necessarily invoke theology and thereby reveal and institutionalize religion. Focusing on this imagined condition and period of human history, even if extant sources and historical evidence could not confirm it, enabled Renaissance jurists to step outside of and away from a fundamental aspect of traditional jurisprudence that permeated the 'Western legal tradition' for most of its history—real and imagined—namely, the appeal to God's eternal will and plan and how this was revealed to man in and by civil laws. Civil laws infused institutions and authorities with moral authority in much the same way that appealing to *ius gentium* did. However, they also carried corruptions stemming from *ius commune*, which were tearing Europe apart by the sixteenth century and wreaking havoc in the Atlantic world in the wake of European expansion and incursion.

Reaching beyond *ius commune* and anchoring their ideas outside theological or biblical ideas of man's original condition allowed the Renaissance jurists to do two things. First, it helped them to bracket religious dogma or at least try to circumvent it. Even though this took on a new urgency from the onset of the Reformation onwards, it is essential to remember that the attempt to bracket or circumvent religion, as part and parcel of modern state formation, helped to create the tinderbox that the Reformation set ablaze in the first place. Second, by using the state of nature as a metaphor and history to reimagine the past—to create an ersatz nostalgia—to address problems in their present, Renaissance jurists were able to offer a vision for the future rooted in that past. Whether the future that they imagined was immediate (Zasius and Vitoria) or remote (More and Bodin), the path to it required returning to a time when *ius gentium* mediated and moderated the actions of humankind in families and communities. That the vision of the past embodied by it likely never existed was inconsequential. What mattered was that the idea of that past and the images invoked to present it could be used to suggest and even effect change in their present. The past that they appealed to was rooted in, and synonymous with, the state of nature.

Renaissance jurists were so adept at using collective memory and ancient sources to recast images and features of man's condition before the establishment of civil society that their ideas helped transform Western legal and political thought at their core. Combining images embedded in and transmitted by *ius gentium* with familiar stories and knowledge to frame, structure, and support their arguments also allowed them to transliterate theories rooted outside the state into legal histories of state formation. A vital component of this transliteration was their infusion of the state of nature—even as they conceded it was imagined—with historical and moral authority so that they could invoke it, in turn, to define (and defend) the line between sovereignty and tyranny. Furthermore, they used the metaphor to anchor their arguments about the inviolability of rights and the universal obligation of rulers and subjects alike to respect and protect them; they used it to set out the limits of authority while accounting for its origins. Indeed, Renaissance jurists and lawyers used the idea of the state of nature as a preface and preliminary to help invent the modern rule of law, which was grounded in and defined by rights and obligations that existed before states were created and between them once they were.

References

Bartleson, Jens. "Double Binds: Sovereignty and the Just War Tradition." In *Sovereignty in Fragments: The Past, Present and Future of a Contested Concept*, edited by Hent Kalmo and Quentin Skinner, 81–95. Cambridge: Cambridge University Press, 2010.

Bellomo, Manlio. *The Common Legal Past of Europe, 1000–1800*, 2nd ed., Translated by Lydia G. Cochrane. Washington, DC: The Catholic University of America Press, 1995.

Berman, Harold Joseph. *Law and Revolution I: The Formation of the Western Legal Tradition*. Cambridge, MA: Harvard University Press, 1983.

Berman, Harold Joseph. *Law and Revolution II: The Impact of the Protestant Reformation on the Western Legal Tradition*. London: Belknap, 2004.

Black, Antony. *Political Thought in Europe, 1250–1450*. Cambridge, UK: Cambridge University Press, 1992.

Bodin, Jean. *Six Books of the Commonwealth (Six livres de la République)* [1576], Edited by Kenneth Douglas McRae. Cambridge, MA: Harvard University Press, 1962.

Bodin, Jean. *Colloquium of the Seven about Secrets of the Sublime* (*Colloquium Heptaplomeres de Rerum Sublimium Arcanis Abditis*). Translation with Introduction by Marion Leathers and Daniels Kuntz. Princeton, NJ: Princeton University Press, 1975.

Brett, Annabel S. *Changes of State: Nature and the Limits of the City in Early Modern Natural Law*. Princeton, NJ: Princeton University Press, 2011.

Brundage, James A. *The Medieval Origins of the Legal Profession: Canonists, Civilians, and Courts*. Chicago: University of Chicago Press, 2008.

Canning, Joseph. *Ideas of Power in the Late Middle Ages, 1296–1417*. Cambridge, UK: Cambridge University Press, 2014.

Canning, Joseph. "Ideas of Empire in the Thought of the Late Medieval Roman Law Jurists." In *Empire and Legal Thought: Ideas and Institutions from Antiquity to Modernity*, edited by Edward Cavanagh, 280–299. Leiden: Brill, 2020.

Cicero, Marcus. *De inventione, de optimo genere oratorum, topica*, Translated by H. M. Hubbell. Cambridge, MA: Harvard University Press, 1949.

Covell, Chris. *The Law of Nations in Political Thought: A Critical Survey from Vitoria to Hegel.* New York: Palgrave Macmillan, 2009.

Davies, Kathleen. *Periodization and Sovereignty: How Ideas of Feudalism and Secularization Govern the Politics of Time.* Philadelphia: University of Pennsylvania Press, 2017.

D'Entreves, A. P. *Natural Law: An Introduction to Legal Philosophy.* London: Hutchinson University Library, 1972.

Fasolt, Constantin. *The Limits of History.* Chicago: University of Chicago Press, 2014.

Fedele, Dante. "*Jus gentium*: The Metamorphoses of a Legal Concept (Ancient Rome to Early Modern Europe)." In *Empire and Legal Thought: Ideas and Institutions from Antiquity to Modernity*, edited by Edward Cavanagh, 213–250. Leiden: Brill, 2020.

Halme, Miia and Pamela Slotte (eds.). *Revisiting the Origins of Human Rights.* Cambridge, UK: Cambridge University Press, 2015.

Herzog, Tamar. *A Short History of European Law: The Last Two and a Half Millenia.* Cambridge, MA: Harvard University Press, 2018.

Hobbes, Thomas. *Leviathan* [1651]. Cambridge: Cambridge University Press, 1991.

Hobbes, Thomas. *De Cive* [1642; 1651]. Cambridge: Cambridge University Press, 1998.

Ishay, Micheline. *The History of Human Rights: From Ancient Times to the Globalization Era.* Berkeley, CA: University of California Press, 2008.

Johnson, James Turner. "Then and Now: Medieval Conception of Just War Versus Recent Portrayals of the Just War Idea." In *Medieval Foundations of International Relations*, edited by William Bain, 117–133. London: Routledge, 2017.

Justinian. *Institutes*, Translated by J. A. C. Thomas. Amsterdam: North-Holland Pub. Co., 1975.

Justinian. *The Digest of Justinian*, 2 vols., translated by Alan Watson. Philadelphia: University of Pennsylvania Press, 1998.

Kantorowicz, Ernst. *The King's Two Bodies: A Study in Mediaeval Political Theology.* Princeton, NJ: Princeton University Press, 1967.

Koskenniemi, Martti. "Vitoria and Us." *Rechtsgeschichte/Legal History* 22 (2014): 119–138.

Koskenniemi, Martti. *The Gentle Civilizer of Nations: The Rise and Fall of International Law, 1870–1960.* Cambridge: Cambridge University Press, 2002.

Koskenniemi, Martti. *To the Uttermost Parts of the Earth: Legal Imagination and International Power 1300–1870.* Oxford: Oxford University Press, 2021.

Lauren, Paul Gordon. *The Evolution of International Human Rights: Visions Seen*, 3rd ed. Philadelphia, PA: University of Pennsylvania Press, 2011.

Longfield Karr, Susan. *Jus Gentium in Humanist Jurisprudence: On Justice and Right.* Leiden: Brill, 2022.

Luscombe, D. E. "The State of Nature and the Origin of the State." In *The Cambridge History of Later Medieval Philosophy: From the Rediscovery of Aristotle to the Disintegration of Scholasticism, 1100–1600*, edited by Anthony Kenny, Eleonore Stump, Jan Pinborg, and Norman Kretzmann, 757–770. Cambridge: Cambridge University Press, 1982.

Martines, Lauro. *Power and Imagination: City-States in Renaissance Italy.* New York: Vintage Books, 1979.

Martines, Lauro. *Lawyers and Statecraft in Renaissance Florence*. Princeton, NJ: Princeton University Press, 1968.
More, Thomas. *Utopia*, Rev. ed., Edited by George M. Logan and Robert. M. Adams. Cambridge: Cambridge University Press, 2002.
Padoa-Schioppa, Antonio. *A History of Law in Europe: From the Early Middle Ages to the Twentieth Century*, Translated by Caterina Fitzgerald. Cambridge: Cambridge University Press, 2017.
Pagden, Anthony (ed.). *Lords of All the World: Ideologies of Empire in Spain, Britain, and France c.1500–1800*. New Haven, CT: Yale University Press, 1995.
Pagden, Anthony (ed.). *The Languages of Political Theory in Early-Modern Europe*. Cambridge: Cambridge University Press, 1987.
Pennington, Kenneth. *The Prince and the Law 1200–1600: Sovereignty and Rights in the Western Legal Tradition*. Berkeley: University of California Press, 1993.
Pollmann, Judith. *Memory in Early Modern Europe, 1500–1800*. Oxford: Oxford University Press, 2017.
Rousseau, Jean-Jacques. *The Discourse on the Origin of Inequality*, Translated by Maurice Cranston. New York: Dover Publications, 2004a.
Rousseau, Jean-Jacques. *The Social Contract*, Translated by Maurice Cranston. London: Penguin Books, 2004b.
Russell, Frederick H. *The Just War in the Middle Ages*. Cambridge, UK: Cambridge University Press, 1975.
Skinner, Quentin. *The Foundations of Modern Political Thought: Volume I: The Renaissance*. Cambridge: Cambridge University Press, 1978a.
Skinner, Quentin. *The Foundations of Modern Political Thought: Volume 2: The Reformation*. Cambridge: Cambridge University Press, 1978b.
Somos, Mark and Anne Peters (eds.). *The State of Nature*. Leiden: Brill, 2021.
Stein, Peter. *Roman Law in European History*. Cambridge, MA: Cambridge University Press, 1999.
Stein, Peter. "The *Ius Commune* and Its Demise." *The Journal of Legal History* 25, no. 2 (August 2004): 161–167.
Tierney, Brian. *The Idea of Natural Rights: Studies on Natural Rights, Natural Law, and Church Law, 1150–1625*. Atlanta, GA: Scholars Press, 1997.
Tuck, Richard. *Natural Rights Theories: Their Origin and Development*. Cambridge: Cambridge University Press, 1979.
Vitoria, Francisco de. "De Indis." In *Vitoria: Political Writings*, edited by Anthony Pagden and Jeremy Lawrance, 231–292. Cambridge: Cambridge University Press, 1991.
Witte, Jr., John. "A Short History of Western Rights." In *God's Joust, God's Justice: Law and Religion in the Western Tradition*, edited by John Witte, Jr., 31–48. Grand Rapids, MI: Wm. B. Eerdmans Publishing Company, 2006.
Zasius, Ulrich."In laudem legum oratio." In *Lucubrationes*, 1–4. Basel: Ioannem Frobenium, 1518.
Zasius, Ulrich. "De iustitia et iure (Lecture)." In *Opera omnia*, edited by Johann Ulrich Zasius and Joachim Münsinger von Frundeck, Facsímil., 1 cols., 241–269. Lyon: Sebastianum Gryphium, 1550.

10 Jefferson's preambles, prefaces, and persistence

Matthew Crow

1 Prefaces

The historian Gordon Wood once described Thomas Jefferson as "a Pollyanna about everything." Jefferson, so the argument goes, lacked any deep appreciation for the substance of the legal and intellectual traditions at stake in the major questions of his day, and in his own work, Wood has always emphasized the purportedly more serious constitutional theorizing of James Madison and John Adams.[1] This is by and large the impression of Jefferson's legal and political thinking that still governs scholarly accounts of early American intellectual history. What remains a largely triumphalist and provincial conversation about American constitutional interpretation and its history rarely pauses to take seriously the alternative routes for this history that Jefferson explored.[2] As a result, he remains something of a marginal figure in the intellectual history of law.[3] Jefferson tried to balance the persistence of the constitutional tradition that had produced him and his context with the necessity of a revolutionary openness to taking apart and reassembling that tradition.

In experimenting with how to strike this balance, Jefferson dealt with fundamental questions of authorship and identity, both individual and collective. This was the stuff, for him, of which constitutions were made. Constitutions needed to be understood, in this Jeffersonian framing, not simply as authoritative or fundamental written texts but also as representations—or inscriptions, one might say—of a particular form of collective political life. While we tend to assume constitutionalism and actively participatory politics are in tension if not mutually exclusive, the eccentric ways that Jefferson composed constitutional text show that for him, constitutions are where political communities

1 Gordon S. Wood, "The Disappointments of Thomas Jefferson," August 13, 1981, accessed www.nybooks.com/articles/1981/08/13/the-disappointments-of-jefferson/.

2 See, for example, Gordon S. Wood, *Power and Liberty: Constitutionalism in the American Revolution* (Oxford: Oxford University Press, 2021); Akhil Reed Amar, *The Words That Made Us: America's Constitutional Conversation, 1760–1840* (New York: Basic Books, 2021).

3 For a survey of Jefferson's constitutional thought, see David N. Mayer, *The Constitutional Thought of Thomas Jefferson* (Charlottesville: University of Virginia Press, 1994).

DOI: 10.4324/9781003534815-12

can be at their most radically democratic. This vision had two critically important conditions, which were that constitutions be presented in such a way that made them amenable to this ideal and that the people who showed up to put his theory into practice were those who he considered the right kind of people. As always with Jefferson, that was the rub.

Certainly, Jefferson's direct involvement with the institution of slavery and his contributions to the racial ideology that allowed this institution to persist, spread, and solidify in the early republic accounts for a good deal of his present marginality, and probably justifiably so. He wrote rather bald-facedly, at great length, and in public about the legality and ethics of the legal ownership of Black people, about race and empire, about his need for recognition and his anxieties about recognizing others as sharing a legal history with him, and about his fears of justice and revolt. Jefferson let his mind wander into questions that were at the very heart of what was going on in his world. His thinking forces modern accounts of the origins of American constitutionalism to confront how narratives of civil government in his time were crumbling and transforming across the age of revolutions and how slavery and empire were not only lived realities that troubled ideal theory but also central problems in the legal and political thinking of the day. The still prominent distinction in early American studies between the rarified air of founding constitutional history and the history of political thought, on the one hand, and the lived experience of everyone and everything else, on the other hand, is inadequate, and it has been this way for some time. We need to more fully integrate the histories of legal and imperial intellectual culture and of racial ideology into our accounts of early American thought, politics, and law and into broader histories of constitutionalism.

Jefferson compels us to think about legal and intellectual culture, about ideology, and about the simple fact—discomforting for many historians—that a thinker is not usually in firm control of what they are doing in their thinking and writing. This is the case even when a thinker is trying to assert such control and, especially in Jefferson's case, to wrest some kind of independence from the weight of the legal and intellectual history in which he found himself thinking and acting. This was Jefferson's project in his eccentric and uniquely lengthy prefaces to drafts of legal, constitutional, and diplomatic text. Jefferson spent the decade surrounding his drafting of the Declaration of Independence by burying himself in what he considered the fractious archive of Virginia's colonial legal history and in early modern theories of law, and he poured that reading into drafting legal and constitutional text.

For an apparently fitful optimist who urged his fellow Americans to always look away from the past, Jefferson spent a great deal of time not only immersed in the past but also putting that immersion front and center.[4] Indeed, in his

4 This aspect of this thinking is uniquely appreciated by Michael Knox Beran, *Jefferson's Demons: Portrait of a Restless Mind* (New York: Free Press, 2003); on Jefferson's historical thought, see

most public writing and thinking, even in his drafts of state constitutions for Virginia, Jefferson foregrounded both history and the politics of representing that history. The prefaces and additional commentaries to these documents, in the Declaration of Independence, his constitutional provisions, legal arguments, legislative revisions and diplomatic reports bare out a history of Jefferson's struggle to come to terms with the inseparability of American constitutionalism and his place in it from the British Atlantic and colonial world of an unevenly shared common law legal culture. This struggle, for personal and intellectual as much as political independence, appeared nowhere more directly than in his efforts to draft constitutional text that could take stock of this history and put it to use while at the same time, perhaps always incompletely, putting its sanctioned authority in its proper place: namely, the past. This was a struggle that directly shaped his thinking about race and belonging and about who was subject to whom and when, where, and why, and it is a struggle that illuminates a more rich and dynamic, albeit admittedly a little weird but kind of interesting if not entirely edifying, intellectual world of the American founding.

2 Collecting constitutional culture

Jefferson grew up on the periphery of Anglican Virginia, a self-consciously provincial periphery to the British Atlantic world in its own right.[5] The governing elite of the colony had an anxious, nearly obsessive dedication to what Karl Marx and Friedrich Engels would go on to describe in their Communist Manifesto as chartered freedoms, a premodern and in a sense distinctively Anglo-American faith in the power of legal texts to guarantee individual and public liberty, from fundamental statutes such as Magna Carta to minor conveyances such as charters, bills of sale, and contracts.[6] Colonial historians and writers like Robert Beverley endeavored to demonstrate that the planter class of a colony—which they did not hesitate to describe as the most ancient and loyal in the empire—was directly tied to the protection of the English common

Hannah Spahn, *Thomas Jefferson, Time, and History* (Charlottesville: University of Virginia Press, 2011); Ari Helo, *Thomas Jefferson's Ethics and the Politics of Human Progress: The Morality of a Slaveholder* (Cambridge: Cambridge University Press, 2013); Matthew Crow, *Thomas Jefferson, Legal History, and the Art of Recollection* (Cambridge: Cambridge University Press, 2017).

5 On the provincial enslaving and planter contexts of Jefferson's politics on a Virginian and national scale, see Alan Taylor, *The Internal Enemy: Slavery and the War in Virginia, 1772–1832* (New York: Norton, 2013); Annette Gordon-Reed and Peter S. Onuf, *Most Blessed of the Patriarchs: Thomas Jefferson and the Empire of the Imagination* (New York: Liveright, 2016); Onuf, *Jefferson and the Virginians: Democracy, Constitutions, and Empire* (Baton Rouge: Louisiana State University Press, 2018).

6 Karl Marx and Fredrich Engels, *The Communist Manifesto*, Edited by Gareth Stedman Jones (London: Penguin Classics, 2002), 222; see also Gary Wills, *Inventing America: Jefferson's Declaration of Independence* (New York: Norton, 1978).

law through the history of charters and subsequent legislation since the founding of the colony.[7] After the Virginia Company had landed at Jamestown in 1607, the early history proved bleak for settlers, as violent conflict with the Powhatan Confederacy and even within the beleaguered settler community itself led to the withdrawal of the company charter and the issuance of a royal charter in 1624. This instituted the office of a royal governor who wielded the power of the royal prerogative in the colony, and it created the beginnings of a distinctive historical narrative that tried to balance provincial particularity with imperial legal translation and conformity. In the wake of the Glorious Revolution in 1688–1689 and the rise of parliamentary supremacy in the imperial constitution, this project of shaping and controlling the narrative of legal and constitutional history became a principal goal of eighteenth-century colonial Virginian political and intellectual life. It was that culture, and Jefferson's creative reception of it and his awareness of his uncertain place at the receiving end of it, that gave his tinkering with inherited materials of legal and constitutional history its intense and peculiar virtuosity.

Jefferson became a collector of long-standing efforts on the part of the Virginia governing elite to frame their legal history as suited for their particular needs in local and imperial affairs. They looked to the colonial charters, which they read as royal promises that their colony was a distinct political body whose planting subjects enjoyed the protections of the laws and liberties of England. They spent a great deal of the eighteenth century asserting their powers of local legislative authority in the House of Burgesses and the Governor's Council and at times, in heated conflict with the appointed royal governor. The location, possession, and power of interpreting the law was one of the chief subjects of these kinds of disputes. Assembled bodies of legal texts were questions of immense political importance. Seizures on the orders of Stuart monarchs of the legal notes and writings of common law judges such as Sir Edward Coke provided a historical framework in which successive attempts on the part of governors and imperial officials to take possession of legislative records were understood by Virginia planters, who were actively engaged in protecting what they viewed as their rightfully primary role in making and interpreting law in the colony.

Economic interests were no doubt driving factors in these disputes. The planter elite feared an emergent discourse of political economy that increasingly saw commercial society supplanting what were understood to be feudal relations. Even as they sought to advance their own place in the commerce of the Atlantic empire, the hybrid jurisprudence of Virginia had grafted medieval

7 See Robert Beverley, *The History and Present State of Virginia*, Edited by Susan Scott Parrish (Chapel Hill: University of North Carolina Press, 2013); see also Peter C. Messer, *Stories of Independence: Identity, Ideology, and History in Eighteenth Century America* (Dekalb: University of Northern Illinois Press, 2005); Alexander B. Haskell, *For God, King, and People: Forging Commonwealth Bonds in Renaissance Virginia* (Chapel Hill: University of North Carolina Press, 2017).

English legal statuses of serfs and villeins onto the colonial law of slavery.[8] Powers of taxation, even before the imperial crisis, were another subject of constitutional conflict, as were Virginia's expectations for and speculations in westward expansion. There was something else going on, too. These manifold disputes also involved constitutional identity, recognition, and the assertion of having and making history. These anxieties were shaping forces in Jefferson's constitutionalism.

For historian Jack Greene, this was part of a broader process of colonial cultural and institutional development, Anglicization, and even "political mimesis."[9] Mimesis, of course, is a loaded concept in ethnography, aesthetic theory, legal theory, and beyond. It captures the ways in which continuity and identity shape our sense of reality and how society reproduces itself, which by and large it seems to do seamlessly. But Jefferson came of age intellectually in a world where the mimetic function of customary legal and constitutional authority felt like it was fracturing. History was pushing back on the increasingly desperate assertions on the part of colonials to have their sense of their own legal history confirmed on the other side of the Atlantic. Jefferson became aware, early on, of a kind of fracturing in constitutional time. He collected volumes of the original manuscript copies of colonial laws, and he did so to such an extent that, along with the patriot pamphleteer Richard Bland, he came to be known as an antiquarian. Collecting manuscripts and books on a scale nearly beyond his means (and later in life, well beyond them), he obtained commonplace books of literature, equity jurisprudence, common law doctrine, and political thought. He purchased the libraries of other colonial attorneys and their own collections of notes and legal manuscripts. He was prized by his mentor in the law, George Wythe, as both a careful student of law's history and a partner in the enjoyment of a kind of virtuosic culture of legal humanism. Jefferson and his closest peers in law and politics styled themselves as early modern legal scholars, that is, Renaissance men, and this styling was not merely cynical or ridiculous, although it could at times be both. It was its own kind of mimesis, to be sure, of translating and imitating, but as Jefferson went further into his thinking about how the colonial legal past would be interpreted in a new commonwealth, he began to see, emphasize, and celebrate discontinuity everywhere he looked.

8 See A. G. Roeber, *Faithful Magistrates and Republican Lawyers: Creators of Virginia's Legal Culture, 1680–1810* (Chapel Hill: University of North Carolina Press, 1981); Thomas D. Morris, *Southern Slavery and the Law, 1619–1860* (Chapel Hill: University of North Carolina Press, 1996); Christopher Tomlins, *Freedom Bound: Law, Labor, and Civic Identity in Colonizing English America, 1580–1685* (Cambridge: Cambridge University Press, 2010).

9 Jack P. Greene, *Negotiated Authorities: Essays in Colonial Political and Constitutional History* (Charlottesville: University of Virginia Press, 1994), 190; see Eric Auerbach, *Mimesis: The Representation of Reality in Western Literature* (Princeton: Princeton University Press, 1955); see also William Mazzarella, *The Mana of Mass Society* (Chicago: University of Chicago Press, 2017).

Underneath the narrative of legal continuity in which Virginians claimed rights of English liberty as they understood them, Jefferson started to focus on the ways that representations of law served to cover and displace genuinely political moments in history. His drafting of legal and constitutional text aimed, first and foremost, at instituting a constitutional culture that could hold on to something of its political life and its openness to rereading and rewriting, as well as to remodeling the body politic itself. In his draft of the Declaration of Independence, Jefferson went on at some length indicting the Crown and Parliament for their respective failure over the previous decade to see the Americans as legitimately sharing in the power and responsibility of that kind of rewriting and remodeling. The King, Jefferson laments, "has dissolved Representative houses repeatedly & continually, for opposing with manly firmness his invasions of the rights of the people," and so "legislative powers, incapable of annihilation, have returned to the people at large for their exercise;" this observation is absolutely elemental for Jefferson.[10] Just two years earlier, in his *Summary View of the Rights of British America*, he had directly addressed the King and suggested that the crown "was surrounded by British counselors," having taken none from America who might be more "amenable to the laws on which they are to give you advice;" Jefferson's auditioning for the role is predicated on his assertion that "great principles of right and wrong are legible to every reader" and that if established institutions failed to do the reading and do it well, this specifically constitutional, interpretive power would be retained and practiced by others.[11] For Jefferson, the official responsibility for participating in interpretation and legislation had seeped out of its designated repositories, and there is a profound ambivalence here, not only about the need to be recognized by the distant Royal father figure but also about what it meant to be living in a moment of loss for the traditional authority of law and legal interpretation. That anxious ambivalence about the questions not only of who holds and reads the law and what they do with it but also of whether if it is everybody then is it really anybody at all is a shaping force of Jefferson's constitutional theorizing.

When the Continental Congress directed colonial legislatures to write new state constitutions, Jefferson was one of several men who thought that they might take a crack at it. Jefferson, however, did so from the standpoint of an early modern (as well as ancient and medieval) assumption that authorship was not so separable from collecting, commenting, and editing as would become the case in the nineteenth century. His attempts at constitutional authorship grew out of his thinking of himself less as an author or a writer and more as a compiler, who compiled and recompiled in a moment when the problem of

10 Thomas Jefferson, "Original Rough Draft," *The Papers of Thomas Jefferson*, vol. 1, Edited by Julian P. Boyd (Princeton: Princeton University Press, 1950), 424.

11 Jefferson, "Summary View of the Rights of British America," *Papers of Thomas Jefferson*, vol. 1, 134.

who gets to do this compiling and what they have in their pile had become a political question of the highest importance.

The first draft of his proposed constitution for Virginia, written in the months before the Declaration in 1776, contains a similarly exhaustive list of legal indictments of the Crown and Parliament, many of which are identical. But what is such a framework doing at the beginning of a constitution in the first place? Jefferson clearly felt a very personal need to register the indictment against George, the "Geulph King of Great Britain," in any forum that he could. Of all of the constitutional drafts for states written across the rebelling colonies, Jefferson's is unique in its need to spend its first pages disentangling sovereignty, which was defined in the legal theory of the day as the power to make and define the law that resided in Parliament, from the sovereign. In this preamble of the first draft, Jefferson turns to the Elizabethan charter given to Sir Walter Raleigh in 1584 by noting that the charter warns that any act of hostility by Raleigh and his heirs against the Crown would put them "out of allegiance and protection." Jefferson goes on to suggest that this is as good a ground as any on which to find that in their rebellion against British rule and in the Royal response to the declared causes of taking up arms, "it follows by the sd. charter that, from & after time of such putting out, ourselves, and the places within our habitation, possession, & rule are not subject to him." Jefferson thus located the legitimacy of the rebellion in the charters and other records of colonial rule and took the chance to show off his self-styled erudition and familiarity with these charters and records.[12]

In two subsequent drafts, the lengthy legal indictment fades, possibly because by the time of their drafting, Jefferson had gotten the chance to think about relocating them to other texts, namely, the Declaration of Independence. A shortened version of the preamble still remains, announcing that the text is a "Bill for new modelling the form of government and for establishing the Fundamental principles of our future Constitution."[13] There is a space left in the manuscript copy for the preamble, but Jefferson never fills it. The eccentricities of his draft texts, however, are still apparent. His draft calls for jury trials in all cases, including, notably, in a proposed Court of Chancery and in cases of admiralty and ecclesiastical law. Even more surprisingly, he borrows the idea of a privy council from the British government, which is appointed by the lower house of the representative body, to give advice to the prospective holder of a relatively weak office, not a governor, but an administrator with no veto power or any other common executive prerogatives. Most tellingly, he includes an amendment and approval process that requires a canvassing of specially elected county meetings to approve ratification and subsequent changes.

The actual structure proposed in these drafts is moderate, at best, even as it no doubt shaped the bicameral, limited republican constitution with an even

12 Jefferson, "First Draft," *Papers of Thomas Jefferson*, vol. 1, 337–340.
13 Jefferson, "Second Draft," *Papers of Thomas Jefferson*, vol. 1, 347.

more limited governor (as Jefferson would discover upon being elected to the office) that ended up being approved along with a secondary preamble. It was George Mason's more elegant and fitting with the general tenor of the times preamble and list of rights that won priority. That text stated famously, from the Virginia Declaration of Rights, that

> all men are by nature equally free and independent, and have certain inherent rights, of which, when they enter into a state of society, they cannot, by any compact, deprive or divest their posterity; namely, the enjoyment of life and liberty, with the means of acquiring and possessing property, and pursuing and obtaining happiness and safety.[14]

Jefferson remained self-consciously tied to a very particular and frankly eccentric reading of English ancient constitutionalism, that is, an understanding of constitutions as assemblages of texts and their history of use. His preambles to proposed constitutional text in the revolutionary period went to great lengths to hold on to this ideology and to demand that his participation in its history and his mastery of its materials be acknowledged. Notably, he avoided the references to natural rights in property, opting for the prosaic pursuit of happiness in the Declaration and an English, legal constructivist understanding of property in his state constitutional proposals. He went so far as to suggest that the state should provide property to white men who lacked it as a way of making them fully staked citizens in the new polity. All of this grew out of Jefferson's borderline frenetic obsession with bringing the politics of representing and interpreting legal history and images of law's textuality to the center of what it meant to make and maintain constitutions as something like forms of collective life. For Jefferson, this process consisted of cycles of reading and rereading and writing and rewriting law, fundamental or otherwise.

Appointed to a committee charged with the revisal of the existing body of Virginia law, Jefferson drew up 126 proposed revision bills, many of which were laden with his insistence on keeping the common law tradition and a glossator's approach to legal text and commentary as part of the purportedly new, republican constitutional culture. His draft of the crime bill, to take the most extreme example, contained extensive historical citations in its margins to common law precedents dating back to the earliest memorials of written law and legal interpretation in the British Isles.[15] He was disappointed to discover that no one else thought that printing actual laws that looked like scrapbooks was a good idea or that tying the new commonwealth to a racialized account

14 "The Constitution of Virginia, 1776," accessed https://encyclopediavirginia.org/entries/the-constitution-of-virginia-1776/.

15 Thomas Jefferson, "A Bill for Proportioning Crimes and Punishments in Cases Heretofore Capital," in *The Papers of Thomas Jefferson*, vol. 2, ed. Juian P. Boyd (Princeton: Princeton University Press, 1950), 492–507.

of its imagined origins in early medieval English villages was so essential. The substance of the crime bill, taken as a whole, like his constitutional proposals, is unremarkable, save for its relative conservatism. What concerns us here is that for Jefferson, the substantive details and effects of these proposals were of secondary importance when compared to the apparently, for him, more weighty questions of how they appeared in print and of the culture of interpretive practice that these peculiar textualities would institute. Sure enough, it would be easy to see these eccentric practices as little more than aristocratic vanity and a planter's tunnel vision of his assumptions and preferences as the center of every story in which he finds himself. If for nothing else, Jefferson might be useful here for helpfully reminding academics that critical problematizing and virtuosic reframing are not in and of themselves radical or emancipatory political acts.

What remains notable and little appreciated by so much of the best scholarship on Jefferson and his thinking about the world he lived in was that Jefferson, perhaps naively, potentially quite radically, came to think of citizenship as something like participating in collective projects of virtuosic reframing and remodeling of the legal history, as represented in text, that makes the polity a polity in the first place. He did what he could to hold on to something of the pliable and palimpsest-like quality that he associated with his manuscripts as a way of thinking about constitutional texts in a republic. Moreover, he spent a great deal of the rest of his life castigating more successful draftsmen of lasting constitutional texts for not attending to what for him, was the absolute necessity: keeping those texts more physically open than they have proven to be to new readings, new uses, and in short, to legal history as something not just inherited but made and remade in the course of human events.

3 Constitutions between criticism and capacity

As Hannah Arendt appreciated about Jefferson, memory, or more precisely, remembrance or recollection, was at the center of Jefferson's thinking about constitutions and about what, in his view, was lost as much as gained in the founding. The "book-learning and thinking in concepts" that had characterized the intellectual history of the imperial crisis leading up to 1776, Arendt argues, "dried up almost immediately" after independence had been achieved. Arendt, like Tocqueville, notes the absence of a theoretical interest in politics in American thought, and she suggests that this is less a defining feature than a kind of mistake, an accident of a particular "failure of thought and remembrance" in the wake of the revolution.[16] This not only has left the American Revolution "sterile in terms of world politics" relative to its French counterpart and of no apparent lasting relevance to speculative political thought but also leaves the United States without what Arendt thought of as its

16 Hannah Arendt, *On Revolution* (New York: Penguin Classics, 2006), 211.

greatest potential contribution to political theory, its attention to the work of remembrance.

> Experiences and even the stories which grow out of what men do and endure, of happenings and events, sink back into the futility inherent in the living world and the living deed unless they are talked about over and over again,

and "this incessant talk" itself "remains futile unless certain concepts, certain guideposts for future remembrance, and even for sheer reference, arise out of it."[17] The late colonial concern for a particular narrative attachment to British constitutionalism in the Atlantic world can be understood as a reflection of this insight and this need, a practical, political and deeply personal need for a history from which to act—and to be seen to act—in time.

This was no doubt a specific experience of history tied to this particular moment, caught as it was between the neoclassical and civic humanist, imperial culture of the early modern world and that of the quintessentially modern, bourgeois citizen, namely, of a past irrevocably made *past* by an experience of history as progress beyond the cyclical ruination and reconfiguration of the polity, specifically, decline and fall. In the problem of founding lasting institutions, Arendt suggests, the Americans failed to remember that it was less a state and still less a text that would need to endure but politics itself, the "revolutionary spirit" of collective action. To survive, this spirit would need to hold on to something of this opening in time, this experience of being caught, productively, between the past and the future, and a particular referentiality of the past for use in the present. "On the American scene," Arendt argues, "no one has perceived this seemingly inevitable flaw in the structure of the republic with greater clarity and more passionate preoccupation than Jefferson."[18] On this point, she is right. Increasingly, as the years wore on, Jefferson cultivated an occasionally searing critique of the U.S. constitutional order, precisely for its inattentiveness to the capacity of the citizenry to think and act anew and to recollect their history and rework it by rereading and rewriting its materials. This capacity, for Jefferson, was just about the only thing that had a laudatory claim to lasting persistence from the age of democratic revolutions that he had helped begin, and the law continued to be the medium, for Jefferson, for the maintenance and exercise of that capacity.

He began leveling his developing constitutional criticism before the war for independence was even over. He had submitted his respective drafts of constitutional text for Virginia as bills outlining principles of government under the assumption that as the Burgesses had not called a special constitutional convention and were meeting in legislative session, nothing like a document

17 Arendt, *On Revolution*, 212.
18 Arendt, *On Revolution*, 225.

of fundamental law could be authorized. In his *Notes on the State of Virginia*, Jefferson argued that while the broader context of a war made exigency and efficiency necessary, the adoption of a state constitution under such circumstances was a violation of the republican principles at stake in that war. The powers of prerogative, Jefferson inferred, had not been taken apart so much as relocated to the legislature, which, as the example of Parliament proved well enough for him, could be as despotic as any king or governor acting in the king's stead. No doubt, Jefferson is settling scores here and using the opportunity to respond to queries from a French official about the respective states in the union to philosophize at great length about natural history, race and identity, and law and politics. This included taking shots at Virginia's legislature, which had censured him as governor for fleeing the state capitol when under British attack. In Queries XIII and XIV, written between 1780 and 1782 and published in 1787, Jefferson engaged in an extensive theorization of what was right and what was wrong, in his view, with the experiment in republican government going on in the states.

In his theorizing, he remained almost entirely focused less on the actual policies or structures than on their legitimacy as he understood it, namely, the manner in which texts were acknowledged and maintained as authoritative. He had begun the query on constitutions by discussing the charters that had become founding documents for the colonists, detailing the original letters and charter for Sir Walter Raleigh and subsequent charters and grants. Query XXIII detailed the colonial charters, official records, and colonial histories written from those records, and Jefferson continued to insist that Virginia was a civil polity as measured by its archive, which demonstrated that it had been such a polity all along and that its governing elite was in possession of a history of counsel and legislation. This history, the implication went, was not being honored amidst current events. In its ratification of a new state constitution, the legislature, Jefferson reasoned, had been "seduced in their judgment by the example of an ancient republic" and by the idea that the sovereign power had to sit somewhere and especially in times of emergency, and this, Jefferson mourned, displayed a tragic lack of faith in the capacity of the state's citizens to help hold the state together and wait for Jefferson's favored process of collective deliberation, canvassing, and editing of constitutional text to play out.[19] He ends the query on constitutions by calling for a new constitutional convention, arguing that one is necessary to ensure that the exigencies of popular acquiescence to the government not become a bad precedent, a failure to remember.

The next query on the laws of the state builds on the same set of governing assumptions that had characterized Jefferson's revolutionary-era constitutional theorizing. It was less concerned with policy than with its appearance in print

19 Thomas Jefferson, *Notes on the State of Virginia*, Edited by Frank Shuffleton (New York: Penguin Classics, 1999), 135.

and the possible relationships created and foreclosed between the public and their texts. He summed up the project for the revisal of the laws as a historical one: "It was thought dangerous to attempt to reduce it to a text: it was therefore left to be collected from the usual monuments of it."[20] These monuments were precisely the archives of legal records and histories, official and unofficial, held in public and private hands, including Jefferson's, which Jefferson was so concerned to put at the center of any seriously republican understanding of the legislated constitution. That some of these were in his own growing private library highlights the already fraught connections between his own sense of himself and his place in the new political class and his wider membership in an Atlantic republic of letters. He continued to perform and promote his erudition as a felt precondition for being taken intellectually and politically seriously by others, and this continued to be tied to a sense of the importance of curating a legal identity for Virginia and more broadly, the United States.

Just a year after the publication of the *Notes on the State of Virginia*, in his capacity as minister to France, Jefferson would issue his report on the impacts of the revolutionary war and British and French mercantile policy on the American whaling industry, giving a lengthy introduction on the history of European whaling in the Atlantic world dating back to the Basques.[21] The audience for the report, which included the French Council of State and the U.S. Congress, probably did not need a history lesson, but that is what they got. Within a year, he watched with excitement as the early stirrings of the French Revolution surfaced around him in Paris, and he let this excitement shock his friends John and Abigail Adams and James Madison. As Madison wrote to update Jefferson on the progress of the ratification debates for the new U.S. Constitution, Jefferson responded by questioning whether constitutions can legitimately outlast the generation that makes them, once again leveling his critique of the very idea of fundamental law as reflective of an overly rigid and impoverished textuality.[22] Some "look at constitutions with sanctimonious reverence, & deem them like the arc of the covenant," he would later

20 Jefferson, *Notes on the State of Virginia*, 144; see also Jefferson, *The Autobiography of Thomas Jefferson, 1743–1790*, Paul Leicester Ford, ed. (Philadelphia: University of Pennsylvania Press, 2005), pp. 64–71.

21 Jefferson, "Observations on the Whaling Industry," in *The Papers of Thomas Jefferson*, vol. 14, ed. Julian P. Boyd (Princeton: Princeton University Press, 1958), 242–256; see Matthew Crow, "Jefferson's Whale: Race, Climate, and Commerce in Early America," *Journal of the Early Republic* 40 no, 3 (Fall 2020), 435–463.

22 Jefferson to Madison, 6 September 1789, *Papers of Thomas Jefferson*, Vol. 15; p. 384–99; see also Merrill D. Peterson, *Adams and Jefferson: A Revolutionary Dialogue* (Oxford: Oxford University Press, 1976), 37–61; Eric Slauter, *The State as a Work of Art: The Cultural Origins of the Constitution* (Chicago: University of Chicago Press, 2009); Mary Sarah Bilder, *Madison's Hand: Revising the Constitutional Convention* (Cambridge, MA: Harvard University Press, 2015).

write, "too sacred to be touched."[23] He did not share this view. Imperfectly at best, his project, all the same, had been concerned with instituting a textual culture that lent itself to being revised and reinstituted, where notions of authorship and intention were at most marginal to jurisprudence, questions of use were much more front and center, and some space was created that was not free of the past so much as it might have hoped to reach a point where the past was delivered to the possibilities of reference, that is, to new use and new arrangement. This was, in a sense, what Jefferson considered the materials of constitutional politics to consist of in the first place.

4 Conclusion

For Jefferson, citizenship was thus something like a historical practice, and republican constitutionalism was something like a peculiarly material and textual culture of public historiography. The ideal citizen in such a culture was not only shaped by laws and institutions, perhaps more than by anything else, but also capable of participating to varying degrees in shaping them. This made who was deemed to possess that capacity a—if not the—central question of political thought in the revolution and founding. This was certainly true for Jefferson, who turned shortly after his discussion of the revisal, in his query on laws in the *Notes on the State of Virginia*, to slavery. This was not a coincidence. For Jefferson, slavery was not, among other things, just a legal and economic institution and the material basis for his own capacity to collect and legislate and that of many of his contemporaries. Race was an elemental structuring fact of political life, or indeed of the very possibility of it, because of the troubling question of who remembers what and of what recollections count as properly civic and political. Why not incorporate Black people into the state and make them citizens, Jefferson is asked, and he responds: "Deep-rooted prejudices" among whites, and more importantly perhaps, "ten thousand recollections" on the part of the enslaved of their oppression and endurance.[24] In a polity sustained by what Abraham Lincoln would go on to call in his first inaugural address the mystic chords of memory and what for Jefferson was a critical component of citizenship, specifically, the active sharing of a legal history, counter-history was perceived as a radical threat, liable in Jefferson's reckoning to produce a conflict that could only lead to a race war. For all of the racist declarations of natural intellectual inferiority that famously follow in the *Notes*, it needs to be remembered that what Jefferson feared most was not just revolt and conflict, although he certainly did fear both, but also

23 Jefferson to Samuel Kercheval, 12 July 1816, *The Papers of Thomas Jefferson: Retirement Series*, Vol. 10, J. Jefferson Looney, ed., p. 226.

24 Jefferson, *Notes on the State of Virginia*, p. 145; see Christopher P. Iannini, *Fatal Revolutions: Natural History, West Indian Slavery, and the Routes of American Literature* (Chapel Hill: University of North Carolina Press, 2012), Ch. 5.

remembrance. He feared a disruption to precisely the kind of anxiously theorized, curated, and mediated relationship between past and present that he saw as the substance of civic life, and he went to war, in the pages of the *Notes*, to protect his sense of himself and his idealized vision of his fellow citizens as having an exceptional capacity to master the materials of their history. He was deeply troubled, haunted even, that this desperately imagined mastery could be questioned and challenged and that the people with whom he shared space in his plantation and the people with whom he shared a continent were just as capable of thought and remembrance and politics as he was, and maybe in a sense even more so.

Jefferson, it warrants repeating, was grossly wrong about so much, but his written work helps us see that, as the historian J.G.A. Pocock suggests, if politics is the art of making and managing history, then the people who inhabit the U.S. have a lot of political and historical work to do.[25] But what would this work look like? It might entail remodeling the inscribed and built environment of civic culture and even taking down a few monuments. Even then, we would have to confront some of the same problems that purportedly monumental figures and their texts have served to resolve for established history in the past, for example, problems about the historical foundations of legality and identity, about collective agency and memory, and the relationship between the two. It would surely have to be a good deal more than quietly reframing the founding texts or tinkering with their appearance. All the same, Jefferson's eccentric willingness to put the collected and constructed history of law up front in his constitutions and his discussions about them warrant recollection today as something like what the philosopher Gillian Rose calls a "poetics of law." This poetics would be an attention to the material practices of legal and political theorizing that, in its illumination of both the constructed and constructive qualities of law's power, might help us, as she puts it, "to rediscover politics."[26] If there is any path for Americans to have more productively political relationships with their past and present and, thus, a more liberating and imaginative jurisprudence, then Thomas Jefferson might be found to have left some guideposts along the way.

References

Amar, Akhil Reed. *The Words That Made Us: America's Constitutional Conversation, 1760–1840*. New York. Basic Books, 2021.

Arendt, Hannah. *On Revolution*. New York: Penguin Classics, 2006.

25 J.G.A. Pocock, "The Politics of History: The Subaltern and the Subversive," in *Political Thought and History: Essays in Theory and Method* (Cambridge: Cambridge University Press, 2009), 239–256.

26 Gillian Rose, *Mourning Becomes the Law: Philosophy and Representation* (Cambridge: Cambridge University Press, 1996), 76.

Auerbach, Eric. *Mimesis: The Representation of Reality in Western Literature*. Princeton: Princeton University Press, 1955.

Beran, Michael Knox. *Jefferson's Demons: Portrait of a Restless Mind*. New York: Free Press, 2003.

Beverley, Robert. *The History and Present State of Virginia*, Edited by Susan Scott Parrish. Chapel Hill: University of North Carolina Press, 2013.

Bilder, Mary Sarah. *Madison's Hand: Revising the Constitutional Convention*. Cambridge, MA: Harvard University Press, 2015.

Crow, Matthew. *Thomas Jefferson, Legal History, and the Art of Recollection*. Cambridge: Cambridge University Press., 2017.

Crow, Matthew. "Jefferson's Whale: Race, Climate, and Commerce in Early America." *Journal of the Early Republic* 40, no. 3 (2020): 435–463.

Gordon-Reed, Annette and Peter S. Onuf. *Most Blessed of the Patriarchs: Thomas Jefferson and the Empire of the Imagination*. New York: Liveright, 2016.

Greene, Jack P. *Negotiated Authorities: Essays in Colonial Political and Constitutional History*. Charlottesville: University of Virginia Press, 1994.

Haskell, Alexander B. *For God, King, and People: Forging Commonwealth Bonds in Renaissance Virginia*. Chapel Hill: University of North Carolina Press, 2017.

Helo, Ari. *Thomas Jefferson's Ethics and the Politics of Human Progress: The Morality of a Slaveholder*. Cambridge: Cambridge University Press, 2013.

Iannini, Christopher P. *Fatal Revolutions: Natural History, West Indian Slavery, and the Routes of American Literature*. Chapel Hill: University of North Carolina Press, 2012.

Jefferson, Thomas. *The Papers of Thomas Jefferson*, Edited by Julian P. Boyd et al. Princeton: Princeton University Press, 1951.

Jefferson, Thomas. *Notes on the State of Virginia*, Edited by Frank Shuffleton New York: Penguin Classics, 1999.

Jefferson, Thomas. *The Autobiography of Thomas Jefferson, 1743–1790*, Edited by Paul Leicester Ford. Philadelphia: University of Pennsylvania Press, 2005.

Jefferson, Thomas. "The Constitution of Virginia, 1776." https://encyclopediavirginia.org/entries/the-constitution-of-virginia-1776/.

Marx, Karl and Friedrich Engels. *The Communist Manifesto*, Edited by Gareth Stedman Jones. London: Penguin Classics, 2022.

Mayer, David N. *The Constitutional Thought of Thomas Jefferson*. Charlottesville: University of Virginia Pres, 1994.

Mazzarella, William. *The Mana of Mass Society*. Chicago: University of Chicago Press, 2017.

Messer, Peter C. *Stories of Independence: Identity, Ideology, and History in Eighteenth Century America*. Dekalb: University of Northern Illinois Press, 2005.

Morris, Thomas D. *Southern Slavery and the Law, 1619–1860*. Chapel Hill: University of North Carolina Press, 1996.

Onuf, Peter S. *Jefferson and the Virginians: Democracy, Constitutions, and Empire*. Baton Rouge: Louisiana State University Press, 2018.

Peterson, Merrill D. *Adams and Jefferson: A Revolutionary Dialogue*. Oxford: Oxford University Press, 1976.

Pocock, J. G. A. "The Politics of History: The Subaltern and the Subversive." In *Political Thought and History: Essays in Theory and Method*. Cambridge: Cambridge University Press, 2009.

Roeber, A. G. *Faithful Magistrates and Republican Lawyers: Creators of Virginia's Legal Culture, 1680–1810*. Chapel Hill: University of North Carolina Press, 1981.

Rose, Gillian. *Mourning Becomes the Law: Philosophy and Representation*. Cambridge: Cambridge University Press, 1996.

Slauter, Eric. *The State as a Work of Art: The Cultural Origins of the Constitution*. Chicago: University of Chicago Press, 2009.

Spahn, Hannah. *Thomas Jefferson, Time, and History*. Charlottesville: University of Virginia Press, 2011.

Taylor, Alan. *The Internal Enemy: Slavery and the War in Virginia, 1772–1832*. New York: Norton, 2013.

Tomlins, Christopher. *Freedom Bound: Law, Labor, and Civic Identity in Colonizing English America, 1580–1685*. Cambridge: Cambridge University Press, 2010.

Wills, Gary. *Inventing America: Jefferson's Declaration of Independence*. New York: Norton, 1978.

Wood, Gordon S. "The Disappointments of Thomas Jefferson." August 13, 1981. www.nybooks.com/articles/1981/08/13/the-disappointments-of-jefferson/.

Wood, Gordon S. 2021. *Power and Liberty: Constitutionalism in the American Revolution*. Oxford: Oxford University Press.

11 Martens Clause and ambiguity at the birth of modern humanitarian law

Daimeon Shanks-Dumont

1 Introduction

On May 18, 1899, at the behest of Tsar Nicholas II, delegates from twenty-six nations gathered in The Hague to discuss "[t]he maintenance of general peace and a possible reduction of the excessive armaments which weigh upon all nations."[1] Foreign ministries were doubly surprised by the invitation: first, that Russia, who had up to this time been enthusiastic participants in the arms race that contributed to the collapse of the Concert of Europe, were now seeking peace through disarmament, and second, when the proposed conference program was circulated, that it had little to do with the Tsar's stated goals. The regulation of the *conduct* of war and the extension of the 1864 Geneva Conventions to naval warfare dominated the proposed agenda. It was to be a war conference, and the duplicity was lost on no one.[2]

But amid the agreements and compromises that were produced at the Hague Conference was an unassuming clause that would lead to the modernization of one of the oldest fields in the law of nations: international humanitarian law (IHL), the rules that regulate the conduct of armed forces during hostilities.[3] The traditional story is that the principles of IHL first expressed

1 "Russian Circular Note Proposing the First Peace Conference," in *Reports to the Hague Conferences of 1899 and 1907*, ed. J. B. Scott (Oxford: Clarendon Press, 1917).

2 "German Note. XV. 141," in *German Diplomatic Documents 1871–1914*, vol. 3, ed. E. T. S. Dugdale (Royal Institute of International Affairs, 1930), 74 ("[The proposed conference] greatly surprised the German Government and was in sharp contrast with Russia's attitude up to that time and with the continuous massing of troops on the German eastern frontier during the Tsar's reign"); letter from Bertha von Suttner to Henry Dunant on 9 May 1899, cited in André Durand, "The Development of the Idea of Peace in the Thinking of Henry Dunant," *International Review of the Red Cross* 250 no. 26 (1986): 16, 38 ("[A]ll the military men, statesmen and governments, who do not want to hear a word about the end of wars, entrench themselves behind the Red Cross and the Geneva Conventions to obstruct the entire Conference of the Hague. They are going to discuss additional articles to deal with the evils of future massacres, so as not to have to concern themselves with the means of avoiding such massacres.").

3 Traditionally referred to as *ius in bello* (the laws in/of war), these rules are in contrast to *ius ad bellum* (the right to [wage] war), the rules that govern a state's resort to war, such as the

DOI: 10.4324/9781003534815-13

in the Hague Conventions would begin a process of humanizing war and tempering the worst of humanity's most evil impulses.

The so-called "Martens Clause," named for Feodor Martens, the Russian lawyer tasked with operationalizing the Tsar's peace initiative, is the ninth paragraph of the preamble to the 1899 Hague Convention (II) on the Regulation of the Laws and Customs of War on Land:

> Until a more complete code of the laws of war has been issued, the high contracting Parties deem it expedient to declare that, in cases not included in the regulations adopted by them, the inhabitants and the belligerents remain under the protection and the rule of the principles of the law of nations, as they result from the usages established among civilized peoples, from the laws of humanity, and from the dictates of the public conscience.[4]

The Clause has taken an outsized importance in international law. As one of international law's foundational "myths," it has come to represent the first expression that humanitarian considerations should be given binding legal effect during armed conflict.[5] The Clause has been restated in international agreements,[6] cited by international tribunals and domestic courts,[7] and invoked by scholars and judges alike as expanding on, or creating entirely new, sources of international law.[8]

---

customary and treaty norms concerning the right of self-defense. For an accessible historical survey of the development of *ius ad bellum*, see Oona A. Hathaway and Scott J. Shapiro, *The Internationalists: How a Radical Plan to Outlaw War Remade the World* (New York: Simon & Schuster, 2017).

4 "Preamble, Convention No. II with Respect to the Laws and Customs of War on Land," in *Reports to the Hague Conferences*, 126. The clause would be replicated, in nearly the same terms, in the preamble to the 1907 Hague Convention IV.

5 Antonio Cassese, "The Martens Clause: Half a Loaf or Simply Pie in the Sky?," *European Journal of International Law* 11 no. 1 (2000): 187.

6 Geneva Convention for the Amelioration of the Condition of the Wounded and Sick in Armed Forces in the Field, Aug. 12, 1949, 75 U.N.T.S. 31, at art. 63 ("Geneva I"); Geneva Convention for the Amelioration of the Condition of Wounded, Sick and Shipwrecked Members of Armed Forces at Sea art. 62, Aug. 12, 1949, 75 U.N.T.S. 85, at art. 62 ("Geneva II"), Geneva Convention Relative to the Treatment of Prisoners of War, Aug. 12, 1949, 75 U.N.T.S. 135, at art. 142 ("Geneva III"); Geneva Convention Relative to the Protection of Civilian Persons in Times of War, Aug. 12, 1949, 75 U.N.T.S. 287, at art. 158 ("Geneva IV"); Protocol Additions to the Geneva Conventions of 12 August 1949, and Relating to the Protection of Victims of International Armed Conflicts, June 8, 1977, at art. 1 ("Protocol I").

7 *Military and Paramilitary Activities in and Against Nicaragua (Nicar. v. U.S.)*, Judgment, 1986 I.C.J. Rep. 14, ¶ 218 (June 27); *Prosecutor v. Kupreskic*, Case No. IT-95-16, Judgment, ¶ 525–26 (Int'l Crim. Trib. for the Former Yugoslavia Jan. 14, 2000); Colombia: Final Agreement to End the Armed Conflict and Build a Stable and Lasting Peace preamble, Nov. 24, 2016, www.refworld.org/docid/5b68465c4.html.

8 Cassese, "The Martens Clause," 189 fn. 5.

However, Martens' intent in drafting the Clause had little to do with humanitarian concerns.[9] Rather, what inspired Martens' language was a contest of wills between the lesser and great European powers over the rights accorded to belligerent occupiers. The former group, led by the Belgian delegation, wished to preserve a legal right of armed insurgency in the event of invasion. The latter, nominally headed by Martens but reflecting the will of Europe's ascendant superpower, Germany, wanted to limit lawful status to regularized military forces—effectively criminalizing civilian resistance and legitimating draconian reprisal practices. The negotiations regarding the first and second articles of the proposed convention,[10] concerning the legal status of combatants, ground to a halt as Great Britain and Switzerland joined the Belgians, and Germany backed Russia.

Martens has been hailed for his "pioneering and conciliatory role" in proposing the declaration that broke the impasse,[11] but the proposed compromise was little more than a retrenchment of the Russian and German position and a face-saving opportunity for the Belgians to capitulate. Why was this compromise position accepted? The conference proceedings do little to show the concerns that motivated the delegates in attendance; however, it is clear from the records that Martens—an adept international lawyer and savvy political operative[12]—was at the center of the debate and crucial to its resolution. The aim of this chapter is to recover the events surrounding the drafting of the Martens Clause to expose its shaky foundation as a source of normative legal doctrine by challenging the traditional narrative that it had indeed been proposed with "a humanitarian goal in mind."[13] The chapter explores the conference records and the larger legal and geopolitical backgrounds in which the

9 Within the conventional teleologically-oriented understanding of humanitarian law, our anachronistic conception of the Martens clause is exactly the type of "myth" that Quentin Skinner identifies as resulting from traditional historicism—the reification of a doctrine (i.e., humanitarianism) that the historian expects an author (i.e., Martens) to have articulated, even though the author did not or even could not intend to give the text such a meaning. Quentin Skinner, "Meaning and Understanding in the History of Ideas," in *Meaning & Context: Quentin Skinner and His Critics*, ed. James Tully (Cambridge UK: Polity Press, 1988), 29–67. In this instance, the idea that humanitarian constraints on warfare was in some sense an imminent intellectual tradition throughout history, or at least in the nineteenth century, has led to a hagiographic quality that imbues much of the Martens literature. For example, see V. V. Pustogarov, *Our Martens: F.F. Martens—International Lawyer and Architect of Peace*, Translated by W. E. Butler (London: Simmonds & Hill Pub., 2000); Arthur Eyffinger, "Feodor Martens, Architect of the Hague Tradition of International Law," *Journal of Social Sciences of U Nord. Tallinn* 17 (2009).

10 Articles 1 and 2 of the Hague Convention (II) were recodifications of Articles 9 and 10 of the Brussels Declaration of 1874, and, as such, were usually referred to as Articles 9 and 10 during the Conference debates.

11 Eyffinger, "Feodor Martens, Architect," 35.

12 Arthur Nussbaum, "Frédéric de Martens, Representative Tsarist Writer on International Law," *Nordisk Tidsskrift International Ret* 22 (1952): 51.

13 Cassese, "The Martens Clause," 193, 198.

conference was held to provide insight into the delegates' acceptance of the compromise position. It does so by contextualizing Martens himself through an examination of the political and intellectual environment surrounding the Russian liberal elite of St. Petersburg, of whom Martens was a leading figure. The objective is to uncover the motivations behind Martens' own project in an effort to reconcile the conflicting accounts of his role at the birth of international humanitarian law.

The literature that examines Martens' role in the genesis of IHL generally falls into two opposing positions: laudatory or skeptical. The former lavishes praise on Martens as a humanitarian ahead of his time;[14] some go so far as to ascribe to his work precursor ideations of modern human rights.[15] The latter denigrates Martens as little more than an apologist for Tsarist policy and a political opportunist.[16] It is true that Martens used his considerable legal acumen and diplomatic tact to achieve Russian political objectives at The Hague, but at times, these purely political maneuvers were belied by apparently inconsistent ideological obstinacy.[17] Martens—one-part international jurist, one-part diplomat—had his own project, the appreciation of which helps shed light on the ambiguous legacy of his contributions to the laws of armed conflict.

Feodor Feodorovich Martens (1845–1909) was in many ways a paradox himself. Born to ethnically Estonian parents in the Western borderlands of the Russian Empire, Martens was sent to the imperial capital of St. Petersburg when he was orphaned at the age of nine. Educated in German, Martens would become an influential professor of international law at St. Petersburg University while simultaneously serving as a counselor at the Russian Ministry of Foreign Affairs.[18] As a prominent figure in the Russian school of international law, Martens was an advocate for European integration and was prototypical of the cadre of Russianized Baltic German scholars and diplomats who held

14 For examples, see Pustogarov, *Our Martens*; Eyffinger, "Feodor Martens, Architect," 35.

15 See, for example, Lauri Mälksoo, "F.F. Martens and His Time: When Russia Was an Integral Part of the European Tradition of International Law," *European Journal of International Law* 25 no. 3 (2014): 824.

16 Nussbaum, "Martens, Representative Tsarist Writer," 22. Often these positions reflect the political commitments of their authors, for example, Mälksoo has characterized Pustogarov's work as "engaged . . . only relatively little with Martens' international legal theory," "occasionally emphatically defensive-patriotic," and "anti-Nussbaum." Mälksoo, "F.F. Martens and His Time," 818. Nussbaum, for his part, stated that "de Martens considered it his professional duty as a scholar and writer on international law to defend and back up the policies of his government at any price . . . Obviously his motivation was overwhelmingly, if not exclusively, political and patriotic." Nussbaum, "Martens, Representative Tsarist Writer," 60.

17 This was the case in the Conference's Third Committee, where Martens vehemently opposed the American proposition that arbitral awards should be subject to secondary review on ideological grounds. Frederick W. Holls, *The Peace Conference at the Hague* (New York: The Macmillan Company, 1900), 286–303 (Holls was a delegate from the United States and sat on the *comité d'examen* alongside Martens).

18 Lauri Mälksoo, *Russian Approaches to International Law* (Oxford: Oxford University Press, 2015), 42.

influential positions in the capital.[19] His status as both a political insider and an ethnic outsider and prominent position in academic and political spheres made him an easy target for Russophile critics in the nascent nationalist movements of the late nineteenth century.

Russia's precarious position as a great military and economic power during this period as the "family of civilized nations" concretized[20] and the retrenchment of an autocratic, repressive social order that followed Alexander II's short-lived reforms following the Crimean War (1853–1856) resulted in considerable tensions and uncertainties for the Tsarist regime both internationally and domestically. This generated a bifurcation of political ideologies among the liberal elite of St. Petersburg.[21] Martens was a prominent member of one faction who idealized the West and understood the Russian intellectual tradition as being decidedly European. In opposition were the Slavophiles, who saw Russia as the head of a distinct "historical-cultural type," whose ethnic and historical conditions put it in direct opposition to Western Europe.[22] Martens' writings are best understood as being in direct discourse with the polemics of the Slavophile camp. And the idiom that he used in this dialogue was international law—a distinctly Western, positivist international law.[23]

19 Lauri Mälksoo, "The Science of International Law and the Concept of Politics: The Arguments and Lives of the International Law Professors at the University of Dorpat/Iur'ev/Tartu 1855–1985," *British Yearbook of International Law* 76 no. 1 (2005): 383.

20 Gerrit Gong, *The Standard of "Civilization" in International Society* (Oxford: Clarendon Press, 1984), 24–35.

21 This period of economic uncertainty and social repression would also spawn the socialist movements that would eventually overthrow the imperial regime, to whom Martens gave short shrift: he considered socialists as political criminals who desired and celebrated the "instincts bestiaux de l'homme." Martii Koskenniemi, *The Gentle Civilizer of Nations* (Cambridge: Cambridge University Press, 2004), 68.

22 Lauri Mälksoo, "The History of International Legal Theory in Russia: A Civilizational Dialogue with Europe," *European Journal of International Law* 19 no. 1 (2008): 221–22. Prominent among these intellectuals was Nikolai Danilevski (1822–1885), whose highly influential book *Russia and Europe* was widely read throughout imperial Russia, particularly as the Balkan crisis of 1875–1878 became a focal point of political debate. N. Ya. Danilevski, *Rossia i Evropa. Vzgljad na kul'turnye i politicheskie otnoshenia Slavjanskogo mira k Germano-Romanskomu*, 5th edn (St. Petersburg: Paneleevs, 1895, first print in 1869). Ethnic Slav uprisings in the Ottoman-controlled Balkan regions were supported, and in some cases fomented, by Russia, which would lead to the Russo-Turkish War of 1877–1878. Alexis Heraclides and Ada Dialla, *Humanitarian Intervention in the Long Nineteenth Century: Setting the Precedent* (Manchester: Manchester University Print, 2015), 169–196. Danilevski argued that the West would only ever consider Germanic-Romanic civilizations as truly European, thereby excluding Russia and the rest of the Slavic world as natural rivals and mere "ethnographic material" for the West. Danilevski, *Rossia i Evropa*, 50, 59, 131–132.

23 Russian international lawyers of the era, of whom Martens was the most prominent, were staunch proponents of Westernization in this respect and considered themselves the "translators and transferors of Western European international law scholarship." Mälksoo, "The History of International Legal Theory in Russia," 213.

Martens' Westernizing project entailed three primary facets. First, Europeanization of the cultural and political spheres of the capital elite represented the continuation of modernization efforts that had begun in the early eighteenth century under Peter the Great.[24] For Martens, the internal domestic order and external international conduct of a state were co-constitutive;[25] thus, Russia's engagement with the international community as a member of the "family of nations" constructed Russia's status as a civilized people as much as it reflected actual societal conditions.[26] In overtly appropriating the classical European approach to international law, Martens promoted the idea that Russia was itself civilized, which, for the Westernizers, was coterminous with the political and social conditions of European nations.[27]

Second, Martens' contributions to the "civilizing mission" of the late nineteenth century strongly supported the Tsar's imperialist projects in Central Asia and the Balkans. Like most of his contemporaries, Martens ascribed to "civilized" states the unequal privileges afforded under the legalized hegemonic and liberal anti-pluralistic international order that defined the nineteenth century.[28] Martens posited that non-civilized nations (essentially, all non-European states) could only become civilized by Europeanizing their internal domestic order, just as Russia had. In this view, pre-Petrine Muscovy had been an uncivilized country before it undertook a process of aggressive modernization in the early eighteenth century,[29] the continuation of which Martens saw as his own mission.[30]

24 Arnulf Becker Lorca, "Universal International Law: Nineteenth-Century Histories of Imposition and Appropriation," *Harvard International Law Journal* 51, no. 2 (2010): 540–541.

25 Lorca, "Universal International Law," 542–543.

26 Martens was not ignorant of the conditions in which the majority of Russians lived. In many ways, he understood international law as a "gentle civilizer" within Russia's borders, as much as it was a means of regulating external relations. Mälksoo, *Russian Approaches to International Law*, 46 (citing Koskenniemi, *The Gentle Civilizer of Nations*). For example, Martens wrote in his diary that "in Russia despotism is reaching the limits of mindless arbitrariness" and that "the systematic persecution of the Jews, Finns and Baltic Germans had considerably increased the centrifugal tendencies in the Russian Empire." V. V. Pustogarov, *Our Martens*, 208.

27 "[T]he Russian people begin to understand their deficiencies, their backwardness, become aware of themselves and seek to achieve the level of civic life and culture on which stand *other more enlightened peoples*." Martens, *Modern International Law*, 157–158 (emphasis added). Among the most prominent "enlightened peoples" were, for him, the Germans. Ibid., 137.

28 Gerry Simpson, *Great Powers and Outlaw States* (Cambridge: Cambridge University Press, 2004).

29 Mälksoo, "The History of International Legal Theory in Russia," 221.

30 Moreover, Martens' view that the Ottoman Empire and other Central Asian states lay outside the international community buttressed the Russian desire to recover Constantinople from the Turks, lost after the Crimean War, and to abrogate the 1865 Treaty of Paris that prohibited Russia from keeping warships and arsenals in the Black Sea. John Lowe, *The Great Powers, Imperialism and the German Problem, 1865–1925* (Taylor and Francis, 1994), 8–9.

The third aspect of Martens' project was the programmatic expression of these philosophical commitments, which was on full display at the 1899 Hague Peace Conference. He did not see it as his diplomatic and scholarly duty to unreflectively justify the Tsar's autocratic regime but rather to demonstrate Russia's civilized behavior among Europeans through professional engagement. And Martens' scholarly output was prodigious, publishing the first comprehensive Russian treatise on international law,[31] a fifteen-volume annotated collection of imperial Russian treaties,[32] and numerous other books and articles that were widely read and translated.[33] Professionally, he served as a member of the *Institut de droit international*,[34] sat on various arbitration tribunals,[35] and represented Russia at the 1874 Brussels Conference, the 1885 Conference of Berlin, both Hague Peace Conferences, and the 1905 Russo-Japanese peace negotiations.[36] In many ways, Martens' involvement in that period's obsession with codifying international law "demonstrate[ed] more enthusiasm than the Europeans."[37]

It is through these lenses that Martens' actions at The Hague begin to gain coherence. Martens was perfectly willing to equivocate or dissemble when it served his purpose,[38] just as he could be obdurate when circumstances called

31 F. F. Martens, *Sovremennoe mezhdunarodnoe pravo tsivilizovannykh narodov (Modern International Law of Civilized Peoples)*, vol. 1 and 2, Edited by L. N. Shestakova (Moscow: Yuridicheskii Kollodzh MGU, 1996).

32 F. F. Martens (ed.), *Sobranie traktatov i konventsii, zaklijuchennykh Rossieyu s inostrannymi derzhavami* (St. Petersburg: A. Böhnke, 1874–1909).

33 Peter Holquist, "The Russian Empire as a 'Civilized State': International Law as Principle and Practice in Imperial Russia, 1874–1878," *National Council for Eurasian and East European Research*, Working Paper (July 14, 2004), 1–37.

34 For a comprehensive overview of Martens' professional work, see Mälksoo, "F.F. Martens and His Time," 826–829.

35 This included the infamous Anglo-Venezuelan arbitration. Martens' role as the president of this arbitral tribunal, which occurred contemporaneously with the 1899 Hague Peace Conference, has been called into question as allegations of impropriety and fraud were levied against him. The validity of the arbitral award is now the basis of a dispute between Guyana and Venezuela before the International Court of Justice. *See* Federica Paddeu and Brendant Plant, "The Dispute between Guyana and Venezuela Over the Essequibo Region," *EJIL: Talk!*, April 11, 2018, accessed www.ejiltalk.org/the-dispute-between-guyana-and-venezuela-over-the-essequibo-region/.

36 Mälksoo, "F.F. Martens and His Time," 826–829.

37 Becker Lorca, "Universal International Law," 540–541.

38 For example, Martens academic writing presented a coherent and consistent position with respect to the legal requirement to declare war prior to the commencement of hostilities. Pursuant to this view, Japan's surprise attack at the outset of the Russo-Japanese War was deemed illegal by Martens. F. F. Martens, "Les Hostilités sans Déclaration de Guerre à Propos de la Guerre Russo-Japonaise," *Revue Générale de Droit International Public* 111 (1904): 148–150. However, he duplicitously argued that the Russian surprise naval action against Sinop in 1853 was distinguishable as there existed a *de facto* condition of war prior to the attack, demonstrating his ambivalent attitude toward ideological consistency. Ibid.

for it.[39] His objectives in constructing the conference agenda and as Chair of the Second Commission were to facilitate Russia's inclusion in the "family of civilized nations" through the use of international law, signaling both internationally and domestically that Russia was, and should be, considered a Western polity. Codification was the goal by (almost) any means necessary. To understand the reception of Martens' contributions and not just his actions, however, we must first take a short detour to discuss the general state of international law around the turn of the century.

2 Prologue: the legal context

The meaning of the Martens Clause is not exhausted by reference to Martens' intentions; rather, one must consider the legal contexts in which the international lawyers present at the conference would have understood the proposed text. In particular, the tradition of legal positivism as a mode of legal thought is put forward as a partial explanation for the acceptance of the Martens Clause compromise, inasmuch as it was drafted in a style that recalled earlier conceptions of natural law and, consequently, would not have been understood as imposing a binding obligation.

Positivism, as a mode of legal thought, is best understood in relation to that which it displaced: natural law, the norms and principles that can be deduced from religion, nature, reason, or abstract conceptions of justice.[40] Positivism, by contrast, assumes no source for law outside the enactments of a sovereign recognized as authoritative; that is, all legal facts are ultimately determined by social facts alone.[41] Beginning as part of a larger movement of "positive philosophy" that began with August Comte (1798–1857) in the early nineteenth century, positivism gained prominence in jurisprudence through the writing of British lawyer John Austin (1790–1859), whose sanction theory of law posited that law was whatever the sovereign commanded, backed up by a legitimate threat of sanction; that is, law could be inductively identified through observation rather than by deductive reasoning from abstract, general norms.[42] Inspired by the successes of the natural sciences, the overarching goal of positivism was, as a historical movement, to transform law into a science properly understood.

Although there were many variations of positivism in international law, three core tenets were shared by most positivist lawyers of the era.[43] First

39 For example, see Holls, *The Peace Conference at the Hague.*

40 Alexander Orakhelashvii, "Natural Law and Justice," in *Max Planck Encyclopedias of International Law*, last modified August 2007, accessed https://opil.ouplaw.com/view/10.1093/law:epil/9780199231690/law-9780199231690-e730?rskey=pcc4Et&result=1&prd=MPIL.

41 Scott J. Shapiro, *Legality* (Cambridge, MA: Belknap Press, 2011), 27–30.

42 Stephen C. Neff, *Justice Among Nations: A History of International Law* (Cambridge, MA: Harvard University Press, 2014), 223–224.

43 Neff, *Justice Among Nations*, 224.

and foremost, positive international law as a science entailed the wholesale rejection of natural law as a proper source of obligation; in place of abstract concepts, positivist lawyers looked to the will of states to determine what the rules were. There was agreement on the "centrality of *will* over *reason* in the making of law," inasmuch as it was a "body of law that was made *by* the states themselves *for* their own purposes" rather than a "reflection of transcendental, universal, eternal norms, as natural lawyers held."[44] Second, positivism was understood as a *method* for identifying existing rules and creating new law rather than a fixed system of universal concepts and principles. Third and finally, positivism insisted on the strict separation of law from morality, that is, the method of international law was meant solely for the discovery of what the law *is*; questions about what the law *ought* to be were properly the domain of moral philosophy.

The implications of positivism for international law were numerous, but three are of importance to this discussion, with the latter two deriving from the first. To begin with, the fundamental principle of the sovereign equality of states—still the primary coordinating principle of international law today[45]—meant not only that states were independent but also that no law was binding unless the concerned state consented to the rule by its own free will.[46] On this understanding, states coexist in a kind of anarchical society; international law, for the positivist, is merely a practical means of mediating states' interactions such that peaceful coexistence is possible.[47] Flowing from the principle of the equality of states came the notion of states as possessors of rights: because sovereigns were not subject to duties derived from nature or reason meant that states, instead, possessed fundamental permissive rights by virtue of the absence of external constraints (operating in a manner similar to the so-called "domestic analogy"—a metaphor of man in a pre-political Hobbesian state of nature—which was the basis for natural law jurisprudence).[48] Chief among these rights was self-preservation, stylized as self-defense.[49]

Lastly, and as a consequence of the principles of equality and possession of rights, was the understanding of international law as a contractual system. Because no state could arbitrarily force its will on another and states retained

44 Neff, *Justice Among Nations*, 225.
45 For example, see James Crawford, *Brownlie's Principles of Public International Law*, 8th ed. (Oxford: Oxford University Press, 2012), 448–449.
46 See Matthew J. Lister, "The Legitimating Role of Consent in International Law," *Chicago Journal of International Law* 11 no. 2 (2011): 663–691: Neff.
47 Hedley Bull, *The Anarchical Society: A Study of Order in World Politics*, 3rd ed. (New York: Columbia University Press, 2002).
48 Hedley Bull, "The Grotian Conception of International Society," in *Diplomatic Investigations*, eds. Herbert Butterfield and Martin Wight (London: Allen & Unwin, 1966). On the domestic analogy, specifically as it applied in a secular natural law jurisprudence, see Richard Tuck, *The Rights of War and Peace: Political Thought and the International Order from Grotius to Kant* (Oxford: Oxford University Press, 1999).
49 Neff, *Justice Among Nations*, 246.

all of the inherent rights that they did not voluntarily divest, the basis of legal obligation could only be sourced through positive obligations, that is, agreements.[50] Usually grouped under the rubric "the principle of freedom" or the "Lotus principle" (named for a Permanent Court of International Justice case in which the principle was later expounded), two further implications arise from this contractual conception: first, that in the absence of an agreement, no rule of international law could be said to exist; and, second, that in the absence of a prohibitory rule, state conduct must be deemed permissible.[51]

By the time of the 1899 Hague Peace Conference, the hegemony of positivism as a mode of legal thought was near its apogee. Codification of the rules of armed conflict was but one aspect of this flourishing but nevertheless represented an important element in the project to transform international law into a body of scientific knowledge, so much so that the international lawyers present at The Hague were given the auspicious title of "scientific delegates" in the conference proceedings.

3 The conference debates

The working structure of the 1899 Hague Peace Conference closely reflected the subjects proposed by the Russian Circular Note that had proposed the gathering, with the First and Third Commissions addressing the reduction or prohibition of armaments and the pacific settlements of disputes, respectively. Martens presided over the Second Commission, which was tasked with the revision of an earlier, unsuccessful attempt at codification of the laws and customs concerning the conduct of warfare, the 1874 Brussels Declaration.[52] Following the Franco-Prussian War of 1870–1871, the Brussels Conference, which produced the Brussels Declaration, was the brainchild of Martens, and it had catapulted the international lawyer and mid-level diplomate to a place of prominence in the Russian foreign service, setting him up as the obvious choice to lead the Russian delegation at The Hague.[53] On June 6, during the proceedings of the Second Sub-Commission, the attendees took up the questions that had frustrated the widespread acceptance of the Brussels

50 Rules of customary international law were readily accepted by even the staunchest positivists; after all, they still represent a state's positive agreement to be bound through tacit consent. The difficulty lay, and still lies today, with what counts as evidence of such tacit consent. Monica Hakimi, "Making Sense of Customary International Law," *Michigan Law Review* 118 no. 8 (2020).

51 *Case of the S.S. "Lotus" (Fr. v. Turk.)*, 1927 P.C.I.J. (ser. A) No. 10 (Sept. 7).

52 Regarding articles 5, 6, and 7 of the Circular Note. Scott, *Reports to the Hague Conferences of 1899 and 1907*; see generally Tracey Leigh Dowdeswell, "The Brussels Peace Conference of 1874 and the Modern Laws of Belligerent Qualification," *Osgood Hall Law Journal* 54 no. 3 (2017): 805.

53 John Fabian Witt, *Lincoln's Code: The Laws of War in American History* (New York: Free Press, 2012), 343–344.

Declaration—and directly inspired the Martens Clause—namely, the rights and duties applicable during military occupation.[54]

At the outset of the debate, Auguste Beernaert, Minister of State and delegate of Belgium, voiced his strong opposition to the codification of Chapters I, II, and IX of the Brussels *projet*, which dealt with the legal rights of occupiers. "In my opinion," he stated,

> there are certain points which cannot be the subject of a convention and which it would be better to leave, as at present, under the governance of that tacit and common law which arises from the principles of the law of nations.[55]

In a lengthy speech, Beernaert spoke against the disparate treatment that codification would afford "small countries which in the nature of the things cannot be invaders but are subject of being invaded."[56] His opposition centered on a two-prong argument. First, the proposed articles would grant extensive civil powers to occupying belligerents. Beernaert conceded that these situations were a normal occurrence during occupation but argued that it was wrong to bestow advance treaty-based rights to conquering armies, thus preemptively organizing "a régime of defeat."[57]

The second, more contentious issue concerned the qualification of lawful belligerents.[58] The proposed articles 1 and 2 of the Convention's Annex detailing the convention's regulations were word-for-word identical to Articles 9 and 10 of the Brussels Declaration, which set forth the criteria of lawful combatant status, with an additional recognition of civilians engaged in *levée en masse* (the mass conscription of regular citizens to repel invasion).[59] Moreover, Article 11 vested, in the event of capture, "the rights of prisoners of war" to those who fulfilled the formal requirements laid out in Article 9. Beernaert argued that in defining lawful combatants, it necessarily proscribed the right of citizens to resist occupation, unless they were conscripted into regularized

54 Beernaert (Belgium), "Second Commission: Second Subcommission, Sixth Meeting, June 6, 1899," in *The Proceedings of the Hague Peace Conferences, Translation of the Official Text*, ed. J. B. Scott (New York: Oxford University Press, 1920–1921), 502 ("I am afraid that if we wish to regulate everything and to decide everything conventionally, we shall meet the same difficulties as before.").

55 Beernaert, "Second Commission," 502.

56 Beernaert, "Second Commission," 504.

57 Beernaert, "Second Commission," 503.

58 Rotem Giladi, "The Enactment of Irony: Reflections on the Origins of the Martens Clause," *European Journal of International Law* 25 no. 3 (2014): 852.

59 "Preamble, Convention No. II with Respect to the Laws and Customs of War on Land," in *Reports to the Hague Conferences*, arts. 1 & 2.

standing armies. The Belgian minister exhorted his fellow delegates to consider that

> [B]y undertaking to restrict war to States only, the citizens remaining to a certain extent only mere spectators, would not the risk be run of reducing the factors of resistance by weakening the powerful mainspring of patriotism? Is it not the first duty of a citizen to defend his country, and is it not to the fulfillment of this duty that we all owe the most beautiful pages of our national history?[60]

Beernaert's position was self-evident, given Belgium's precarious geographical location between Germany and its principal rivals, France and Great Britain, and its treaty-imposed neutrality.[61] Moreover, in replicating the Brussels formulation, the delegates present knew that they would be codifying provisions that advantaged occupying forces so greatly that their previous iteration had been known in European ministries as "The Code of Conquest."[62]

What was left unsaid—but omnipresent in the subtext of the debate—were the political considerations that had helped to frustrate the ratification of the Brussels Declaration.[63] Germany, recently unified behind the powerful Prussian state, became the principal military presence on the European continent after its defeat of Napoleon III in 1871, destabilizing the existing balance of powers.[64] Led by the statesman Otto von Bismarck, Germany had "turned the international system inside out,"[65] embarking on an ambitious coalition-building project in the 1870s that resulted in the Triple Alliance of Germany, Italy, and Austria-Hungary while maintaining normalized relations with Russia and mediating St. Petersburg's rivalry with Austria-Hungary over

60 Beernaert (Belgium), *Proceedings of the Hague Peace Conferences*, 504.

61 Belgium's strict neutrality was imposed by the great powers of Britain, France, Russia, Austria-Hungary, and Prussia by the 1839 Treaty of London. C. P. Sanger and H. T. J. Norton, *England's Guarantee to Belgium and Luxemburg, with the Full Text of the Treaties* (London: G. Allen & Unwin Ltd., 1915), 139–141.

62 The British representative to the Brussels Conference, Savile Lumly, in a letter to Lord Derby, described the response to the articles as a "general feeling of uneasiness . . . Created by the consideration of [the] propositions, which have been aptly designated as the 'Code of Conquest.'" 7 July 1875. FO 83/481, Foreign Office Archives, Public Record Office (PRO). The French ambassador to the Court of St James wrote that "all the measures seem calculated to guarantee conquering armies the advantages of their organization and their invading marching masses, and, on the other hand, to diminish the means of defence of populations surprised by such an invasion. It is, in truth, a code of conquest rather than one of defence." Letter from La Rochefoucauld to the Minister of Foreign Affairs, 26 June 1874. Brussels, Légations Fond A 25.

63 Karma Nabulsi, *Traditions of War* (Oxford: Oxford University Press, 1999), 6.

64 For example, see Michael W. Doyle, *Empires* (Ithaca, NY: Cornell University Press, 1986), 242–248.

65 Doyle, *Empires*, 245–246.

the Balkans.[66] Containment of the ascendant military and economic power of Germany became of central importance to the rest of the European powers, spurring Russia to forge the Franco-Russian Alliance in 1894.[67] Great Britain, which had fallen out with France as both vied for influence in Egypt[68] and was increasingly at odds with both Russia and other European rivals over its colonial holdings,[69] found itself somewhat isolated and in an ever-increasing naval arms race with the Germans.[70] Policies of containment shaded international diplomacy in the last quarter of the nineteenth century, including at Brussels in 1874 and in The Hague twenty-five years later.

Thus, the lesser powers such as Belgium, along with the great powers Great Britain and France, had opposed the codification of Prussia's occupation policies of 1870–1871, which is largely what the Brussels Declaration represented in the popular imagination.[71] The then-existing doctrines of occupation were severe, governed by the vague mandates of military necessity and *Kriegraison*. Civilians who participated in hostilities, such as the French guerilla fighters known as *francs-tireurs* (literally *free-pullers*, referring to the action of a trigger) that had resisted Prussian occupation, were considered outlaws rather than combatants. As the Russian's proposed text for the Brussels Declaration in 1874 ominously affirmed, such unlawful combatants were to be "delivered to justice."[72]

The idealized conception of warfare in the nineteenth century was reserved to the exclusive domain of professional armies who fought "with more than a trace of the sporting ethos."[73] Professional soldiers were ostensibly "technicians" who participated in war as a political event, with an absence of personal animosity on either side.[74] During periods of occupation, however, this idealized code of conduct gave way to widespread civilian participation in resistance efforts. The use of such forces to repel invasion became commonplace during the nineteenth century—indeed, it was the Spanish paramilitary tactics during the Peninsular War (1808–1814) that gave English the term *guerilla*

66 Doyle, *Empires*, 248–250.
67 William L. Langer, *The Franco-Russian Alliance (1890–1894)* (Oxford: Oxford University Press, 1925).
68 John Darwin, *The Empire Project: The Rise and Fall of the British World System, 1830–1970* (Cambridge: Cambridge University Press, 2009), 70–74.
69 Doyle, Empires, 253.
70 Paul Kennedy, *The Rise and Fall of the Great Powers: Economic Change and Military Conflict from 1500 to 2000* (New York, NY: Random House, 1987), 211–212.
71 Nabulsi, *Traditions of War*, 6.
72 Nabulsi, *Traditions of War*, 16.
73 Stephen C. Neff, *War and the Law of Nations* (Cambridge: Cambridge University Press, 2005), 189.
74 Neff, *War and the Law of Nations*. For an illustrating examination of the philosophical considerations undergirding individual exculpation for acts performed during war and in service of a sovereign authority, see Christopher Kutz, *On War and Democracy* (2016): 37–62.

fighter[75]—but it was in the Franco-Prussian War that the use of irregular militias gained notoriety. Led by the Kingdom of Prussia, the emerging German Empire quickly routed the French regular army early in the war, winning a string of decisive encounters and capturing Emperor Napoleon III on the battlefield of Sedan in September of 1870.[76] A popular uprising ensued, following which the French parliament set up a provisional government in Paris, the Government of National Defence, to continue the war effort for a further five months by calling on irregular forces to bolster their devastated regiments. The *francs-tireurs* came out in large numbers, engaging in guerrilla warfare tactics such as sabotage and ambush in defense of their homeland.[77]

As a means of repressing resistance, invading armies in the nineteenth century regularly used highly coercive measures called reprisals against civilian populations, even as they were obliged under the law of nations to extend certain protections to lawful combatants taken as prisoners or were otherwise *hors de combat*.[78] For example, both Germany and France were parties to the recently-signed 1864 Geneva Convention when hostilities broke out; thus, they were subject to positive-law duties to respect the neutrality of medical personnel and the care and repatriation of wounded enemy soldiers.[79] Civilians, however, were granted no such protections if they engaged in hostilities as unlawful combatants.[80] German reprisal practices against such civilians during the invasion of France were notoriously draconian, consisting of summary executions, vicarious and collective punishment, hostage-taking, and a complete disregard for norms of due process if trials were granted.[81] During the ensuing occupation, Germany issued a proclamation declaring that combatants not possessing the distinguishing marks of the regular army were liable to penalty of death,[82] whose determination was a matter of discretion for the occupying power—both as a practical matter and because prior to the 1874 Brussels Conference, there had been no systematic attempt to define what would be considered adequate identification.

Martens knew full well the explosive potential of the underlying dispute concerning the qualification of lawful belligerents as it had, after all, thwarted

75 Nabulsi, *Traditions of War*, 48–52.
76 Dowdeswell, "The Brussels Peace Conference of 1874," 808.
77 Dowdeswell, "The Brussels Peace Conference of 1874," 808–809.
78 Nabulsi, *Traditions of War*, 27–33.
79 Geneva Convention for the Amelioration of the Condition of the Wounded in Armies in the Field, Aug. 22, 1864, https://ihl-databases.icrc.org/en/ihl-treaties/gc-1864?activeTab=historical.
80 A strikingly similar argument was wielded by the Bush Administration during the U.S.'s war on terror. See, for example, *Hamdan v. Rumsfeld*, 548 US 557 (2008).
81 Nabulsi cites a 1911 treatise on the laws of war in which reprisals are addressed in a chapter titled, "Under Martial Law the Guilt of the Accused is Assumed." Ibid., 32 (citing J. M. Spaight, *War Rights on Land* (London: Macmillan, 1911), 349–350).
82 W. Hall, *A Treatise on International Law* (Oxford: Clarendon Press, 1924), 496.

the ratification of the Brussels *projet*.[83] In his response to Beernaert, Martens extolled the virtue of complete regulation, including the comprehensive definition of lawful combatant status. "Is this uncertainty [about the definition] advantageous to the weak? Do the weak become stronger because the ***duties*** of the strong are not determined?" he implored. "Do the strong become weaker because their ***rights*** are specifically defined and consequently limited?"[84] Ironically, he was claiming to advocate on behalf of the lesser powers by promoting the position that they were opposing. Perhaps anticipating that his intervention would not win the day, Martens made one last appeal before it was agreed to table the discussion of these "two theses"—the rights and duties of occupiers and the qualification of lawful belligerents—for a future session. "It is for you to answer this question," remarked Martens, "To whom will doubt and uncertainty be of advantage, to the weak or to the strong?"[85]

It would be a full two weeks before the Second Commission would take up the contentious articles again.[86] Each side prepared for the debate. Germany remained obstinate, as it had little interest in attending the conference in the first place[87]—it was the world's great military power and suffered none of the financial straits that had partly motivated the call to disarmament—but if it were to participate, it wanted the most propitious terms possible.[88] Germany's military delegate Colonel Gross von Schwarzhoff, who had been a strident opponent of arms limitations and the proposed armament moratorium,[89] steered the German retinue and led the fierce opposition to Beernaert's suggestion to leave the rules of occupation to the vagaries of the law of nations.

Despite its wariness of German militarism,[90] Russia found itself on their side—partly due to its own military stance and partly because Martens knew

83 Pustogarov, *Our Martens*, 108.

84 Pustogarov, *Our Martens*, (emphasis in the original).

85 Pustogarov, *Our Martens*, 508.

86 "Second Commission: Second Subcommission, Eleventh Meeting, June 20, 1899," in *Proceedings of the Hague Peace Conferences*, 545.

87 'Willy' (Kaiser Wilhelm II), upon receiving news of the Tsar's invitation, directly telegrammed his first cousin 'Nicky' (Tsar Nicholas II): imagine "a Monarch holding personal command of his Army, dissolving his regiments sacred with a hundred years of history . . . and handing over his towns to Anarchists and Democracy." Barbara W. Tuchman, *The Proud Tower: A Portrait of the World Before the War, 1890–1914* (Westminster: Random House Publishing Group, 1966), 241.

88 Tuchman cogently argues that Russia's motivations in calling the Conference were largely driven by both an inability to finance their participation in the precipitous arms race engulfing the modernizing world and fear of widespread social upheaval that would follow a modern war, as formulated in Ivan Bloch's influential *The Future of War* (1898). Tuchman, *The Proud Tower*, 229–251.

89 In response to grandiloquent economic appeals for disarmament, he brusquely replied that the German people "were not crushed beneath the weight or armament expenditures . . . They are not hastening toward exhaustion and ruin." Tuchman, *The Proud Tower*, 258.

90 There was little love lost between the Russian and German delegations. Andrew White, the American delegate, recounted a conversation with Count Münster, who "said the calling of

that the proposed articles were necessary for Germany's support for codification. France, despite its treatment in 1870–1871, stayed out of the dispute, likely due to a recently inked alliance with the Tsar.[91] The United States, for its part, remained disinterested throughout the debate.[92]

Switzerland, as a small power, was a natural ally to Belgium and supported Beernaert. Less self-evident was Great Britain's position, despite the geopolitical balance of powers. On the one hand, the British Empire had sent a strong military and naval delegation in the persons of Major General Sir John Ardagh and Admiral Sir John Fisher, neither of whom could be mistaken for pacifists.[93] Moreover, as the most ardent imperialists, the British government forcefully opposed military and especially naval limitations.[94] In a previous session, Ardagh had restated the British position towards codification in general, asserting that it was their "intention . . . to embody in our manual of instruction, literally, if possible, all the articles of the Declaration," that were "in accordance with which we have thus far regulated our acts." However, such rules were to remain inferior to British regulations, with Ardagh stating that the "full liberty to accept or modify the articles is of supreme importance to us."[95]

On the other hand, London was heavily invested in Belgian neutrality due to its geographic location and the UK's increasing political and military isolation.[96] Britain's position as an island had traditionally been the nation's first and strongest line of defense against continental rivals, and the fear of Germans appropriating the Belgian ports, in such close proximity to British shores, incentivized their support for the Low Countries' inviolability.[97]

---

the conference was simply a political trick—the most detestable trick ever practiced. It was done . . . mainly to embarrass Germany, to glorify the young Russian Emperor, and to put Germany and nations which Russia dislikes into a false position." Andrew W. White, *The First Hague Conference* (Boston: The World Peace Foundation, 1912), 63–64.

91 Norman Rich, *Great Power Diplomacy 1814–1914* (New York: McGraw-Hill, 1992), 260–262.

92 William R. Crozier, a military delegate for the U.S., would later write of the dispute that he "took the guiding principle that the United States itself did not fear invasion but could afford to be as humane towards invaded countries as anybody." Letter from W. Crozier to General Corbin, July 19, 1899, Hay Papers, Library of Congress.

93 Tuchman recounts how Lord Salisbury, the British prime minister who had selected Fisher to serve as delegate, remarked that he had no doubt Fisher would fight at the Peace Conference. "So I did," wrote Fisher, "though it was not for peace." Tuchman, *The Proud Tower*, 255.

94 Ardagh vigorously opposed the prohibition of 'dumdum' bullets, as he argued they were necessary to produce "shock sufficient to stop the stricken soldier and put him immediately *hors de combat*." Ardagh (Great Britain), "First Commission, Third Meeting, June 22, 1899," in *Proceedings of the Hague Peace Conferences*, 276–278. Tuchman quotes Ardagh providing his unvarnished yet still droll opinion: "Your fanatical barbarian, similarly wounded, continues to rush on, spear or sword in hand; and before you have had time to represent to him that his conduct is in flagrant violation of the understanding relative to the proper course for the wounded man to follow—he may have cut off your head." Tuchman, *The Proud Tower*, 262.

95 Ardagh (Great Britain), "Second Commission: Second Subcommission, Eighth Meeting, June 10, 1899," in *Proceedings of the Hague Peace Conferences*, 517.

96 Lowe, *The Great Powers*, 4.

97 The British and German military rivalry was already tense in 1899. The Kaiser considered sea power an essential lever in making Germany a *Weltmacht* (world power), which placed

In advance of the debate, Great Britain and Switzerland laid on the table two proposals to amend the controversial articles.[98] The Swiss revision would expressly prohibit the use of reprisals during occupation, while the British amendment was formulated as a without-prejudice clause affirming "the right belonging to the population of an invaded country to fulfill its duty of offering by all lawful means, the most energetic patriotic resistance against the invaders."[99] While lesser states such as Belgium and Switzerland could likely be browbeaten into submission, the British position must have greatly troubled Martens, as it was to a great extent British intransigence on this very subject that had sunk the Brussels *projet* twenty-five years earlier.[100]

In opening the Second Commission on June 20, 1899, Martens changed tact and reversed himself. The crafty lawyer *qua* statesmen, before discussions could begin, availed himself of his prerogative as President of the Commission to "make some observations" in regard to the objectives of Articles 1 and 2.[101] Out was the need for comprehensive regulation, and in was a proposal designed to be amenable to the Belgian and British delegation yet vague enough to be acceptable to the Germans.

Martens opened by reiterating that governments had "as a sacred duty to do all in their power in an endeavor to diminish the evils and calamities of war" and that "[i]t is in view of this sublime purpose that the defensive forces should be organized and disciplined."[102] "However,"—here is the reversal—the codes were "not intended to deny the right of populations to defend themselves. This right is sacred."[103] Martens argued that this right was not *precluded* through regulation but actually *enabled* by it:

> It was in order to fulfill this duty that the Russian Government in 1874 proposed to all the States that they adopt conditions easy of fulfillment in order to enable the populations to take part in the operations of war.

---

it in direct competition with Britain, the extant global naval super-power. The resulting Anglo-German naval race would appreciably heighten the political tensions that led to World War I. For example, see Geoffrey Wawro, *Warfare and Society in Europe, 1792–1914* (New York: Routledge, 2000), 176–187.

98 "Nothing in this chapter shall be considered as tending to lessen or abolish the right belonging to the population of an invaded country to fulfill its duty of offering by all lawful means, the most energetic patriotic resistance against the invaders" (Great Britain); "No Acts of Retaliation Shall be Exercised against the Population of the Occupied Territory for Having Openly Taken Up Arms against the Invader," in *Proceedings of the Hague Peace Conferences* (Switzerland), 550.

99 Ibid.

100 Giladi, "The Enactment of Irony," 860.

101 Martens (Russia), "Second Commission: Second Subcommission, Eleventh Meeting, June 20, 1899," in *Proceedings of the Hague Peace Conferences*, 547.

102 Martens, "Second Commission".

103 Martens, "Second Commission".

His position was that prescribing strict legal criteria for combatant status was not tantamount to sanctioning the reprisal policies of occupying armies (it was) but simply established easily-met conditions for "those who desire legally to fight for their country." Moreover, these codes were intended to "afford populations more guaranties than had existed up to that time" because, he added, "no less sacred is the duty of Governments not to sacrifice useless victims in the interest of the war."[104] As he had done two weeks earlier, Martens was championing the small states' cause by co-opting it.

The following is where the official proceedings document Martens' reversal:

> The Brussels Conference [was] by no means intended to abolish the right of defense, or to create a code which would abolish this right. It was, on the contrary, imbued with the idea that heroes are not created by codes, but that the only code that heroes have is their self-abnegation, their will and their patriotism.
>
> . . .
>
> [I]t must be remembered that it is not the purpose of these provisions to codify all cases that might arise. They have left the doors open to the heroic sacrifices which nations might be ready to make in their defense; a heroic nation is, like heroes, above codes, rules, and facts.[105]

Martens' perorations were intended not only to win over Beernaert but also to pre-empt the British and Swiss amendments. To this effect, Martens read his declaration, which contained an almost complete iteration of the now-famous Martens Clause:

> The Conference is unanimous in thinking that it is extremely desirable that the usages of war should be defined and regulated. In this spirit it has adopted a great number of provisions which have for their object the determination of the rights and of the duties of belligerents and populations and for their end a softening of the evils of war so far as military necessities permit. It has not, however, been possible to agree forthwith on provisions embracing all the cases which occur in practice.
>
> On the other hand, it could not be intended by the Conference that the cases not provided for should, for want of a written provision, be left to the arbitrary judgment of the military commanders. Until a perfectly complete code of the laws of war is issued, the Conference thinks it right to declare that in cases not included in the present arrangement, populations and belligerents remain under the protection and empire of the principles of international law, as they result from the usages established

104 Martens, "Second Commission".
105 Martens, "Second Commission".

> between civilized nations, from the laws of humanity, and the requirements of the public conscience.
>
> It is in this sense especially that Articles 9 and 10 adopted by the Conference must be understood.[106]

Beernaert, perhaps reading the writing on the wall, announced that despite the fact that Articles 1 and 2 "[did] not come up to what he would have wished," he would vote for them on the condition that Martens' declaration, as expressive of the "unanimous sentiment of the assembly," be "inserted both in the minutes of the meeting and in the final protocol, or else in the general act which is to crown the work of the Conference."[107] Seeing Beernaert retreat from the fight, the Swiss delegate, Arnold Künzli, attempted to resuscitate the debate, only to be quickly shot down by Martens. With little more fanfare, Articles 1 and 2 were unanimously adopted; it seemed as though Martens had prevailed.

Sir John Ardagh, however, was not finished with the matter. Asked whether Martens' declaration had satisfied the military delegate from Great Britain, Ardagh responded that he would prefer the adoption of an additional article, worded exactly as his earlier proposed amendment, and requested that it be put to a vote.[108] Künzli once again took the floor to support Ardagh's proposal, imploring that

> [a]s it is not within your power to close up the temple of Janus forever, at least do not expose yourselves to the reproach of having maintained in our enlightened days usages and customs of war which no longer belong to our time.[109]

Martens retreated to his earlier talking points: it was not the objective of the Conference to "codify the heroic acts of individuals or populations. Our task is much simpler: we wish to save the life and property of the *weak*, the *unarmed*, and the *inoffensive*," that is, to save populations from their own bloodthirsty governments bent on futile resistance, not from invading armies.[110]

At this point, the Germans had had enough. Cutting through the grandiloquent rhetoric, von Schwarzhoff, who had been silent up to this point, declared that he could not go along with Ardagh's proposal. The proposition, he said, "At first sight . . . appears harmless, almost anodyne, as it speaks only of lawful means. But what are lawful means? According to me, they are only

106 Martens, "Second Commission," 547–548.
107 Martens, "Second Commission," 548.
108 Martens, "Second Commission," 550.
109 Martens, "Second Commission," 551.
110 Martens, "Second Commission" (emphasis in the original).

those which conform to the conditions prescribed" in Articles 1 and 2.[111] But if Ardagh's proposal did *not* contemplate anything further, von Schwarzhoff asserted, then it would be completely "superfluous." "It is time to remember," he continued, "that soldiers are also men, and have a right to be treated with humanity."[112] In what could only be considered a veiled threat, the colonel reminded the assemblage that, despite his "grave objections" to Article 2 (regarding the legal status of civilians participating in *levée en masse*), he had "in a spirit of conciliation," remained silent and refrained from blocking its passage. "However," he continued, "the concessions should stop here."[113]

This was the showdown that Martens had feared. Von Schwarzhoff's position was immediately endorsed by Colonel Gilinsky, the Russian military advisor, and, somewhat surprisingly, E.N. Rahusen of the Netherlands.[114] Ardagh, for his part, remained adamant and insisted that his proposition be inserted as a separate article and that it be submitted to a vote.

The impasse was broken by Russia's newly minted ally, France. By insisting that the substance of Ardagh's proposal and Martens' declaration were one and the same, the French delegate proposed that Martens' declaration be inserted in the final protocol, which, in fact, had been Beernaert's earlier suggestion. Discussion ensued, but in the end, at the behest of Martens, Ardagh acknowledged the "unanimous approval" of his principle as expressed in Martens' declaration, and "out of a spirit of conciliation," he withdrew his proposed amendment. Thereby Articles 9 and 10 of the Brussels Declaration on the conditions required for civilians to participate legally in hostilities were codified as Articles 1 and 2 of the Hague Regulations annexed to the Second Convention.

Feodor Martens had gotten what he wanted—Russian success where he and his compatriots had failed in Brussels twenty-five years earlier. The Clause made its way into the preamble of the 1899 Hague Convention (II), but in an era of high legal positivism, its admonition to respect the "principles of humanity" and the "dictates of the public conscience" would have been understood as little more than hortatory.

111 Martens, "Second Commission," 552.
112 Martens, "Second Commission," 552–553.
113 Martens, "Second Commission".
114 The Dutch position at the Hague is somewhat of a puzzle, and the official proceedings do not shed much light on their motivations. Despite being similarly situated as Belgium vis-à-vis the great powers, they nevertheless wholeheartedly supported Martens' declaration and the Germans' opposition to Ardagh. Ibid., 549, 553. Perhaps, as the Conference's host nation, they were as spurred as Martens himself in seeing a successful result by whatever means were expedient, as a failure might reflect poorly on the Kingdom. But this is merely speculation.

4 Coda: an ambiguous legacy

The upshot is that Beernaert's appeal to leave the rules of occupation to that "tacit and common law which arises from the principles of the law of nations" would have been understood as invoking an out-of-favor appeal to natural law, in which the basis for obligation was made by reference to abstract, universal principles—to laws that were found rather than made. This was also true of Martens' clause, which echoed Beernaert's words by appealing to the vague notions of humanity and public conscience. If anything, Martens' reference to the "principles of international law, as they result from the usages established between civilized nations," would have *sanctioned* reprisal regimes as permissible state practice as a matter of positive law, given Germany's widespread use of reprisals as a means of repressing civilian resistance. In effect, Germany had been exercising its fundamental right of self-preservation in 1870–1871, which, in the absence of an express prohibition, was in accordance with the principle of sovereign freedom.

The lawyers—the "scientific delegates"—present at The Hague would have recognized that, absent a precise definition of the content of the "laws of humanity" and the "dictates of public conscience," to which states gave their affirmative consent, the preamble to the Second Convention would carry little weight as a counterbalance to Articles 1 and 2 of the Regulations. Germany and Russia did not think so and neither did Great Britain. Sir John Ardagh summed up the sentiment neatly: "If anything was required to show the need for some article of the kind" codifying protections for civilians, Ardagh is reported to have said, it was the "bitter resistance of the Germans and Russians which accomplished the amendment's defeat."[115] The Martens Clause would be reproduced in the 1907 Hague Convention (IV) and numerous subsequent agreements, almost invariably without its original coda: "They declare that it is in this sense especially Articles 1 and 2 of the Regulations must be understood."[116]

It was not only the Clause but also these two articles of the 1899 Regulations that were reproduced word-for-word in the 1907 revision, leaving the legality of reprisal regimes indefinite on the eve of the First World War. As the Germans marched through the Ardennes in August 1914, their treatment of Belgian civilians echoed the French experience of the three decades earlier. As part of the military strategist Carl von Clausewitz's doctrine of *kriegraison*—a theory of total war that recommended the terrorization of civilian populations to force them to compel their leaders to capitulate quickly and wholly[117]—the Germans justified their reprisal practices as a legally privileged response to

115 Tuchman, *The Proud Tower*, 261.
116 "Preamble, Convention No. II with Respect to the Laws and Customs of War on Land," in *Reports to the Hague Conferences* (arts. 9 & 10 of the Brussels Declaration).
117 Carl von Clausewitz, *Vom Kriege: Vollständige Ausgabe der acht Bücher* (1832).

illegal resistance—*encore les francs-tireurs.*[118] Many hundreds of civilians from the towns and villages through which the Germans marched were rounded up and executed as suspected unlawful combatants, even though actual instances of civilian resistance were sparse and unsubstantiated.

Legal accountability for these killings, which would now be categorized as war crimes, were for the most part unavailable. The Treaty of Versailles of 1919, which ended the war between Germany and the Allied Powers, included draft articles to create an international tribunal to hold Kaiser Wilhelm II and other high-level officials criminally responsible for starting the war and for atrocities committed against Belgian civilians.[119] Notwithstanding the fact that "Murders and massacres; systematic terrorism," "Putting hostages to death," and the "Imposition of collective penalties" were among the proposed crimes to be prosecuted, the tribunal failed to materialize largely due to the legal doctrine of *nullum crimen sin lege*, a general principle of law that prohibits the retroactive punishment of acts that were not criminalized at the time they were committed.[120] Although also the result of political considerations, the lack of will to carry through with the proposed international tribunal was in no doubt related to the uncertainties around its legal foundations. With no other positive legal obligations that could be referenced, the "laws of humanity" and the "dictates of the public conscience" were simply insufficiently precise to conclude that German reprisals were illegal as a matter of contemporary international law.

The import of the Martens Clause has expanded and contracted as its interpretations have reflected the legal and political contexts in which it has been invoked. Although reproduced in the 1925 Geneva Protocol prohibiting the use of poisonous gases,[121] it largely lay fallow until the end of the Second World War. When international lawyers were yet again faced with an uncertain legal basis for prosecuting German atrocities because of the problem of retroactivity, the hegemony of legal positivism had retreated from its high-water mark, making room for vague notions such as "reason" and "justice" to give content to the nascent field of international criminal law. As is made clear in an oft-cited passage from the Nuremberg Tribunal that prosecuted high-level Nazi officials, the lack of precisely codified rules would no longer stand as an absolute bar to accountability:

> [T]he maxim *nullum crimen sine lege* is not a limitation of sovereignty, but is in general a principle of justice. To assert that it is unjust to punish

118 See Barbara W. Tuchman, *The Guns of August* (New York: The Macmillan Company, 1962), 313–324.

119 See generally William A. Schabas, *The Trial of the Kaiser* (Oxford: Oxford University Press, 2018).

120 Schabas, *The Trial of the Kaiser*, 174–197. The presumption against retroactive punishment is now enshrined as Article 11(2) of the Universal Declaration of Human Rights (1948).

121 The Geneva Protocol for the Prohibition of the Use in War of Asphyxiating, Poisonous or other Gases, and of Bacteriological Methods of Warfare, June 17, 1925, 94 L.N.T.S. 65, at arts. 1 & 3.

> those who in defiance of treaties and assurances have attacked neighbouring states without warning is obviously untrue, for in such circumstances the attacker must know that he is doing wrong, and so far from it being unjust to punish him, it would be unjust if his wrong were allowed to go unpunished.[122]

The post-war efflorescence of the Martens Clause is related to this re-emergence of natural law sensibilities in the professional field of international law not only in the limited domain of international criminal law but also most importantly in the jurisprudence of human rights. The U.N. Charter in 1945 and the Universal Declaration of Human Rights that followed in 1948 affirmed the modern idea that "natural rights are the rights that people have, not by virtue of any particular role or status in society, but by virtue of their very humanity."[123] Importantly, and unlike the maxim *nullum crimen sin lege*, human rights *are* a limitation on sovereignty in that they are meant to operate as an external check on the principle of sovereign freedom; that is, they exist as a non-positivistic source of international law in and of themselves.[124] Moreover, just as human rights have re-introduced an element of morality to the general rules of international law, the Martens Clause has come to perform a similar function in the specific field of IHL, both as a general interpretive guideline and through the incorporation of human rights norms into the rules of armed conflict.[125]

Whether understood as an interpretive tool, a constraint on *a contrario* arguments, or a positive source of binding obligation,[126] the construction of the Martens Clause has proved remarkably malleable in recent decades: it has been restated in international agreements, including the Geneva Conventions and its Additional Protocol I that codifies the rules of international armed conflict,[127] cited by international tribunals and domestic courts, such as the

122 *France et al. v. Goring et al.* (1948), 22 Trial of the Major War Criminals before the International Military Tribunal, 14 November 1945–1 October 1946 (IMT) 203, p. 462.

123 Brian Tierney, *The Idea of Natural Rights: Studies on Natural Rights, Natural Law, and Church Law: 1150–1625* (Wm. B. Eerdmans Publishing, 1997), 2 fn. 4.

124 See supra note 51 and accompanying text. See also S. James Anaya, *Indigenous Peoples in International Law*, 2nd ed. (Oxford: Oxford University Press, 2004).

125 For example, the International Criminal Court for the Former Yugoslavia (ICTY) relied on the Martens Clause to categorize the prohibition against torture as a principle of humanity. *Prosecutor v. Anto Furund'ija*, IT-95–17/1-T, Judgement, ¶ 137 (Int'l Crim. Trib. for the Former Yugoslavia Dec. 10, 1998).

126 Cassese surveys these interpretive moves in "The Martens Clause."

127 Geneva Convention for the Amelioration of the Condition of the Wounded and Sick in Armed Forces in the Field, Aug. 12, 1949, 75 U.N.T.S. 31, at art. 63 ("Geneva I"); Geneva Convention for the Amelioration of the Condition of Wounded, Sick and Shipwrecked Members of Armed Forces at Sea art. 62, Aug. 12, 1949, 75 U.N.T.S. 85, at art. 62 ("Geneva II"), Geneva Convention Relative to the Treatment of Prisoners of War, Aug. 12, 1949, 75 U.N.T.S. 135, at art. 142 ("Geneva III"); Geneva Convention Relative to the Protection of Civilian Persons in Times of War, Aug. 12, 1949, 75 U.N.T.S. 287, at art. 158 ("Geneva IV"); Protocol Additions to the Geneva Conventions of 12 August 1949, and

International Court of Justice (ICJ)[128] and the International Tribunal for the Former Yugoslavia,[129] and invoked by scholars and judges alike as expanding on or creating entirely new sources of international law.[130]

Perhaps the high-water mark of this malleability came in 1994 when the UN General Assembly requested an advisory opinion from the ICJ on the legality of the threat or use of nuclear weapons.[131] After a lengthy deliberation, the Court was evenly split with respect to the most pressing question, but the opinion was considered adopted by virtue of the Court's president voting in the affirmative:

> [I]n view of the current state of international law, and of the elements of fact at its disposal, the Court cannot conclude definitively whether the threat or use of nuclear weapons would be lawful or unlawful in an extreme circumstance of self-defence, in which the very survival of a State would be at stake.[132]

In coming to this lack of a conclusion, the Court grappled with the meaning of the Martens Clause and the legacy of both positivism and international humanitarian law as it had developed over the past century.

The majority opinion affirmed that the Martens Clause, particularly as it was expressed in the Geneva Conventions, constituted an "intransgressible principle[] of international customary law" that had proven to be an "effective means of addressing the rapid evolution of military technology" yet was vague in the specifics as to how the Clause itself should apply to the question before the Court.[133] The dissenting opinion of Judge Shahabuddeen, to the contrary, provided an extensive discussion of the Martens Clause as a normative source of legal obligation, putting forward that it "lays down some norm of State conduct" that does not "exist wholly *dehors* the Clause."[134] Shahabuddeen's reading of the travaux préparatoires was that the Martens Clause was "*intended* to fill gaps left by conventional international law and to do so in a

---

Relating to the Protection of Victims of International Armed Conflicts, June 8, 1977, at art. 1 ("Protocol I").

128 *Military and Paramilitary Activities in and Against Nicaragua (Nicar. v. U.S.)*, Judgment, 1986 I.C.J. Rep. 14, ¶ 218 (June 27).

129 For example, see *Prosecutor v. Kupreskic*, Case No. IT-95-16, Judgment, ¶ 525–26 (Int'l Crim. Trib. for the Former Yugoslavia Jan. 14, 2000); Colombia: Final Agreement to End the Armed Conflict and Build a Stable and Lasting Peace preamble, Nov. 24, 2016, www.refworld.org/docid/5b68465c4.html.

130 Cassese, "The Martens Clause," 189 fn. 5.

131 Legality of the Threat or Use of Nuclear Weapons, Advisory Opinion, 1996 I.C.J. Rep. 226, ¶ 105 ("Nuclear Weapons Advisory Opinion").

132 Ibid.

133 Nuclear Weapons Advisory Opinion, ¶ 78–79.

134 Legality of the Threat or Use of Nuclear Weapons, Advisory Opinion, 1996 I.C.J. Rep. 226, 405 (July 8) (dissenting opinion by Shahabuddeen, J.).

practical way," because Beernaert, after objecting to the adoption of Articles 1 and 2, "immediately announced that he could because of this declaration vote for them."[135] This is, indeed, a strained interpretation of the record. Under this reading, the laws of humanity and dictates of public conscience were principles of international law that had created obligations of a legal character at the outset, whose precise content was to be ascertained in light of the changing conditions of warfare and armaments.[136] As to what this content might be, he did not venture an opinion, only that the Court *could* come to a determination on the legality of nuclear weapons—one way or the other—with the legal materials available.

That neither the majority nor Judge Shahabuddeen explicated the content of the Martens Clause, notwithstanding its development over the twentieth century into an "intransgressible principle" of humanitarian law, is not surprising because its meaning is not exhausted by its origin story (or at least one version of that story). Rather, its development has come piecemeal, as its meaning has been determined and re-determined in local contexts and in response to what circumstances have demanded.

5 Conclusion

My intent in problematizing the Martens Clause as a foundational piece of international law relates to a larger set of questions regarding the desirability of legalizing warfare altogether. Does compliance with IHL condone or even commend warfare as a legitimate means of inter-state conflict resolution? Has this legitimation paradoxically resulted in perverse outcomes; that is, is the destruction of human life not only permitted but also now legally privileged? Most importantly, do the received histories of IHL give it an imprimatur of coherence that make it difficult to challenge the regime as an orienting framework? Many of the conventional history-as-progress narratives that populate international law texts take it as a given that the development of IHL has been normatively desirable[137] and do not seriously engage with the paradoxes inherent in the "humanization of warfare."[138]

135 Ibid., 406, 408–09.
136 Ibid., 406.
137 For example, see *Humanizing the Laws of War: The Red Cross and the Development of International Humanitarian Law*, eds. Geiß, Zimmermann, and Haumer (Cambridge: Cambridge University Press, 2017).
138 For example, see Hilaire McCoubrey, *International Humanitarian Law* (Routledge, 1990), 2–3. McCoubrey dedicates three scant paragraphs to this paradox before dismissing it out of hand. One notable exception has been the work of David Kennedy. David Kenney, *The Dark Side of Virtues: Reassessing International Humanitarianism* (Princeton: Princeton University Press, 2005); David Kennedy, *Of War and Law* (Princeton: Princeton University Press, 2006).

The conclusion of the 1899 Hague Convention did not bring about disarmament on the continent, and it did not succeed as a geopolitical strategy to rebalance the European powers and avert the hemoclysm of 1914–1918. In fact, the reprisal regimes and related war crimes that were deployed by the Germans in 1870–1871, which had so worried the Belgians at The Hague, were a fixture of Germany's march through the Low Countries in the early months of the First World War.[139] In the interwar years, jurists struggled to reconcile the positivist permission of war-as-politics and a growing unease with its attendant humanitarian implications within institutions such as the League of Nations and through multilateral treaty initiatives such as the Kellogg-Briand Pact (1928). It was not until the horrors of a second World War and the Holocaust gave way to the U.N. Charter and an outright prohibition on the use of force. In the subsequent years, war has become viewed as a necessary evil, fought in collective self-defense in compliance with Charter principles, and in the name of humanitarian intervention and the Responsibility to Protect, even as the doctrine of "preemptive self-defense" and the Russian invasion of Ukraine (2014–) testify as to how even the patently unlawful can be justified as legally permitted.[140]

The Martens Clause has been invoked and re-invoked during these developments as a malleable tool useful in novel legal and political contexts, with each successive iteration recalling the spirit of 1899 as if Martens' phrasing were a talismanic incantation—linguistically closed yet substantively underdetermined. Such appeals to the origin of international law as authority serves a double movement: both as support for tendentious arguments about what the law *is* and as a means of avoiding the difficult task of justifying one's position about what the law *ought* to be. For such genealogy to evade the pitfalls of genetic fallacy, historical argument should attend not only to the intersubjective meanings that something like the Martens Clause carried at its creation but also to how such meanings have changed as times have changed. The Clause's ambiguity worked to placate, or at least mollify, both sides of a bitter dispute; but this self-same ambiguity has given it an afterlife that few could have envisioned as the legalization of war has developed.

Its invocation by both the majority and dissenting opinions of the ICJ's Nuclear Weapons Advisory Opinion demonstrates this plasticity—Judge Shahabuddeen interpreted Feodor Martens' intentions at The Hague to be more than they were and simply more than they could have been, given the contexts in which Martens made his declaration. Yet Shahabuddeen's argument could have been made without appealing to a fixed and essentialized understanding

139 Barbara W. Tuchman, *The Guns of August* (New York: Macmillan, 1962), 310–324.

140 On the legality of the U.S.'s invasion of Iraq, see Philippe Sands, *Lawless World: America and the Making and Breaking of Global Rules* (Allen Lane, 2005); on Russia's legal justifications for the invasion of Ukraine, see Marko Milanovic, "What is Russia's Legal Justifications for Using Force against Ukraine?," EJIL: Talk!, July 2, 2023, accessed www.ejiltalk.org/what-is-russias-legal-justification-for-using-force-against-ukraine/.

of the "particularly ambiguous" and "very loosely worded" sentiment. In the end, the meaning of the Martens Clause is that which we ourselves supply and must continually re-negotiate as the laws of humanity and the dictates of public conscience evolve.

References

Anaya, S. James. *Indigenous Peoples in International Law*, 2nd ed. Oxford: Oxford University Press, 2004.

Butterfield, Herbert and Martin Wight (eds.). *Diplomatic Investigations.* London: Allen & Unwin, 1966.

Cassese, Antonio. "The Martens Clause: Half a Loaf or Simply Pie in the Sky?" *European Journal of International Law* 11, no. 1 (2000).

Colombia: Final Agreement to End the Armed Conflict and Build a Stable and Lasting Peace Preamble, November 24, 2016. www.refworld.org/docid/5b68465c4.html.

Convention (II) with Respect to the Laws and Customs of War on Land and Its Annex: Regulations Concerning the Laws and Customs of War on Land, July 29, 1899, 187 CTS 429.

Crawford, James. *Brownlie's Principles of Public International Law*, 8th ed. Oxford: Oxford University Press, 2012.

Crozier, W. Letter to General Corbin, July 19, 1899, Hay Papers, Library of Congress.

Danilevski, N. Ya. *Rossia i Evropa. Vzgljad na kul'turnye i politicheskie otnoshenia Slavjanskogo mira k Germano-Romanskomu*, 5th ed. First print 1869. St. Petersburg: Paneleevs, 1895.

Dowdeswell, Tracey Leigh. "The Brussels Peace Conference of 1874 and the Modern Laws of Belligerent Qualification." *Osgood Hall Law Journal* 54, no. 3 (2017).

Doyle, Michael W. *Empires.* Ithaca, NY: Cornell University Press, 1986.

Dugdale, E. T. S. (ed.). *German Diplomatic Documents 1871–1914*, vol. 3. Royal Institute of International Affairs, 1930.

Durand, André. "The Development of the Idea of Peace in the Thinking of Henry Dunant." *International Review of the Red Cross* 250, no. 26 (1986).

Eyffinger, Arthur. "Feodor Martens, Architect of the Hague Tradition of International Law." *Journal of Social Sciences of U Nord. Tallinn* 17 (2009).

Geiß, Robin, Andreas Zimmermann, and Stefanie Haumer. *Humanizing the Laws of War: The Red Cross and the Development of International Humanitarian Law.* Cambridge: Cambridge University Press, 2017.

Geneva Convention for the Amelioration of the Condition of the Wounded in Armies in the Field, August 22, 1864. https://ihl-databases.icrc.org/en/ihl-treaties/gc-1864?activeTab=historical.

Geneva Convention for the Amelioration of the Condition of the Wounded in Armies in the Field. (I) for the Amelioration of the Condition of the Wounded and Sick in Armed Forces in the Field, August 12, 1949, 75 U.N.T.S. 31.

Geneva Convention for the Amelioration of the Condition of the Wounded in Armies in the Field. (II) for the Amelioration of the Condition of Wounded, Sick and Shipwrecked Members of Armed Forces at Sea art. 62, August 12, 1949, 75 U.N.T.S. 85.

Geneva Convention for the Amelioration of the Condition of the Wounded in Armies in the Field. (III) Relative to the Treatment of Prisoners of War, August 12, 1949, 75 U.N.T.S. 135.

Geneva Convention for the Amelioration of the Condition of the Wounded in Armies in the Field. (IV) Relative to the Protection of Civilian Persons in Times of War, August 12, 1949, 75 U.N.T.S. 287.

Geneva Protocol Additions (I) to the Geneva Conventions of 12 August 1949, and Relating to the Protection of Victims of International Armed Conflicts. Protocol for

the Prohibition of the Use in War of Asphyxiating, Poisonous or Other Gases, and of Bacteriological Methods of Warfare, June 17, 1925, 94 L.N.T.S. 65.
Geneva Protocol Additions (I) to the Geneva Conventions of 12 August 1949, and Relating to the Protection of Victims of International Armed Conflicts, June 8, 1977.
Giladi, Rotem. "The Enactment of Irony: Reflections on the Origins of the Martens Clause." *European Journal of International Law* 25, no. 3 (2014).
Gong, Gerrit. *The Standard of "Civilization" in International Society.* Oxford: Clarendon Press, 1984.
Hakimi, Monica. "Making Sense of Customary International Law." *Michigan Law Review* 118, no. 8 (2020).
Hall, W. *A Treatise on International Law*. Oxford: Clarendon Press, 1924.
Hathaway, Oona A. and Scott J. Shapiro. *The Internationalists: How a Radical Plan to Outlaw War Remade the World.* New York: Simon & Schuster, 2017.
Heraclides, Alexis and Ada Dialla. *Humanitarian Intervention in the Long Nineteenth Century: Setting the Precedent.* Manchester: Manchester University Print, 2015.
Holls, Frederick W. *The Peace Conference at the Hague.* New York: The Macmillan Company, 1900.
Kennedy, David. *The Dark Side of Virtues: Reassessing International Humanitarianism.* Princeton: Princeton University Press, 2005.
Kennedy, David. *Of War and Law*. Princeton: Princeton University Press, 2006.
Kennedy, Paul. *The Rise and Fall of the Great Powers: Economic Change and Military Conflict from 1500 to 2000.* New York, NY: Random House, 1987.
Koskenniemi, Martii. *The Gentle Civilizer of Nations.* Cambridge: Cambridge University Press, 2004.
La Rochefoucauld. Letter to the Minister of Foreign Affairs, 26 June, 1874. Brussels, Légations Fond A 25.
Lowe, John. *The Great Powers, Imperialism and the German Problem, 1865–1925.* Taylor and Francis, 1994.
Lister, Matthew J. "The Legitimating Role of Consent in International Law." *Chicago Journal of International Law* 11, no. 2 (2011).
Lorca, Arnulf Becker. "Universal International Law: Nineteenth-Century Histories of Imposition and Appropriation." *Harvard International Law Journal* 51, no. 2 (2010).
Lumly, Savile. Letter to Lord Derby, 7 July 1875. FO 83/481, Foreign Office Archives, Public Record Office (PRO).
Mälksoo, Lauri. "The Science of International Law and the Concept of Politics: The Arguments and Lives of the International Law Professors at the University of Dorpat/lur'ev/Tartu 1855–1985." *British Yearbook of International Law* 76, no. 1 (2005).
Mälksoo, Lauri. "The History of International Legal Theory in Russia: A Civilizational Dialogue with Europe." *European Journal of International Law* 19, no. 1 (2008).
Mälksoo, Lauri. "F.F. Martens and His Time: When Russia Was an Integral Part of the European Tradition of International Law." *European Journal of International Law* 25, no. 3 (2014).
Mälksoo, Lauri. *Russian Approaches to International Law*. Oxford: Oxford University Press, 2015.
Martens, F. F. *Sobranie traktatov i konventsii, zaklijuchennykh Rossieyu s inostrannymi derzhavami.* St. Petersburg: A. Böhnke, 1874–1909.
Martens, F. F. "Les Hostilités sans Déclaration de Guerre à Propos de la Guerre Russo-Japonaise." *Revue Générale de Droit International Public* 111 (1904).
Martens, F. F. *Sovremennoe mezhdunarodnoe pravo tsivilizovannykh narodov (Modern International Law of Civilized Peoples)*, vol. 1 and 2., Edited by. L. N. Shestakova. Moscow: Yuridicheskii Kollodzh MGU, 1996.

McCoubrey, Hilaire. *International Humanitarian Law*. Routledge, 1990.
Milanovic, Marko. "What Is Russia's Legal Justifications for Using Force against Ukraine?" *EJIL: Talk!*. Accessed July 2, 2023. www.ejiltalk.org/what-is-russias-legal-justification-for-using-force-against-ukraine.
Nabulsi, Karma. *Traditions of War*. Oxford: Oxford University Press, 1999.
Neff, Stephen C. *War and the Law of* Nations. Cambridge: Cambridge University Press, 2005.
Neff, Stephen C. *Justice Among Nations: A History of International Law*. Cambridge, MA: Harvard University Press, 2014.
Nussbaum, Arthur. "Frédéric de Martens, Representative Tsarist Writer on International Law." *Nordisk Tidsskrift International Ret* 22 (1952).
Orakhelashvii, Alexander. "Natural Law and Justice." *Max Planck Encyclopedias of International Law*. Last modified August 2007. https://opil.ouplaw.com/view/10.1093/law:epil/9780199231690/law-9780199231690-e730?rskey=pcc4Et&result=1&prd=MPIL.
Paddeu, Federica and Brendant Plant. "The Dispute between Guyana and Venezuela over the Essequibo Region." *EJIL: Talk!*. Accessed April 11, 2018. www.ejiltalk.org/the-dispute-between-guyana-and-venezuela-over-the-essequibo-region/.
Pustogarov, V. V. *Our Martens: F.F. Martens—International Lawyer and Architect of Peace*, Translated by W. E. Butler. London: Simmonds & Hill Pub., 2000.
Rich, Norman. *Great Power Diplomacy 1814–1914*. New York: McGraw-Hill, 1992.
Sands, Philippe. *Lawless World: America and the Making and Breaking of Global Rules*. Allen Lane, 2005.
Sanger, C. P. and H. T. J. Norton. *England's Guarantee to Belgium and Luxemburg, with the Full Text of the Treaties*. London: G. Allen & Unwin Ltd., 1915.
Scott, J. B. (ed.). *Proceedings of the Hague Peace Conferences*. New York: Oxford University Press, 1920–1921.
Scott, J. B. (ed.). *Reports to the Hague Conferences of 1899 and 1907*. Oxford: Clarendon Press, 1917.
Shabas, William A. *The Trial of the Kaiser*. Oxford: Oxford University Press, 2018.
Shapiro, Scott J. *Legality*. Cambridge, MA: Belknap Press, 2011.
Simpson, Gerry. *Great Powers and Outlaw States*. Cambridge: Cambridge University Press, 2004.
Spaight, J. M. *War Rights on Land*. London: Macmillan, 1911.
Tierney, Brian. *The Idea of Natural Rights: Studies on Natural Rights, Natural Law, and Church Law: 1150–1625*. Wm. B. Eerdmans Publishing, 1997.
Tuchman, Barbara W. *The Guns of August*. New York: The Macmillan Company, 1962.
Tuchman, Barbara W. *The Proud Tower: A Portrait of the World Before the War, 1890–1914*. Westminster: Random House Publishing Group, 1966.
Tuck, Richard. *The Rights of War and Peace: Political Thought and the International Order from Grotius to Kant*. Oxford: Oxford University Press, 1999.
Tully, James and Annabell Brett (eds.). *Meaning & Context: Quentin Skinner and his Critics*. Cambridge, UK: Polity Press, 1988.
U.N. General Assembly. Universal Declaration of Human Rights, December 10, 1948, 217 A (III).
von Clausewitz, Carl. *Vom Kriege: Vollständige Ausgabe der acht Bücher*. Berlin: Ferdinand Dümmler, 1832.
Wawro, Geoffrey. *Warfare and Society in Europe, 1792–1914*. New York: Routledge, 2000.
White, Andrew W. *The First Hague Conference*. Boston: The World Peace Foundation, 1912.
Witt, John Fabian. *Lincoln's Code: The Laws of War in American History*. New York: Free Press, 2012.

12 Searching for meaning in the Utah Constitution's Free Market Preamble[1]

Jorge L. Contreras

1 Introduction

Though the United States Constitution is the most prominent constitutional document in the United States, each of the fifty states has its own unique constitution that exists alongside, and in addition to, the federal constitution. State constitutions attract far less attention from scholars, policymakers, and the public than the federal constitution does, but several state constitutions predate the federal constitution by a century or more and often extend to their citizens important rights beyond those guaranteed by the federal constitution. In this regard, state constitutions exemplify the American system of federal government and serve as fertile grounds for policy experimentation and differentiation among the states. State constitutional preambles announce to the citizens of a state, courts, policymakers, and the broader citizenry of the United States policies that a state wishes to enshrine in its constitutional charter. This chapter closely examines one such pronouncement—the "Free Markets" Clause of the Utah Constitution, a unique textual enactment that reflects both the distinctive historical evolution of this western state and broader national concerns with business expansion and oppression during the late nineteenth century.

Article XII, Section 20 of the Utah Constitution, enacted in 1895 immediately prior to Utah's admission to the Union, relates to antitrust law and monopolies. A century after its initial enactment, the preamble to this section was amended to state that

> It is the policy of the state of Utah that a free market system shall govern trade and commerce in this state to promote the dispersion of economic and political power and the general welfare of all the people.

1 This chapter is based on Jorge L. Contreras, "Free Market State (Of Mind): Antitrust Federalism, John J. Flynn and the Utah Constitution's Free Market Clause," *Utah Law Review* (2023): 279–335.

DOI: 10.4324/9781003534815-14

Utah's so-called Free Market Clause links a "free market system," not to economic efficiency or pricing considerations—mainstays of modern antitrust law—but to distributive justice and general public welfare. It is an invitation to Utah's antitrust authorities (and courts) to consider a broad range of social and economic factors when evaluating the legality of business practices under the antitrust laws.

But despite the creation of this seemingly powerful tool for reform, the Free Market Clause has not been adopted in any other state. Moreover, it appears that in the three decades since its adoption, both the Utah courts and its practicing bar have lost sight of the origin, meaning, and potential of this unique constitutional guaranty. The most telling sign of this institutional lapse of memory is evidenced by *Tesla Motors v. Utah Tax Commission*,[2] in which the Utah Supreme Court denied the justiciability of the Free Market Clause, thereby rendering it unenforceable. This chapter traces the strange journey of the Utah Free Market Clause from an ambitious tool for progressive legal reform to a legal irrelevancy and asks whether any substance can be poured back into this once-promising constitutional preamble.

2 Utah's 1895 Constitution: the road to statehood, free markets, and antitrust

Though the federal Sherman Antitrust Act is often viewed as the principal antitrust law of the United States, there is a long history of state-level antitrust regulation in the U.S. The earliest state laws prohibiting conspiracies in restraint of trade were enacted in the 1820s, largely to quell the activity of labor unions.[3] The economic boom that followed the Civil War resulted in the accumulation of market power by large business combinations or "trusts" in industries such as steel, cotton, sugar, railroads, and, most notably, oil. Public and legislative concern over the aggressive business practices of these trusts reached a significant level by the early 1880s.[4] Congress's enactment of the Sherman Act in 1890 was the best-known response to the ascendancy of the trusts, but numerous state legislatures also sought to curb the trusts' growing power. Thus, by the time that Congress enacted the Sherman Act, fourteen states had already incorporated anti-monopoly provisions into their state

2 *Tesla Motors UT, Inc. v. Utah Tax Commission*, 2017 UT 18, 398 P.3d 55, 66 (Utah 2017).

3 James May, "Antitrust Practice and Procedure in the Formative Era: The Constitutional and Conceptual Reach of State Antitrust Law, 1880–1918," *University of Pennsylvania Law Review* 135 (1987): 495, 498, notes 6–7.

4 David K. Millon, "The First Antitrust Statute," *Washburn Law Journal* 29 (1990): 141, 142–143.

constitutions,[5] and thirteen had enacted separate antitrust statutes.[6] Today, all fifty U.S. states, the District of Columbia, Guam, Puerto Rico, and the U.S. Virgin Islands have some form of antitrust legislation on their books,[7] and nineteen include antitrust provisions in their state constitutions.[8]

Utah's road to statehood was a long and circuitous one. Though already home to a substantial indigenous population, the territory that today constitutes the state of Utah was first "settled" in 1847 by Mormon pioneers fleeing religious persecution in the eastern United States. When these settlers arrived, the territory was formally part of Mexico, but in 1848, it was ceded to the United States under the Treaty of Guadalupe Hidalgo, which ended the U.S.-Mexican War. In 1849, the settlers sought admission to the Union as a state and drafted a constitution for this purpose. The statehood proposal was rejected by Congress, which instead created the Utah Territory, a large region including modern Utah, most of Nevada, and parts of California, Wyoming, Colorado, Oregon, New Mexico, and Arizona.[9]

Utah's territorial legislature drafted further constitutions in 1856, 1862, 1872, 1882, and 1887, each in support of a new bid for statehood.[10] But issues surrounding polygamy, slavery, and religion in the largely Mormon territory effectively blocked Utah's admission to the Union for the first half-century of its territorial existence.[11] In a final effort to appease opponents in the U.S. Congress, the leaders of the Mormon church officially rejected the practice of polygamy in 1890, and the Utah Territory outlawed it in 1892. This concession led (after two more unsuccessful attempts) to the passage of the Utah Enabling Act by Congress in July 1894, authorizing a new constitutional convention.[12] In early 1895, the convention drafted a new constitution that borrowed language from the state constitutions of Nevada, Washington, Illinois, and New York.[13] The new constitution was approved by the voters

5 Legislation, "A Collection and Survey of State Anti-Trust Laws," *Columbia Law Review* 32 (1932): 347, 347 n.2; Steven G. Calabresi and Larissa C. Leibowitz, "Monopolies and the Constitution: A History of Crony Capitalism," *Harvard Journal of Law & Public Policy* 36 (2013): 983, 1073–1081.

6 See Legislation, "Collection," 347 (citing earlier compilations); and May, "Antitrust Practice," 499–500 (cataloging prohibited activities and penalties).

7 Rocky C. Tsai et al. (eds.), *1 State Antitrust Practice and Statutes*, 5th ed. (Chicago: American Bar Association, 2014), 1–28.

8 See Calabresi and Leibowitz, "Monopolies," 1067.

9 See Jean Bickmore White, *The Utah State Constitution* (2011).

10 See Flynn, 1966, 314–321; White, *Utah State Constitution*, 4–12.

11 See Flynn, 1966, 314–321; White, *Utah State Constitution*, 4–12; Christine Durham, Daniel J. H. Greenwood, and Kathy Wyer, "Utah's Constitution: Distinctively Undistinctive," in *The Constitutionalism of American States*, eds. George E. Connor and Christopher W. Hammons (2006): 649, 653–654.

12 Enabling Act, ch. 138, 28 Stat. 107 (1894).

13 Flynn, 1966, 323; White, *Utah State Constitution*, 12.

of the Utah Territory in November 1895, and on January 4, 1896, President Grover Cleveland admitted Utah to the Union as the 45th state.

Economic issues played a major role in the deliberations over Utah's 1895 Constitution.[14] The national economic depression of the 1890s had a severe effect on employment and income in Utah's agricultural and mining sectors—the Territory's principal industries.[15] The Utah constitutional delegates thus sought to foster a legal and business environment that would "attract eastern capital and build industrial prosperity,"[16] an attitude that was not uncommon among nineteenth-century constitutional drafters in the Western states.[17]

However, like lawmakers across the United States, the Utah delegates feared the growing power of the trusts and sought to equip the state legislature to "deal with the powerful corporations they hoped to attract."[18] Accordingly, Article XII of the new constitution included numerous provisions that constrained the power of corporations, including by authorizing the use of eminent domain to take corporate property (Section 11), prohibiting the corporate use of "armed bodies or individuals" (i.e., Pinkertons) (Section 16), and banning the corporate practice of "blacklisting" employees who sought to organize (Section 19).[19]

Another area addressed by Article XII was the regulation of business combinations—what is now referred to as antitrust law. Though the Utah Constitution was approved five years after the enactment of the federal Sherman Act, the delegates nevertheless wished to include protections against the growing power of the trusts. The railroad trusts, in particular, were of concern, given their critical role in transporting goods, raw materials, and settlers to and from the remote western territory. But some delegates feared that regulating trusts too harshly could stymie growing Utah industries such as sugar production.[20] Economic issues were thus among the most divisive issues debated at the constitutional convention,[21] resulting in "a patchwork of compromises" in the final text.[22] The 1895 Utah constitutional antitrust clause borrows heavily from earlier state constitutions, notably those of Idaho[23] and Montana,[24] both of which use similar language to prohibit combinations and contracts entered for the purpose of fixing prices or regulating production.

14 White, *Utah State Constitution*, 12.

15 White, *Utah State Constitution*, 12–13.

16 White, *Utah State Constitution*, 12.

17 See generally G. Alan Tarr, *Understanding State Constitutions* (1998): 116.

18 Jean Bickmore White, *Charter For Statehood: The Story Of Utah's State Constitution* (1996): 74.

19 Utah Const., Art. XII (1895).

20 White, *Utah State Constitution*, 20 and 155–56; Matthew C. Godfrey, *Religion, Politics, and Sugar: The Mormon Church, the Federal Government, and the Utah-Idaho Sugar Company, 1907 to 1921* (2007).

21 See White, *Utah State Constitution*, 13.

22 Id. at 20.

23 Idaho Const. art. XI, § 18 (1890).

24 Mont. Const. art. XV, § 20 (1889).

Utah's 1895 Constitution directed the new state legislature to pass laws for the enforcement of Article XII, Section 20. Accordingly, two months after achieving statehood, the Utah legislature enacted an Act to Prevent Pools and Trusts.[25] Section 2 of this Act made it illegal to create any combination, pool, agreement, or trust to fix prices or limit production of any article manufactured, mined, produced, or sold in the state while Section 3 also made it illegal to "monopolize any part of trade or commerce" within the state.[26] Thus, one year after the enactment of Article XII, Section 20 of the Utah Constitution, the legislature expanded the scope of Utah's antitrust law to condemn not only concerted action but also unilateral conduct in the form of monopolization. In this regard, the Utah Antitrust Act more closely hewed to the contours of the federal Sherman Act and leapfrogged other state antitrust statutes that failed to prohibit anticompetitive unilateral conduct.[27]

Despite the trust-busting fervor with which Utah's 1896 Act was enacted, relatively few actions were brought under it. The scarcity of actions under the Utah antitrust laws contrasts starkly with the number of actions brought in Utah under the federal antitrust laws, which offered clearer avenues for private recovery, larger damages awards, and recovery of costs and fees.[28] As one pair of commentators put it, the notable lack of activity under the 1896 Act "show[ed] both the inadequacy and inertia of that body of law."[29]

Responding to criticisms like these, the Utah legislature in 1979 repealed the 1896 Act and replaced it with a new antitrust law[30] "designed to vitalize state antitrust law."[31] Substantively, the 1979 Act more closely mirrors the language of Sections 1 and 2 of the federal Sherman Act than its 1896 predecessor. But most interestingly, it also includes a preamble explicitly linking the existence of a "free market system" in Utah to economic advancement, lower prices, allocative equity, and the preservation of democratic political and social institutions. This preliminary framing is in stark contrast to the federal Sherman Act, which, to the consternation of courts and commentators alike, contains no preamble language and scant legislative history. What, then, was the intellectual source of Utah's Free Market Preamble?

In his seminal 1971 work, *A Theory of Justice*, political theorist John Rawls lays out the foundations for a just society. His principal focus is not

25 Act of Mar. 9, 1896, Laws of Utah, 1896, 1st Session, ch. XXXIX, p. 125 [hereinafter 1896 Act].

26 1896 Act, at §§ 2–3 (codified at Utah Code § 73–1–3 (1933 compilation)).

27 See, for example, Millon, "First Antitrust Statute," 146–147.

28 See Don A. Stringham, "Antitrust and Unfair Trade Practice Regulation in Utah," *Utah Law Review* 8 (1963): 353–355.

29 Jonathan A. Dibble and James S. Jardine, "The Utah Antitrust Act of 1979: Getting into the State Antitrust Business," *Utah Law Review* (1980): 78; Flynn, 1979, 479–80; May, "Antitrust Practice," 498.

30 1979 Antitrust Act.

31 Dibble and Jardine, "Utah Antitrust Act," 78.

on economics, but Rawls addresses economic matters briefly "to illustrate the content of the principles of justice."[32] As compared to socialist and command economies, Rawls finds market-based systems to be both more efficient and more supportive of "equal liberties and fair equality of opportunity."[33] He explains that properly functioning market systems both decentralize the "exercise of economic power" and obviate the need for direct governmental control—features tending to enhance individual liberty.[34]

Professor John J. Flynn at the University of Utah, writing four years later, considered the implications of Rawls's theories on the practical achievement of distributive justice.[35] Flynn agreed with Rawls that a key element necessary to the preservation of liberty and equality of opportunity was a properly operating "free market system."[36] Nevertheless, viewing the social, political, and economic disarray afflicting the U.S. during the early 1970s, Flynn expressed "considerable doubt as to the existence of a free market system . . . in vast sectors of the American economy."[37] He pointed to the emergence of "giant corporations,"[38] the capture of regulation by private interests, and the concentration of wealth as "imposing inefficiencies, limiting equality of opportunity, and posing substantial risks to the equality of individual liberties."[39] He echoed the progressive critiques of the second decade of the twenty-first century when he concluded that

> [w]here the unchecked growth of concentrated economic power converts the economy from one of free choice to dictated choice, individual mobility, freedom of choice, and individual liberty are greatly lessened. Recent events in the political and economic sphere, when coupled with the pervasive scope of economic concentration in the American economy, clearly indicate the need either to reestablish a competitive market economy in the United States and other major areas of the world or to pay an ever increasing price in the form of resource misallocations, arbitrary wealth transfers, overall economic inefficiencies, and a decline in equality of opportunity and individual liberty.[40]

Flynn thus advocates a restoration of the free market as envisioned by Rawls rather than by Hayek, Friedman, and the Chicago School—a market that is not distorted by wealth inequality and corporate power. Moreover, the means

32 John Rawls, *A Theory of Justice* (Harvard University Press, 1971, rev. ed. 1999), 234.
33 Rawls, *A Theory of Justice*, 240–241.
34 Rawls, *A Theory of Justice*, 241.
35 Flynn, 1975.
36 Id., 156.
37 Id., 155.
38 Id., 154.
39 Id., 155–56.
40 Id., 156.

for achieving this desirable market state, Flynn argues in a 1979 article, is a reinvigoration of state economic regulation intended not only to restrict anticompetitive corporate practices but also to address public interests such as "[e]nvironmental pollution, energy, and raw materials shortages, uncontrolled inflation, and unfair economic exploitation."[41]

A second major current underlying John Flynn's advocacy was his vocal opposition to the neoclassical economic approach to antitrust law espoused by Professor Robert Bork and the Chicago School,[42] an approach that was encapsulated in Bork's influential 1978 book *The Antitrust Paradox*.[43] Flynn, in his work on antitrust federalism, had long believed in "permitting states to serve as laboratories for social and economic experiments."[44] Yet by the 1970s, federal courts and enforcement agencies were increasingly restricting the ability of states to enact regulations intended to address these issues by relying on broad interpretations of the Commerce Clause, the Supremacy Clause, Due Process, Equal Protection, and even the First Amendment.[45] Part of the problem, Flynn found, was the cramped view that the Chicago School held of the purpose of antitrust law—"removing private arrangements restricting output" to the exclusion of any other market regulation.[46] In Flynn's view, in order for antitrust regulation to achieve its broader social and economic potential, it must break free from this "neo-classical model of economic theorizing."[47]

The insertion of the Free Market Clause into Utah's 1979 Antitrust Act was a step toward recognizing this broader scope. It expressly establishes that the purpose of the statute includes economic advancement, lower prices, allocative equity, and the preservation of democratic political and social institutions. The Utah statute thus seems to reject the constraints on antitrust law espoused by the Chicago School and the federal courts and instead adopts the broader view embraced by progressives such as John Flynn.

3 A new Free Market Preamble

By the mid-twentieth century, there was a growing consensus in Utah legal circles that the state's 1895 Constitution required updating. One of the chief proponents of this view was John Flynn. He denigrated Utah's constitution as a "'horse and buggy' constitution"[48] and observed that its complex patchwork

41 Flynn, 1979, 508.
42 Flynn, 1979; Flynn, 1983; Flynn, 1988.
43 Robert H. Bork, *The Antitrust Paradox: A Policy at War With Itself* (1978).
44 Flynn, 1979, 508.
45 Flynn, 1965; Flynn, 1979; May, "Antitrust Practice".
46 Flynn, 1983, 270.
47 Flynn, 1979, 508.
48 Flynn, 1966, at 351.

of pseudo-legislative provisions offered "a basic framework of government designed to prevent government from governing."[49]

In his January 1965 address to the joint houses of the Utah Legislature, Governor Calvin Rampton urged the legislature to call for a new constitutional convention, referring to Utah's 172-page 1895 Constitution as "a relic of the 19th Century."[50] Shortly thereafter, the Utah Senate and House each passed a resolution to place a constitutional convention on the Utah ballot.[51] However, the voters in 1966 rejected the proposal by a wide margin of 85% to 15%.[52]

As an alternative to a full constitutional convention, the Utah constitution may also be amended through a specially constituted commission that submits recommended amendments to the legislature and then to the voters for approval.[53] At the urging of Flynn and others,[54] Utah created a temporary Constitutional Revision Study Commission in 1969,[55] which was given permanent status in 1977.[56] The purpose of the 16-member Commission was to "make a comprehensive examination of the constitution of the state of Utah . . . and thereafter to make recommendations to the governor and the legislature as to specific proposed constitutional amendments."[57]

Numerous constitutional amendments were approved by Utah voters following the creation of the Commission.[58] The formal process for amending Article XII of the Utah Constitution, however, did not began until the 1987 General Session of the legislature[59]—eighteen years after the formation of the Commission and eight years after enactment of the 1979 Antitrust Act.

The Commission began a comprehensive study of Article XII in June 1988 and recommended that most of its provisions be repealed as unnecessary and duplicative of statutory law.[60] In late 1989, the Commission recommended, among other things, that the price fixing prohibition contained in Section 20

49 Flynn, 1966, at 311.

50 Governor's Message, Senate Journal, Thirty-Sixth Session of the Legislature of the State of Utah, 42, 50 (1965) [hereinafter Senate Journal 1965].

51 S.J.R. 3 (passed Jan. 20, 1965), Senate Journal 1965, supra note 107, at 136; and H.J.R. 1 (passed Jan. 25, 1965), Senate Journal 1965, supra note 107, at 186.

52 Ballotopedia, Utah Proposition No. 2: Constitutional Convention Call (1966), https://ballotpedia.org/Utah_Proposition_No._2:_Constitutional_Convention_Call_(1966).

53 Utah Const., Art XXIII. *See also* Kimball, supra note 104, at 392 (discussing Utah Constitutional Commission).

54 Holographic letter from John Flynn to Rita and Jefferson Fordham, dated Mar. 4, 1969.

55 Constitutional Study Commission, Utah Laws 1969, ch. 89 (S.B. 1), Feb. 25, 1969.

56 Constitutional Revision Study Commission, Utah Laws 1977, ch. 159 (S.B. 128), Mar. 10, 1977.

57 Commission Charter 1969, *supra* note 112, § 3.

58 White, *Utah State Constitution*, 22–25.

59 Report of the Constitutional Revision Commission Submitted to the Governor and the 49th Legislature of the State of Utah, Jan. 1992, at 15 [1992 Commission Report].

60 1992 Commission Report, 15.

be repealed,[61] probably due to its overlap with Utah's 1979 Antitrust Act. The repeal of Article XII, Section 20 would have resulted in the removal of any antitrust provision from the Utah Constitution, an approach taken by other states.[62]

The repeal of Section 20, however, was opposed by the new Antitrust Unit of the Utah Attorney General's Office, as well as "a University of Utah College law professor" (undoubtedly John Flynn).[63] As reported by the Commission, these advisors argued that the prohibition against price fixing contained in the 1895 Constitution provided "a fundamental protection of the competitive market system, an economic system upon which the nation is founded, and therefore should be retained in the constitution."[64] This position echoed Flynn's earlier writings on the potential power of state antitrust rules to shape both the economic and social fabric of the state.

Members of the Commission were divided. Some argued that the price-fixing prohibition of the 1895 clause was too narrow to merit inclusion in the constitution, and others argued that a broader antitrust provision would hamper changes to the law that might be necessitated by changing economic conditions. Finally, others—the prevailing group—argued that the narrow 1895 price-fixing provision should be replaced by a broader prohibition on anticompetitive activity, along the lines of the Federal Sherman Act and the 1979 Utah Antitrust Act.[65]

A subcommittee of the Commission was formed to draft language to this effect; it submitted its proposal to the full Commission in September 1990. The 1990 subcommittee redraft of Section 20 retained the title of the original 1895 clause, "Trusts and combinations prohibited," but replaced the remainder of the 1895 ban on price fixing with substantive provisions broadly prohibiting anticompetitive concerted and unilateral conduct similar to the Federal Sherman Act and the 1979 Utah Antitrust Act.

After debate within the Commission, the draft was revised to change, among other things, its preamble language.[66] In January 1992, the Commission submitted another proposed revision of Article XII to the General Legislature. This time, it was accepted and filed as a Senate Joint Resolution,[67] which was approved by both houses of the legislature on February 6. The amendment was included as Proposition 2 on the ballot of the November

61 Id.

62 For example, Montana included an anti-monopoly clause similar to Utah's in its 1889 constitution (Art. XV, § 20) but removed this provision upon enacting comprehensive antitrust legislation in 1973 (Mont. Code Ann. §§ 30–14–101 to 30–14–142).

63 1992 Commission Report, 15.

64 Id., 15–16.

65 Id., 16.

66 Id.

67 Utah S.J.R. 7.

1992 general election.[68] The amendments passed by comfortable margins and became effective as of January 1, 1993.

Article XII Section 20, as enacted, contains the following preamble:

> It is the policy of the state of Utah that a free market system shall govern trade and commerce in this state to promote the dispersion of economic and political power and the general welfare of all the people.

The remainder of Section 20, as enacted, mirrors the prohibitions on agreements in restraint of trade and monopolization contained in the Sherman Act. Yet the Free Market Clause that serves as its preamble does more and intentionally so.[69] Like the preamble language of both the 1979 Antitrust Act and the 1990 subcommittee draft, the Free Market Clause of the 1992 amendment establishes that the purpose and scope of Utah's antitrust law go beyond considerations of output restriction and price that are espoused by the neoclassical Chicago School and the federal courts.

When taken together, the 1992 Amendment and the 1979 Antitrust Act define the scope of Utah's antitrust laws as encompassing goals of distributive justice and the preservation of democratic political and social institutions, in addition to more traditional economic goals associated with consumer prices, product quality, progress and general welfare.

4 Co-option of the Free Market Clause

One can imagine the Free Market preambles of the Utah Antitrust Act and the Antitrust Clause of the Utah Constitution as experiments set in motion by antitrust federalism's great innovator, John Flynn. Could an express statement of broad social and distributive justice goals embedded within the text of a state's antitrust legislation persuade courts interpreting those statutes to broaden their focus beyond the narrow consumer welfare standard espoused by the Chicago School? Could such statements free Utah's and other states' antitrust laws from the shackles imposed by the federal courts' narrow readings of the Sherman Act, a statute that lacks any such explanatory language or legislative history of its own? And if so, might those broader interpretations eventually come to fill the interpretive vacuum of the Sherman Act itself, eventually supplanting the cramped reading given to the federal antitrust laws by the Chicago School and the courts?

Regrettably, nearly thirty years later, these questions have still not been answered, as the enforcement of state antitrust laws did not experience the revival that Flynn and others had hoped, and the Free Market Clause has gone down a road with several unexpected turns. Beginning in the 1970s,

68 Utah Voter Information Pamphlet, General Election, November 3, 1992.

69 Utah Senate, Floor Debate, Jan. 22, 1992, Statement of Sen. Haven Barlow.

state antitrust enforcement expanded significantly across the United States.[70] Various explanations have been offered for this expansion, including the enactment of the Hart-Scott-Rodino Antitrust Improvements Act of 1976, which authorizes states to bring federal antitrust claims on behalf of their citizens *parens patriae*,[71] and the concurrent decline in federal antitrust enforcement during the hands-off Reagan-Bush era.[72]

In 1983, the National Association of Attorneys General (NAAG), the leading association of state antitrust enforcement officials, formed a Multistate Antitrust Task Force, which facilitated the coordination of joint investigations and antitrust enforcement by states.[73] By 1993, forty-five states and the District of Columbia brought monopolization claims against a group of cable operators,[74] twenty states joined the Department of Justice (DOJ)'s massive antitrust case against Microsoft in 1998,[75] and since 2019, nearly every state, the District of Columbia, Puerto Rico, Guam, and the U.S. Virgin Islands has gotten involved in investigating or suing Google and Meta over a variety of alleged anticompetitive practices.

However, with a few exceptions, the significant growth of state antitrust enforcement over the past thirty years has not led to a comparable increase in claims under state antitrust law. This discrepancy exists largely because state attorneys general participating in federal antitrust cases often focus on the enforcement of federal antitrust laws. Likewise, multistate actions requiring cooperation and coordination among multiple states tend to emphasize common elements of state claims rather than doctrines and interpretations that are unique to a particular state. Thus, even when state law claims accompany federal claims in a lawsuit, the state law claims are often viewed as subsidiary and are not the focus of significant independent analysis or argumentation.

This is not to say, however, that there are not some areas in which state antitrust law differs substantively from federal law. For example, according to one recent report, twenty-five states and the District of Columbia have enacted legislation overriding the Supreme Court's decision in *Illinois Brick Co. v. Illinois*,[76] which prohibits recovery by indirect purchasers under the

70 See James May, "The Role of the States in the First Century of the Sherman Act and the Larger Picture of Antitrust History," *Antitrust Law Journal* 59 (1990); Juan A. Arteaga and Jordan Ludwig, "The Role of US State Antitrust Enforcement," *Global Competition Review* (November 19, 2019); Tsai et al. (eds.), *State Antitrust Practice*, 1–27.

71 Hart-Scott-Rodino Antitrust Improvements Act of 1976 ("HSR Act"), Pub. L. 94–435, Title III, 90 Stat. 1394, codified at 1 5 U.S.C. §15c.

72 See Arteaga and Ludwig, "Role of US State Antitrust."

73 Tsai et al. (eds.), *State Antitrust Practice*, 1–13 to 1–14.

74 *New York ex rel. Abrams v. Primestar Partners*, 1993–2 Trade Cas. (CCR) 170,404 (S.D.N.Y. 1993).

75 *New York v. Microsoft Corp.*, 224 F. Supp. 2d 76 (D.D.C. 2002); *United States v. Microsoft Corp.*, 253 F.3d 34 (D.C. Cir. 2001).

76 *Illinois Brick Co. v. Illinois*, 431 U.S. 720 (1977).

federal antitrust laws.[77] Likewise, a number of states continue to view resale price maintenance as per se illegal under state antitrust laws,[78] notwithstanding the Supreme Court's application of the "rule of reason" to this practice under the Sherman Act in *Leegin Creative Leather Prods. v. PSKS*.[79] Nevertheless, to date, no federal or state case has invoked the Free Market Clauses of the Utah Constitution or Antitrust Act to challenge the application of the consumer welfare standard that has been adopted by the federal courts.

Despite the dearth of litigation over Utah's Free Market Clause, it has attracted notice outside of the state. The American Legislative Exchange Council (ALEC), founded in 1973, is, according to its website, "America's largest nonpartisan, voluntary membership organization of state legislators dedicated to the principles of limited government, free markets and federalism."[80] One of ALEC's principal activities is the drafting and dissemination of "model" legislation that can be introduced in state legislatures. The creation of model legislation is a time-honored practice that arose long before ALEC. For example, the non-profit Uniform Law Commission (ULC), founded in 1892, has drafted numerous model laws, such as the Uniform Commercial Code, that have been adopted in nearly all states. But in recent years, the production of model legislation has become controversial as partisan organizations (often conservative-leaning) have facilitated adoption of state laws relating to hot issues such as abortion, gun ownership, asbestos litigation, scientific evidence, education, immigration, environmental protection, voter registration, and taxation.[81]

ALEC is among the most prolific and successful of these organizations.[82] According to one study, between 2010 and 2018, bills based on ALEC model legislation were introduced in state legislatures and the U.S. Congress more than 2,900 times, with 600 of such bills becoming law.[83] ALEC is also unabashedly in favor of reducing governmental regulation, criticizing the heavy financial burdens of regulatory compliance on businesses and attributing slowed economic growth, among other things, to "regulatory accumulation."[84]

77 Arteaga and Jordan, "Role of US State Antitrust."

78 Tsai et al. (eds.), *State Antitrust Practice*, 1–15.

79 551 U.S. 877 (2007).

80 Am. Legis. Exchange Council, About ALEC, www.alec.org/about/.

81 See Rob O'Dell and Nick Penzenstadler, "Copy, Paste, Legislate: You Elected Them to Write New Laws: They're Letting Corporations Do It Instead," *USAToday* (June 19, 2019).

82 See Yvonne Wingett Sanchez and Rob O'Dell, "What is ALEC? 'The Most Effective Organization' for Conservatives, Says Newt Gingrich," *USAToday* (April 5, 2019); Mike McIntire, "Conservative Nonprofit Acts as a Stealth Business Lobbyist," *NY Times* (April 21, 2012); Nancy Scola, "Exposing ALEC: How Conservative-Backed State Laws Are All Connected," *The Atlantic* (April 14, 2012); John Nichols, "ALEC Exposed," *The Nation* (July 12, 2011); People for the American Way, *ALEC and the Battle of the States* (2003).

83 Sanchez and O'Dell, "What is ALEC?".

84 Am. Legislative Exchange Council, Regulatory Reform, www.alec.org/issue/regulatory-reform/.

ALEC has long had an affinity with the traditionally conservative state of Utah. In 2012, ALEC held its annual meeting in Salt Lake City and named Utah as the state having "the strongest economic outcome in the nation," an honor that the state has received multiple times.[85] In 2009, ALEC adopted a model "Free Market Constitutional Amendment." The model clause is nearly identical to the preamble of Article XII, Section 20 of the Utah Constitution:

> It is the policy of the state of __________ that a free enterprise system shall govern trade and commerce in this state to promote the dispersion of economic and political power and the general welfare of all the people.[86]

The model amendment was drafted by Tennessee State Representative Susan Lynn, Chair of the ALEC Commerce Task Force.[87] In addition to drafting the ALEC model constitutional amendment, Representative Lynn also sought to have it adopted in her own state of Tennessee. She explained that

> By definition, a free enterprise economy is an economic system controlled chiefly by individuals and private companies; not the government.
>
> Characteristics include economic freedom which allows people to decide how they will earn and spend their income; goods and services are produced and allocated through supply and demand by voluntary exchanges; private ownership of property and of the means of production is the key; and profit is not a bad word but greeted [sic] by freedom.[88]

Lynn further noted that "[t]o date, only Utah has such a reassuring clause in their state Constitution."[89] The Tennessee amendment appears to have died in committee,[90] and no other state has yet taken up the ALEC model amendment or adopted a Free Market Clause similar to Utah's.

Political watchdog the Center for Media and Democracy, which publishes a feature known as "ALEC Exposed," has taken specific aim at ALEC's Free Market Clause, claiming that it

85 Ron Scheberle, "ALEC Members Gather to Advance Economic Work in the States," *Deseret News* (July 24, 2012).

86 Am. Legislative Exchange Council, Free Market Constitutional Amendment www.alec.org/model-policy/free-market-constitutional-amendment/ (visited Jan. 9, 2021).

87 Susan Lynn, "Free Enterprise Constitutional Amendment," *Cannon Courier*, February 16, 2010, accessed www.cannoncourier.com/free-enterprise-constitutional-amendment-cms-1789.

88 Susan Lynn, "Free Enterprise Constitutional Amendment," *Cannon Courier*, February 16, 2010, accessed www.cannoncourier.com/free-enterprise-constitutional-amendment-cms-1789.

89 Lynn, "Free Enterprise Constitutional Amendment."

90 Tenn. *HJR0722*, introduced January 14, 2010 (Lynn), accessed http://wapp.capitol.tn.gov/apps/BillInfo/default.aspx?BillNumber=HJR0722&GA=106.

> is likely intended to provide a basis for overturning state policies that conflict with right-wing ideology. For example, minimum wage laws, zoning and land use laws, race- or gender- conscious policies, housing subsidies or rent controls, and perhaps even environmental standards may all arguably interfere with the "free market" and be found unconstitutional if this proposed Amendment were adopted.[91]

In response to a reporter's inquiry on whether ALEC's Free Market clause was intended to eliminate all regulations on business, Representative Lynn responded that it was not. "Do we approve of stealing, of fraud, or abuse of natural resources[?] No, whether done by an individual or a business such actions clearly violate the Constitutional rights of others."[92] Instead, Rep. Lynn insisted that the Free Market Clause that she introduced was intended only to curb "the free-market killing regulations we see being enacted today."[93]

However one wishes to interpret ALEC's or Rep. Lynn's intentions with respect to the Free Market Clause, it seems abundantly clear that the ideals of distributive justice and social equality espoused by John Rawls and John Flynn do not enter into their calculus. Rather than promoting positive state regulation to ensure that all people have equal access to the fruits of the market (i.e., free access to markets), ALEC and Lynn appear to interpret the Free Market Clause as discouraging positive economic regulation and instead allowing businesses to operate in an unencumbered, laissez-faire manner. In this, they would likely go even further than the Chicago School in eviscerating antitrust law through their version of the Free Markets Clause.

This gloss on "free markets," while different than that espoused by Rawls and Flynn, is not wholly disingenuous. The protean term "free market" is susceptible to multiple, sometimes opposing, meanings. In fact, the term today is most closely associated with a laissez-faire approach to markets that seeks to minimize governmental intervention, as promoted by the Free Market Study established at the University of Chicago in 1946 and more fully realized by Frederich Hayek's Mont Pèlerin Society founded in 1947.[94] Robert Bork also invokes the term "free market" as a condition of limited governmental intervention, writing that

> Antitrust was originally conceived as a limited intervention in free and private processes for the purpose of keeping those processes free.

91 Center for Media and Democracy, *ALEC Exposed—Free Market Constitutional Amendment*, accessed www.alecexposed.org/wiki/Free_Market_Constitutional_Amendment_Exposed.

92 Lynn, "Free Enterprise."

93 Lynn, "Free Enterprise."

94 Angus Burgin, *The Great Persuasion: Reinventing Free Markets Since the Depression* (Harvard University Press 2012), 56, 125; Robert Van Horn, "Chicago's Shifting Attitude Toward Concentrations of Business Power (1934–1962)," *Seattle University Law Review* 34 (2011): 1527, 1537–1540.

> It tempered laissez-faire in order to preserve a free-market system . . . The conception was one of free markets with minimal government involvement.[95]

Thus, the concept of a "free market" can be used in the sense of Rawls and Flynn, namely, a market that is open and accessible to all competitors, large and small, on an equal basis, or in the sense used by Hayek and Bork, specifically, a laissez-faire market that is free from governmental regulation and oversight. The Utah provisions, shaped by Flynn, were likely intended to indicate the former. However, even Flynn must have realized by the 1980s that the sense of this term was shifting toward the right. For this reason, Flynn was likely behind the proposals in Utah to modify the "free market" language of the 1992 constitutional amendment to refer instead to a well-functioning competitive process.[96] Yet this modification was never enacted, perhaps intentionally and perhaps not.

5 The final indignity: Tesla and non-justiciability

If ALEC's interpretation of the Free Market Clause goes against that of the drafters of the Utah Clause, then at least it is an interpretation. In a recent case, the Utah Supreme Court declined even to interpret the Free Market Clause, holding that it was too vague "to sustain a justiciable constitutional standard."[97]

In *Tesla Motors v. Utah Tax Commission*,[98] a wholly owned subsidiary of California-based electric vehicle manufacturer Tesla Motors applied to the Utah Motor Vehicle Enforcement Division for a license to sell new Tesla vehicles from a retail showroom in Salt Lake City. The Division denied the application, citing two Utah statutes that prohibit a vehicle manufacturer from owning an interest in its retail franchisee.[99] Tesla appealed the Division's decision all the way to the Utah Supreme Court. It argued, among other things, that the motor vehicle franchise requirement violated the Free Market Clause of the Utah Constitution. This was the first case invoking Utah's Free Market Clause, either under the Constitution or the Antitrust Act, and, thus, the first opportunity for the Utah courts to interpret this unique legislative pronouncement.[100]

95 Bork, *Antitrust Paradox*, 435.
96 Contreras, "Free Market," 310.
97 *Tesla Motors UT, Inc. v. Utah Tax Commission*, 2017 UT 18, 398 P.3d 55, 66 (Utah 2017).
98 Id.
99 Motor Vehicle Business Regulation Act (Licensing Act), Utah Code § 41-3-101, and New Automobile Franchise Act, *id.* §3-14-101.
100 In *Summit Water Distrib. Co. v. Summit County*, 2005 UT 73, 123 P.3d 437 (Utah 2005), one party argued that the Antitrust Clause of the Utah Constitution (Art. XII, Sec. 20) was not self-executing. However, the Court declined to reach this issue. Id. at 452.

In the case, Tesla argued as follows:

> By prohibiting Tesla from selling new cars in the Utah retail new car market unless it enters into franchise agreements with local independent dealers, the Commission has significantly interfered with the free market, constrained consumer freedom and entrenched incumbent economic interests. This type of clear interference with the free market can only be sustained if the [Division] can demonstrate it furthers a legitimate state interest.
>
> The [Division] did not show any legitimate interest at the hearing, nor can it. The only purpose of forbidding a non-franchising manufacturer from selling directly to consumers is to protect local independent dealers from competition from a manufacturer selling a different brand of automobile, a policy that inevitably leads to less consumer choice and higher prices among different automobile brands.
>
> Because there is no legitimate justification for excluding Tesla from the retail new car market, the Commission's Final Decision and its interpretation and application of the Acts must be rejected as violating the Free-Market Provision of the Utah Constitution.[101]

Tesla also introduced evidence that prohibiting it from selling vehicles directly to consumers (i.e., through its wholly owned subsidiary) would likely have the effect of increasing consumer prices, reducing consumer choice, adversely impacting the environment, and reducing jobs for Utah residents.[102] Tesla concluded that the only apparent purpose of the restrictions was "economic protectionism for local independent dealers," an impermissible justification, it contended, for violating the Free Market Clause.[103]

The Utah Supreme Court was not sympathetic. Without considering any of Tesla's substantive arguments regarding the Free Market Clause, it held that the clause was non-justiciable under the constitutional self-execution doctrine. As the Court explained,

> Not every provision of the constitution states an enforceable limitation on our government. Some provisions are non-justiciable: They are stated at so high a level of generality or aspiration that they require legislation to establish a limitation enforceable in our courts. . . . The quoted language of the Free Market Clause is such a provision. This clause articulates only a "policy." And it frames the policy in terms that identify only a "general principle" with no justiciable standard or "means for putting

101 *Tesla Motors UT, Inc. v. Utah Tax Commission*, Appeal No. 20150792-SC, Utah Supreme Court, Brief of Petitioner/Appellant at 38 (filed Jan. 27, 2016).

102 Id., 46–48.

103 Id., 48.

> [it] into effect." We know from the Free Market Clause that our charter for state government is in favor of a "free market." But we know little more than that.
>
> The general aspiration for a "free market" is too vague a policy to sustain a justiciable constitutional standard. So without any implementing legislation, we deem this provision non-justiciable.[104]

Thus, in one fell swoop, the Utah Supreme Court rendered the state's unique Free Market Clause non-justiciable—a jurisprudential dead letter.

6 Conclusion

The Free Market Clause of the Utah Constitution and its predecessor in the Utah Antitrust Act expressly link a free market system to the achievement of goals relating to distributive justice and the preservation of democratic political, and social institutions. As such, they reflect the thinking of progressive antitrust theorist John Flynn, who sought to orchestrate a direct assault on the cramped reading given to the antitrust laws by the Chicago School and the federal courts. By expanding the express scope of the antitrust laws in Utah beyond neoclassical economic analysis, Flynn may have hoped to influence not only state jurisprudence but also the broader interpretation of antitrust law, particularly the Sherman Act, throughout the United States.

Yet this project never achieved its goal. The terminology of free markets was co-opted by the right to represent, not the open and accessible markets envisioned by Flynn, but laissez-faire unregulated markets that could be dominated by large firms without consequences. Moreover, in the most recent case to interpret the Free Market Clause, the Utah Supreme Court seemingly abdicated its interpretive responsibility by holding that the clause was non-justiciable.

What, then, should one make of Utah's lofty Free Market Clause—the preamble to its constitutional antitrust provisions? Should later courts interpret the clause, and if so, how should they read it? Constitutional jurisprudence today, at least at the federal level, is dominated by a textualist, originalist tendency.[105] Such an approach might lead one to Flynn's conception of free markets or it might not, as the intentions of the actual adopters of the clause—the legislators and voters—might have held a more Hayekian view of the term "free market." Given this interpretive coin toss, is the Utah Supreme Court's refusal to interpret the Free Market Clause the better course? It is not. Rather, it is the role of the courts to offer an interpretation—to decide, one way or another, the meaning of constitutional text. And courts do this all of the time

104 398 P.3d at 66.

105 Diarmuid F. O'Scannlain, "'We Are All Textualists Now:' The Legacy of Justice Antonin Scalia," *St. John's Law Review* 91 no. 2 (2017): 303–313.

with equally vague (or lofty) constitutional text from the guarantee of freedom of expression to the ban on cruel and unusual punishment.

Invariably, any interpretation of a constitutional text will cause dissatisfaction among some stakeholders. Yet if this is the case, those stakeholders at least have a clear pathway forward: to seek to amend the constitutional text in a manner that is more to their liking. But at least the path forward will be clear rather than, as in the case of the Utah Free Market Clause, the murky void through which it currently runs.

References

Arteaga, Juan A. and Jordan Ludwig. "The Role of US State Antitrust Enforcement." *Global Competition Rev.*, November 19, 2019.

Bork, Robert H. *The Antitrust Paradox: A Policy at War With Itself.* New York: Basic Books, 1978.

Burgin, Angus. *The Great Persuasion: Reinventing Free Markets Since the Depression.* Harvard University Press, 2012.

Calabresi, Steven G. and Larissa C. Leibowitz. Monopolies and the Constitution: A History of Crony Capitalism, 36 Harv. J.L. & Pulb. Pl'y 983, 2013.

Contreras, Jorge L. "Free Market State (Of Mind): Antitrust Federalism, John J. Flynn and The Utah Constitution's Free Market Clause." *Utah Law Review* 2023, no. 2 (2023): 279–335.

Dibble, Jonathan A. and James S. Jardine. "The Utah Antitrust Act of 1979: Getting into the State Antitrust Business." *Utah Law Review* (1980): 73.

Durham, C. J. Christine, Daniel J. H. Greenwood, and Kathy Wyer. "Utah's Constitution: Distinctively Undistinctive." In *The Constitutionalism of American States*, edited by George E. Connor and Christopher W. Hammons (2006): 649.

Flynn, John J. "The Crisis of Federalism: Who Is Responsible?" *ABA J.* 51 (1965): 229.

Flynn, John J. "Federalism and Viable State Government—The History of Utah's Constitution." *Utah Law Review* (1966): 311.

Flynn, John J. "Trends in Federal Antitrust Doctrine Suggesting Future Directions for State Antitrust Enforcement." *The Journal of Corporate Law* 4 (1979): 479.

Flynn, John J. "Reaganomics and Antitrust Enforcement: A Jurisprudential Critique." *Utah Law Review* (1983): 269.

Flynn, John J. "The Reagan Administration's Antitrust Policy, Original Intent and the Legislative History of the Sherman Act." *The Antitrust Bulletin* 33 (1988): 259.

Flynn, John J. and Piero Ruffinengo. "Distributive Justice: Some Institutional Implications of Rawls 'A Theory of Justice.'" *Utah Law Review* (1975): 123.

Legislation. "A Collection and Survey of State Anti-Trust Laws." *Columbia Law Review* 32 (1932): 347.

May, James. "Antitrust Practice and Procedure in the Formative Era: The Constitutional and Conceptual Reach of State Antitrust Law, 1880–1918." *University of Pennsylvania Law Review* 135 (1987): 495.

May, James. "The Role of the States in the First Century of the Sherman Act and the Larger Picture of Antitrust History." *Antitrust Law Journal* 59 (1990): 93.

Millon, David K. "The First Antitrust Statute." *Washburn Law Journal* 29 (1990): 141.

O'Scannlain, Diarmuid F. "'We Are All Textualists Now': The Legacy of Justice Antonin Scalia." *St. John's Law Review* 91, no. 2 (2017): 303–313.

Stringham, Don A. "Antitrust and Unfair Trade Practice Regulation in Utah." *Utah Law Review* 8 (1963): 339.

Tsai, Rocky C. et al. (eds.). *State Antitrust Practice and Statutes*, 5th ed. Chicago: American Bar Association, 2014.
Van Horn, Robert. "Chicago's Shifting Attitude Toward Concentrations of Business Power (1934–1962)." *Seattle University Law Review* 34 (2011): 1527.
White, Jean Bickmore. *Charter for Statehood: The Story of Utah's State Constitution*. Salt Lake City: University of Utah Press, 1996.
White, Jean Bickmore. *The Utah State Constitution*. Oxford University Press, 2011.

Appendix

Selected source material

Chapter 2: The preambles to archaic Greek interstate treaties at Olympia: a study in the diffusion of diplomatic language

Bronze inscription of the treaty between the Eleans and Ewaoioi:[1]

> The agreement of the Eleans and the Ewaoioi. There will be an alliance for one hundred years. It will begin from this year. If there is any need, either in word or in deed, they shall stand together in all things, especially in war. If they do not stand together, the wrong-doers shall pay a talent of silver to Olympian Zeus for dedication. If anyone does harm to this writing, whether the community or an official or private citizen, he shall be liable to the sacred penalty which here is written down.

Bronze inscription for the treaty between the Sybarites and Serdaioi:[2]

> The Sybarites and their allies and the Serdaioi agreed to friendship, faithful and without deceit, forever. The protectors are Zeus, Apollo, the other gods, and the city of Poseidonia.

Bronze inscription for the treaty between the Anaitoi and Metpioi:[3]

> The agreement between the Anaitoi and the Metapioi: friendship for fifty years. And if either side violates the compact, let both the protectors and the priests expel them from the altar. If they transgress the oath, judgment shall belong to the priest at Olympia.

1 Translation by Nicholas Cross. See image in Jeffery and Lilian Hamilton, *The Local Scripts of Archaic Greece* (Oxford: Clarendon Press, 1961), 42 n. 6.

2 Translation by Nicholas Cross. See image in Margherita Guarducci, *Epigrafi di carattere pubblico* (Roma: Istituto poligrafico dello Stato, 1969), 94.

3 Translation by Nicholas Cross. See Dosuna and Julián Méndez, "La clause finale de l'accord entre les Anaitiens et les Métapiens (*IvO* 10 = *IÉD* 14, L. 5–7)," *Zeitschrift für Papyrologie und Epigraphik* 184 (2013): 148.

Chapter 4: The conservative case for warrior law: legal change in medieval Japan

Hōjō Yasutoki's first letter: regarding the list of precedents[4]

In the judgment of various lawsuits, even those of the same type, the strong get [their claims] heard while the weak go ignored. These articles were drafted so that, even if [the judge] acts with care, the severity [of judgments] will not be dependent on [the social power or political influence of] the parties. I include one copy [of the List with this letter].

Such matters should be based and judged solely on the provisions of [existing] law, but there is not even one in a thousand or ten thousand in the countryside who understand this way [of law]. If a crime is committed, even those that should be immediately punished like robberies or night attacks, there are many who scheme and do others bodily harm. And when someone who is not familiar with the specifics of the law becomes involved [with a trial] and encounters an opinion that cites it, it is as though they are wandering into a mountain full of deer traps and unknowingly fall into them.

For this reason, in the time of the Great General [Minamoto no Yoritomo], there were no judgments referencing [classical] law. As this was not done by successive generations of shogun, the precedent is still followed at present. After all, if followers devote their loyalty to their masters, children have filial devotion for their parents, and wives obey their husbands, then those with crooked hearts will be rejected and the upright will be rewarded, and the people naturally will be at peace. In thinking this, we created [this List], although I am apprehensive and embarrassed that there will surely be those around the capital who will scorn it, scoffing that it was compiled by ignorant country bumpkins. It shall be implemented because if [such principles] are not established in advance, [judgment] will depend on [the social position of] the parties.

I want you to widely proclaim this to the Kantō housemen, military governors, and local law enforcement officials, and ensure they understand my thinking. Now, copy and distribute [the List] to each military governor, and have them clearly explain it to the local law enforcement officials and housemen in their provinces. If there are oversights, supplements shall be written and added. Respectfully yours,

[Jōei 1st year (1232)] 8th month, 8th day
Governor of Musashi [Hōjō Yasutoki]
[To:] Governor of Suruga [Hōjō Shigetoki]

4 Translation by Christoffer Bovbjerg.

Hōjō Yasutoki's second letter: regarding the list of precedents[5]

A document that records articles of how judgments ought to be made should be called a "catalog" (mokuroku), but given that it records substance of governance as well, the drafters wisely titled it "Articles of Precedents" (shikijō). But I found this name to be overwrought and so have renamed it "The List of Precedents" (shikimoku). Please understand this.

There will surely be those [in the capital] who will criticize the making of this List of Precedents and ask what is its textual authority. In truth, it does not rely on any original text; it was written only in keeping with reason (dōri). As [such principles] have not yet been established, [judges] either ignore the right and wrong of the matter and proceed based on the [social] strength and weakness of those involved, or forget prior decisions and rule [on the same matters] again. Due to such conditions, a body of judgments has been established. The particulars have been recorded so that judgments will be rendered impartially, without discrimination between high and low.

This text deviates from the teachings of [existing] law in some minor ways. However, when it comes to reading classical law and its amendments, even those who can read Chinese characters can recognize the individual characters [but cannot grasp the text's overall meaning]. For those who only know the Japanese syllabary, when they are confronted with Chinese characters, it is as though their eyes have gone blind. As there are many in the world who only know the Japanese syllabary, this List of Precedents was made to be easily understood by the people far and wide [and so is written in the syllabary]. It is also only for the management of warriors. For these reasons, it shall not in any way alter the authority of Kyoto's courts or the rules of classical law.

While generally the teachings of [existing] law are certainly to be exalted, looking at the practices of the warriors and common people, there are not even one or two in a hundred or a thousand who can understand it. Accordingly, when [an incident occurs] and many people are ignorant of the law, court clerks are suddenly tasked with considering right and wrong based on the law and inconsistently cite texts on the severity [of punishment]. As a result, legal opinions are not uniform. We hear that the people are confused. Given this state of affairs, this List of Precedents has been recorded so that those who cannot read can understand it and so that judgments do not deviate [from this standard].

If there are people in Kyoto who criticize this [List], be knowledgeable of these principles and respond. Respectfully yours,

[Jōei 1st year (1232)] 9th month, 11th day
Governor of Musashi [Hōjō Yasutoki]
[To:] Governor of Suruga [Hōjō Shigetoki]

5 Translation by Christoffer Bovbjerg.

Chapter 5: Bodies of law in early medieval England and Scotland

THE INJURY SCHEDULE IN THE *LEGES INTER BRETTOS ET SCOTTOS*, CAP. 212[6]

	De emenda iniurarium et percussionum fienda	*On restitution for injuries and blows*
[1]	Per legem diuinam caput pro capite manus pro manu oculos [sic] pro oculo.	According to divine law, a head for a head, a hand for a hand, eyes for an eye.
[2]	Per legem humanam pro uita hominis ix^{xx} uacce.	According to human law, for a man's life, 180 cows.
[3]	Pro pede una marca; pro manu tantum.	For a foot, one mark; the same for a hand.
[4]	Pro oculo dimidia marca; pro aure tantum.	For an eye, half a mark; the same for an ear.
[5]	Pro dente xii. d.	For a tooth, 12 *denarii.*
[6]	Pro quolibet pollice longitudinis plage xii d.	12 *denarii* also for each thumbs-length of a wound.
[7]	Pro quolibet pollice latitudinis plage xii d.	12 *denarii* also for each thumbs-length of width of a wound.
[8]	Pro ictu sub aure xvi d.	For a blow below the ear, 16 *denarii.*
[9]	Pro ictu cum baculo viii d. et si ceciderit cum ictu illo xvi d.	For a blow with a staff, 8 *denarii,* and if he was knocked over by the blow, 16 *denarii.*
[10]	Pro wlnere in facie dabit ymaginem auri.	For a wound to the face, he shall give a gold image.
[11]	Et lex humana pro fractura ossium ii oras.	And [according to] human law, for broken bones, 2 ores.
[12]	Item si sub tegimento wlneratus fuerit quis xii d.	*Item*, if someone is wounded under his garment, 12 *denarii.*
[13]	Si autem habeat manicam xv d.	Moreover, if he has sleeves, 15 *denarii.*
[14]	Pro qualibet uisibili plaga excepta facie xv d.	For any visible wound, except on the face, 15 *denarii.*
[15]	Item pro uita hominis xii marce supra anelitum v s. sub anelitu xl d.	*Item*, for a man's life, 12 marks; 5 shillings above the neck, and 40 *denarii* below the neck.
[16]	Pro ictu cum pede xl d.	For a blow with a foot, 40 *denarii.*
[17]	Pro extractione sanguinis xxv.s ultra mare vi uacce.	For the shedding of blood, 25 shillings or, across the sea, 6 cows.

6 Text taken from Alice Taylor, *The Laws of Medieval Scotland* (Edinburgh: The Stair Society, 2019). Translation by Andrew Rabin.

4.2.A. The Injury Schedule in Sir John Skene's *Regiam Maiestatem*, 1609[7]

	De pretio sanguinis et injuriam satisfactione	*On the price of satisfaction for blood and injuries*
[1]	Item per legem terrae in Scotia pro vita hominis, novies viginti vaccae.	*Item*, according to the law of the land in Scotland, for a man's life, 180 cows.
[2]	Pro pede, una marca.	For a foot, one mark.
[3]	Pro dente, duodecim denarii.	For a tooth, 12 *denarii.*
[4]	Pro qualibet plaga longitudinis pollicis, duodecim denarii.	For each thumbs-length of a wound, 12 *denarii.*
[5]	Pro ictu sub aure, sexdecim denarii.	For a blow below the ear, 16 *denarii.*
[6]	Pro ictu cum baculo, octo denarii et si percussus ceciderit, sedecim denarii.	For a blow with a staff, 8 *denarii,* and if he was knocked over by the blow, 16 *denarii.*
[7]	Item pro vulnere in facie, vulnerans dabit unam peciam auri vidilicet unam imagine mauri.	For a wound to the face, a gold coin, that is, a gold image.
[8]	Pro fractura ossium, quinque orae.	For a broken bone, 5 ores.
[9]	Pro vulnere sub vestibus, duodecim denarii.	If someone is wounded under his garment, 12 *denarii.*
[10]	Si ante manicam, sexdecim denarii	If before his sleeves, 15 *denarii.*
[11]	Pro qualibet visibili plaga, excepta facie, quindecim denarii.	For any visible wound except on the face, 15 *denarii.*
[12]	De plaga super anhelitum, quinque solidi.	For a wound above the windpipe, 15 *solidi.*
[13]	Sub anhelitu, quadraginta denarii.	Below the windpipe, 40 *denarii.*
[14]	Pro ictu cum pede, quadraginta denarii.	For a blow with a foot, 40 *denarii.*
[15]	Pro ictu cum palma pro quolibet digito, duodecim denarii	For a blow with the palm, for each finger [i.e. with a fist], 12 *denarii.*
[16]	Pro ictu cum pugno clausu, duodecim denarii.	For a blow with a closed fist, 12 *denarii.*
[17]	Pro extractione sanguinis, viginti quinque denarii ex parte maris Scotici, scilicet ultra mare. Et ex alia parte ejusdem maris, sex vaccae.	For the shedding of blood, 25 *solidi* south of the Scottish sea [i.e., the Firth of Forth]. And on the other side of the sea, 6 cows.
[18]	Sed in his usus et consuetudo observatur.	But in these instances, practice and custom should be observed.

7 Text taken from Thomas Mackay Cooper, *Regiam Majestatem and Quoniam Attachiamenta*, Stair Society (Edinburgh: J. Skinner and Co., 1947). Translation by Andrew Rabin.

Chapter 6: Promises and Perils of Macaulay's Preface to the Indian Penal Code

Excerpts from: A PENAL CODE Prepared by the Indian Law Commissioners, and published by Command of the Governor-General of India in Council[8]

TO THE RIGHT HONOURABLE GEORGE LORD AUCKLAND, C.C.C.B.

MY LORD,

The Penal Code which, according to the orders of Government of the 15th of June 1835, we had the honour to lay before your Lordship in Council on the 2nd of May last, has now been printed under our superintendence, and has, as well as the Notes, been carefully revised and corrected by us while in the press.

The time which has been employed in framing this body of law will not be thought long by any person who is acquainted with the nature of the labour which such works require, and with the history of other works of the same kind. We should, however, have been able to lay it before your Lordship in Council many months earlier, but for a succession of unfortunate circumstances against which it was impossible to provide. During a great part of the year 1836, the Commission was rendered almost entirely inefficient by the ill-health of a majority of the members and we were altogether deprived of the valuable services of our colleague Mr. Cameron, at the very time when those services were most needed.

It is hardly necessary for us to entreat your Lordship Council to examine with candour the work which we now submit to you. To the ignorant and inexperienced the task in which we have been engaged may appear easy and simple. But the members of the Indian Government are doubtless well aware that it is among the most difficult tasks in which the human mind can employed; that persons placed in circumstances far more favourable than ours have attempted it with very doubtful success; that the best Codes extant, if malignantly criticised, will be found to furnish matter for censure in every page; that the most copious and precise of human languages furnish but a very imperfect machinery to the legislator; that, in a work so extensive and complicated as that on which we have been employed, there will inevitably be, in spite of the most anxious care, some omissions and some inconsistencies; and that we have done as much as could reasonably be expected from us if we have furnished the

8 Taken from the full address of T. B. Macaulay et al., "Prefatory Address to the Right Honourable George Lord Auckland, C.C.C.B., Governor-General of India in Council," *The Indian Penal Code: As Originally Framed in 1837* (1888).

Government with that which may, by suggestions from experienced and judicious persons, be improved into a good Code.

Your Lordship in Council will be prepared to find in this performance those defects which must necessarily be found in the first portion of a Code. Such is the relation which exists between the different parts of the law, that no part can be brought to perfection while the other parts remain rude. The Penal Code cannot be clear and explicit while the substantive civil law and the law of procedure are dark and confused. While the rights of individuals and the powers of public functionaries are uncertain, it cannot always be certain whether those rights have been attacked, or those powers exceeded.

Your Lordship in Council will perceive that the system of penal law which we propose is not a digest of any existing system, and that no existing system has furnished us even with a groundwork. We trust that your Lordship in Council will not hence infer that we have neglected to inquire, as we are commanded to do by Parliament, into the present state of that part of the law, or that in other parts of our labours we are likely to recommend unsparing innovation, and the entire sweeping away of ancient usages. We are perfectly aware of the value of that sanction which long prescription and national feeling give to institutions. We are perfectly aware that lawgivers ought not to disregard even the unreasonable prejudices of those for whom they legislate. So sensible are we of the importance of these considerations, that, though there are not the same objections to innovation in penal legislation as to innovation affecting vested rights of property, yet, if we had found India in possession of a system of criminal law which the people regarded with partiality, we should have been inclined rather to ascertain it, to digest it, and moderately to correct it, than to propose a system fundamentally different.

But it appears to us that none of the systems of penal law established in British India has any claim to our attention, except what it may derive from its own intrinsic excellence. All those systems are foreign. All were introduced by conquerors differing in race, manners, language and religion from the great mass of the people. The criminal law of the Hindoos was long ago superseded, through the greater part of the territories now subject to the Company, by that of the Mahomedans, and is certainly the last system of criminal law which an enlightened and humane Government would be disposed to revive. The Mahomedan criminal law has in its turn been superseded, to a great extent, by the British Regulations. Indeed, in the territories subject to the Presidency of Bombay, the criminal law of the Mahomedans, as well as that of the Hindoos, has been altogether discarded, except in one particular class of cases; and even in such cases, it is not imperative on the judge to pay any attention to it. (pages vii-ix)

. . .

Thus widely do the systems of penal law now established in British India differ from each other: nor can we recommend any one of the three systems as furnishing even the rudiments of a good Code. The penal law of Bengal and of the Madras Presidency is, in fact, Mahomedan law, which has gradually been distorted to such an extent as to deprive it of all title to the religious veneration of Mahomedans, yet which retains enough of its original peculiarities to perplex and encumber the administration of justice. In substance it now differs at least as widely from the Mahomedan penal law, as the penal law of England differs from the penal law of France. Yet technical terms and nice distinctions borrowed from the Mahomedan law are still retained. Nothing is more usual than for the Courts to ask the law officers what punishment the Mahomedan law prescribes in a hypothetical case, and then to inflict that punishment on a person who is not within that hypothetical case, and who by the Mahomedan law would be liable either to a different punishment, or to no punishment. We by no means presume to condemn the policy which led the British Government to retain, and gradually to modify, the system of criminal jurisprudence which it found established in these provinces. But it is evident that a body law thus formed must, considered merely as a body law, be defective and inconvenient. (page x)

. . .

It would have given us great pleasure to have found that Code such as we could with propriety have taken as the groundwork of a Code for all India. But we regret to say that the penal law of the Bombay Presidency has over the penal law of the other Presidencies no superiority, except that of being digested. In framing it, the principles according to which crimes ought to be classified and punishments apportioned have been less regarded than in the legislation of Bengal and Madras. (page xi)

. . .

In the meantime the population which lives within the local jurisdiction of the Courts established by the Royal Charters is subject to the English Criminal Law, that is to say, to a very artificial and complicated system,—to a foreign system,—to a system which was framed without the smallest reference to India,—to a system which even in the country for which it was framed is generally considered as requiring extensive reform,—to a system finally which has just been pronounced by a Commission composed of able and learned English lawyers to be so defective that it can be reformed. only by being entirely taken to pieces and reconstructed.

Under these circumstances we have not thought it desirable to take as the groundwork of the Code any of the systems of law now in force in any part of India. We have, indeed, to the best of our ability, compared the Code with all those systems, and we have taken suggestions from all; but we have not adopted a single provision merely because it formed a part of any of those systems. We have also compared our work with the most celebrated systems of Western jurisprudence, as far as the very scanty means of information which were accessible to us in this country enabled us to do so.

We have derived much valuable assistance from the French Code, and from the decisions of the French Courts of Justice on questions touching the construction of that Code. We have derived assistance still more valuable from the Code of Louisiana, prepared by the late Mr. Livingston. We are the more desirous to acknowledge our obligations to that eminent jurist, because we have found ourselves under the necessity of combating his opinions on some important questions. (pages xiii-xiv)

. . .

One peculiarity in the manner in which this Code is framed will immediately strike your Lordship in Council,—we mean the copious use of illustrations. These illustrations will, we trust, greatly facilitate the understanding of the law, and will at the same time often serve as a defence of the law. In our definitions we have repeatedly found ourselves under the necessity of sacrificing neatness and perspicuity to precision, and of using harsh expressions because we could find no other expressions which would convey our whole meaning, and no more than our whole meaning. Such definitions standing by themselves might repel and perplex the reader, and would perhaps be fully comprehended only by a few students after long application. Yet such definitions are found, and must be found, in every system of law which aims at accuracy. A legislator may, if he thinks fit, avoid such definitions, and by avoiding them he will give a smoother and more attractive appearance to his workmanship; but in that case he flinches from a duty which he ought to perform, and which somebody must perform. If this necessary but most disagreeable work be not performed by the lawgiver once for all, it must be constantly performed in a rude and imperfect manner by every judge in the empire, and will probably be performed by no two judges in the same way. We have therefore thought it right not to shrink from the task of framing these unpleasing but indispensable parts of a Code. And we hope that when each of these definitions is followed by a collection of cases falling under it, and of cases which, though at first sight they appear to fall under it, do not really fall under it, the definition and the reasons which led to the adoption of it will be readily understood. The illustrations will lead the mind of the student through the same steps by which the minds of those who framed the law proceeded, and may sometimes show him that a phrase which may have struck him as uncouth, or a distinction which he may have thought idle, was deliberately adopted for the purpose of including or excluding a large class of important cases. In the study of geometry it is constantly found that a theorem which, read by itself, conveyed no distinct meaning to the mind, becomes perfectly clear as soon as the reader casts his eye over the statement of the individual case taken for the purpose of demonstration. Our illustrations, we trust, will in a similar manner facilitate the study of the law.

There are two things which a legislator should always have in view while he is framing laws: the one is, that they should be as far as possible precise; the other, that they should be easily understood. To unite precision and simplicity in definitions intended to include large classes of things, and to exclude others very similar to many of those which are included, will often be utterly impossible. Under such circumstances it is not easy to say what is the best course. That a law, and especially a penal law, should be drawn in words which convey no meaning to the people who are to obey it is an evil. On the other hand, a loosely-worded law is no law, and to whatever extent a legislature uses vague expressions, to that extent it abdicates its functions, and resigns the power of making law to the Courts of Justice.

On the whole, we are inclined to think that the best course is that which we have adopted. We have, in framing our definitions, thought principally of making them precise, and have not shrunk from rugged or intricate phraseology when such phraseology appeared to us to be necessary to precision. If it appeared to us that our language was likely to perplex an ordinary reader, we added as many illustrations as we thought necessary for the purpose of explaining it. The definitions and enacting clauses contain the whole law. The illustrations make nothing law which would not be law without them. They only exhibit the law in full action, and show what its effects will be on the events of common life.

Thus the Code will be at once a Statute book and a collection of decided cases. The decided cases in the Code will differ from the decided cases in the English law books in two most important points. In the first place, our illustrations are never intended to supply any omission in the written law, nor do they ever, in our opinion, put a strain on the written law. They are merely instances of the practical application of the written law to the affairs of mankind. Secondly, they are cases decided not by the judges but by the legislature, by those who make the law, and who must know more certainly than any judge can know what the law is which they mean to make.

The power of construing the law in cases in which there is any real reason to doubt what the law is amounts to the power of making the law. On this ground the Roman jurists maintained that the office of interpreting the law in doubtful matters necessarily belonged to the legislature. The contrary opinion was censured by them with great force of reason, though in language perhaps too bitter and sarcastic for the gravity of a Code. "Eorum vanam subtilitatem tam risimus quam corrigendam esse censuimus. Si enim in præsenti leges condere soli imperatori concessum est, et leges interpretari solo dignum imperio esse oportet. Quis legum ænigmata solvere et omnibus aperire idoneus esse videbitur nisi is cui legislatorem esse concessum est? Ex plosis itaque his ridiculosis ambiguitatibus tam conditor quam interpres legum solus imperator juste existimabitur."

The decisions on particular cases which we have annexed to the provisions of the Code resemble the imperial rescripts in this, that they proceed from the same authority from which the provisions themselves proceed. They differ from the imperial rescripts in this most important circumstance, that they are not made ex post facto, that they cannot therefore be made to serve any particular turn, that the persons condemned or absolved by them are purely imaginary persons, and that, therefore, whatever may be thought of the wisdom of any judgment which we have passed, there can be no doubt of its impartiality.

The publication of this collection of cases decided by legislative authority will, we hope, greatly limit the power which the Courts of Justice possess of putting their own sense on the laws. But we are sensible that neither this collection nor any other can be sufficiently extensive to settle every question which may be raised as to the construction of the Code. Such questions will certainly arise, and, unless proper precautions be taken, the decisions on such questions will accumulate till they form a body of law of far greater bulk than that which has been adopted by the legislature. Nor is this the worst. (pages xiv-xvii)

. . .

In conclusion, we beg respectfully to suggest that, if your Lordship in Council is disposed to adopt the Code which we have framed, it is most desirable that the native population should, with as little delay as possible, be furnished with good versions of it in their own languages. Such versions, in our opinion, can be produced only by the combined labours of enlightened Europeans and natives; and it is not probable that men competent to execute all the translations which will be required would be found in any single province of India. We are sensible that the difficulty of procuring good translations will be great; but we believe that the means at the disposal of your Lordship in Council are sufficient to overcome every difficulty; and we are confident that your Lordship in Council will not grudge anything that may be necessary for the purpose of enabling the people who are placed under your care to know what that law is according to which they are required to live.

We have the honour to be, My Lord,
Your Lordship's most obedient humble Servants,
T. B. MACAULAY.
J. M. MACLEOD.
G. W. ANDERSON.
F. MILLETT.

Indian Law Commission (pages xxi–xxii)

Chapter 7: (Re-)framing Hammurabi's laws: worldbuilding with prologues and epilogues in the Ancient Near East

Excerpts from the Prologue of the Laws of Ur-Namma of Ur (2111–2095 BCE), Sumerian:[9]

When the gods An and Enlil turned over the kingship of the city of Ur to the god Nanna, at that time, for Ur-Namma, son born of the goddess Ninsun, for her beloved house-born slave, according to his (the god Nanna's) justice and truth . . . gave to him

. . . I promoted Namhani to be the governor of the city of Lagash. By the might of the god Nanna, my lord, I returned Nanna's Magan-boat to the quay, and made it shine in the city of Ur.

At that time, the *nusku*-people had control of the fields, the chief sea-captain had control of trade, the herdsman had control over those who held back[10] cattle, held back sheep, and held back asses.

At that time, I, Ur-Namma, mighty man, king of Ur, king of the land of Sumer and Akkad, by the might of the god Nanna, my lord, and by the true command of the god Utu, did indeed establish justice in the land. I did indeed return [. . .]

Freedom was established for those conducting trade (free from) the chief sea-captain, for those who held back cattle, held back sheep, and held back assess (free from) the herdsman, and for the Akkadians and foreigners in the land of Sumer and Akkad.

At that time, Ummar, Marad, GIRkal, Kazallu, Usarum—those cities which had been subjugated by Anšan—by the might of the god Nanna, my lord, I established their freedom.

I established a copper *bariga* vessel and standardized it as 60 *sila* (= c. 60 liters) capacity. I fashioned a copper *ban* measure and standardized it as ten *sila* (= c. 10 liters) capacity. I fashioned a royal *ban* measure of current value made of copper and standardized it as five *sila* (= c. 5 liters) capacity. I fashioned a bronze measure of one *sila* (= c. 1 liter) and standardized it as one mina. I standardized the weight of stones from the pure one shekel weight to the one mina weight.

At that time, I [put in order] river-boat traffic on the banks of the Tigris, on the banks of the Euphrates, and on the banks of all the rivers. I established road stations in [. . .]. I built and planted orchards beside them. I, the king, placed gardeners in charge of them.

9 The first two paragraphs here are adapted from M. T. Roth, *Law Collections from Mesopotamia and Asia Minor* (Atlanta, GA: Scholars Press, 1997), 15ff. The remaining parts of the prologue were translated by Douglas R. Frayne, *Ur III Period (2112–2004 BCE)* RIME 3/2 (University of Toronto Press, 1997), 46ff. The brackets indicate missing content.

10 This means "appropriate."

The orphan was not handed over to the rich man. The widow was not handed over the mighty man. The man of one shekel was not handed over to the man of one mina (60 shekels). The man of one sheep was not handed over to the man of one ox.

I did indeed settle them there—my generals, my mothers, my brothers, and their families, and I will not impose their order (that is, orders on them). I did not impose toil there. I banished there evil, violence, and any cause for complaint. I established justice in the land.

(the laws ensue)

Epilogue: a curse[11]

Whoever erases this inscription and writes his name on it or, because of this curse, forces an outsider (who) erases the inscription and [writes(?)] for him a name not to be written, this person, be he a king, be he an en, be he a governor, . . . [the one who was] pla[ced] on a throne may (now) sit on the dust, may his [people] wander about among reed huts, may his [city] be a city not agreeable to Enlil, may the gates of his town remain wide open, may the young men of his town be blind, may the young women of his town be infertile! May [the gods] of his town, Enki, Iĺkur, and Aĺnan curse it by the sublime [order] of Enlil. May no one build a sheepfold, may [no one . . .] a cattle pen, . . . (rest broken, except for isolated signs; the last-preserved line seems to mention Ur-Namma).

Excerpt from the Prologue and Epilogue of the Laws of Lipit-Ishtar of Isin (1936–1926 BCE), Sumerian:[12]

When great god An, father of the gods, and the god Enlil, king of the lands, the lord who determines destinies, gave a favorable reign and the kingship of the lands of Sumer and Akkad to the goddess Ninisina, child of An, pious lady, for whose reign [. . .] rejoicing, for whose brilliant glance . . . in the city of Isin, her treasure house, established by the god An.

At that time, the gods An and Enlil called Lipit-Ishtar to the princeship of the land. Lipit-Ishtar, the wise shepherd, whose name has been pronounced by the god Nunamnir in order to establish justice in the land, to eliminate cries for justice, to eradicate enmity and armed violence, to bring well-being to the lands of Sumer and Akkad.

At that time, I, Lipit-Ishtar, the pious shepherd of the city of Nippur, the faithful husbandman of the city of UR, he who does not forsake the

11 This epilogue is translated by Miguel Civil, "The Law Collection of Ur-Namma," in *Cuneiform Royal Inscriptions and Related Texts in the Schøyen Collection (CUSAS 17)*, ed. Andrew George (CDL Press, 2011), 252.

12 This portion is adapted from Roth, *Law Collections*, 24ff.

city of Eridu, the befitting lord of the city of Uruk, the king of the city of Isin, king of the lands of Sumer and Akkad, the heart's desire of the goddess Inanna, by the command of the god Enili, I established justice in the lands of Sumer and Akkad.

At that time, I liberated the sons and daughters of the city of Nippur, the sons and daughters of the city of Ur, the sons and daughters of the city of Isin, the sons and daughters of the lands of Sumer and Akkad, who were subjugated [by the yoke], and I restored order.

(the prologue continues, followed by laws)

Epilogue

In accordance with the true word of the god Utu, I made the lands of Sumer and Akkad hold fair judicial procedure. In accordance with the utterance of the god Enlil, I, Lipit-Ishtar, son of Enlil, eradicated enmity and violence. I made weeping, lamentation, shouts for justice, and suits taboo. I made right and truth shine forth, and I brought well-being to the lands of Sumer and Akkad. [. . .]

[. . .] all humankind. When I established justice in the lands of Sumer and Akkad, I erected this stele. He who will not do anything evil to it, who will not damage my work, who will not efface my inscription and write his own name on it—may he be granted life and breath of long days; may he raise his neck to heaven in the Ekur temple; may the god Enlil's brilliant countenance be turned upon him from above.

But he who does anything evil to it, who damages my work, who enters the treasure room, who alters its pedestal, who effaces this inscription and writes his own name, or, because of this curse, induces an outsider to remove it—that man, whether he is a king, an *ēnu*-lord, or an ensi-ruler, [. . . may he be completely obliterated . . .]

(the epilogue continues)

Chapter 8: Prefaces in the legal texts of the crusader Kingdoms of Jerusalem and Cyprus

Preface to the canons of the Council of Nablus, explaining the disasters that had occurred in the crusader states, which the king and church believed needed to be corrected by issuing a set of laws. Translated by the author, from the Latin text in Kedar (1999: 331–332).

> In the year of the incarnation of the Lord 1120, our sins were evident, and the region of Jerusalem was laid waste by great oppression and was forsaken, with its crops consumed both by locusts and mice over the previous four years, and faced with quite frequent attacks and treachery from the Saracens, who killed many pilgrims and citizens. So, the patriarch Warmund, a man of dovelike simplicity and humility, and our son Baldwin, the patron of happiness, second king of the Latins of Jerusalem, busied themselves with pious prayers and works of justice in order to resist the threat of danger to the citizens. Aroused by divine inspiration to improve the condition of the church and the region, together with the prelates and important men of this same church and kingdom, in the second year of Baldwin's reign and of Warmund's patriarchate, they convened a council on the 17th day before the Kalends of February [16 January], at Nablus, the city of Samaria. In this way the needs of the land became clear, and in order to correct the population, which was rushing into ruin, they established decrees, which we have written below. The people of this region have been following decadent pleasures for some time now, which have impaired them and have endangered them with daily misfortunes, and there is only one refuge for them: to call upon the mercy of God and, with a certain measure of justice, to impose some restraint on the sins of the people who are sliding into error. Once they have stopped sinning, as we have read happened to the people of Israel, divine vengeance might cease, and the mercy of God, who does not desire the death but rather the correction of the sinner, might rescue his penitent sons from the imminent danger of the enemy. Indeed, last summer the enemy, that is the Saracens, had killed Roger, the prince of Antioch, along with, alas, almost all of the Christians of the principality of Antioch who had been defeated in battle, and they invaded the region of Jerusalem more frequently than usual. But enough has been said about these things.

Preface to Philip of Novara, explaining to an unnamed friend that he was unworthy of explaining the process of pleading before the court. Philip of Novara, Le Livre de forme de plait, trans. Peter W. Edbury (Cyprus Research Centre, 2009), pg. 205.

> Because of the enduring tender friendship and longstanding prayer of him on whom I am much dependant, and the great hope that I have in his ingenuity, discretion and desire to learn well and, so may it please

God, make good use of all the matters spoken of below, I have undertaken to instruct my lord and friend as best I can of an activity of which I myself know very little. This is the art of pleading: something which is good to know and wrong to engage in unless his need or that of his friend is such that he has to do it out of necessity. Because it is foolishness and most offensive for someone to give instruction as if he were a master when he is not even an average pupil, I beg you that you keep it hidden, since I have done for you what I should not have done for any lord or friend. So I beg you not to show or reveal this writing to anyone. For I have never found any lord or friend who would be prepared to do this for me, and someone could learn something from me that at some point he might use to get the better of me over some wrong I have committed or use it in his own defence.

John of Ibelin explains the legendary history of Godfrey of Bouillon, who supposedly established the courts and the assizes of Jerusalem after the First Crusade. Translated by the author, from John of Ibelin, Livre des Assises, ed. Peter W. Edbury (Brill, 2003), pg. 51–52.

When the holy city of Jerusalem was conquered from the enemies of the cross and put back in the hands and the power of those who have faith in Jesus Christ by the pilgrims, who were incited to come conquer it through the preaching of the cross, which was preached by the exhortation of Peter the Hermit, the princes and barons who had conquered it elected as king and lord of the Kingdom of Jerusalem the duke Godfrey of Bouillon, and he received lordship over it and did not want to be consecrated or anointed as king of the aforementioned kingdom, because he did not want to wear a crown of gold where the King of Kings, Jesus Christ, the son of God, wore a crown of thorns on the day of the Passion. He [Godfrey], who was very attentive and very careful to place the kingdom in a good shape and position, so that his men and his people and all sorts of other people who came and went and remained in the kingdom would be governed, guarded, upheld and preserved, as well as led and judged by right and reason, with the advice of the patriarch of the holy church of Jerusalem and the advice of the princes and barons and the wisest men that he could find, chose wise men to investigate and learn about the customs of the people who had come there from many different lands.

And whatever those whom they had chosen to do this were able to discover or learn, they had it put it writing and brought it to duke Godfrey. And he assembled the patriarch and the aforementioned men and showed it to them, and had it read to them, and afterwards, with their advice and agreement, he advised them about what seemed to be good, and from this he created the assizes and customs that we must now uphold and maintain and use in the kingdom of Jerusalem.

The anonymous author of the burgess assizes explains the concept of justice and law. Translated by the author, from Les Livres des Assises et des Usages dou Reaume de Jerusalem sive Leges et Instituta Regni Hierosolymitani, ed. Édouard H. Kausler (Adolf Krabbe, 1839), pg. 43–44.

> Here begins the book of justice and law, that is, here you will hear about reason and law, and what kind of man the viscount must be, and which men should be jurors in the court, and which men cannot be jurors; and how they should maintain and judge all men and women, and all cases of murder, theft, and selling, purchasing and renting houses and vineyards, and knights and sergeants, and all such things that will come to the attention of the court.
>
> At the beginning of this book we should discuss first of all justice and law, and seek justice, in order to give each man his right. For in Latin justice is described in this way: Justice is a constant and perpetual will, allotting to each man his due. Constant, that is, he must be firm in faith and justice, because he who is firm in faith and justice will live and will never die. As it is said in scripture and in law, Justus ex fide uiuit, that is, the just man lives by faith. Likewise justice should be eternal, as David says: the justice of God lasts forever. Therefore, we must speak first of all about faith and justice, so that by faith and by justice we can provide every man and every woman with their due.

The anonymous author of the Livre contrefais (also known as the "Abrégé" of the burgess assizes) dedicates his work to the Virgin Mary. Translated by the author, from the Abrégé du Livre des Assises de la Cour des Bourgeois, in RHC, Lois, vol. 2 (Académie royal des inscriptions et belles-lettres, 1843), pg. 234.

> So that every person may know for certain that all good comes from omnipotent God, and that no one can properly receive his grace unless through his blessed mother, Our Lady the Virgin Mary, to whom all grace is given and who is perfectly authorized to grant and distribute it at her will and discretion, I, though I am unworthy to dare request or receive this blessed grace, by the very great mercy that exists in she who is full of all good and goodness, and who willingly acquiesces to the small creatures who have hope in her, have placed my hope in her very great humility, which is full of perfect charity, and pray to her with all my heart that she will allow me and give me from her grace the dignity of a small spark, in accordance with my smallness, so that by the very great virtue that exists in her, this spark may perfect my understanding and my accomplishment, and that I, by this very great assistance and marvellous virtue, by the same grace may begin this, my book, and complete and accomplish it perfectly, in such a way that each person can and must know my smallness; on account of this smallness, accompanied by this blessed grace, Jesus Christ can and must be praised and glorified, the blessed son of

> omnipotent God and of the very gentle Virgin Mary, who lives and reigns with God the Father and with God the Holy Spirit, for all time. Amen.

Geoffrey le Tor explains that he wants to describe the law simply and plainly, unlike the "malicious" authors of the longer treatises. Translated by the author, from Livre de Geoffroi le Tor, ed. Auguste-Arthur Beugnot, in RHC, Lois, vol. 1 (Académie royal des inscriptions et belles-lettres, 1841), pg. 444–445.

> This book is based on two verses from the Psalter, which are different and contrary to each other. The subject of one of the verses should be followed by all those who want to be heard properly, and as for the other verse, everyone should avoid its subject. The first verse, the subject of which should be followed, is the one that says: 'The fear of the Lord is the beginning of wisdom.' The subject of this verse is followed by those who intend to do good and to maintain loyalty, right, justice, and judgment, without love, without hate, and without envy. For he who fears God sets about doing all that which is described below, and keeps himself from doing the contrary. The other verse, the subject of which must be avoided, says: 'Why do you glory in malice, you who are powerful in iniquity?' It happens to those who follow this verse that, because they do not fear God and because they have no fear of God at all, they glorify themselves in their malice and are powerful in their iniquity. And because of this, it happens that they put all their weakened sense and understanding in themselves, in order to seek out obscure pleas, so they can steal away and overcome the rights of others with their trickery. And this way they make new judgements, contrary to the law and good customs. And because I want to follow the subject of the verse that says the 'fear of the Lord is the beginning of wisdom', and avoid the sentence in the other bad verse, I want to keep myself from teaching how to plead and demonstrating the subtleties and obscurities. For the malice and envy in people is so great that those who would teach them these things, and write a book about them, would be acting as if he was giving a snake venom to drink; for he would add evil upon evil. And for all these reasons and those mentioned above, I do not want to put anything in this book except what can be used to properly settle the kinds of arguments and disputes that need to be brought before the court and judged there, which the court will need to settle and decide according to the assizes and good usages and customs of the Kingdom of Jerusalem, and which must also be upheld in the Kingdom of Cyprus. And as for issues that are not covered by any assize, usage, custom, I do not want to say anything myself, based on their meaning and their understanding, which is what should be done with new things. If I cannot include in this book all the assizes and good usages and good customs of the Kingdom of Jerusalem, it is no wonder, because they were created and began to be used long ago. But I will include what I have seen being used, and what

> I have heard being argued and spoken in court and outside of court. And it may well happen that not all those who will hear this book will agree with it; and if it may well be that no one sees how damaging this is, either to them or to their friends, so then they may be at the peak of the law and not profit from it; nor to any others who will want to demonstrate that they are wise, if they use trickery to argue subtle and obscure points, contrary to what is said in this book. And I will not make myself an authority about this, for whoever wants to do so will trust me and my book, and whoever does not want to believe it, so be it.

James of Ibelin briefly describes the purpose of his work. Translated by the author, from Livre de Jacques d'Ibelin, ed. Auguste-Arthur Beugnot, in RHC, Lois, vol. 1 (Académie royal des inscriptions et belles-lettres, 1841), pg. 453. Another version of this preface states that James wrote it on his deathbed.

> You have heard and understood above [in John of Ibelin's treatise] the assizes and the customs of the Kingdom of Jerusalem concerning pleading, and now you will be able to hear them purely, without any pleading. These assizes were made by James of Ibelin, may God have true mercy on his soul.
>
> Based on what I have seen and heard before, and what I certainly understand to be the good usages and good customs of the kingdom of Jerusalem, I want to describe them chapter by chapter, just as it will be written hereafter, and so I would begin with the first chapter.

Chapter 10: Jefferson's preambles, prefaces, and persistence

Jefferson's "original Rough draught" of the Declaration of Independence:[13]

A Declaration of the Representatives of the UNITED STATES OF AMERICA, in General Congress assembled.

> When in the course of human events it becomes necessary for a people to advance from that subordination in which they have hitherto remained, & to assume among the powers of the earth the equal & independant station to which the laws of nature & of nature's god entitle them, a decent respect to the opinions of mankind requires that they should declare the causes which impel them to the change.
>
> We hold these truths to be sacred & undeniable; that all men are created equal & independant, that from that equal creation they derive rights inherent & inalienable, among which are the preservation of life, & liberty, & the pursuit of happiness; that to secure these ends, governments are instituted among men, deriving their just powers from the consent of the governed; that whenever any form of government shall become destructive of these ends, it is the right of the people to alter or to abolish it, & to institute new government, laying it's foundation on such principles & organising it's powers in such form, as to them shall seem most likely to effect their safety & happiness. prudence indeed will dictate that governments long established should not be changed for light & transient causes: and accordingly all experience hath shewn that mankind are more disposed to suffer while evils are sufferable, than to right themselves by abolishing the forms to which they are accustomed. but when a long train of abuses & usurpations, begun at a distinguished period, & pursuing invariably the same object, evinces a design to subject them to arbitrary power, it is their right, it is their duty, to throw off such government & to provide new guards for their future security. such has been the patient sufferance of these colonies; & such is now the necessity which constrains them to expunge their former systems of government. the history of his present majesty, is a history of unremitting injuries and usurpations, among which no one fact stands single or solitary to contradict the uniform tenor of the rest, all of which have in direct object the establishment of an absolute tyranny over these states. to prove this, let facts be submitted to a candid world, for the truth of which we pledge a faith yet unsullied by falsehood.
>
> he has refused his assent to laws the most wholesome and necessary for the public good:

13 Reconstructed by Julian P. Boyd (ed.), *The Papers of Thomas Jefferson*, vol. 1, 1760–1776. (Princeton: Princeton University Press, 1950), 245–274.

he has forbidden his governors to pass laws of immediate & pressing importance, unless suspended in their operation till his assent should be obtained; and when so suspended, he has neglected utterly to attend to them.

he has refused to pass other laws for the accomodation of large districts of people unless those people would relinquish the right of representation, a right inestimable to them, formidable to tyrants alone:

he has dissolved Representative houses repeatedly & continually, for opposing with manly firmness his invasions on the rights of the people:

he has refused for a long space of time to cause others to be elected, whereby the legislative powers, incapable of annihilation, have returned to the people at large for their exercise, the state remaining in the mean time exposed to all the dangers of invasion from without, & convulsions within:

he has endeavored to prevent the population of these states; for that purpose obstructing the laws for naturalization of foreigners; refusing to pass others to encourage their migrations hither; & raising the conditions of new appropriations of lands:

he has suffered the administration of justice totally to cease in some of these colonies, refusing his assent to laws for establishing judiciary powers:

he has made our judges dependant on his will alone, for the tenure of their offices, and amount of their salaries:

he has erected a multitude of new offices by a self-assumed power, & sent hither swarms of officers to harrass our people & eat out their substance:

he has kept among us in times of peace standing armies & ships of war:

he has affected to render the military, independant of & superior to the civil power:

he has combined with others to subject us to a jurisdiction foreign to our constitutions and unacknoleged by our laws; giving his assent to their pretended acts of legislation, for quartering large bodies of armed troops among us;

for protecting them by a mock-trial from punishment for any murders they should commit on the inhabitants of these states;

for cutting off our trade with all parts of the world;

for imposing taxes on us without our consent;

for depriving us of the benefits of trial by jury;

for transporting us beyond seas to be tried for pretended offences: for taking away our charters, & altering fundamentally the forms of our governments;

for suspending our own legislatures & declaring themselves invested with power to legislate for us in all cases whatsoever:

he has abdicated government here, withdrawing his governors, & declaring us out of his allegiance & protection:

he has plundered our seas, ravaged our coasts, burnt our towns & destroyed the lives of our people:

he is at this time transporting large armies of foreign merce naries to compleat the works of death, desolation & tyranny, already begun with circumstances of cruelty & perfidy unworthy the head of a civilized nation:

he has endeavored to bring on the inhabitants of our frontiers the merciless Indian savages, whose known rule of warfare is an undistinguished destruction of all ages, sexes, & conditions of existence:

he has incited treasonable insurrections in our fellow-subjects, with the allurements of forfeiture & confiscation of our property:

he has waged cruel war against human nature itself, violating it's most sacred rights of life & liberty in the persons of a distant people who never offended him, captivating & carrying them into slavery in another hemisphere, or to incur miserable death in their transportation thither. this piratical warfare, the opprobrium of **infidel** powers, is the warfare of the CHRISTIAN king of Great Britain. determined to keep open a market where MEN should be bought & sold, he has prostituted his negative for suppressing every legislative attempt to prohibit or to restrain this execrable commerce: and that this assemblage of horrors might want no fact of distinguished die, he is now exciting those very people to rise in arms among us, and to purchase that liberty of which he has deprived them, & murdering the people upon whom he also obtruded them; thus paying off former crimes committed against the **liberties** of one people, with crimes which he urges them to commit against the **lives** of another.

in every stage of these oppressions we have petitioned for redress in the most humble terms; our repeated petitions have been answered by repeated injury. a prince whose character is thus marked by every act which may define a tyrant, is unfit to be the ruler of a people who mean to be free. future ages will scarce believe that the hardiness of one man, adventured within the short compass of 12 years only, on so many acts of tyranny without a mask, over a people fostered & fixed in principles of liberty.

Nor have we been wanting in attentions to our British brethren. we have warned them from time to time of attempts by their legislature to extend a jurisdiction over these our states. we have reminded them of the circumstances of our emigration & settlement here, no one of which could warrant so strange a pretension: that these were effected at the expence of our own blood & treasure, unassisted by the wealth or the strength of Great Britain: that in constituting indeed our several forms of government, we had adopted one common king, thereby laying a foundation for perpetual league & amity with them: but that submission to their parliament was no part of our constitution, nor ever in idea, if history may be credited: and we appealed to their native justice & magnanimity, as well as to the ties of our common kindred to disavow these usurpations which were likely to interrupt our correspondence & connection. they too have been deaf to the voice of justice & of consanguinity, & when occasions have been given them, by the regular course of their laws, of removing from their councils the disturbers of our harmony, they have by their free election re-established them in power. at this very time too they are permitting their chief magistrate to send over not only soldiers of our common blood, but Scotch & foreign mercenaries to invade & deluge us in blood. these facts have given the last stab to agonizing affection, and manly spirit bids us to renounce for ever these unfeeling brethren. we must endeavor to forget our former love for them, and to hold them as we hold the rest of mankind, enemies in war, in peace friends. we might have been a free & great people together; but a communication of grandeur & of freedom it seems is below their dignity. be it so, since they will have it: the road to glory & happiness is open to us too; we will climb it in a separate state, and acquiesce in the necessity which pronounces our everlasting Adieu!

We therefore the representatives of the United States of America in General Congress assembled do, in the name & by authority of the good people of these states, reject and renounce all allegiance & subjection to the kings of Great Britain & all others who may hereafter claim by, through, or under them; we utterly dissolve & break off all political connection which may have heretofore subsisted between us & the people or parliament of Great Britain; and finally we do assert and declare these a colonies to be free and independant states, and that as free & independant states they shall hereafter have power to levy war, conclude peace, contract alliances, establish commerce, & to do all other acts and things which independent states may of right do. And for the support of this declaration we mutually pledge to each other our lives, our fortunes, & our sacred honour.

See also:

First Draft by Jefferson [before June 1776] https://founders.archives.gov/documents/Jefferson/01-01-02-0161-0002

Jefferson's Draft of a Constitution for Virginia, May-June 1783 https://founders.archives.gov/documents/Jefferson/01-06-02-0255-0004

Chapter 11: Martens Clause and ambiguity at the birth of modern humanitarian law

Convention (II) with Respect to the Laws and Customs of War on Land and its annex: Regulations concerning the Laws and Customs of War on Land, 29 July 1899, 187 CTS 429.

Convention with respect to the laws and customs of war on land (HAGUE, II) (29 July 1899)

Entry into Force: 4 September 1900

His Majesty the Emperor of Germany, King of Prussia; [etc.]:

Considering that, while seeking means to preserve peace and prevent armed conflicts among nations, it is likewise necessary to have regard to cases where an appeal to arms may be caused by events which their solicitude could not avert;

Animated by the desire to serve, even in this extreme hypothesis, the interest of humanity and the ever increasing requirements of civilization;

Thinking it important, with this object, to revise the laws and general customs of war, either with the view of defining them more precisely, or of laying down certain limits for the purpose of modifying their severity as far as possible;

Inspired by these views which are enjoined at the present day, as they were twenty-five years ago at the time of the Brussels Conference in 1874, by a wise and generous foresight;

Have, in this spirit, adopted a great number of provisions, the object of which is to define and govern the usages of war on land.

In view of the High Contracting Parties, these provisions, the wording of which has been inspired by the desire to diminish the evils of war so far as military necessities permit, are destined to serve as general rules of conduct for belligerents in their relations with each other and with populations.

It has not, however, been possible to agree forthwith on provisions embracing all the circumstances which occur in practice.

On the other hand, it could not be intended by the High Contracting Parties that the cases not provided for should, for want of a written provision, be left to the arbitrary judgment of the military Commanders.

Until a more complete code of the laws of war is issued, the High Contracting Parties think it right to declare that in cases not included in the Regulations adopted by them, populations and belligerents remain under the protection and empire of the principles of international law, as they result from the usages established between civilized nations, from the laws of humanity, and the requirements of the public conscience;

They declare that it is in this sense especially that Articles 1 and 2 of the Regulations adopted must be understood . . .

. . .

Annex to the Convention

Regulations respecting the laws and customs of war on land

SECTION I.—ON BELLIGERENTS

CHAPTER I.—On the Qualifications of Belligerents

Article 1

The laws, rights, and duties of war apply not only to armies, but also to militia and volunteer corps, fulfilling the following conditions:

To be commanded by a person responsible for his subordinates;

To have a fixed distinctive emblem recognizable at a distance;

To carry arms openly; and

To conduct their operations in accordance with the laws and customs of war.

In countries where militia or volunteer corps constitute the army, or form part of it, they are included under the denomination "army."

Article 2

The population of a territory which has not been occupied who, on the enemy's approach, spontaneously take up arms to resist the invading troops without having time to organize themselves in accordance with Article 1, shall be regarded a belligerent, if they respect the laws and customs of war.

Chapter 12: Searching for meaning in the Utah Constitution's Free Market Preamble

Utah Antitrust Act of 1979, § 2, Utah Code § 76-10-3102:

> The legislature finds and determines that competition is fundamental to the free market system and that the unrestrained interaction of competitive forces will yield the best allocation of our economic resources, the lowest prices, the highest quality and the greatest material progress, while at the same time providing an environment conducive to the preservation of our democratic, political and social institutions.

Constitution of the State of Utah, Article XII, Section 20 (1992):

> It is the policy of the state of Utah that a free market system shall govern trade and commerce in this state to promote the dispersion of economic and political power and the general welfare of all the people.

New States Ice Co. v. Liebmann, 285 U.S. 262, 311 (1932) (Brandeis, J., dissenting):

> It is one of the happy incidents of the federal system that a single courageous State may, if its citizens choose, serve as a laboratory; and try novel social and economic experiments without risk to the rest of the country.

John J. Flynn, Federalism and Viable State Government——The History of Utah's Constitution, 1996 Utah Law Review 311, 314 (1966):

> No other territory experienced the difficulties that Utah encountered in obtaining statehood, for no other territory was settled under such unusual circumstances.

John J. Flynn & Piero Ruffinengo, "Distributive Justice: Some Institutional Implications of Rawls 'A Theory of Justice'," 1975 Utah Law Review 123 (1975):

> [at 124]
> The great and growing inequalities of distribution in America and the world can no longer be justified to most members of our society. One indication of the unjust distribution of goods is the persistent and growing maldistribution of wealth. Although measurement of the degree of economic inequality is crude in light of the countless factors which must be considered, research to date indicates a grossly unjust and unjustifiable distribution of wealth.

[at 154]

[T]he giant corporation has become a principal engine of distributive injustice in our society and a growing threat to individual liberty. It has become such by distributing increments of wealth to those who have done nothing to earn that wealth, contrary to the original legal assumptions of the corporate institution; it has become a source of undue political and economic power on the national and international scene, and its internal organization is leading to a denial of individuality and a rebirth of status rights and liabilities reminiscent of feudalism . . .

[at 157]

We have lost a consensus on an ethic of distributive justice in our culture and, as a result, we risk sinking into a new form of [feudalism] where the rights and dignity of the individual are made subservient to monolithic institutions, a political or economic elite, or a mindless and onrushing technocracy. In grappling with the conundrum of preserving individualism in an ever more complex and interdependent society, which is currently under great economic stress, we need a renewed consensus of justice—one which does not exalt efficiency, meritocracy, or group utility as the primary end of social and economic justice. Rather, we need a consensus which guarantees just institutions capable of restricting inequalities to those inequalities for the reasonable benefit of all, while preserving individual liberty.

Robert H. Bork, The Antitrust Paradox: A Policy At War With Itself (1978, 2021 eBook ed.):

[at 4]

Antitrust was originally conceived as a limited intervention in free and private processes for the purpose of keeping those processes free. It tempered laissez faire in order to preserve a free-market system. . . . The conception was one of free markets with minimal government involvement.

[at 48]

The responsibility of the federal courts for the integrity and virtue of law requires that they take consumer welfare as the sole value that guides antitrust decisions.

[at 51–53]

These notions, which are examples of the theory of the 'social and political purposes of antitrust,' are, to put the matter kindly, a jumble of half-digested notions and mythologies . . . A variety of such themes may be discerned in antitrust case law; they may be referred to collectively as theories of social and political purposes of anti-trust, to distinguish them from the pro-consumer tradition of the law. No matter how they are characterized, however, they have this in common: the idea that the law properly expresses social and political purposes, purposes which should

> be taken into account by courts, always turns out to mean that there are some cases in which protection of inefficient firms or the subsidization of small firms should overrule considerations of efficient resource allocation through the free market. This is a tax upon consumers for the benefit of some producers—a tax levied not by Congress but by the Supreme Court of the United States. The point here is not that these ideas are dubious social policies (which they are), but rather, as our statutes now stand, that they make it impossible antitrust law.

John J. Flynn, The Reagan Administration's Antitrust Policy, Original Intent and the Legislative History of the Sherman Act, 33 Antitrust Bulletin 259, 284 (1988):

> "Consumer welfare" in [Bork's] sense and in the context of reality is a paternalistic concept premised upon a belief in preexisting and absolute property and contract rights and the presumed 'rationality' of producers and sellers, rather than consumer welfare in the sense of unfair wealth transfers caused by a breakdown in the competitive process and the denial to every individual of equality of opportunity in access to and fairness in the operations of the market.

Tesla Motors UT, Inc. v. Utah Tax Commission, 398 P.3d 55, 66 (Utah 2017)

> Not every provision of the constitution states an enforceable limitation on our government. Some provisions are non-justiciable: They are stated at so high a level of generality or aspiration that they require legislation to establish a limitation enforceable in our courts.
>
> The . . . Free Market Clause is such a provision. This clause articulates only a "policy." And it frames the policy in terms that identify only a "general principle" with no justiciable standard or "means for putting [it] into effect." We know from the Free Market Clause that our charter for state government is in favor of a "free market." But we know little more than that.
>
> The general aspiration for a "free market" is too vague a policy to sustain a justiciable constitutional standard. So without any implementing legislation, we deem this provision non-justiciable.

References

Bork, Robert H. *The Antitrust Paradox: A Policy at War with Itself.* New York: Basic Books, 1978, 2021 eBook ed.

Boyd, Julian P. (ed.). *The Papers of Thomas Jefferson*, vol. 1, 1760–1776. Princeton: Princeton University Press, 1950. Accessed via Library of Congress: www.loc.gov/exhibits/declara/ruffdrft.html#:~:text=We%20therefore%20the%20representatives%20of,or%20under%20them%3B%20we%20utterly.

Civil, M. "The Law Collection of Ur-Namma." In *Cuneiform Royal Inscriptions and Related Texts in the Schøyen Collection* (CUSAS 17), edited by Andrew George, 221–286. CDL Press, 2011.

Cooper, Thomas Mackay. *Regiam Majestatem and Quoniam Attachiamenta.* Stair Society. Edinburgh: J. Skinner and Co., 1947.

Dosuna, Julián Méndez. "La clause finale de l'accord entre les Anaitiens et les Métapiens (*IvO* 10 = *IÉD* 14, L. 5–7)." *Zeitschrift für Papyrologie und Epigraphik* 184 (2013): 147–155.

Flynn John J. "The Reagan Administration's Antitrust Policy, 'Original Intent' and the Legislative History of the Sherman Act." *Antitrust Bulletin* (1988): 259–307.

Flynn, John J. and Piero Ruffinengo. "Distributive Justice: Some Institutional Implications of Rawls 'A Theory of Justice'." *Utah Law Review* 123 (1975): 123–157.

Frayne, Douglas R. *Ur III Period (2112-2004 BCE)* RIME 3/2. University of Toronto Press, 1997.

Guarducci, Margherita. *Epigrafi di carattere pubblico.* Roma: Istituto poligrafico dello Stato, 1969.

Jeffery, Lilian Hamilton. *The Local Scripts of Archaic Greece.* Oxford: Clarendon Press, 1961.

Kedar, Benjamin K. "On the origins of the earliest laws of Frankish Jerusalem: The canons of the Council of Nablus, 1120." *Speculum* 74 (1999): 331–332.

Macaulay, T. B., J. M. Macleod, G. W. Anderson, and F. Millett. "Prefatory Address to the Right Honourable George Lord Auckland, C.C.C.B., Governor-General of India in Council." In *The Indian Penal Code: As Originally Framed in 1837.* Madras: Higginbotham and Co., 1888.

Philip of Novara. *Le Livre de forme de plait*, ed. and trans. Peter W. Edbury. Nicosia: Cyprus Research Centre, 2009.

Roth, M. T. *Law Collections from Mesopotamia and Asia Minor.* Atlanta, GA: Scholars Press, 1997.

Taylor, Alice. *The Laws of Medieval Scotland.* Edinburgh: The Stair Society, 2019.

Index

Kolibri 360 GmbH
Ferdinand-Jühlke-Straße 7
99095 Erfurt, Deutschland
produktsicherheit@kolibri360.de